John Mansfield
Murrinhpatha Morphology and Phonology

Pacific Linguistics

Managing editor
Bethwyn Evans

Editorial board members
Wayan Arka
Mark Donohue
Nicholas Evans
Gwendolyn Hyslop
David Nash
Bill Palmer
Paul Sidwell
Jane Simpson
Andrew Pawley
Malcolm Ross

Volume 653

John Mansfield
Murrinhpatha Morphology and Phonology

DE GRUYTER
MOUTON

ISBN 978-1-5015-2442-4
e-ISBN (PDF) 978-1-5015-0330-6
ISBN (EPUB) 978-1-5015-0310-8
ISSN 1448-8310

Library of Congress Control Number: 2018967116

Bibliographic information published by the Deutsche Nationalbibliothek
The Deutsche Nationalbibliothek lists this publication in the Deutsche Nationalbibliografie; detailed bibliographic data are available on the Internet at http://dnb.dnb.de.

© 2020 Walter de Gruyter Inc., Boston/Berlin
This volume is text- and page-identical with the hardback published in 2019.
Typesetting: Integra Software Services Pvt. Ltd.
Printing and binding: CPI books GmbH, Leck
Photo credit: John Mansfield

www.degruyter.com

For Damien and Heather Mansfield

Acknowledgements

I would like to thank the many Murrinhpatha speakers who shared their language with me. In Wadeye I have a constant feeling of support and encouragement from local residents, who receive warmly all my efforts to speak Murrinhpatha, and clearly go out of their way to make sure that I'm getting practice. For more concentrated Murrinhpatha instruction and elicitation I would like to thank Desmond Pupuli, Luke Parmbuk, Raphael Tunmuck, Keith Mardigan, Anne-Marie Nadjulu, Mark Ninnal, Samuel Longmair and William Parmbuk. Dozens of other Murrinhpatha speakers allowed me to record their stories and conversation on various occasions, and I thank them all for their openness and trust.

I also owe great thanks to a non-Aboriginal resident of Wadeye, Mark Crocombe, who provided staunch support, wisdom and fascinating bush trips. I also received help and support in Wadeye from Tony 'Tjithay' Goodfellow, Will Peartree, Steven Wenzel, Marie Klesch.

This research began during my PhD, in which Jane Simpson and Linda Barwick offered invaluable mentorship. As a junior researcher, Rachel Nordlinger has continued this mentorship, while I have enjoyed the friendship and intellectual engagement of other Murrinhpatha researchers, especially Joe Blythe, Lucy Davidson, Bill Forshaw and Michael Walsh. Chester Street, who sadly passed away during the preparation of this book, provided advice based on a deeper knowledge of Murrinhpatha than I can ever hope to attain. The manuscript for this book was improved substantially thanks to comments from Rachel Nordlinger, Adam Tallman, Claudia Mansfield and an anonymous reviewer.

The research leading this book received institutional support from the University of Melbourne, Australian National University and the University of Sydney. Additional support in Wadeye was received from the Thamarrurr Corporation and Batchelor Institute.

Finally, I would like to acknowledge the unflagging love and support of my parents, Heather and Damien Mansfield, to whom I dedicate this book.

Contents

Acknowledgements —— VII

List of Tables —— XIV

List of Figures —— XV

Abbreviations and glossing conventions —— XVI

1 Introduction —— 1
1.1 The morphology and phonology of Murrinhpatha —— 1
1.2 A brief sketch of Murrinhpatha —— 2
1.3 Previous work on Murrinhpatha —— 6
1.4 Previous work on word structure in Australian languages —— 8
1.5 Data sources used in this study —— 9
1.6 What I mean by phonology —— 10
1.7 What I mean by morphology —— 11
1.7.1 Morphological description, cognitive representation and gradience —— 13
1.7.2 What I mean by 'word' —— 15
1.7.3 Constructions: Abandoning the grammar–lexicon split —— 16
1.7.4 Summary —— 20
1.8 Prosodic constituency —— 21
1.9 Chapter outline —— 23

2 Social setting and language ecology —— 25
2.1 Introduction —— 25
2.2 Traditional language ecology —— 26
2.2.1 Neighbouring languages —— 27
2.3 Traditional social organisation —— 29
2.4 Contact and settlement —— 31
2.5 Post-missionary Wadeye —— 32
2.6 Contemporary language ecology of Wadeye —— 35
2.6.1 Status of neighbouring Aboriginal languages —— 36
2.6.2 Youth speech —— 38
2.6.3 English and Kriol —— 39
2.6.4 Digital diglossia —— 40
2.7 Summary —— 41

3	**Segmental sound patterns** — 42	
3.1	Introduction — 42	
3.2	Segmental inventory — 43	
3.3	Word and syllable shapes — 44	
3.3.1	Restrictions by word and syllable position — 46	
3.3.2	Consonant cluster constraints — 48	
3.4	Obstruent voicing, closure and length — 51	
3.4.1	Voicing and closure contrasts — 52	
3.4.2	Positional neutralisations — 53	
3.4.3	Phonetic realisation of contrasts — 54	
3.4.4	Word-medial obstruent lengthening — 57	
3.5	Geminate sonorants and voiced stops — 60	
3.6	The intermediate status of retroflexion — 63	
3.7	Connected speech processes — 67	
3.7.1	Progressive consonant assimilation — 68	
3.7.2	Degemination — 70	
3.8	Loanwords and lexico-phonological strata — 71	
3.9	Summary — 75	

4	**Morphologically specific sound patterns** — 76	
4.1	Introduction — 76	
4.2	Morphological categories and their phonological shape — 77	
4.2.1	Open lexical classes: Nominals and coverbs — 80	
4.2.2	Finite verb stems and semi-regular inflectional elements — 82	
4.2.3	Bound grammatical morphs — 84	
4.3	The prosodic word — 85	
4.4	Prosodic phrases and prominence — 87	
4.4.1	The pitch accent — 89	
4.4.2	Prosodic adjuncts — 92	
4.4.3	Prosodic phrase mapping to syntactic phrases — 94	
4.4.4	Previous descriptions of Murrinhpatha stress — 96	
4.4.5	Comparison to other Australian prosodic systems — 97	
4.5	Prosodically internal juncture effects — 98	
4.5.1	Voiceless obstruent lenition — 98	
4.5.2	Nasal spreading — 101	
4.5.3	Cluster harmonisation — 103	
4.5.4	Non-syllabifiable clusters — 109	
4.6	Summary — 110	

5 Finite verb stem inflection —— 111

- 5.1 Introduction —— 111
- 5.2 Morphological structure in the finite verb stem —— 112
- 5.2.1 Basic and reflexive/reciprocal verb stems —— 114
- 5.2.2 Stem paradigms —— 114
- 5.2.3 Eroded inner stems and lexical identity —— 117
- 5.3 Inflectional paradigms and inflectional classes —— 118
- 5.3.1 Inflection by intersecting formatives —— 118
- 5.4 Intersecting formatives in the finite verb stem —— 120
- 5.4.1 PrefC —— 121
- 5.4.2 PrefV —— 123
- 5.4.3 Suffix —— 124
- 5.4.4 Inner stems —— 125
- 5.5 Unpredictable exponence and cross-linguistic comparison —— 130
- 5.6 Variation and change in inflectional paradigms —— 133
- 5.7 Whole-form storage or morphological structure? —— 134
- 5.8 Summary —— 136

6 Predicate inflectional suffixes —— 137

- 6.1 Introduction —— 137
- 6.2 The prosodically internal layer —— 138
- 6.2.1 Pronominal number categories —— 140
- 6.2.2 Single-argument verbs —— 144
- 6.2.3 Reflexive/reciprocal valency —— 146
- 6.2.4 Object and oblique arguments —— 148
- 6.2.5 Ethical datives —— 151
- 6.2.6 Verb stems and valency —— 152
- 6.3 The prosodically external layer —— 152
- 6.3.1 Paucal and dual number —— 153
- 6.3.2 Tense/modality —— 155
- 6.3.3 Imperfective —— 156
- 6.3.4 Adverbial clitics —— 158
- 6.3.5 Variable sequencing —— 159
- 6.4 Representational schemata for verb inflection —— 161
- 6.5 Predicating nominals —— 162
- 6.5.1 Syntactic strategies for nominal predication —— 163
- 6.5.2 Morphological argument indexing —— 164
- 6.5.3 Grammaticalisation of /ma/ 'hand' —— 165
- 6.6 Summary —— 166

7	**Nominal and phrasal morphology** —— 167	
7.1	Introduction —— 167	
7.2	Affixes and clitics —— 167	
7.3	Noun phrases, nominal compounds and classifier nouns —— 170	
7.3.1	Noun phrases and generic–specific relations —— 170	
7.3.2	NOM-NOM Compounds —— 172	
7.3.3	From compounds to class prefixes —— 176	
7.3.4	Classifiers with verbs —— 179	
7.3.5	Negative nominal prefix —— 179	
7.4	Nominal derivations —— 180	
7.5	Case clitics —— 181	
7.5.1	Prefixing of comitative case —— 184	
7.6	Adverbial clitics —— 184	
7.6.1	Promiscuous attachment —— 186	
7.6.2	Demonstrative and interrogatives hosting adverbials —— 188	
7.7	Discourse clitics —— 190	
7.8	Summary —— 192	
8	**Complex verbs and compounding** —— 193	
8.1	Introduction —— 193	
8.2	Simple, phrasal and compound verbs —— 194	
8.3	The verbiness of verb stems —— 196	
8.3.1	Finite verb stems or inflection-class prefixes? —— 200	
8.3.2	Psychological status of finite verb stems in compounds —— 201	
8.3.3	A recent history of grammaticalisation —— 202	
8.4	Coverbs —— 203	
8.5	Compounding body part nominals to coverbs —— 205	
8.5.1	Relation to independent nominals —— 206	
8.5.2	Compounding relations —— 206	
8.5.3	Fossilised compounds —— 209	
8.5.4	Body-part applicatives —— 210	
8.6	Pluractional coverbs —— 211	
8.7	Prosodic compounding —— 215	
8.7.1	Coverb attachment to a prosodic anchor —— 216	
8.7.2	Recursive PWord constituency —— 217	
8.7.3	Incoporating coverbs into the verb schemata —— 218	
8.8	Representing compound verb lexemes —— 219	
8.9	Summary —— 221	

9	**Murrinhpatha wordhood and gradient morphology** — **222**	
9.1	Introduction — **222**	
9.2	Murrinhpatha phonology — **222**	
9.3	Murrinhpatha morphology — **224**	
9.4	Three types of word in Murrinhpatha — **226**	
9.5	Morphology, gradience, and methods of quantification — **228**	
9.5.1	Number of words sharing a pattern — **229**	
9.5.2	Proportional coverage of syntactic/semantic feature — **230**	
9.5.3	Phonological transparency — **231**	
9.5.4	The status of stems — **231**	
9.5.5	Semantic transparency — **232**	
9.5.6	Lexicon, morphology and syntax — **232**	
9.6	Concluding comments: Wordhood and polysynthesis — **233**	

Appendix I — **235**

Appendix II — **275**

References — **278**

Index — **292**

List of Tables

Table 1.1	Fragment of the verb stem paradigm /ru/ 'go'	6
Table 1.2	Fragment of the verb stem paradigm /ma/ 'say, do'	6
Table 3.1	Murrinhpatha consonant inventory (inherited stratum).	44
Table 3.2	Consonant position types analysed according to transitions	46
Table 3.3	C_1 consonants: Syllable onset, either word-initial or post-consonantal.	47
Table 3.4	Syllable coda (including word-final) consonant inventory	47
Table 3.5	Contemporary Murrinhpatha consonant inventory.	74
Table 4.1	Disagreements about prosodic prominence.	97
Table 5.1	Examples of finite verb stem forms	113
Table 5.2	Murrinhpatha finite verb stems, and sharing of inflectional paradigms.	115
Table 5.3	Inflectional paradigm of /na/ 'use fire'	116
Table 5.4	Sample verb stem inflection paradigm illustrating semi-regular formatives	121
Table 5.5	Allomorphy of PrefC.	122
Table 5.6	Sample of a PrefC formative paradigm	122
Table 5.7	Sample of a PrefV formative paradigm	123
Table 5.8	Sample paradigm for a verb stem analysed as having a consistent /u/ allomorph for PrefV	124
Table 5.9	Suffix allomorphy for finite verb stems	125
Table 5.10	Sample suffix formative paradigms	125
Table 5.11	Sample verb stem illustrating the GEMINATE InnerC alternation in PL forms	127
Table 5.12	Sample verb stem illustrating the RHOTIC InnerC alternation in PL forms	127
Table 5.13	Sample paradigm exhibiting 2SG apicalisation of InnerC	128
Table 5.14	Sample paradigm exhibiting highly irregular alternations	129
Table 5.15	Sample paradigm exhibiting InnerVH and InnerVF alternations	130
Table 5.16	Complete Paradigm Prediction scores for cross-linguistic sample	132
Table 6.1	Labels for number categories with varying degrees of specificity	141
Table 6.2	Murrinhpatha grammatical number distinctions	142
Table 6.3	Murrinhpatha verb stem transitivity classes	153
Table 6.4	Verb tense categories and external tense suffixes	155
Table 6.5	Verb stems used as IMPF suffix	157
Table 7.1	Affix/clitic categorisation according to four widely used criteria.	169
Table 7.2	Classifier nouns	171
Table 7.3	Nominal case clitics	182
Table 7.4	Adverbial clitics.	185
Table 7.5	Murrinhpatha demonstratives and interrogatives.	188
Table 8.1	Discourse frequency of three verb types.	195
Table 8.2	Lexical verbs and some examples of compounds	197
Table 8.3	Light verbs and some examples of compounds	197
Table 8.4	Semantic classifiers and examples of compounds	198
Table 8.5	Pseudo-classifiers and examples of compounds	199
Table 8.6	Comparison of phrasal forms recorded in 1959 with contemporary forms	203
Table 8.7	Bound body parts	205

List of Figures

Figure 1.1	Example of Murrinhpatha prosodic constituent hierarchy	22
Figure 2.1	Murrinhpatha and surrounding languages	27
Figure 2.2	Front page of a Melbourne newspaper, 23 May 2006	34
Figure 3.1(a)	Spectrogram for /putput/ 'pregnant'	54
Figure 3.1(b)	Spectrogram for /burbur/ 'cold'	55
Figure 3.2(a)	Word-medial intervocalic /p/	55
Figure 3.2(b)	Word-medial intervocalic /b/	56
Figure 3.3(a)	Acoustic realisation of laminal fricative /ð/	56
Figure 3.3(b)	Acoustic realisation of dorsal fricative /ɣ/	57
Figure 3.4(a)	Short initial /p/	58
Figure 3.4(b)	Long medial /p/ in [t̪ap:ak] 'fog'	58
Figure 3.5	Right-most obstruent lengthening in [ŋapap:a] 'sugar glider'	59
Figure 3.6(a)	Singleton /n/	62
Figure 3.6(b)	Geminate /nn/	62
Figure 3.7(a)	Alveolar apical lateral	64
Figure 3.7(b)	Retroflex lateral	64
Figure 3.8(a)	Alveolar apical obstruent	65
Figure 3.8(b)	Retroflex obstruent	65
Figure 3.9(a)	/t̪unu-bat/ 'throw it!'	66
Figure 3.9(b)	/t̪ani-pat̪/ 'leave it!'	66
Figure 3.10	Contemporary Murrinhpatha vowel inventory	75
Figure 4.1	Example of Murrinhpatha prosodic constituent hierarchy	86
Figure 4.2	Prosodic constituency for a compound verb forming a single PWord	88
Figure 4.3	Monosyllabic PWord	90
Figure 4.4	Disyllabic PWord	90
Figure 4.5	Trisyllabic PWord	91
Figure 4.6	Quadrisyllabic PWord	91
Figure 4.7	Spectrogram for (59): PPhrase containing two PWords	92
Figure 4.8	Spectrogram for (62), illustrating smooth pitch declension in external suffixes	93
Figure 4.9	Spectrogram and pitch contour for (63), illustrating single pitch peak in a polysyllabic verb	94
Figure 5.1	Sample of English verbs categorised according to Stem vowel and suffix formatives applying in past tense	119
Figure 5.2	Intersection of PrefV and Suffix formative allomorphs on a sample of verb stems	120
Figure 6.1	Verb stem and its internal predicate suffixes	138
Figure 6.2	Number category specification by pronominals and number suffixes	143
Figure 7.1	Illustrative fragment of the ontological hierarchy in the Murrinhpatha noun lexicon	172

Abbreviations and glossing conventions

Murrinhpatha words often have complex morphological structure, requiring dense morphological glossing in examples. A balance between clarity and concision has been sought in these glosses. Some glossing conventions are explained here, and the list of abbreviated grammatical category glosses is given below.

Murrinhpatha has lexical types that have highly grammaticalised functions. Lexemes of this type are glossed in plain font where they have a lexical meaning, and in CAPITALS in their grammaticalised roles. This applies to the 'pseudo-verb' subset of finite verb stems (§8.3), as well as finite verb stems suffixed as imperfective markers (§6.3.3), and to classifier nouns when attached as class prefixes (§7.2).

Finite verb stems are usually presented without segmentation, since there is no direct relationship between morphological formatives and grammatical categories (§5.5). Segmentation is only shown where the formative structure is under discussion. On the other hand, compound coverbs are always segmented in this book, even where there is not semantic compositionality of the parts. For example /ṭi-ðal/ 'bottom-open = slip over' is shown as a segmented compound. Previous work on Murrinhpatha has generally glossed these as single units.

An affix/clitic distinction is drawn in this book, and as is conventional, the double-hyphen '=' is used to mark clitic attaching, and the single hyphen '-' for affixes. However one unusual property of Murrinhpatha clitics is that they can be hosted inside affixes (§7.5, §7.7), resulting in somewhat unfamiliar glosses of the form stem=clitic-affix.

Prosodic constituency, where relevant, is marked in the example form using brackets like [[baŋam-ṭawi-bu]$_\omega$-ḍim]$_\varphi$. Syntactic constituency, where relevant, is marked in the morphological glossing line, like [foot there-LOC-TOWARDS]NP.

Examples that exhibit a phenomenon that has not been accepted in the Murrinhpatha literature, or otherwise with unusual characteristics, are cited with corpus source for transparency. On the other hand, examples illustrating common words or morphological constructs are not associated with any particular corpus source. Corpus citations take the form (XY, Date_Label), where XY is an abbreviated speaker code, Date is the date of recording, and Label is used to distinguish multiple recordings made on the same date, e.g. (AMN, 2015-01-30_Pr3-D1-EC1). The corpus is archived at the Pacific and Regional Archive for Digital Sources in Endangered Cultures (PARADISEC), as collection JM4, and research access can be granted by application to PARADISEC.

Abbreviations

ADJZ	adjectiviser
ADVERS	adversative
AGENT	agentive
ANAPH	anaphora
ANIM	animate
APPL	applicative
ATTEMPT	attemptative
C (for verb inner stems)	consonant alternant
CLS	clause ending
COMIT	comitative
COND	conditional
CONTR	contrastive
COR	coronal
CST	constituent ending
DAT	dative
DEDUCE	deductive
DIM	diminutive
DUAL.SIBL	dual sibling
EMPH	emphatic
ESS	essive
F	feminine
FUT	future
GEN	genitive
IMPF	imperfective
INCL	inclusive
INTJ	interjection
INSTR	instrumental
IRR	irrealis
ITER	iterative
LANG	language (noun class)
LOC	locative
M	masculine
NEG	negator
NFUT	non-future
NUM	number
OBJ	object
OBL	oblique
PAUC	paucal (specific)
PC	paucal (broad)
PER	peripheral
PERL	perlative
PERS	person (noun class)
PL	plural (broad)
PLUR	plural (specific, pronominal), pluractional (coverb)
PROX	proximal

PRSL	presentational
PST	past
PSTIRR	past irrealis
RECOG	recognitional
RR	reflexive, reciprocal
SEQ	sequential
SG	singular
SON	sonorant
TNS	tense
UNDESIR	undesired
UNEXP	unexpected
UNK	unknown
VEG	vegetable (noun class)
VF (for verb inner stems)	vowel frontness
VH (for verb inner stems)	vowel height
VIOL	violence (noun class)

1 Introduction

1.1 The morphology and phonology of Murrinhpatha

This book is a detailed study of morphological and phonological patterns in the Murrinhpatha language of northern Australia, and especially of how these two structural dimensions intersect. It is a study of how words are structured in this typologically interesting language.

The nature of words differs enormously among languages of the world, so much so that if we wish to use the concept 'word' in describing diverse languages we find that we must stretch its definition to cover a diverse range of linguistic phenomena. A word in Vietnamese (Austroasiatic) is a single syllable of lexical meaning (Schiering, Bickel, & Hildebrandt, 2010), while a word in Galo (Tibeto-Burman) almost always combines more than one monosyllabic morpheme by derivation or compounding (Post, 2009). In Cayuga (Iroquoian), a single lexical root can be deployed in hundreds of complex words that derive their meaning from that root (Sasse, 2002). German noun compounding very freely combines clusters of otherwise independent nouns into a single prosodic word, e.g. *sée-alp-weg* 'mountain lake path'. Conversely, in Cree (Algonquian: Russell, 1999) a verb that is made up of highly interdependent subparts may be pronounced as a sequence of distinct prosodic word units, e.g. *nikî-máci-pamihikónânak* 'they looked after us badly' (Russell, 1999, p. 205). Cross-linguistically, a word is some kind minimal utterance where phonological structure (sound patterns) and morphological structure (meaningful sub-parts) intersect. But the nature of this intersection can be very different from language to language, and it has often been noted that 'word' is a rather elusive concept, for which linguists fail to agree on any clear definition (Bickel & Zúñiga, 2017; Bloomfield, 1933; Dixon, 2002b; Haspelmath, 2011). This book may be thought of as a study of words, but it does not propose any essential definition of 'word'. As explained later in this chapter, I do not consider 'word' to be a principled natural category in Murrinhpatha, and this book could more accurately (and unmarketably) have been titled *Patterns of sound and meaning in the more tightly dependent combinatoric structures of Murrinhpatha*.

Polysynthetic languages, found throughout North America, the Arctic, the Caucasus and northern Australia, present varieties of 'sentence-words' in which many meaningful elements are strung together into a single, unbreakable unit of speech (Evans & Sasse, 2002). Polysynthetic languages have drawn much attention for their deviation from the more conventional concept of 'word', but to fully appreciate the nature of this deviation, we must carefully examine the interaction of morphological and phonological structures in these languages. This book presents such a study, for the Murrinhpatha language of northern Australia. The structure of words in Murrinhpatha, just as for Vietnamese or Galo, is quite unique, and deserving of sustained linguistic analysis. In fact Murrinhpatha word structures exhibit some characteristics that have not been described for any other language to the best of my knowledge.

In this chapter I first introduce the Murrinhpatha language, then introduce the concepts of morphology and phonology that underpin this book.

1.2 A brief sketch of Murrinhpatha

This book is not a general grammar of Murrinhpatha, but rather focuses on a more detailed analysis of morphology, phonology, and the interaction between the two. There is some discussion of phrase constituency (in particular, noun phrases and verb phrases), but only inasmuch as these are necessary to understand word structure (§4.3), or to define the domain of attachment for bound morphology (§7). 'Higher level' topics in syntax, semantics and pragmatics are not addressed (but see e.g. Blythe, 2009; Nordlinger, 2011b; Walsh, 1976). However, to provide some context as to how Murrinhpatha words fit into sentences, I here provide a brief grammatical sketch of both word and sentence phenomena.

Murrinhpatha has a fairly simple phoneme inventory, with four vowels and 22 consonants. Like most Australian languages, its consonants have an extensive range of place contrasts, but rather restricted manner contrasts. Syllables are CV(C)(C), and combine into monosyllabic or polysyllabic words. Prosodic prominence involves one pitch accent in each (short) phonological phrase, with the accent anchored to the penultimate syllable or monosyllable of the last word in the phrase (1–4). However, much of the bound morphology is excluded from the determination of accentual anchoring (5, 6).

(1) wák 'crow'
(2) pálŋun 'woman'
(3) kaṉṯáṉin 'sweet'
(4) maḷuk múnṯak 'old didgeridoo'
(5) líṯ puɾ=ɻe 'with an axe'
    axe=INSTR
(6) púɾu-ŋime 'let's go!'
    go.1INCL.IRR-PAUC.F

As mentioned in the previous section, Murrinhpatha words may have elaborate morphological structure. This is most common for verbs (7, 8), though nouns may also exhibit substantial complexity, especially when they play the predicating role in a clause (9). The details of these morphological structures are the main subject matter of this book.

(7) nuŋam-ṭi-ðaḷ=waḓa=kaṭu-wuran
use.feet.3SG.NFUT-bottom-open=SEQ=FROM-GO.IMPF
now he's slipping as he comes (LCh, 2015-07-01_2-3)

(8) ṉini=waḓa dani-ṉi-maḓa-wur-dini
ANAPH=SEQ PIERCE.3SG.PST-1SG.OBJ-belly-discomfort[1]-SIT.IMPF
because of that, I was feeling angry (MaNi, 2015-02-07_Pr2D1)

(9) kaḓu-ma-kuɹa-ŋan-ðaj
PERS-NEG-water-1PL.OBJ-mouth
we are non-drinkers (MaMi, 2015-07-21)

While the configurations of morphological structure within the verb are particularly elaborate, there are only simple configurational structures at the phrase level. There is a clear noun phrase structure of the [head modifier+] type (10), and a verb phrase of the form [NEG coverb verb] (11). Note that object or other argument NPs are not included in the configurational verb phrase.

(10) [kaḓu-kiɣaj paŋkuj perkenku]$_{NP}$
PERS-young.man tall two
two tall young men

(11) [meɹe walalajiŋka kaṉi-ṉime]$_{VP}$
NEG wave be.3PL.IRR-PAUC.F
they are not waving

A single preposition /ŋaɾa/ can introduce either a locative NP (12) or a relative clause (13), although relative clause relations are more often simply implied by parataxis (14) (Walsh, 1976, p. 287ff.).

(12) ŋaɾa [ḓa-ṯalput ŋay]$_{NP}$
LOC PLACE-house 1SG
at my house

---

[1] Compound coverbs often have non-compositional semantics (§8.5). In previous Murrinhpatha literature, including Street's (2012) dictionary, these are presented as fused units. But in this work I segment them, with the aim of demonstrating the important role of body-part compounding in the coverb lexicon – and to avoid making arbitrary decisions about where to draw the line between compositionality and lexicalisation.

(13) ŋara [puŋam-wur-pibim=ka]_REL
    REL   push.RR.3PL.NFUT-eject=CST
    ṭaŋku-ða   kuɹa   puḍḍam-wul
    what-FROM   WATER   IMPEL.RR.3PL.NFUT-return
    when they come out (of prison), why do they go back to drinking?
    (AMN, 2015-01-29_T2-D2-SC2)

(14) bam-ŋkaḍu   [ṭalput   ṉini   dim-panṭa]_REL
    AFFECT.1SG.NFUT-see   house   ANAPH   sit.3SG.NFUT-split
    I saw that the house had split open   (KeMa, 2012-06-20_28)

Other than these NP, VP and PP/REL structures, no other configurational phrase structures have been observed in Murrinhpatha. SOV and SV are the most frequent word orders for uncontextualised declarative sentences (i.e. not taking into account discursive context), though research on this topic is at an early stage (Mujkic, 2013, p. 56; Walsh, 1976, p. 276ff.). Other orders are also acceptable (15, 16), and in practice one or more arguments are generally elided, or dislocated into separate intonational units.

(15) S O V
    ku-kananṭuṭuṭ   ku-ŋulmil   baŋam-lele
    ANIM-crocodile   ANIM-fish   AFFECT.3SG.NFUT-bite
    the crocodile bit the fish   (JoCo, 2011-07-26_2-11)

(16) V O S
    baŋam-lele-ḍim   ku-weɹe   ku-puṭikat=ṭe
    AFFECT.3SG.NFUT-bite-SIT.IMPF   ANIM-dog   ANIM-cat=AGENT
    the cat is biting the dog   (DP, 2011-07-21_3-12)

While (16) uses an agentive enclitic to distinguish thematic roles (see §7.3 for other such case markers), explicit NP role marking of this type is in fact rather rare. It is more common for sentences to use overt nominal arguments for only a subset of the participants, and for their roles to be contextually understood, as in (15) above. Only high-animacy participants (humans, and sometimes animals) are marked on the verb using pronominal morphology. But verbs have a tendency to specify not just events but entities, sometimes obviating the need for nominal arguments (17, 18).

(17) pan-wun-ŋka-pul   ṭu-kaṭ
    SLASH.3SG.NFUT-3PL.OBJ-EYE.APPL-sun.rise   VIOL-cards
    the sun came up on them still playing cards   (LuPa, 2012-06-30)

(18) Jeŋkul=mani=ka   mam-ŋka-ṯum   ṯama-ja   jilele
     [NAME]=ATTEMPT=CST do.3SG.NFUT-EYE.APPL-dry say.2SG.IRR father
     how about Yengkul, the one who <u>stirs up dust in his truck</u>, who you call father?   (SL, 2012-06-12)

Verbal morphology marks three syntactic categories of pronominals: *subject*, *direct object* and *oblique*. Direct objects are unmarked for third singular, and obliques are in competition with direct objects for a single morphological slot, with free variation as to which pronominal marker should win out (Bill Forshaw, *p.c.*).[2] The system of grammatical number is rather complicated, with singular, dual, paucal and plural at the maximal level of distinction, and category mergers occurring among the non-singular types in various grammatical contexts (§6.2). Free and bound pronouns also have special forms to distinguish groups of people who are siblings in the system of kinship classification (Blythe, 2013; Walsh, 1976, p. 151ff.).

Both the nominal and verbal parts of the lexicon are dominated by compound forms, which are discussed extensively in this book. For nominals this most prominently involves a set of 10 nouns that have very broad meanings, and combine with other nominal lexemes that provide more specificity, typically in a hypernym–hyponym relationship (19, 20). The 10 nouns used as heads of compounds in this way can be labelled 'classifier nouns', because they can be seen as 'classifying' the nominal lexicon into semantic categories (Walsh, 1997). In previous work on Murrinhpatha the classifier nouns are written as separate words, but in this book they are treated as parts of compound words, based on prosodic evidence.

(19) ku-walet
     animate-fruitbat
(20) mi-kileṉ
     vegetable-green.plum

For verbs there are 39 finite verb stems, each of which appears in a paradigm of 42 inflected forms. The inflectional patterns of these paradigms are highly irregular. Fragments of two verb stem paradigms are shown in Tables 1.1 and 1.2.

Some finite verb stems (including the two below) can be used as simple verbs, but most are compounded with coverbs to produce more specific predicates.

---

2 In earlier work, Walsh (Walsh, 1976, p. 207) found that the object won out over oblique. It is not clear how or why his data differs from elicitation conducted by Forshaw.

Table 1.1: Fragment of the verb stem paradigm /ru/ 'go'.

	IRR	NFUT	PST
1SG	ŋuru	ŋuran	ŋurini
2SG	ṭuru	ṭuran	ṭurini
3SG	kuru	wuran	wurini

Table 1.2: Fragment of the verb stem paradigm /ma/ 'say, do'.

	IRR	NFUT	PST
1SG	ŋama	ŋamam	me
2SG	ṭama	nam	ne
3SG	kama	mam	me

Coverbs are an open lexical class, though there are limits on the productivity of verb-coverb compounding (21). There may in addition be recursive compounding of a body part nominal with the coverb, modifying the predicate by specifying an affected body part or various metaphorical extensions thereof (22).

(21) waʃiŋ   pillaŋam-biḷbiḷ-paŋam
   wash   wipe.3PL.NFUT-shine.PLUR-BE.IMPF
   they are polishing the car

(22) naṉti-tɻak wuḍam-ŋka-biḷ
   THING-vehicle IMPEL.RR.3SG.NFUT-eye-shine
   the car has come back to life (i.e. started working again)

The finite verb stems vary from those that make a clear lexico-semantic contribution to predicates, to those that contribute more grammaticalised valency or aktionsart content, to those that are semantically opaque. The most semantically opaque are glossed using somewhat arbitrary labels, CAPITALSISED as in (22) above. The semantics of compound verbs is rather elusive and yet to be thoroughly investigated. In this book I limit semantic analysis to an overview of variations in their degree of lexico-semantic compositionality (§8.3).

1.3 Previous work on Murrinhpatha

Murrinhpatha has an intermediate level of available documentation and analysis. Various linguistic studies have become available since the 1970s, but there is so far no comprehensive reference grammar, and many core elements of the language, such as the morpho-phonological structures described in this book, have not been analysed in detail.

The most extensive and general study of Murrinhpatha is Walsh's (1976) doctoral thesis, which provides an overview of most elements of the grammar. Street (1987) is a partial overview, intended as a learner's guide rather than as a linguistic analysis. Further broad descriptions, discussing selected elements of the grammar, are included in later doctoral theses by Blythe (2009) and Mansfield (2014). There is also an early, unpublished description of the grammar by one of the Catholic priests who was among the first non-Aboriginal people to learn any Murrinhpatha (Flynn, 1950). Flynn provides some valuable time depth to our knowledge of the language, though he did not have all the analytic tools of modern linguistics at his disposal. The most extensive published dictionary, with some 2500 headwords, was collected by Street (2012).

There is a substantial number of articles and chapters dealing with specific topics in Murrinhpatha. There is an overview of segmental phonology and stress (Street & Mollinjin, 1981), an instrumental study of the obstruent voicing contrast (Butcher, 2004), and a description of how English loanwords have been integrated into the phonology (Mansfield, 2015b). Walsh has investigated in more detail the classifier nouns, predicating nominals, and the compounding of body part nominals with coverbs (Walsh, 1996a, 1996b, 1997). Street has added further analyses of verbal arguments, tense/aspect/mood, and reduplication (Street, 1980a, 1980b, 1996), while with Kulampurut he describes a system of 'existential' verb inflections (Street & Kulampurut, 1978), which Mansfield re-interprets as markers of the speaker's epistemic stance (Mansfield, forthcoming). Nordlinger and Caudal (2012) provide a more nuanced view on the tense/aspect/mood system, while Nordlinger has produced more detailed morphological studies of templatic structure in the verb, transitivity, reciprocal verbs, applicatives, serial verbs, and an overview of verbal inflection (Nordlinger, n.d., 2010a, 2010b, 2011a, 2011b, 2015). Mansfield has added morphological studies of free variation in sequencing among certain verb suffixes, light verbs and verbal loanwords, semi-regular inflectional patterns in the finite verb stems and prosodically anchored verb compounding (Mansfield, 2015c, 2016a, 2016b, 2017). Finally, there are recent sub-theses exploring noun phrase constituency, stress, discourse markers, and further exploring body-part compounding (Clemens, 2013; Forshaw, 2011; Mujkic, 2013; Wilmoth, 2014).

With so many papers already discussing Murrinhpatha morphology, why do we need another study? The current study provides substantial new insights by exploring not just the grammatical features encoded in Murrinhpatha words, but the ways in which these are phonologically realised. This study provides a comprehensive, rigorous and explicit description of morphological structures in

Murrinhpatha, and in doing so departs somewhat from the analyses offered in previous studies of particular structures.

There are also studies of Murrinhpatha looking beyond the standard elements of grammatical description. The lenition of obstruents has been studied as a sociophonetic variable correlated with speaker age and clan background (Mansfield, 2015a), while intergeneration changes in verb stem inflection have been argued to exhibit incremental demorphologisation (Mansfield & Nordlinger, 2019). Blythe has produced a series of studies looking at interactional patterns, grammatical structure, and especially the development of grammatically encoded kinship categories (Blythe, in press, 2010b, 2010c, 2013, 2015). Blythe has also proposed a historical reconstruction for how the dual suffix derived from an ethical dative pronominal suffix (Blythe, 2010a), while Green reconstructs some finite verb paradigms to show a shared heritage with the nearby Ngan'gi language (Green, 2003). Forshaw and colleagues investigate how polysynthetic verb morphology is acquired by children (Forshaw, 2016; Forshaw et al., 2017).

Murrinhpatha society has been studied by one of the most celebrated figures of Australianist anthropology, W.E.H. Stanner, who wrote a series of influential articles discussing kinship, totemism, religion, naming and colonial contact (Stanner, 1936, 1937, 1959, 1966). The Falkenbergs produced further detailed work on kinship, totemism and marriage (A. Falkenberg & Falkenberg, 1981; J. Falkenberg, 1962). More recently, Mansfield has studied the idiosyncratic heavy metal subculture developed by Murrinhpatha youth, and the neo-totemic form of social organisation built upon this (Mansfield, 2013, 2014a). Musicological works by Barwick, Marett and others describe traditional song and ceremonial cycles (Barwick, 2011; Barwick, Marrett, Blythe, & Walsh, 2007; Marett, 2005). There are also recent doctoral dissertations describing contemporary music production (Furlan, 2005), and the crisis of political authority (Ivory, 2009).

1.4 Previous work on word structure in Australian languages

Most grammatical descriptions include some information on the interaction of morphology and phonology, but it is only in recent decades that a more advanced analytical toolkit has allowed us to describe morphology in terms of prosodic constituency. These developments were initiated by theories of Lexical Phonology (Borowsky, 1993; Kiparsky, 1982; Mohanan, 1986), and have been further developed as Prosodic Morphology (McCarthy & Prince, 1993; Nespor & Vogel, 2012; Peperkamp, 1997; Selkirk, 1984). In the description of Australian languages, the concept of a 'phonological word', 'prosodic word' or 'root-level morphology' has been used to develop analytical insights into various languages, including Lardil (Wilkinson, 1988), Warray (Harvey & Borowsky, 1999), Limilngan (Harvey, 2001, pp. 27–28), Warlpiri (Baker & Harvey, 2003; Pentland & Laughren, 2005), Arrernte (Henderson, 2002), and Dalabon (Evans, Fletcher, & Ross, 2008). There is also an overview on cross-linguistic morpho-phonological patterns across the continent (Baker, 2014).

The most detailed previous investigation of morpho-phonological interaction in an Australian language is for Ngalakgan (Baker, 2008). Ngalakgan is a Gunwinyguan language of eastern Arnhem Land, not demonstrably related to Murrinhpatha. It has two fairly distinct levels of morphological structure: an inner 'root' level and an outer 'word' level, which map onto prosodic word and phrase constituents respectively. Root constructions may be semantically opaque, i.e. 'lexicalised', and use elements that cannot be productively attached to coinages or borrowings (Baker, 2008, pp. 101ff., 129ff.). Root constructions have the same prosodic structure as simplex words, and must bear at least a secondary stress (p. 88ff.). By contrast, word constructions have more productive, semantically transparent elements. Baker calls these constructions 'compounds' (p. 85), but they have mixed characteristics of what might be pre-theoretically thought of as 'words' or 'phrases'. Word constructions as a whole host some elements of inflectional morphology (i.e. are word-like), but speakers sometimes pause at their internal boundaries in extra-careful renditions (i.e. are phrase-like). Baker labels their phonological realisation a 'prosodic phrase', hosting a tonic pitch accent on a primary stressed syllable (p. 88).

Some of the main themes apparent in Baker's study of Ngalakgan are re-iterated in Murrinhpatha. Much of the analysis in this book is built around prosodic word and phrase constituents, with the former mapping onto more semantically opaque, lexicalised constructions, and the latter onto transparent, productive constructions. However there is also a good deal of transparent, regular morphology within the Murrinhpatha prosodic word, and some opaque structures outside it. The Murrinhpatha analysis is also complicated by recursive prosodic constituency, and by more extensive morpho-phonological assimilations.

1.5 Data sources used in this study

This study takes advantage of quite extensive collections of Murrinhpatha recordings and transcriptions. My own collections come to about 50 hours of recorded speech including elicited words and phrases, narratives, informal conversation and translations from English. Approximately five hours of this material has been transcribed and translated. Further language data has been generously shared with me by Andrew Butcher, Joe Blythe, Mark Crocombe, Lucy Davidson, Bill Forshaw, Rachel Nordlinger, Chester Street and Michael Walsh, together more than doubling the quantity of transcribed speech available. Many of the illustrative examples in this book are drawn from corpus data, and are referenced to recordings listed in Appendix II. Other examples, illustrating common words or phrases, are not associated with any particular corpus source.

1.6 What I mean by phonology

Phonology refers to the sound patterns of language, and in this book, the sound patterns specific to a particular language. The pattern of vowels and consonants in Murrinhpatha is not exactly the same as any other language, though it follows many of the typical patterns observed in languages worldwide, and of Australian languages in particular. The same can be said of its 'supra-segmental' sound patterns, involving rhythm and intonation.

In the generativist tradition, phonology involves categorical mental representations of sound patterns, while phonetics involves the physical realisation of these representations as gradient gestures and soundwaves in physical space. The theory of phonological categories is supported by experimental evidence showing that acoustic signals arranged on a smooth cline are categorised in a bimodal distribution by listeners, implying that the gradient signal is processed as variant exemplars of categorical representations. These findings have been made both for segmental categories (e.g. Liberman, 1957; Lisker & Abramson, 1967) and supra-segmental categories (e.g. Gussenhoven & Rietveld, 2000; Pierrehumbert & Steele, 1989). More fundamentally, if there were no abstract categories in phonology, then we would not find any of the orderliness and repetition of patterns that we observe in language. However, categoriality is not equally well supported for all phonological features: for example, vowel space appears to be less categorical than stop voicing space (Holt & Lotto, 2010; Pisoni, 1973). Furthermore, there is evidence that phonological production cannot be reduced to segmental and supra-segmental categories being passed to a phonetic realisation module. On the contrary, details of phonetic realisation have been found to be word-specific, relating to the words' frequency (Bybee, 2001; Pierrehumbert, 2001), contextual predictability (Jurafsky, Bell, Gregory, & Raymond, 2001) and morphological structure (Pluymaekers, Ernestus, Baayen, & Booij, 2010). Some results also show idiosyncratic lexical effects that go beyond frequency, predictability or morphology (Jurafsky, Bell, & Gir, 2000; J. A. Walker, 2012). There is also evidence for not just word-specific phonetics, but phrase-specific phonetics, for example in lenition patterns specific to the phrase 'I don't know' (Bybee & Thompson, 1997). In summary, phonology is not a redundancy-free translation of phonological categorical representations into phonetic output. Aside from empirical evidence, language change gives us an *a priori* reason to assume that phonology is not purely categorical. If phonology changes over time in speech communities (Labov, 1994) or in individuals (Harrington, Palethorpe, & Watson, 2000), then we might expect that change is facilitated by gradient intermediate stages, rather than a sudden switch from one category to another. Ultimately, phonology seems to involve a system of representational categories, as well as gradient representations specific to words or phrases (Pierrehumbert, Beckman, & Ladd, 2000). In other words, phonology and phonetics do not study different phenomena, but rather study the same phenomena using different methods: phonology focuses on the high-level, broad patterns; phonetics focuses on the details of implementation, which in some cases feed back to affect the categorical representations (J. Blevins, 2004; Ohala, 1983).

Phonological analysis, therefore, should investigate the representational categories underlying speech production and perception – but should not assume that all phenomena can be reduced to redundancy-free categories. These principles guide the practice followed in this book. I aim to describe the major contrastive categories in the sound patterns of Murrinhpatha words, with occasional reference to some higher-level phrasal patterns. However I do not propose that every lexical representation is exhaustively specified by these categories. There are some important generalisations, which nonetheless do not hold for every word in the lexicon, or every word in a class. Some words exhibit intermediacy or variation in segmental types (e.g. retroflexion §3.6, loan phonology §3.8). Perhaps most importantly for this study, morpho-phonological phenomena are better characterised as stronger or weaker patterns in the lexicon, rather than rules (e.g. cluster reduction §4.4, §8.6). The phonological focus of this book is 'lexical phonology' (Kiparsky, 1982; Mohanan, 1986), describing sound patterns that relate specifically to certain morphological constructs. It is in this spirit that the book is titled 'morphology and phonology'.

1.7 What I mean by morphology

Morphology is the study of relationships between words that share systematic commonalities in their sound and meaning (Anderson, 2015; J. P. Blevins, 2016). Depending on the theoretical approach, morphological analyses may conclude from such relationships that there are meaningful sub-parts of words, labelled 'morphemes' (Bloomfield, 1933). The greater part of this book is concerned with specific morphological phenomena in Murrinhpatha, but I here lay out some of my assumptions about the nature of morphology in general. I argue that morphology is a gradient phenomenon, associated with degrees of regularity or predictability in the form–meaning relations among words.

Various phenomena described in this book beg the question, 'Is this really morphology?' One such phenomenon is the inflectional structure of finite verb stems, which is characterised by highly irregular paradigmatic patterns (§5). Another is the wealth of compounding within coverbs and in verb stem + coverb combinations. These structures are in many cases semantically opaque or 'lexicalised', so that one might question what is 'really a compound' and what is a historical relic of a compound (§8). Yet another instance is clitics, which I include in my morphological analysis, but might by some criteria be treated as independent words (§7). These phenomena might be treated as pure, unanalysable lexicon on the one hand (verb stems, compounds), or as syntactic phrase structure on the other (clitics). I include all these structures in my description of Murrinhpatha morphology, but only because I take a profoundly gradient view of lexicon, morphology and syntax. I propose below, and again in the final chapter of the book, that lexicon, morphology and syntax can be seen as a cline based on the degree of independence in their internal structural elements. Degrees of morphologicality within words can be equated with mental representations of word relationships, whereby patterns that show stronger cognitive effects in tasks like prime–target reaction times are 'more morphological'. In the discussion below I draw a careful distinction between 'cognitive morphology' of this sort, and purely descriptive morphology, as featured in this book. While I assume that morphology is gradient, I do not have the means to quantify this gradience in the structures I describe in this book. I assume that degrees of morphology are in some way linked to regularity or predictability of patterning, and in the final chapter of this book I discuss some possible approaches to quantifying such patterns (§9.5).

This sub-sections below discuss general concepts of morphology, with reference to theoretical literature. The morphological analyses presented in this book are not framed in a particular formal theory, though I argue here that they are more compatible with some theories than others. In particular, my approach is more compatible with theories that focus on analogical relations between words (e.g. J. P. Blevins, 2006; J. L. Bybee, 2001; Paul, 1888; Skousen, 1989), and those that conceive of linguistic constructions as existing on a cline from grammar to lexicon (e.g. Booij, 2010; Croft, 2001; Goldberg, 2006). Conversely, my approach is inimical to generative theories that assume an essentialist distinction between lexicon and grammar, where the lexicon is a redundancy-free list of atomic units, and the grammar a system of fully predictable combinatoric algorithms.

1.7.1 Morphological description, cognitive representation and gradience

I here propose a distinction between 'descriptive morphology' and 'cognitive morphology', where the former refers to systematic sound–meaning relations among words as identified in linguistic analysis, while the latter refers to patterns that are in some way represented in the minds of speakers. Cognitive representation may involve the use of morphological patterns in parsing or producing new words, or connections between known words that cause morphologically related words to co-activate each other. Most of the field of linguistic morphology is in these terms descriptive morphology, while cognitive morphology has only more recently begun to be investigated by psycholinguists and neurolinguists.

In works of descriptive morphology, and indeed theoretical frameworks for morphology, it is often unclear whether the phenomena described are also being posited as cognitive phenomena. The current work is almost purely descriptive, and in general, its analyses of morphological structure do not imply any claim about cognitive processing. I offer this work as a study of morphological patterns that could be candidates for cognitive activation, in the hope that this and similar descriptions will fuel further developments in psycholinguistic research.

Psycholinguistic experiments have repeatedly shown that morphological structures of many types are cognitively represented, as evidenced especially in priming relations between words (e.g. Cutler, 2012; Gagné, 2017; Jarema, 2007; Marslen-Wilson, 2007; Taft & Forster, 1975; papers in Baayen & Schreuder, 2003). One of the main techniques for illustrating cognitive morphology is by priming of lexical retrieval. A subject hears or sees a prime word (e.g. *able*), before being exposed to a target word (e.g. *ability*) and judging its acceptability. Where the prime and target are morphologically related (as in *able–ability*), participants judge the acceptability of the target more quickly than if the prime word were a random filler. Degrees of relatedness among words can therefore be measured by the average effect they have on reaction time. To distinguish morphological relations from purely phonological or grammatical relations, experimental controls are provided by words that are merely phonologically similar (e.g. *ability, ablative*) and words that are related semantically and/or grammatically, but not morphologically (e.g. *accuracy, precision*). Experiments of this type have shown that morphologically related words facilitate cognitive access to one another, even when the semantic relation is opaque (e.g. Boudelaa & Marslen-Wilson, 2015; Gagné, 2017) or the morphological structure irregular (Baayen & Moscoso del Prado Martín, 2005; Clahsen, Sonnenstuhl, & Blevins, 2003; De Jong, Schreuder, & Baayen, 2000). There remains a great deal of work to do in extending psycholinguistic research into more diverse language types, especially highly synthetic languages such as Murrinhpatha. But nonetheless, existing studies indicate that a range of morphological structures are active in our cognitive architecture. The studies also find highly variable degrees of retrieval facilitation, depending on types of morphological relations. This variation can be interpreted as showing that cognitive morphology is a gradient phenomenon. The morphological structures that produce high degrees of co-activation can be regarded as being 'more morphological' than those that produce lesser co-activation.

In works of descriptive morphology, cognitive representation is often suggested by reference to morphological 'productivity'. Morphological structures are said to be productive if speakers apply them to either borrowed or nonce lexical stems, i.e. stems that are not already established in the language (Aronoff, 1980). For example, the English -s plural can be applied to new nouns by both adult and child speakers (Berko, 1958). This shows that the structure is cognitively accessible to speakers, rather than being a merely descriptive fact about the learnt lexicon. Productivity is usually associated with structures that apply to a large number of stems in the lexicon, though there are some instances in which lexical type frequency does not align well with productivity. For example, the German -en plural is dominant in the established lexicon, but is unproductive for borrowings (Dahl, 2004, p. 297ff.). Conversely, English past tense vowel ablaut applies to a limited set of established lexemes, but nonetheless can be applied by speakers to nonce forms (Bybee & Moder, 1983). It is not always clear whether casual mentions of productivity in descriptive morphology reflect informal observations of lexical frequency, or true tests of applicability to novel lexemes. There is also the question of gradience in productivity, either because speakers disagree on the acceptability of a form, or because their judgements are on a gradient scale (i.e. *'It sounds a bit odd, but okay'*). Productivity shows one type of evidence for cognitive representation, but not the only type. As discussed above, cognitive representation is also evident in priming relations among known words, and these findings include representation of irregular, unproductive morphology.

The morphological structures described in this book presumably range from some that are highly morphological in cognitive terms, to some that are barely morphological or not at all. At the most morphological pole, we should expect to find those inflectional affixes that apply to every stem in an open lexical class, and the compound structures that are semantically transparent. For example, the suffix /-ɲime/ PAUC.F can be applied to any of thousands of verbs of the appropriate number category (§6.3). At the least morphological pole, we should expect to find inflectional exponences (both affixational and suprasegmental) that apply to highly restricted sets of stems. For example, a /d-/ prefix appears on 3SG finite verb stems, but only in nine of the thirty-nine stem classes, and only in a subset of tense categories (§5.5). It is not clear whether speakers cognitively cross-activate these /d-/ words such as /diraŋanmat̪/ 'she watches' and /dammut/ 'she gives' any more than they associate 3SG verbs in general, or words that begin in /d-/ in general. Similarly, Murrinpatha has compound stems that are both semantically opaque and appear in only a few combinations. For example the compound coverb /ṭe-pup/ ear-sit, 'hear', is semantically opaque, and furthermore never appears independently, but only in finite verb + coverb compounds such as /dinṭepup/ 'you heard' (§8.5). The element /wiṉi/ appears only in a series of compound coverbs, which have no consistent semantic element among them. Again, it is unclear whether these elements of descriptive morphology are cognitively activated or not.

1.7.2 What I mean by 'word'

The discussion above refers crucially to relations between 'words', and yet rather than being a solid conceptual grounding, the word is a theoretical quagmire. There have been some attempts to provide a principled definition of the word, which might clearly distinguish words from either word-parts on the one hand, or phrases on the other (e.g. Bloomfield, 1933; Robins, 1959). Criteria for wordhood generally relate to *distributional independence*: words can be separated and spoken alone, word-parts cannot. Phrases can be broken up by intervening word-level material, words cannot. Thus *albatross* is a word because it forms a meaningful utterance alone, does not itself contain anything word-like, and shows substantial independence in how and where it appears in sentences. But *-ed* PST cannot be uttered alone, and must always be adjacent to a verb stem.

More recent studies of wordhood have noted that there are several possible tests of independence, which do not always align (e.g. Bickel & Zúñiga, 2017). Non-alignment tends to occur in clitics, lexical compounds and in tightly bound phrases (Haspelmath, 2011). Clitics may show highly mobile positioning, yet fail as independent utterances. Compounds contain word-like elements within them, but show mixed results for distributional separability. Only some phrase types allow extraction or interruption. Furthermore, distributional criteria are sometimes compared to phonological criteria for wordhood, whereby words have a higher level of prosodic constituency than word-parts, but a lower level than phrases (see next section). But phonological criteria simply provide further dimension of potential non-alignment, especially where the 'prosodic word' does not align with morphosyntactic tests of wordhood (Bickel, Hildebrandt, & Schiering, 2009; Dixon, 2002b; Russell, 1999).

The non-alignment of various tests of independence undermines the hope for a simple, essentialist definition of wordhood. We might select one single criterion and simply decree it to be our theoretical definition of 'word', but this would be a merely terminological gambit, rather than a source of theoretical insight.

Alternatively, we might allow that 'word' has a fuzzy definition, pointing to the clustering of dependency phenomena within a certain subset of linguistic structures, which we identify as the words of a language. But it is yet to be shown cross-linguistically, or for any particular language, that dependency phenomena do indeed cluster into two levels, words and phrases (Haspelmath, 2011).

Murrinhpatha exhibits non-alignment phenomena that make any principled distinction of wordhood arbitrary. For example, there are adverbial elements that are highly mobile in their positioning, are not tightly bound prosodically, and have independent meanings. But the adverbials are never uttered without being post-posed to a host, and in verbs they may occur in the midst of a structure that otherwise shows characteristics of being a unified word (§6.3.4, §7.5). Thus the wordhood status of both adverbials and verbs exhibits criterial non-alignment. Compounding plays a major role in Murrinhpatha, and introduces typical non-alignment effects. For example, 'classifier nouns' can be independently meaningful utterances, but also appear in combination with other nouns, where they may be semantically bleached to various degrees, and some exhibit evidence of prosodic dependence (§7.2). These combinations could be labeled 'noun phrases' or 'noun–noun compounds', depending on the criteria selected. Thus Murrinhpatha does not exhibit two clearly distinct levels of structural dependency, but rather has a range of combinatoric structures, each with particular dependency phenomena. Accordingly, I do not posit an essential wordhood category in this book. In the final chapter I return to this question, giving a more detailed account of criterial non-alignment (§9.4). In the main text, however, linguistic and orthographic convention requires that I should present some differentiation between (at least) spaced and hyphenated elements. I apply this distinction in a discretionary way, with discussion of the distributional and prosodic properties of each structure designed to clarify why it has been annotated as a word or a phrase. Additionally, I use the term 'clitic' and annotate elements with a '=' symbol to distinguish those phenomena that show the greatest non-alignment of wordhood criteria, namely case markers, adverbials and discourse tags (§7.4–§7.6). These orthographic conventions should not be taken to imply a principled theoretical distinction between words, phrases and clitics.

1.7.3 Constructions: Abandoning the grammar–lexicon split

Analysing language without an essential word–phrase distinction begs the question of how we might distinguish morphology from syntax (Haspelmath, 2011). One solution to this is offered by Distributed Morphology, where all combinatoric principles are in a unified syntax, while sound–meaning pairings of any level are stored as a Vocabulary, be they independent words or bound word-parts (Embick, 2015, p. 15ff.; Halle & Marantz, 1993). A different approach is offered by Construction Grammar, where a language consists of a mixture of concrete and schematic 'constructions', which encompass both morphology and syntax (Booij, 2010; Croft, 2001; Fillmore, Kay, & O'Connor, 1988; Goldberg, 2006; Jackendoff, 2008 inter alia). Though this book is not a study in Construction Grammar, some discussion of its basic principles can further clarify what I mean by morphology.

Languages consist of both highly productive combinatoric patterns, and structures that apply to just a few lexical items, or that produce idiosyncratic meanings from their parts. These more specific structures have led to theories that posit language as a network of 'constructions', some of which are highly abstract and generalisable, and others of which are more lexically or categorically specific. All linguistic theories allow that such structures exist, but while generative theories posit a sharper separation between regular combinatorics in 'the grammar' and idiosyncratic sound–meaning pairs in 'the lexicon' (e.g. Chomsky, 1970; Di Sciullo & Williams, 1987), construction theories instead posit different *degrees* of constructional generality, with no essential grammar-lexicon split. To take an example from syntax, construction grammar posits a highly general schema in English that produces a sentence with a subject and a predicate of the form [[__]$_{NP}$ [__]$_{VP}$]s. Another type of construction, but one that is far less general, produces a VP with two serialised verbs and a prepositional phrase, of the form [[__]$_{V1}$ [__]$_{V2}$-ing [__]$_{PP}$]$_{VP}$. The V_1 position in this construction can only be filled by a limited set of verbs of movement, including *come, go, run, take off, take* and *bring*, for example *'Go laughing down the street', 'Bring him struggling into the room'* (Goldberg, 2006, p. 50). This conception of language allows for gradience in degrees of generality, according to how general or specific are the requirements of schematic slots. Constructions are hierarchically nested within one another: for example the PP element in the example above is itself a construction. This hierarchy goes down to the level of unanalysable lexical stems, which are 'constructions' without internal structure (Goldberg, 2006, p. 5). In morphological constructions, we can see an example of both generality and nesting in the schemata [[__]$_V$-able]$_A$ e.g. *climbable*, which has a fairly productive V slot, and [un-[[__]$_V$-able]$_A$]$_A$ e.g. *unclimbable*, which inherits the former schema (Booij, 2010, p. 42). A more specific schema would be [[__]$_{A,V}$-th]$_N$, e.g. *width, growth*, which has a fairly small set of A,V slot-fillers.

Theories that separate lexicon and grammar have developed two approaches to morphology. The first is the 'syntactic' approach, as in Distributed Morphology, where morphological word-parts are all sound–meaning pairs stored in the lexicon (or Vocabulary). These are combined to form words that merge the individual meanings of all the morphological parts (Chomsky, 1957; Embick, 2015;

Halle & Marantz, 1993). In the second approach, 'realisational morphology', the lexicon contains lexical stems only, and there is a morphological module, distinct from syntax, where word-formation rules derive complex words from lexical bases by applying various phonological operations (Anderson, 1992; Aronoff, 1994; Stump, 2001). The constructional approach to morphology is somewhat akin to realisational morphology, since it does not separate out affixes from the word structures in which they appear (Booij, 2010). Affixal word parts are represented, and are meaningful, only as part of constructional schemas. But construction grammar divides language in a different way, with no direct equivalents of lexicon, morphology and syntax. Instead, construction grammar has some constructions that are fully specified with semantic and phonological content (e.g. [jogging shoes]$_N$), some that are fully abstract schemas (e.g. [[__]$_{Det}$ [__]$_A$ [__]$_{NP}$]$_{NP}$), and some partially-specified schemas such as [jog [__]$_{NP.ANIM}$'s memory]$_{VP}$ and [[__]$_V$-able]$_A$ (Goldberg, 2006, p. 5). As in analogy-based theories of grammar (e.g. J. P. Blevins, 2006; J. L. Bybee, 2001; Paul, 1888), construction grammar treats abstract representations as being closely related to concrete exemplars. A partially-abstract schema such as [[__]$_V$-able]$_A$ is emergent from fully specified exemplars such as [[break]$_V$-able]$_A$, [[walk]$_V$-able]$_A$ and [[dance]$_V$-able]$_A$.

Construction grammar is perhaps best known for its applicability to semantically opaque idioms (e.g. *spill the beans*), or to idioms that contain fossil words (e.g. *without further ado*). These inherit phrasal structure from abstract schemata, without inheriting all (or any) of the semantic combinatorics. But this treatment of complex structures without compositional meaning is also useful in morphology (Booij, 2010). English contains many derived and compound words in which stem semantics are opaque (e.g. *hard-ly*), and others where stems are not independently meaningful lexemes. Examples such as *cran-berry* and *ruth-less* exemplify clear morphological patterns (c.f. *blueberry, strawberry; loveless, mindless*) but are built on stems *cran* and *ruth* that have no independent meaning. The problem is much more widespread in Latinate vocabulary such as *negoti-ate*, *negoti-able*, which are semantically related, derived words, but for which the bare stem *negot* is not independently meaningful. These phenomena sit awkwardly in a grammar that has lexical stems as atomic sound–meaning pairs in one module, and generative combinatorics in the other. Either these words contain lexical stems that are deficient in their essential sound–meaning properties, or these words actually have no morphological structure, and their apparent connection to compound or derivational word families is an illusion. In construction grammar, on the other hand, these words are linked to partially specified word schemata ([[__]$_{N,A}$-berry]$_N$, [[__]$_N$-less]$_A$, [[__]$_V$-able]$_A$ etc.). Like phrasal idioms, they inherit a schematic structure, while only partially inheriting its semantic combinatorics.

A construction approach also holds great appeal for representing complex inflectional paradigms. In some languages the inflected forms of a noun or verb involve alternations to the form of the stem, as well as affix allomorphs, both of which exhibit arbitrary patterns associated with particular lexemes. Under a theory with a lexicon/grammar split, the lexical entry for these words must include complex diacritic information about inflectional exponence. This is an unintuitive solution, but is necessary if the lexicon is the repository of all that is unpredictable, while the grammar is completely regular. Meanwhile a constructional approach, emancipated from the lexicon/grammar split, represents inflectional paradigms as whole-word forms sharing schematic structure. Examples of such schemata will be illustrated in this book (§5.7). In some inflectional systems, such as Estonian, Georgian, and indeed Murrinhpatha, there are complex dependencies between stem alternations and affixal allomorphs. As Blevins (2006) points out, storing this information in a whole-form unit keeps these phenomena unified in a single representation, whereas the separation into lexical specification and word-formation procedure artificially breaks apart pieces of information that are in practice always encountered together.

The morphological phenomena discussed above are all highly prevalent in Murrinhpatha. There are many compound structures where one element has no independent meaning (§8), and finite verb stem inflection patterns are characterised by large numbers of stem alternants, some of which interact with affixational allomorphy (§5). These phenomena can be fairly simply represented as constructional schemata, abstracted by analogy from sets of exemplar forms. Representing them as lexical entries and word-formation routines would require semantically empty lexical entries, and complex specifications for generating affixation. One may object that the simplicity of constructional schemata comes at the cost of multiplying the number of constructions that must be stored, as opposed to the redundancy-free lexicon of generative grammar. However it is not clear at what point mass storage becomes a limitation in language processing. I consider that Murrinhpatha morphological phenomena are more amenable to construction morphology than other theories, and what I mean by morphology can be understood in a constructional framework. I presume that Murrinhpatha speakers process morphology by analogy between related exemplars, and on some level adduce abstract constructional schemata. I do not presume a modular separation of lexicon and word-formation, as is often assumed in linguistic theory.

While my theoretical inclinations tend to the constructional, the morphological glossing provided in this book follows standard conventions of aligning a meaning with each morphological word-part. This should be understood as a notational convenience, rather than a theoretical claim. As mentioned above, Murrinhpatha has many word parts that are not independently meaningful.

In the case of 'cranberry morphs', I gloss these with the meaning of the larger construction in which they appear. For example, where the recurrent but meaningless coverb compound element /wiɲi/ appears, I gloss it with the meaning of the entire compound (23). In the case of semantically opaque combinations, such as /ṭe-pup/ ear-sit, 'hear', I gloss each element with the meaning it has in independent occurrence, even if that meaning is not present in the compound (24). In the case of finite verb stem inflection, I generally do not show morphological segmentation, except for in the chapter that analyses these inflectional patterns (§5).

(23) dam-wiɲi-maḍa-pak
 PIERCE.3SG.NFUT-pour.into-belly-put
 she poured it in
(24) bim-ṭe-pup
 HEAR.3SG.NFUT-ear-sit
 she heard it

1.7.4 Summary

This book describes systematic sound–meaning relationships among words in Murrinhpatha, which may be thought of as having distinct 'degrees of morphologicality', inasmuch as some are very widespread patterns, while others are specific to small sets of words. The descriptions of morphology herein generally make no claim to psychological reality for Murrinhpatha speakers, though based on what we know from psycholinguistic studies in other languages, we might expect that most of these patterns, even some that are not productive, play an active role in cognitive processing.

The 'words' among which I analyse relationships are not a strictly defined category, and more accurately I might delimit this book's scope to be 'the more tightly inter-dependent combinatoric structures of the language'. The various structures described each have different dependency properties in terms of morphosyntactic distribution and prosodic constituency, and there is no clear, generalised division between dependent and independent elements. In my orthographic representations I use conventional affix, clitic and word segmentation, though I do this to make the material legible and roughly comparable to other works, rather than as a matter of principle. I also use the term 'word', as an imprecise shorthand, meaning a tightly bound structure.

This book is not framed in terms of any theoretical formalism, though I have argued that the construction grammar approach captures some of my key assumptions about language structure – namely, that there is no principled distinction between lexicon and grammar, that meaning may be specified on various levels of nested structure, and that a complex structure may contain another structure, either with or without inheritance of its meaning. As with 'word', I use the terms 'lexical' and 'lexicon' for convenience, referring to specific as opposed to schematic constructions.

1.8 Prosodic constituency

The main focus of this book is the morphology–phonology interface in Murrinhpatha. If morphology is the study of word relations, then this study is particularly concerned with the phonological form of those relations. Other works of morphology are more concerned with the semantic or syntactic properties of morphology, and most of the previous work on Murrinhpatha morphology is more in this vein (§1.3).

'Prosodic structure' as the term is used here refers to the hierarchical bundling of speech sounds into nested units. Segments are bundled into syllables (or morae), syllables into feet, feet into prosodic words, words into phrases, and phrases into utterances (Hayes, 1995; Nespor & Vogel, 2012; Selkirk, 2011). Note that 'prosodic' in some literature refers more specifically to intonational phenomena (e.g. Jun, 2005, 2014), which are determined primarily on the utterance level. Its usage here has more to do with segmental phenomena than intonation, and it is prosodic words and short phrases with which we will be concerned, rather than utterance-level phenomena.

Morphosyntactically defined units (stem, word, clitic, XP) form the domains in which multiple phonological phenomena intersect. For example, the morphosyntactic word may be the domain for maximal consonant contrasts at its left edge, for metrical stress defined from the right edge and for vowel harmony. This domain is thus labeled the 'prosodic word'. The NP or VP may be the domain for word-juncture assimilations, a phrasal tone pattern, and phonetic lengthening of the final syllable. This domain is thus labeled the phonological phrase. We posit these domains as abstract prosodic constituents, capturing the observation that diverse phonological and morphosyntactic properties intersect in these units. Morphological elements usually have a constant prosodic constituency, though we also find occasional instances where the same morphological element has different prosodic constituency in different constructions (e.g. Baerman, 2001). We also find some instances of this in Murrinhpatha (§7.5.2, §8.7.1).

The use of common labels such as 'syllable', 'prosodic word' and 'phonological phrase' captures the fact that we tend to find fairly similar prosodic constituents in many different languages. However languages do not share exactly the same prosodic hierarchy. In particular, the interpretation of prosodic words is highly problematic in some languages (Schiering et al., 2010), and the prosodic levels between word and utterance ('accentual phrase', 'intermediate phrase', either of which may elsewhere be labelled 'phonological phrase') also appear to be typologically diverse (Jun, 2005, 2014). Some languages lack metrical foot structure between syllable and word (Himmelmann, 2018; Hyman, 2014), and I will argue that this is the case for Murrinhpatha (§4.3).

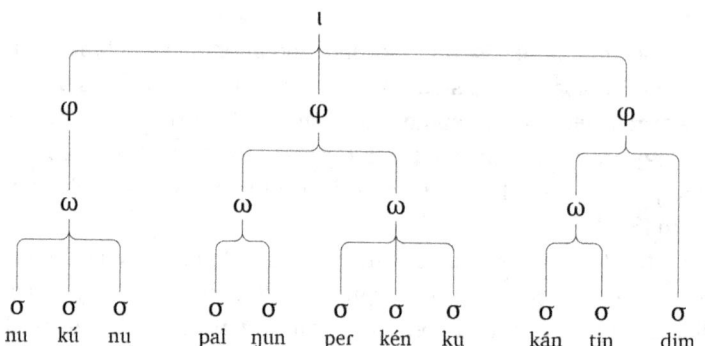

Figure 1.1: Example of Murrinhpatha prosodic constituent hierarchy.

(25) [[nukúnu]ω]φ [[palŋun]ω [perkénku]ω]φ [[káṉtin]ω-dim]φ
     he   woman   two   have.3SG.NFUT-SIT.IMPF
     he has two women   (LP, 2015-09-16_AT)

Figure 1.1 and (25) illustrates the prosodic constituency of a Murrinhpatha utterance, with syllables (σ), prosodic words (ω), phonological phrases (φ) and an intonational phrase (ι). Some earlier views of prosodic structure argued for 'strict layering' in which each constituent is built up solely and exhaustively from constituents on the level immediately below – e.g. φ must be exhaustively composed of daughter ω constituents, [[_]ω [_]ω]φ (Nespor & Vogel, 2012; Selkirk, 1984). However it has more recently been acknowledged that many languages deviate from strict layering in two respects: they exhibit prosodic recursion, e.g. where ω contains a ω, [[σ σ]ω σ]ω, and 'level-skipping', e.g. where φ contains σ that is not part of any ω, [[σ σ]ω σ]φ (Selkirk, 2011). Another name for level-skipping is 'prosodic adjunction', where the lower-level sibling, e.g. the σ that is a direct daughter of φ, is the 'adjunct', and is 'adjoined' to a sibling on the higher level (Bennett, Elfner, & McCloskey, 2016, p. 198). Figure 1.1 illustrates prosodic adjunction, which features prominently in my analysis of Murrinhpatha (§4.4.2, §6.3).

Prosodic constituency, like all linguistic systems, is crucial for language processing even though we have little conscious awareness of its operation. The chunking of the sound stream into nested bundles has an information-packaging function that facilitates sound → meaning processing (Carlson, Frazier, & Clifton, 2009; Christiansen & Chater, 2015; Cutler, 2012, p. 227ff.; Vallduvi & Engdahl, 1996). It has been argued that complex systems in general require hierarchical chunking to provide efficiency and resilience (Simon, 1962). But compared to other linguistic systems, prosodic constituency has been rather late to receive descriptive or theoretical attention. The syntax and semantics of meaning have been extensively studied; the segments and tones of sound patterns equally so; yet prosodic constituency, the abstract glue that binds these two faces of language together, has as yet only been thoroughly addressed in a small number of languages. In attempting to understand the sound–meaning interface in Murrinhpatha I have found it essential to map out the prosodic structure that mediates the relationship. The extension of prosodic constituency research to a wider range of languages helps us more fully understand the structural diversity of human language, as exemplified by studies of Axininca Campa (McCarthy & Prince, 1993), Chácobo (Tallman, 2016), Galo (Post, 2009), Vietnamese and Limbu (Hildebrandt, 2007; Schiering et al., 2010), Ngalakgan (Baker, 2008) and the several languages treated in collected volumes (Dixon & Aikhenvald, 2002; Jun, 2005, 2014).

1.9 Chapter outline

The structure of this book flows broadly from social setting, to phonology, to morphology, and finally returning to some theoretical considerations.

Chapter 2 lays out the social and historical context in which Murrinhpatha is spoken, drawing particular attention to the multilingual ecology in which it existed up until the 1940s, before settlement of the town of Wadeye [wadéje] brought about a sudden convergence of Aboriginal clans shifting to the Murrinhpatha language, now in a diglossic relationship with English.

Chapter 3 commences the linguistic analysis by describing segmental sound patterns, drawing particular attention to certain consonant contrasts that are unusual among Australian languages, or have an intermediate status in Murrinhpatha. The chapter also briefly describes phonetic connected-speech phenomena, and the integration of loanwords from Jaminjung and English. The latter topics are not crucial to understanding the core morpho-phonological interactions of Murrinhpatha, but are necessary to bridge the gap between structures represented in this book, and the actual flow of discourse in real-life Murrinhpatha speech. Chapter 4 builds on the segmental description by showing how it is deployed in morphological structures, both lexical word classes and bound morphology. The core structures of prosodic word and phrase are introduced, and morpho-phonological assimilations that occur within the prosodic word are described.

Chapter 5 describes the inflected forms of finite verb stems, which are highly irregular and opaque. This chapter presents a more detailed analysis of these complex inflectional patterns than has been previously presented in the literature, and argues that this phenomenon can be more naturally represented in a constructional approach than in theories with an essentialist lexicon/grammar split. Chapter 6 describes inflectional suffixes hosted by predicating lexemes, which may be a verb or a nominal, so that these suffixes are not distinguished as being either 'verbal' or 'nominal'. This description includes an account of the complex system of number marking in verbs, which interacts with pronominal arguments and with prosodic constituency in interesting ways. Chapter 7 describes semantic and morphological aspects of noun phrases, and phrase-level morphology. This chapter shows that compounding is prolific in the Murrinhpatha noun lexicon, and that phrase-level 'clitic' elements also play a prominent role in the language.

Chapter 8 describes complex verbs, which combine finite verb stems with coverbs, either as phrases or as morphological compounds. It explores the cline of lexicalisation, from the most transparent compounds to the most opaque, highlighting the fact that this suggests alternative versions of how stem – inflection structure should be represented. The chapter also describes derivational reduplication in the coverb, and recursive compounding of body-part nominals with coverbs, the whole unit in turn being compounded with a finite verb stem. The prosodic constituency of compound verbs is described, showing that compounding uses a prosodic edge as an anchor point for the coverb, with inflectional morphology appearing either to the left or right of the coverb, depending on its prosodic status. 'Prosodic compounding' of this type has not been attested for any other language as far as I know. This chapter again argues that a construction grammar offers an intuitive approach to these phenomena.

Chapter 9 provides a summary of some phonological and morphological highlights from the book. Drawing on these, I then return to the theoretical questions raised in this introduction regarding the nature of wordhood and morphology. I argue that the concept of 'word' does not fit neatly in Murrinhpatha, and that within word-like structures, there is no clear cut-off between morphology and pure, unanalysable lexicon. I sketch some possible approaches to how we might quantify relative degrees of morphologicality, and finally reflect on the question of what makes 'polysynthetic' languages special.

2 Social setting and language ecology

2.1 Introduction

In this chapter I set the scene for the grammatical description that follows, by describing the social situation in which Murrinhpatha is spoken. The Murrinhpatha people lived until relatively recently as semi-nomadic hunter gatherers in the tropical savannah of northern Australia, in the region to the south-west of the Daly River (see map, Figure 2.1 below). The region was very linguistically diverse, with several quite distinct languages (not to mention more fine-grained dialects) spoken within a radius of 100 kilometres (Nordlinger, 2017; Tryon, 1974). Sedentary living and permanent contact with non-Aboriginal people was established from 1939, when the Port Keats Mission was founded on Murrinhpatha land by Jesuit missionaries. The mission became home to not just the seven clans that spoke Murrinhpatha, but also to another dozen or so clans speaking other Aboriginal languages of the region (Pye, 1972).

The establishment of the mission set in motion a series of radical changes in Murrinhpatha society, the consequences of which are still unfolding. Since 1975 the mission has been replaced by secular governance, and the town renamed Wadeye. In some respects the Murrinhpatha people have taken on typical sedentary, urbanised ways of living; but in other respects they remain deeply connected to the social and spiritual structures of their recent hunter-gatherer past. The transition to settlement life has not been easy, and development of the town of Wadeye is frustrated by chronic social problems, and outbursts of public disorder. The nature of 'Murrinhpatha' as an ethno-linguistic identity is also undergoing rapid change, as the language is now spoken by many Aboriginal people who are not of Murrinhpatha clan heritage.

Section §2.2 describes the traditional language ecology of Murrinhpatha, and section §2.3 describes pre-contact forms of social organisation. Section §2.4 and §2.5 describe the establishment of contact with colonial Australia, and the secularisation of the mission, respectively. Section §2.6 describes the contemporary language ecology of Murrinhpatha.

2.2 Traditional language ecology

The Murrinhpatha language (also spelled Murrinh Patha[3]) is spoken by virtually all Aboriginal people in the town of Wadeye in northern Australia, as well as smaller numbers of Aboriginal people in other regional locations, giving it a total speaker population of around 3000. This makes it one of the most vibrant Australian Aboriginal languages, and also one of very few that are still being learnt by children as their first language. Traditionally, Murrinhpatha has been spoken by at least four patrilineal clans: Dimirnirn, Kirnmu, Maninh and Nangu (Ward, 1983). A further three clans – Kura Thipmam, Madjalindi and Wunh – are identified as speakers of *Murrinh Kura*, which is generally agreed to be a variety of Murrinhpatha. A further four clans – Kura Ngaliwe, Papa Ngala, Piru Pangkuy and Pulampa – identify primarily with other Aboriginal languages, but secondarily with Murrinhpatha or Murrinh Kura. Some or all of these clans can be considered to 'own' the language. Different clan members may give different views on language affiliation, showing that clan–language affiliations in the region are not always stable or deterministic (cf. Sutton, 1978). Aboriginal people of the Daly region were traditionally multilingual, speaking not just their own patrilineal clan language but also those of their extended exogamous kin network (J. Falkenberg, 1962, p. 13). However all Aboriginal people of the region, not just those of the clans cited above, now speak Murrinhpatha, and in most cases remember little of their traditional clan languages (§2.6).

The linguistic history of the Daly region has not been comprehensively reconstructed, and may be complicated by a high degree of areal diffusion associated with regional inter-marriage, ceremonial links and multilingualism (Dixon, 2002a, pp. 674–676). Murrinhpatha was for some decades treated as a linguistic isolate, until Green (2003) showed that it is genetically related to the nearby Ngan'gi (Reid, 1990). Apart from Ngan'gi, none of the Daly languages have been shown to have a genetic relationship with Murrinhpatha. Therefore Murrinhpatha is currently classified as a 'Southern Daly' language along with Ngan'gi, and beyond that as one of the 'non-Pama-Nyungan' languages of the northern Australian tropical fringe, which are defined negatively as not belonging to the Pama-Nyungan family occupying the rest of the continent (Evans, 2003c; Koch, 2014).

---

[3] The single-word form 'Murrinhpatha' has been preferred by the Wadeye school and church since about 2009, though it is rather inconsistent with general Murrinhpatha orthography, where noun classifiers are written as separate words, e.g. *murrinh thelerrdhe* 'news' (Street 2012). Other spellings include 'Murrinh-patha' and 'Murriny Patha'. Some older records (e.g. work by Stanner) use the spelling 'Murinbata'.

2.2.1 Neighbouring languages

The most widely recognised neighbouring language varieties are illustrated on the map in Figure 2.1. Attempting to delimit bordered clan or language territories is in itself a very difficult task (cf. Sutton, 1978), so I here mark an indicative central point for the range of each language. This is not an undisputed list of languages in the area, as there is not always clear agreement about which varieties count as the same language and which count as different (Mühlhäusler, 2002; Sutton, 1991). However, there is substantial convergence in contemporary local views, and in the documentary record, on this set of named varieties as the languages whose speakers populate the town of Wadeye.

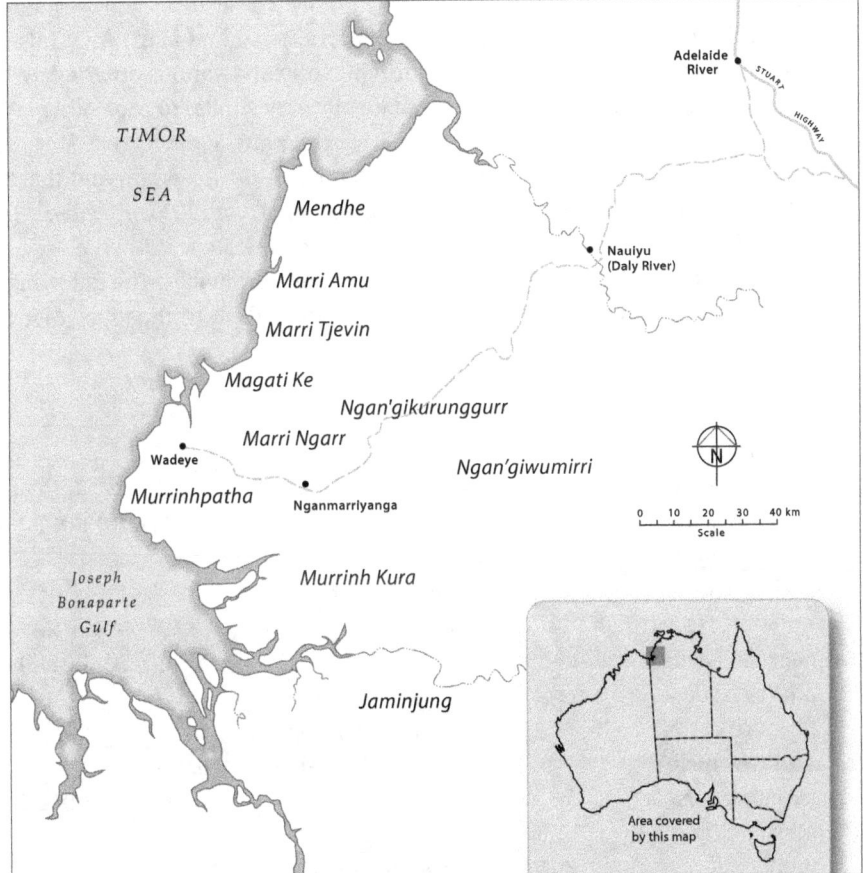

Figure 2.1: Murrinhpatha and surrounding languages (Barwick et al., 2009; Blythe, 2009; Furlan, 2005; Reid, 1990; Ward, 1983).

Murrinh Kura is a variety closely related to Murrinhpatha. It is almost totally undocumented, and is unfortunately now almost extinct. Most people at Nganmarriyanga, the town nearest to Wadeye, identify as Murrinh Kura speakers, though only a handful of elderly people can recall any differences between traditional Murrinh Kura and Murrinhpatha dialects. The only clear difference I have been able to establish is a distinct inflectional prefix for first-person inclusive finite verb stems (§5.5).

As noted above, the Ngan'gi languages are the only other languages demonstrably related to Murrinhpatha (Green, 2003). Ngan'gi is phonologically and grammatically similar to Murrinhpatha (Reid, 1990), though the lexicon is quite distinct and they are not mutually intelligible. Murrinhpatha people do not see Ngan'gi as being particularly similar to their own language.

To the north and east of Murrinhpatha there are a series of fairly closely related languages making up the Western Daly family. These are Marri Ngarr and Magati Ke (in a close dialectal relationship), Marri Tjevin and Marri Amu (also close to each other), then further to the north Mendhe and various other related varieties (Green, 1989). All these are grammatically very similar to each other, as well as being fairly similar to Murrinhpatha. For the pairs Marri Ngarr / Magati Ke and Marri Tjevin / Marri Amu, there is also great lexical overlap, and these languages are recognized by speakers as being similar (Tryon, 1974, pp. xiii–xiv). Translation between Murrinhpatha and any of these languages is often close to a morph-by-morph calque, but with very few cognate morphemes. The following are translation equivalents provided by a fully bilingual Murrinhpatha / Marri Tjevin speaker:

(1) *Marri Tjevin*
   a-kani-pir̺-a   t̪uwuyina
   ANIM-stand.3SG.R-fish-PST   yesterday
   he went fishing yesterday   (CD, 2013-01-15)

(2) *Murrinhpatha*
   ku-kaḍi-ku-ða   kuɲiniɻe
   ANIM-be.3SG.PST-fish-PST   yesterday
   he went fishing yesterday   (CD, 2013-01-15)

(3) *Marri Tjevin*
   t̪a-mur̺uka   kiriŋki-βut̪-kar̺ki-ja
   THING-vehicle   use.hands.1PL.R-have-SIT.IMPF-PST
   we had a vehicle   (CD, 2013-06-25)

(4) *Murrinhpatha*
   naṉti-tɻak   ŋume-bat̪-t̪a-ŋaḍi
   THING-vehicle   use.hands.3PC.PST-have-PST-BE.IMPF
   we had a vehicle   (CD, 2013-06-25)

This grammatical isomorphism would no doubt make language acquisition easier for speakers of one Daly language learning another, and may have been the result of long-term convergence in a Daly sprachbund.

Jaminjung (Schultze-Berndt, 2000) is from an altogether separate Mirndi language family, separate to the south by the Fitzmaurice River (Harvey, 2013). However there is some Jaminjung multilingualism in the older generation at Wadeye, many of whom travelled to work on cattle stations in Jaminjung country. Unfortunately, little has been documented about the linguistic situation on stations where Murrinhpatha and Jaminjung people worked together, or indeed the degree of Jaminjung bilingualism among Murrinhpatha people of the cattle station generation.[4] Murrinhpatha–Jaminjung bilingualism is evident in the Jaminjung lexico-phonological stratum of Murrinhpatha (§3.8).

2.3 Traditional social organisation

Before European contact, Murrinhpatha people were semi-nomadic hunter-gatherers. They established a series of camps on their clan territories, moving in accordance with tropical wet and dry seasons, and the various food sources associated with each. Traditional residence groups numbered a few dozen people at most, and were somewhat fluid in their composition (J. Falkenberg, 1962, p. 124ff.). Like all Australian Aboriginal societies, Murrinhpatha people structure their social interactions around kinship. One's father and his brothers are of the same category (*yile*, 'father'), and one's mother and her sisters are of the same category (*kale*, 'mother'), which means that one has many classificatory 'fathers' and 'mothers', and all their children are one's 'sisters' and 'brothers'. Meanwhile patrilineal and matrilineal grandparents are distinguished, so that one has four categories of kin in this generation, which in turn provides the basis for a more finely specified range of uncles, aunts and cousins (Blythe, in press; J. Falkenberg, 1962). The importance of kin relations in social interaction is reflected in the Murrinhpatha verb inflection system, which has special inflectional categories for referring to groups of people who are classificatory brothers or classificatory sisters (§6.2) (Blythe, 2013).

---

[4] On one occasion Claver Dumoo, an elderly Wadeye man who usually speaks Murrinhpatha or Marri Tjevin, was present at a recording session where I elicited sentences from an elderly Jaminjung speaker. The latter was somewhat frail and struggling to enunciate his words, but Dumoo assisted by enunciating, with apparent ease, the Jaminjung sentences on his behalf.

Most social categories are built on kin relationships. The patrilineal clan is the fundamental traditional social category, both in the sense that others can be derived from it, and in terms of functional importance. Clans own tracts of country and are associated with totemic species that are found in that country. For example, the Kura Thipmam clan come from a stretch of country encompassing named sites including Ngudaniman, Yerrpilam and Kulthil. Their name references dark silty water that enters the sea at Yerrpilam, and they are alternatively known as Kulthil clan. Their totems include *ku balli* 'mud crab' and *ku kanamkek* 'Rainbow Serpent' (Ward, 1983). In some cases neighbouring clans share one or more totems.

Clans can be grouped into tribes or 'language groups' according to self-identification as speaking the same language. For example, Kuy and Yederr clans both identify their language as Magati Ke and agree that they speak the same language, although furthermore, and without contradiction, these clans may identify their languages more specifically as Magati Kuy and Magati Yederr. (For all the language names treated here except Jaminjung, the first part means 'speech': *murrinh, marri, magati, ngan'gi*.) The categorization of clans into language groups is not always straightforward, as some clans identify with two or three neighbouring languages either simultaneously, or at different points in time. For example the Papa Ngala clan is recorded as Murriny Kura by Ward (1983), but later in Barwick et al (2009) identified as Ngan'giwumirri; the Pulampa clan is identified by Ward as both Marri Ngarr and Ngan'giwumirri. But other clans are identified consistently with one language. For example the Nangu and Maninh clans are unambiguously identified as Murrinhpatha people; Wakal Bengkunh and Wudipuli clans are unambiguously Marri Ngarr people. Adding to the difficulty of a stable taxonomy, most clans can be referred to by more than one name, and some of the languages also have multiple designations (Sutton, 1991).

Another superordinate grouping for clans is 'ceremony groups', which are activated for initiation rites as well as funerary smoking ceremonies and any other events involving traditional song and dance. The importance of these groups in ceremonial exchange and in transactions with the spirit realm has been extensively documented by Marett (2005) and Barwick (2006, 2011). The situation with ceremony groups is much as with language groups, with some clans identifying with more than one ceremony group, or changing group over time. The groups Djanba, Wangga and Lirrga are the most solidly attested, though in recent times some clans also identify as Balga or Wurlthirri, each of which may or may not be distinct from Djanba. All of these group names can also be regarded as the names of song and dance genres.

Moiety and subsection groups have also been used at Wadeye, but these categories have both fallen into disuse. *Kartthin* 'chicken hawk' and *tiwungku* 'eagle hawk' were the patrilineal moieties, seemingly well-established in the social structure at the time of earliest documentation (Stanner 1936). It is unclear why moieties have ceased to be recognised in Wadeye. Subsections, on the other hand, were an innovation only briefly borrowed in the early twentieth century from the Jaminjung and other groups to the south, being discarded after just a few decades' currency (Blythe, in press). Around the same time, some Wadeye men experimented with the penile subincision ceremony they had encountered among people to the south. This too proved a rather brief fad (Mark Crocombe, *p.c.*).

2.4 Contact and settlement

Murrinhpatha peoples' contact with European (mostly British) colonisers began in the late nineteenth and early twentieth centuries, but at this stage amounted to only brief and sporadic encounters when Australian settlers stopped off at their coastline on journeys of exploration or commerce (Walsh, 2011). More extensive contact probably came from Murrinhpatha people themselves travelling, especially to the cattle stations that had already been established in Jaminjung country to the south. But at this stage there were no non-Aboriginal people resident in Murrinhpatha country.

In 1935 Father Richard Docherty founded the first Catholic mission in the area at a site behind some coastal dunes named Werntek Nganayi, in Kirnmu (Murrinhpatha) clan territory. After four years, it was decided that an alternative site was superior, a few kilometres to the north in Dimirnirn (also Murrinhpatha) clan territory. At this site, on the high ground between the Wadeye creek and a system of mangrove inlets, the permanent Port Keats Mission was founded, which later became the contemporary town renamed Wadeye (Pye, 1972, n.d.). The decision to site the mission here on Murrinhpatha country would later prove propitious in supporting the survival of the language, while other languages around it ceased to be spoken. Offering rations of flour, tea and tobacco, as well as respite from inter-clan territorial disputes, the mission soon attracted all clans from within about a 50km radius. At first there were not sufficient resources to provide for the demand, and clans were therefore allotted alternating fortnights staying at the mission, and returning to the bush. Later the mission grew large enough that the clans were able to settle there permanently (Pye, 1972, n.d.).

Though spear-fights were not unknown at the mission (Pye, 1972, p. 30), life was fairly harmonious. The mission received basic goods imported by barge from Darwin, but otherwise was largely cut off from urban Australia, as overland travel to Wadeye was arduous in the dry season, and impossible in the wet season. The Murrinhpatha people shared in the missionaries' vision of improving living conditions with housing, medical treatment and literacy, and the ideology of spiritual improvement through salvation in Christ. In fact the Murrinhpatha proclaimed that Jesus and the Virgin Mary were already known to them, having appeared to the Dimirnirn man Mollinjin in a dream before Docherty's arrival (Reynolds, 1999, pp. 74–78). Another Dimirnirn man, Ngiparl Boniface Perdjert, became the first Australian Aboriginal deacon. In this way the Dimirnirn's ownership of the land on which Wadeye was founded became partly transferred into authority within the new spiritual regime. The mission instituted a rather paternalistic regime of farm work and church attendance for adults, and school attendance for children. This must have been a great contrast from semi-nomadic bush life, which responded to vagaries of weather and food availability, rather than relying on a structured regime of agriculture and imports. Murrinhpatha people also now found themselves living in a much larger permanent group than they had ever experienced in the bush, at first numbering a few hundred, but soon growing into the thousands. Perhaps the most drastic life change was that imposed on children, who spent week-days living under the care of the missionaries in girls' and boys' dormitories, forming gendered peer groups that cut across clan and tribal affiliations. Children who had spoken a range of Aboriginal languages as their first language all learnt Murrinhpatha as a peer lingua franca in the dormitory, anticipating what would soon become a generalised language shift.

2.5 Post-missionary Wadeye

In 1975 the mission was dissolved and the secularised town was officially renamed as Wadeye. The new form of governance combined mainstream Australian bureaucracy and jurisdiction together with a local Aboriginal council, first Kardu Numida ('one people') established in 1978, which later disintegrated, and was replaced by a new council Thamarrurr ('gathering of delegates'), which persists at the time of writing (Ivory, 2009). The town population continued to grow rapidly, reaching its current level of some 2500 people (Taylor, 2010). The original town now has two outlying 'suburbs', Manthathpe and Nilinh. A small plane transports people and goods to and from Darwin twice a day, while road access is much improved, at least in the dry season. There are now several shops selling food, clothes and hardware in the Wadeye main street, a large medical clinic has been built, and the school is expanded.

Local leaders and some non-Aboriginal educators or public servants have worked strenuously to develop social cohesion and economic development in the town. However, their best efforts have at times been frustrated by social problems and civil disturbances, for which Wadeye has been somewhat notorious (Bailey & Coren, 1988; Brady, 2017, p. 107ff.; Ivory, 2009, p. 270ff.). Neither Australian government bodies nor the local Thamarrurr council are able to fully impose their authority on the town, and there is an unfortunate lack of employment or economic activity to help the Murrinhpatha people make sense of settlement life. Hunting and ceremonial activities persist, but somewhat peripherally, no longer providing core subsistence or substantial integration of a body politic. As in other remote Aboriginal communities, the lives of many Wadeye residents are restricted by economic stagnation and welfare dependency (Pearson, 2000).

Boredom and lack of authority in post-missionary Wadeye frequently foment open conflict between kin groups. Medical care has greatly reduced birth mortality, but has not substantially improved life expectancy, so that youth outnumber the elderly by around ten to one (Taylor, 2010, p. 12). During the 1980s and 1990s the availability of alcohol at a licensed canteen in Wadeye exacerbated violent conflict, until a local anti-alcohol group took matters into their own hands and destroyed the canteen with a front-end loader (Brady, 2017, p. 118ff.). Alcohol was subsequently banned from the town, which to this day does not permit drinking by Aboriginal people. Some alcohol is still consumed in a covert manner, though it is not especially common.

The persistent power vacuum in Wadeye, and its bottom-heavy age demographic, has created space for young men to develop their own unsanctioned forms of social organisation and conflict. Their groups have been labelled 'gangs' in scandalised newspaper reports (e.g. Murdoch, 2006, Figure 3), though they are unlike classical urban crime gangs, and in fact have much in common with traditional totemic kinship groups (Mansfield, 2013). Perhaps the most striking thing about these groups is that they name themselves after heavy metal bands seen on television. The gangs have names like Judas Priest, Slayer, Megadeth and Iced Earth. Revolving around heavy metal, marijuana, nocturnal street-fights and intense alienation from mainstream institutions, Wadeye youth have created an idiosyncratic local subculture with which most identify to some extent (Mansfield, 2014a, 2018). These alienated youth speak Murrinhpatha as their main language, like almost all Aboriginal residents of Wadeye.

Chronic fighting among the heavy metal gangs, especially the enduring war between Judas Priest and Evil Warriors, brought particularly negative attention to bear on Wadeye in the years 2006–2008. The Prime Minister of Australia visited the town to see the problem, and together with his Minister for Indigenous Affairs (*not* an Indigenous man), launched the Northern Territory Emergency Response, a package of crisis measures designed to combat what was seen as an epidemic of violence and abuse in remote Aboriginal communities (Altman & Hinkson, 2010; Toohey, 2008).

Figure 2.2: Front page of a Melbourne newspaper, 23 May 2006.

Conflict in Wadeye has been somewhat alleviated since the crisis intervention, and the greater attention has brought improved funding for housing and education. However conflict between kin groups still flares up intermittently, and the major underlying problem of unemployment persists. Despite secularisation of town governance, and the general lack of public order, the church continues to have a very active role in the community, and most of the population are devout believers in Christian salvation. One of my Murrinhpatha friends, himself a proud affiliate of Megadeth gang and a fierce fighter, always wears rosary beads, and wishes me goodnight with the words *kangkarl-mawu kirranhipe* 'may Jesus (*lit.* the sky-dweller) watch over you'.

2.6 Contemporary language ecology of Wadeye

Murrinhpatha has elsewhere been described as the 'lingua franca' of Wadeye and surrounds (Blythe, 2009, p. 26; Walsh, 1990). However, Murrinhpatha can be seen not just as a lingua franca, but as a sort of 'official language'. The site of Wadeye is in the country of the Dimirnirn clan, and since Murrinhpatha is the language of the Dimirnirn, Murrinhpatha is the proper language for Wadeye (Rumsey, 1993).

Virtually all Aboriginal people at Wadeye speak Murrinhpatha as their primary day-to-day language, and for some young people this is their only fluent language. The main exceptions are Aboriginal people who have recently married into Wadeye, who of course are not fluent in Murrinhpatha, but quickly begin to acquire the language. I do not know how long this acquisition process takes, but I have observed Aboriginal people who have lived at Wadeye for a few years conversing comfortably in Murrinhpatha. I have also heard recently arrived Aboriginal people using Kriol (a northern Australian, English-lexified creole (Sandefur, 1979)), both among themselves and to address Murrinhpatha speakers.

There is a striking contrast between the successful acquisition of Murrinhpatha by Aboriginal in-migrants, and the non-acquisition of Murrinhpatha by non-Aboriginal people. There are only a handful of non-Aboriginals who can speak or understand Murrinhpatha, while other medium-term residents (school or clinic workers who stay for a few years) generally learn a few isolated words. The contrast between Aboriginal and non-Aboriginal people is undoubtedly because of their totally different types of social integration in the community, with Aboriginal people entering into kin relationships and Aboriginal households, while non-Aboriginals remain socially segregated in their own sub-community. But it is perhaps also a testament to Aboriginal peoples' disposition to multilingualism, compared to non-Aboriginal Australians' expectation that the only language they should need to speak is English (and perhaps an immigrant language of their parents).

Murrinhpatha is also spoken by some Aboriginal people outside of Wadeye. The nearest town, Nganmarriyanga (also known as Palumpa), has a population of some 300–400 people who generally speak Murrinhpatha as their main language. This is despite Nganmarriyanga not lying on traditional Murrinhpath land, and the main resident clans not being Murrinhpatha clans. Nganmarriyanga appears to have taken up Murrinhpatha as its main language under the influence of its larger neighbour Wadeye. There is further 'diasporic' use of Murrinhpatha: around 25 regular speakers at Kununurra, a few at Peppimenarti, Daly River and Katherine, and a few dozen living in Darwin 'town camps' (Aboriginal housing estates), or living rough in the city's parks. In Darwin, Murrinhpatha is sometimes used with non-Murrinhpatha people from distant tribes, indicating that new forms of multilingualism are developing in this large urban centre.

2.6.1 Status of neighbouring Aboriginal languages

By the time the Port Keats Mission was fully settled, Murrinhpatha people were a minority of the population, and Western Daly language groups the majority (i.e. Marri Ngarr, Magati Ke, Marri Tjevin and Marri Amu people). An early estimate counts 200 Murrinhpatha people and 500 from Western Daly languages (Falkes, Docherty, & Gsell, 1939). But though the majority of the contemporary Wadeye population comes from other Aboriginal language groups, these languages are now moribund. Nor do any of these languages remain vibrant in other locations. Mendhe, Ngan'gi and Jaminjung are all moribund in their homeland communities (Reid & McTaggart, 2008; Schultze-Berndt, 2000, p. 10), while Wadeye was the major place of settlement for Western Daly tribes as a whole. Marri Tjevin and Marri Amu both have just one or two full speakers still living in Wadeye; Marri Ngarr has a few full speakers living at Wudipuli outstation some 40km away, but none as far as I know at Wadeye; Magati Ke has no living full speakers as far as I know; Jaminjung has one or two full speakers living at Wadeye. The actual usage of these other Aboriginal languages in Wadeye is limited to encounters between older Western Daly or Jaminjung speakers, and one-way usage when they speak their own language to address younger kin, who however reply in Murrinhpatha.

The convergence of multiple language groups onto a single language happened very rapidly at Wadeye. Levels of linguistic competence and people's childhood recollections calibrated against their ages suggest that languages other than Murrinhpatha stopped being fully acquired in the 1950s – that is to say, barely a decade after the Mission was settled. An explanation for this rapid language shift can be found in the widespread Aboriginal philosophy of language, wherein the connection between language and place is axiomatic (Rumsey, 1993). As mentioned above, there is a consensus that Murrinhpatha is the proper language for Wadeye, so that even though Murrinhpatha people were not the largest population group, their language became the lingua franca of the Mission. Note however that this process has not been automatic in all multilingual settlements of northern Australia. Rather, it may be that the group on whose land a settlement is built need a certain minimum of political power or assertiveness to stake the claim of their language. For instance Maningrida (est. 1957) was built on Ndjébbana country, but the speakers of this language lacked sufficient political power in the early settlement to give their language the status of lingua franca (Elwell, 1982, p. 86). Maningrida has instead settled on another language, Burarra, as lingua franca, while at the same time remaining highly multilingual (Vaughan, in press).

Rapid language shift to Murrinhpatha was facilitated by the dormitories that children stayed in during the mission days. One of the first acts of the missionaries was to construct two dormitories, one for boys and one for girls, with school children staying there during the week and returning to their family camps for weekends and 'bush holidays' (Pye, 1972). The aim of such dormitories seems to have been to interrupt the socialisation patterns of the Aboriginal people, so that they might be partly re-socialised according to the missionaries' ideas of moral and educational betterment (Choo & McCoy, 2010). But though the Port Keats missionaries were generally supportive of maintaining Aboriginal language (and 'culture', or at least those parts that did not contradict Christianity), their dormitories may have unwittingly also interrupted language socialisation. Several middle-aged Marri Ngarr people have told me that they spoke Marri Ngarr as children, but switched to Murrinhpatha when they went to live in the dormitory.

The last full Magati Ke speaker (PN, 1930–2014) recounted a fateful event in the decline of his language. One day in the early mission era, Magati Ke men were sitting in a public area discussing how they were going to arrange an upcoming ceremony. Some Murrinhpatha men accused them of planning something subversive behind the veil of their own language, and a spear fight ensued, in which the Murrinhpatha men were victorious. After this the Magati Ke people decided not to speak their language at the mission, and from that point on, their children grew up speaking Murrinhpatha (story via Mark Crocombe, *p.c.* 2013-12). There have been other, deeper conflicts between clan and language groups at Wadeye. One Marri Ngarr clan was in chronic conflict with various Murrinhpatha, Marri Tjevin and Marri Amu groups during the mission era (DP 2012-06-20_25). More recently there has been a long-simmering conflict between another Marri Ngarr clan and a Marri Tjevin clan. Since Marri Ngarr are inland, fresh-water people, and the clans with which they have fought are coastal, the long-term enmities in Wadeye are sometimes characterised by Aboriginal people as saltwater versus freshwater conflict. In terms of recent gang fighting, this has been loosely translated into the conflict between Evil Warriors (saltwater) and Judas Priest (freshwater). However there are many youth who affiliate to the group that does not align with their patrilineal language heritage.

The counter-balance to the history of conflict described above is the extensive social intermingling and inter-marriage of all Aboriginal groups at Wadeye, and in particular the kinship ties that allow any individual to relate to any other individual within a very few steps of recognised relatedness. A certain discourse, presumably growing out of these links, centres on statements of unity. The wording in official council or public business is usually *kardu numida, murrinh numida* 'one people, one language', but in informal discourse I have recorded it as *wan darrikardu, wan femili, wan lengwitj thanamngerrenngime* 'one people, one family, we speak one language' (MAK, 2013-07-11_02). But such statements may be made alongside others that draw attention to the differences between various clan groups in Wadeye. Rather than simple assertions of unity, they must instead be seen as assertions of *unity underlying difference*. The following statement was made in a video recording of two youth whose clan heritage is Marri Ngarr, though like all Wadeye youth they speak Murrinhpatha[5]:

> *Kardu kanhi thumemluluruy-thanam kardu da wan len thanamnime. Kardu wan Murrinhpatha thanamngerrennime da purtek karrim kanhi. Neki-kathu-ka rispek pumarrabath pi. Purtkit kanhi-yu, da komuniti ngala kanhi-yu. [...] Neki-ka da manangka da-wa kanhi-yu. Da ngathayida tjirrampunmawu Murrinhpatha mup-nu.*
>
> The people here are always in conflict, (but) we're of the same country. We all speak the same language in this country. This is the Murrinhpatha peoples' place, the two of us respect them. All of us have respect here in Port Keats, the whole community. [...] This country isn't the country of us two. We're just outsiders living here with the Murrinhpatha people. (JL, 2013-06-22_02)

2.6.2 Youth speech

Across northern and central Australia, dozens of Aboriginal languages are becoming moribund as young people grow up speaking Kriol or English, but Murrinhpatha is among the handful that continue to be learnt by children as their first language.[6] Murrinhpatha as spoken by contemporary young people is not identical to the language as it was spoken at the founding of the Mission, but it is still confidently identified by both young and old as 'Murrinhpatha' (Mansfield, 2014b). The speech of young people is not considered to be a separate language variety, but it is widely recognised that youth speak in a 'slang' way, which can be labelled *Murrinh Kura* (lit. 'water language'). This is somewhat confusing, given that this is also the name of a moribund traditional dialect, as mentioned above (§2.2).

The grammar of youth speech does not diverge radically from that of older people, but there are a handful of minor morphological differences, and very occasional insertions of English/Kriol grammatical structures. On the other hand, there is massive lexical borrowing from English/Kriol (Mansfield, 2015b, 2016a). This re-lexicalisation has led to the rapid obsolescence of inherited vocabulary – a topic which is the subject of ongoing corpus research. It has also affected the

---

[5] Both youth have Marri Ngarr heritage, which makes them freshwater people. However they have strong social ties with Murrinhpatha clans (i.e. saltwater), reflected in their affiliation to the Evil Warriors grouping. This may influence their positive comments about the Murrinhpatha language and people.

[6] Other languages still spoken by children include Yolngu varieties, Kunwinjku, Burarra, Wik Mungkan, Anindhilyakwa, Western Desert varieties, Warlpiri, Arrernte varieties and Kala Lagaw Ya (Evans, 2007; Walsh, 2007).

balance between phrasal verb and compound verb structures, giving more prominence to analytic phrases (§8.2). Youth also tend to use a more lenited pronunciation than older people, producing a laconic speech style in keeping with their esoteric subculture (Mansfield, 2015a).

The phonological and morphological structures described in this book apply equally to contemporary youth speech and to 'classical Murrinhpatha', as evidenced in archival recordings from the mission era. The essential phonological and morphological patterns of the language have not changed in this period. However some minor changes observed in youth speech include the loss of word-initial laminal nasals (§3.3.1), changes in inflectional allomorphy in the finite verb stem (§5.6), mergers in tense categories and in number marking on oblique pronominal suffixes (§5.2.2, §6.2.1), the decline of the nominal inflected predicates (§6.5), and the aforementioned shift from compound to phrasal verbs (§8.2).

2.6.3 English and Kriol

There is a wide range of English competence among the Aboriginal population of Wadeye, but usually people over the age of about 40 have a greater command of English, and among young people women have a greater command than men. Overall, English competence among adults ranges from complete fluency, to only basic communication (especially among young men). The heavy use of English lexical borrowings in youth speech is not directly connected to bilingualism. Rather, it is a sociolinguistic style indexing generational consciousness, which can be acquired and deployed by all youth irrespective of their English bilingualism (Mansfield, 2015b, 2016a).

It is rather unusual to observe an Aboriginal community in which use of English is less among the young than the old. The phenomenon is explained by the greater success of non-Aboriginal institutions in the mission era, compared to the post-mission era in which contemporary youth have grown up. Young men speak limited English because they have not spent much time at school or in other English-speaking, non-Aboriginal environments. By contrast, older people attended the mission school regularly, and acquired more English. Lack of English discourages young men from engaging with non-Aboriginal institutions, thus creating a vicious circle of disempowerment and alienation.

For the many young men whose participation in school and work is only fleeting, the main sources of their English exposure are non-institutional contexts. There is substantial mobility of people between Wadeye and Peppimenarti, Daly River, Emu Point, and other small communities inland. Aboriginal people from all these places are likely to speak Kriol, and communicate with Wadeye Murrinhpatha speakers using various mixtures of English, Kriol and Murrinhpatha. It has previously been reported that Kriol is 'by and large ... absent' at Wadeye (Blythe 2009: 30), but it does in fact have some currency, both among temporary visitors and some permanent residents. As a very rough estimate, I would guess that there are a couple of dozen permanent Wadeye residents who primarily use Kriol rather than Murrinhpatha. If Murrinhpatha faces any future threat of language shift, it is from the expansion of this Kriol-speaking population.

2.6.4 Digital diglossia

When we turn to other modalities of linguistic communication the situation is quite different. In mobile digital media there is a most notable switch into English, which I label 'digital diglossia' (Mansfield, 2014b, p. 107ff.). The switch is probably related to literacy: young people have some limited literacy in English, though this might be characterised as 'digital literacy' related to mobile phone use (Kral, 2014). In recorded music Murrinhpatha shares dominance with English-language music, but on television (including DVDs) English dominates.

Print media is not extensively used by Aboriginal people in Wadeye outside of the school and the church, unless we include the prolific use of graffiti under this rubric. A few older people read Darwin newspapers or globally distributed comics that are available at the store. A certain amount of official mail is received, in English, which for many people requires assistance from someone with greater literacy.

A fairly substantial body of educational and religious material in Murrinhpatha has been produced over the years at the Literacy Production Centre attached to the school. More recently books in other local Aboriginal languages have been added to the collection. However I have not observed how these are deployed in the classroom, and it is unclear how much these materials are used outside of the school. Printed songsheets of hymns in Murrinhpatha are used in the church, which is closely associated with the school. Outside of these institutions, the only use of Murrinhpatha print media I have observed is the writing down of secular song lyrics so that they can be correctly remembered for a recording session.

2.7 Summary

In this chapter we have seen that Murrinhpatha was traditionally spoken by semi-nomadic hunter-gatherers of northern Australia. However, since the establishment of a missionary settlement in 1939, creating the town now known as Wadeye, the world of Murrinhpatha speakers has undergone rapid and radical change. Murrinhpatha people are wrestling with a difficult transition to urbanised life, consumer goods and Australian government institutions. Poverty, ill-health and unemployment are rife. However, the Murrinhpatha language remains vibrant as the main everyday language of Wadeye, and continues to be learnt by children as their first language. In fact its speaker numbers are growing, thanks to a high birth rate, and the shift of other language groups to Murrinhpatha. Naturally, the language itself is changing, but the grammatical system in the language of Murrinhpatha youth is essentially the same as that of their forebears. The following chapters present an exposition of the phonological and morphological dimensions of this system.

3 Segmental sound patterns

3.1 Introduction

This chapter describes the phonological building blocks from which Murrinhpatha words are formed – the segmental inventory, and the way in which segments combine into syllables and words. Murrinhpatha phonology fits broadly into familiar patterns of Australian languages, but has a somewhat larger range of segmental and syllabic structures than most Pama-Nyungan languages. In particular, Murrinhpatha has three types of obstruents: voiceless stop, voiced stop and fricative. It also has obstruents in coda position, which produces a wide range of hetero-syllabic clusters. As we will see in later chapters, both the obstruent contrasts and the clusters are subject to extensive morpho-phonological alternations, which contributes to opacity in word structure.

The vowels of Murrinhpatha are few and analytically uncomplicated. The consonants are more complex, exhibiting nuanced distinctions of voicing, closure type and length. The longest section of this chapter is dedicated to describing how these distinctions interact to produce obstruent manner contrasts. Furthermore, there is an interesting lengthening effect rendering some consonants much longer in word-medial position than word-initially. For most obstruents this is not contrastive; however there is contrastive gemination of apical sonorants and voiced stops, but only in a closed class of finite verb stems. Finally, I dedicate some space to describing apical consonant retroflexion, which has an 'intermediate' phonological status, neither wholly contrastive nor wholly predictable.

The last two sections of this chapter describe phenomena that are not crucial to understanding the core segmental structures of the language, but shed light on phonological variation and change. The first of these is the phonetic reduction of connected speech. This phonetic variation sheds light on morpho-phonological alternations described in the next chapter. The second topic here is 'lexico-phonological strata', that is to say, sub-sets of the vocabulary consisting of loanwords that retain segmental patterns from their source languages. The patterns of assimilation and innovation observed here help reinforce some of the main principles of Murrinhpatha's core phonology. Overall, these last two sections explore the gap between systemic segmental phonology, and the actual phonetic speech stream of contemporary Murrinhpatha discourse.

3.2 Segmental inventory

Murrinhpatha has a very simple vowel system, about which little needs to be said. There are four vowels, /i, e, a, u/, realised approximately as [ɪ, ɛ, ɐ, ʊ]. The vowels /i, e/ can be grouped as FRONT vowels, since they have a common effect in palatalising a preceding laminal consonant (§3.8), while /e, a/ can be grouped as LOW vowels, sharing a common ablaut pattern in the formation of some paucal subject agreement morphology (§5.4.4).

It is the consonants that demand most of our attention. These can be divided into four familiar main types: obstruents, nasals, liquids and glides. There are typical peripheral places of articulation: labial /p, b, m/ and dorsal /k, ɣ, ŋ/. Coronal articulations have a core distinction between laminals (/t̪/ etc.) and apicals (/t/ etc.), though within each of these categories there are marginally contrastive place distinctions, discussed in sections below. Apical coronals sometimes exhibit an alveolar/retroflex contrast (/t, ʈ/ etc.), though this is not consistently realised (§3.6). Laminal coronals exhibit a dental/post-alveolar contrast (/t̪, t̠/ etc.), though this is almost entirely restricted to Jaminjung and English lexico-phonological strata (§3.8). In most discussions of phonology throughout this book it is only the core place contrasts, /p, t̪, t, k/ that are relevant. Table 3.1 represents the 'inherited stratum' of Murrinhpatha consonant segments, including the alveolar/retroflex contrast but indicating its intermediate status by shading. An expanded inventory including loanword strata will be presented below (§3.8).

As with other Australian languages, Murrinhpatha's coronal distinctions occur not just in obstruents /t̪, t̠, t, ʈ/ but also in nasals /n̪, ɲ, n, ɳ/. Laterals however lack the laminal articulation (though laminal laterals are found in some neighbouring languages, such as Marri Ngarr). The consonant inventory is completed by a typical Australian inventory of glides /w, ɻ, j/ and a trilled or tapped /r/. The retroflex glide /ɻ/ is somewhat limited in that it only occurs intervocalically, and usually only in morpheme-medial positions.[7]

---

[7] /ɻ/ further occurs to a great extent as the result of lenition at morpho-phonological junctures, e.g. /da-t̪al-t̪al/ → /daɻat̪al/ 'cut it!'. There is also some evidence of it occurring initially in bound morphemes, where it is subject to fortition if preceded by a consonant, e.g. /maɲan-ɻut̠-ɻut̠/ → /maɲantut̠tut̠/ 'he threw the finishing net (repeatedly)' but in many cases there is no definitive evidence for choosing between /t̠, ɻ/ in the phonological representation of a bound stem (§4.4.3).

Table 3.1: Murrinhpatha consonant inventory (inherited stratum). Shading indicates that the alveolar/retroflex contrast is not consistently realised.

		Labial	Laminal	Apical Alveolar	Apical Retroflex	Dorsal
Obstruent	Voiceless	p	t̪	t	ʈ	k
	Voiced	b		d	ɖ	
	Fricative		ð			ɣ
Nasal		m	n̪	n	ɳ	ŋ
Lateral				l	ɭ	
Trill / tap				r		
Glide		w	j	ɻ		

3.3 Word and syllable shapes

I begin here by describing the phonological shape of simple lexical stems in Murrinhpatha, while the next chapter describes the phonology of morphologically complex constructs. Morphologically simple words in Murrinhpatha are usually composed of between one and three syllables, most of which have /CV/ or /CVC/ shapes. There are only a few four-syllable simple words, and none that are longer, though morphologically complex words (as described in subsequent chapters) can be much longer. There are a very few syllables with complex codas, i.e. /CVCC/.

Murrinhpatha words diverge somewhat from a rather restricted sound pattern that has been observed to characterise words in most Australian languages. Three major restrictions are common, either as categorical constraints on a language, or as strong tendencies with only a few lexical exceptions (Baker, 2014, pp. 144–148; Dixon, 1980, p. 127ff.; Hamilton, 1996, p. 75ff.):
(a) Words have two or more syllables;
(b) Syllable codas are sonorant, not obstruent[8];
(c) Word-initial position uses a substantially restricted subset of the consonant inventory, which is therefore only fully exhibited at word-medial position.

The outcome of these restrictions is an inventory of 'standard Australian' word shapes, formulated here using C_1 = initial (restricted) consonant, C_2 = medial intervocalic (unrestricted) consonant, N = sonorant and V = vowel:

---

[8] The 'sonorant coda' restriction has previously been formulated in terms of word-final position rather than syllable codas, due to a resistance to syllabic analyses as described below.

/C₁VC₂V/
/C₁VC₂VN/
/C₁VNC₂V/
/C₁VNC₂VN/

The Australian 'standard' word is heavily biased towards Pama-Nyungan languages; the northern Australian non-Pama-Nyungan languages, including Murrinhpatha, often violate requirements (a, b) i.e. minimally disyllabic words, and sonorant codas (e.g. Ngalakgan: Baker, 2008; Bardi: Bowern, 2004, p. 74ff.; Bininj Gun-wok: Evans, 2003a, p. 89; Limilngan: Harvey, 2001; Marra: Heath, 1981, p. 19; Gooniyandi: McGregor, 1990, p. 74). Murrinhpatha in addition has a less severe than usual version of (c), the restricted set of word-initial consonants, thanks to its unusual word-initial use of obstruent voicing contrasts (§3.4). However we will see in the next chapter that Murrinhpatha word shapes are more diverse only in the open lexical classes, while conforming to the Australian standard in closed classes and in bound grammatical morphology.

The highly standardised shape of words in most languages has given rise to a tradition in Australianist phonology of analysing whole-word shapes rather than syllables, based on the prototypes above in which the first and second 'syllables' have sufficiently different constraints that they should not be treated as iterations of the same unit (Baker, 2014, pp. 143–145; Dixon, 1980, pp. 159–178). However because these constraints don't hold in Murrinhpatha, the syllable remains a valid analytic construct. There are plenty of monosyllabic words /CV/ and /CVC/, obstruent codas are common, and although it is true that the two halves of a /CVC.CVC/ word have somewhat different constraints, they also have much in common. Both open and closed syllables are common in Murrinhpatha, and there are a few complex codas /lk, ḻk, lm, lŋ, ɾk/. Exemplary shapes of morphologically simple words are shown in (1–12). Constraints on consonant clusters at syllable boundaries will be discussed below.

Monosyllables
(1) ke 'shell sp.'
(2) wak 'crow'
(3) buɾk 'excellent'

Disyllables
(4) pa.ṭa 'good'
(5) ṭa.pak 'fog'
(6) kuk.pi 'carpet snake'
(7) kik.muṅ 'wax'

(8) ṯun.piṯ   'red flowering kapok'
(9) walm.pu   'testicles'

Three or four syllables
(10) pi.ɣu.ṉu   'they (pl.)'
(11) ṉuṉ.pa.lin   'black whip snake'
(12) mal.ki.ma.ɾin   'vein'

3.3.1 Restrictions by word and syllable position

We can distinguish three Murrinhpatha word/syllable positions in terms of the consonant types that can occupy them:

C_1 Syllable onset, either word-initial or post-consonantal;
C_2 Syllable onset, intervocalic word-medial;
C_3 Syllable coda.

These positional consonant classes can be configured freely in word shapes:

/C_1VC_2V/
/$C_1VC_2VC_3$/
/$C_1VC_3C_1V$/
/$C_1VC_3C_1VC_3$/
/$C_1VC_2VC_2V$/ ... etc.

Notice that the three position classes can be characterised in terms of whether they have CV and VC transitions, when considered independently of neighbouring words or affixes (Table 3.2).

Table 3.2: Consonant position types analysed according to transitions.

	CV	VC
C_1	y	n
C_2	y	y
C_3	n	y

The perceptual cues produced in these transitions presumably explain the different ranges of consonants that can be distinguished in the three classes (J. Blevins, 2004). As in other Australian languages, the intervocalic C_2 position hosts the full array of consonant contrasts (as in Table 3.1 above). Position C_1, the word-initial or post-consonantal onset, is constrained by lacking the alveolar/retroflex contrast found elsewhere (§3.6), and lacking both 'rhotic' consonants, glide /ɻ/ or trill /r/ (Table 3.3). It is also worth noting that the laminal nasal /ṉ/, while it does occur word-initially, occurs in just three common words, and in these is often phonetically deleted.[9]

Table 3.3: C_1 consonants: Syllable onset, either word-initial or post-consonantal. Shaded /ṉ/ is rare in this position.

		Labial	Laminal	Apical	Dorsal
Obstruent	Voiceless	p	ṯ	t	k
	Voiced	b		d	
Nasal		m	ṉ	n	ŋ
Lateral				l	
Glide		w	j		

Table 3.4: Syllable coda (including word-final) consonant inventory.

	Labial	Laminal	Apical		Dorsal
			Alveolar	Retroflex	
Obstruent	p	ṯ	t	ʈ	k
Nasal	m	ṉ	n	ɳ	ŋ
Lateral			l	ɭ	
Trill / tap			r		
Glide		j			

Position C_3, the syllable coda position, hosts contrastive retroflexion, but altogether collapses the distinctions of obstruent closure and voicing (Table 3.4). The merged coda obstruents are realised as voiceless, unreleased stops. Two of the three glides are also absent: the laminal glide /j/ occurs but neither the labial glide /w/ nor the rhotic glide /ɻ/ occur (unlike in Western Daly, which has coda /ɻ/).

---

9 The only common words with initial /ṉ/ are /ṉini/ and /ṉinta/ (both anaphoric demonstratives), and /ṉini/ 2SG. The demonstratives are often pronounced without their initial nasal, while the 2SG pronoun is pronounced by many younger speakers as /nini/, perhaps under contact influence from Western Daly languages (e.g. Marri Ngarr /niṉ/ 2SG, Marri Tjevin /naṉ/ 2SG). I am grateful for Joe Blythe for first drawing my attention to this alternative pronunciation.

Laminals /t̪, n̪/ in this position have a distinctly palatalised allophone, producing a high-front offglide on the preceding vowel, e.g. /karat̪/ → [karaɪ̯t̪] 'devil'.[10]

3.3.2 Consonant cluster constraints

Further constraints apply to codas and onsets when they occur in heterosyllabic clusters, i.e. /C₁VC₃.C₁VC₃/ (Street & Mollinjin, 1981, p. 204). I focus here on evidence from morphologically simple words, while also introducing evidence from morpho-phonological alternations, which will be more fully explored in the next chapter (§4.4.3). There are two constraints observable in consonant clusters, both of which reiterate patterns found throughout Australian languages, though the possibilities in Murrinhpatha are again more diverse than Pama-Nyungan languages. These are constraints against increasing sonority (*OBS-SON) and peripheral-coronal place sequences (*PER-COR). These are in addition to the cluster constraints that follow directly from positional classes described above (i.e. coda limitations and post-consonantal onset limitations).[11]

The constraint against increasing sonority is both a trans-Australian cluster constraint, and a common global pattern (Murray & Venneman, 1983; Seo, 2011). For many Australian languages this constraint has a quite restrictive version in which only sonorant-obstruent (SON-OBS) clusters are permitted (Hamilton, 1996, p. 155ff.), but for Murrinhpatha there is a more permissive version that also allows equal-sonority clusters (OBS-OBS and SON-SON), and constrains only increasing sonority, i.e. *OBS-SON. However even this is not an absolute constraint in Murrinhpatha; there are a handful of unanalysable roots attested with OBS-SON clusters, including /kikmun/ 'wax' and /ŋut̪ŋen/ 'ordinary'. However these are notably rare in the lexicon compared to clusters with level or decreasing sonority profiles; and of course these few exceptions may indeed represent historical morphology that has become totally opaque.

The second major constraint, against peripheral-coronal place sequences (*PER-COR), is this time a pattern that is endemic to Australian languages (Hamilton, 1996, pp. 109–113), but runs counter to a constraint observed on other continents. Evidence has been adduced from several unrelated languages that there is a

---

10 This palatalisation is the strongest co-articulation allophony I have observed in Murrinhpatha. I suspect that it has a functional motivation in making perceptible the coda distinction /t̪, t/, which would otherwise be very weakly cued in the VC transition (Ohala, 1990).

11 Note also that there is a general scarcity of the palatal glide /j/ in clusters, even though by sonority preferences we might expect to find it in coda position. Some of the few monomorphemic exceptions are /t̪ujkem/ (place name) and /paljir/ 'rock'. This is again a common Australian pattern (Hamilton, 1996, p. 167).

general constraint in the opposite direction, i.e. *COR-PER (J. Blevins, 2004, p. 126; Blust, 1979). For example, it has been observed that English uses regressive place assimilation to avoid *COR-PER (e.g. *footprint* [fʊp.pɹɪnt]), while allowing PER-COR (e.g. *riptide* [ɹɪp.tɑɪd]) (Blust, 1979, p. 103). Australian languages show the opposite tendency, i.e. *PER-COR. In Murrinhpatha, this constraint is quite categorical among unanalysable roots, as there are no roots with /__{p, k, m, ŋ}.{t̪, t, ṉ, n̠}__/ etc. On the other hand, there are a few compound lexemes, even some deeply lexicalised (semantically opaque) ones, in which *PER-COR is violated (13–16).

(13) ŋapkapt̪i
　　　ŋap-ŋap-t̪i
　　　sense-PLUR-bottom
　　　sorcerer who steals kidney fat

(14) kent̪ipt̪ar
　　　kem-t̪ip-t̪ar
　　　sit.3SG.PRSNL-dark-quite
　　　(place name)

(15) bekt̪aj
　　　bek-t̪aj
　　　howl-mouth
　　　open mouth

(16) baŋmant̪aj
　　　baŋ-baŋ-t̪aj
　　　pierce-PLUR-tree
　　　breakable tree

Evidence from morpho-phonological juncture processes confirms both the application of the two constraints, *OBS-SON and *PER-COR, and the non-categorical nature of their enforcement. For both constraints, there is more than one type of resolution that can be used to avert a violation. For *OBS-SON, the most common resolutions affect the C₁ (onset) sonorant, which can either be strengthened to an obstruent to produce a more harmonic OBS-OBS cluster, or deleted altogether so that C₃ becomes a simple, intervocalic onset (17, 18). Also attested, but in fewer constructions, is the deletion of the C₃ (coda) obstruent to produce a simple intervocalic onset (19). Finally, we see that the constraint is not absolute in lexical compounds, as the *OBS-SON contour sometimes is left unresolved (20).

(17) ɲirkkirk
　　　ɲirk-ɲirk
　　　growling　　　　　　　　(Street 2012)

(18) leṯetmam
    leṯ-let-mam
    stick-stick-do.3SG.NFUT
    sticky
(19) puniŋkawal̪aw̲al̪akṯa
    puni-ŋka-wal̪ak̲-w̲al̪ak-ða
    SLASH.3SG.PST-eye-rub-rub-PST
    they fell asleep   (LCh, 2009-11-21_03)
(20) ṯapɲini
    ṯap-ɲini
    touch-body
    physically attractive   (Street 2012)

For *PER-COR, there are again both complex constructions that resolve the constraint, and others that retain a violation. Cases of resolution all target the C3 (coda) position, either assimilating it to the same place of articulation as the C1 onset, or deleting it altogether (21, 22). This pattern supports a cross-linguistic observation of *regressive* place assimilation in consonant clusters, reflecting the domination of CV onset transitions over VC coda transitions (J. Blevins, 2004, p. 118; Gordon, 2016, p. 128). As we might expect from the *PER-COR violations exhibited above for lexicalised constructs, this constraint is also sometimes violated in transparent constructs (23).

(21) nuŋaṉ̪ṯuk
    nuŋam-ṯuk
    use.feet.3SG.NFUT-search
    she searches
(22) kanad̪i
    kanam-d̪i
    be.3SG.NFUT-enter
    she went in
(23) tum̲tum
    tum-tum
    dry-dry

Cluster resolution phenomena in morphological constructs in addition shows some interaction between *OBS-SON and *PER-COR constraints, and most importantly for the current study, some variation depending on the type of morphological construct involved. These matters will be addressed in the next chapter as part of the discussion of morphologically specific phonology (§4.5).

3.4 Obstruent voicing, closure and length

In terms of obstruents, Australian languages can be divided into those with a single obstruent series, and those with contrastive fortis and lenis obstruents. Murrinhpatha and other Daly languages are outliers of the fortis/lenis group. The single obstruent series languages constitute the largest group, especially among Pama-Nyungan languages (Dixon, 1980, p. 132ff.; Evans, 1995). But there is also a substantial number of fortis/lenis languages, where the contrast appears only in word-medial positions and involves a phonetic distinction of both closure duration and voicing (Butcher, 2004; Stoakes, 2013). These languages are found in a genetically diverse cluster in the Top End (e.g. Gupapuyngu, Bininj Gunwok, Wagiman), and in more closely related clusters in eastern central Australia (e.g. Wangkumarra, Adnyamathanha) and in Cape York Peninsula (e.g. Mbiywom, Wik Muminh) (Austin, 1988). The main environment for these contrasts is intervocalic, though in some languages they also occur in clusters after sonorants (nasals, laterals or trills). For some languages they are closely related to distinctive vowel lengths, with the fortis obstruent following short vowels, and the lenis obstruent following long vowels, e.g. /ătౖa, aːɖa/.

The Murrinhpatha fricatives /ð, ɣ/ follow the general pattern of the fortis/lenis systems, in that they are word-medial and weakly articulated. But the Murrinhpatha voiced stops /b, d/ produce a different type of contrast, both in that it is more specifically a voicing contrast between stops, and because it occurs in syllable onsets of any position. This should therefore be seen as a third type of obstruent contrast in Australian languages, a 'true voicing contrast'. As far as I know, the only other clear attestations of a true voicing contrast are in Murrinhpatha's neighbouring languages, the related language Ngan'gi (Reid, 1990, p. 39ff.), and the Western Daly languages (Green, 1989, p. 17ff.).[12]

Previous analyses on Murrinhpatha have posited a simpler voiceless/voiced category distinction (e.g. Street & Mollinjin, 1981; Walsh, 1976), but I here present distributional and realisational evidence for a three-way split: voiceless stops, voiced stops and fricatives. Further, I here explore a non-contrastive pattern of voiceless obstruent lengthening in word-medial positions. This is necessary for fully understanding the system of obstruent contrasts, and the geminate sonorant phenomena described in the following section.

---

[12] Two Paman languages from distant Cape York are also claimed to have a true voicing contrast (Kunjen, Umbuygamu: Sommer, 1969, 1976), but the purported contrast has not been described in detail and it is not clear whether it is operative word-initially. Kala Lagaw Ya does have a well-attested, true voicing contrast, but in general it shows many signs of combining Australian grammatical features with Papuan phonology (Mitchell, 2015).

3.4.1 Voicing and closure contrasts

Voiced stops /b, d̪/ can be distinguished from fricatives /ð, ɣ/ firstly on the grounds of phonetic realisation. The dental fricative is usually realised with actual frication, while dorsal fricative may involve either frication or an approximated constriction. The voiced stops have full closure, but maintain voicing throughout. But there is also a distributional distinction. Voiced obstruents occur in both C_1 and C_2 onset positions (24–26), while fricatives occur only as C_2, i.e. in word-medial intervocalic onsets (27, 28). Note that the latter statement refers only to 'phonologised' fricatives, i.e. those that are consistently realised as continuants. There are phonetic lenition effects that produce variably fricated realisations of voiceless stops in C_1 position (§3.3.1.). Further positional neutralisations that affect all obstruent types will be discussed below.

(24) bamam   'white'
(25) kirikbe   'bird'
(26) pibim   'they are standing'
(27) ŋam-ŋkud̪uk   'I licked it'
(28) kiɣaj   'young man'

In fact the distribution of fricatives is limited not just to C_2, but in most cases is limited to C_2 at the onset of bound morphs. Almost all examples of /ð/ are at the beginning of bound morphs such as /-ðap/ 'shut' and /-ða/ PST, with just a few morph-medial instances such as /-ŋaða/ 'brief' and /kuɻaɣaða/ 'boomerang'.[13] /ɣ/ occurs mostly just in bound coverb onsets such as /-ɣud̪uk/ 'drink' and /-ɣuma/ 'make smoke', though there are also a handful of morph-medials such as /kiɣaj/ 'young man' and /niɣunu/ 'she'.

Aside from distribution in word structure, there is a further morpho-phonological difference between voiced stops and fricatives. Voiced stops are subject to progressive nasalisation in compounds (29) (§3.7), while fricatives in the same position remain as oral obstruents, but lose their manner contrast (30, see below).

(29) demmuɣaḻ
     dem-buɣaḻ
     PIERCE.RR.3SG.NFUT-melt
     it's melted   (DP, 2015-06-29)

---

[13] The rare demonstrative /t̪i ~ ði/ 'there' may be something of an exception, as it often appears to have voicing and/or frication in its initial obstruent, despite it being in word-initial position.

(30) dent̪ap
    dem-ðap
    PIERCE.RR.3SG.NFUT-shut
    it's shut

The contrastive voiced obstruents /b, ɖ/ have a broad distribution and no obvious signs of developing as a result of morpho-phonological process, while the fricatives /ð, ɣ/ have a limited distribution and may be explicable as a result of phonologised lenition in bound morphemes. Further light will be shed on this topic in the sections on phonetic obstruent length (§3.7) and morpho-phonological juncture lenition (§4.4).

3.4.2 Positional neutralisations

Obstruent voicing and closure contrasts, e.g. /p, b/ or /t̪, ð/, occur only in syllable onsets. Coda obstruents are neutralised to a voiceless unreleased stop, [p̚] etc.[14] Further, there are no contrasts in nasal-obstruent clusters, where the only obstruent type is short and has variable voicing. I represent these manner-neutral obstruents using the symbols /p, t̪, t, k/, which in the post-nasal context should be understood as having no voicing or manner specification. When a voiced obstruent is brought into a post-nasal environment at a morphological juncture, the obstruent is either nasalised (§3.7), or realised as a manner-neutral obstruent (31). Bound stems beginning with either voiceless stops or fricatives are realised as manner-neutral (32, 33).

(31) nuŋammat ~ nuŋampat
    nuŋam-bat
    use.feet.3SG.NFUT-throw.weapon
    he threw the weapon
(32) dant̪ap
    dam-t̪ap
    PIERCE.3SG.NFUT-taste
    she tasted it
(33) dant̪ap
    dam-ðap
    PIERCE.3SG.NFUT-close
    she closed it

---

14 There are two apparent exceptions, /ɟebɟeb/ 'food' and /ɟegɟeg/ 'play'.

3.4.3 Phonetic realisation of contrasts

Murrinhpatha voiceless stops are realised with voicing lagging behind stop release by around 20–60 ms, and with an 'aspirated' burst of air. The voiced obstruents, by contrast, have voicing active before release, and have little or no burst. This is consistent with Butcher's (2004) articulatory findings using airflow measurements, which show that Murrinhpatha voiceless obstruents are produced with much higher intra-oral pressure than their voiced counterparts. Measurements and sample spectrograms presented here are typical tokens from careful speech; analysis of the range of phonetic variation is beyond the scope of this study. Figure 3.1 (a, b) shows sample spectrograms from the same speaker, exhibiting the word-initial contrast for /p, b/.

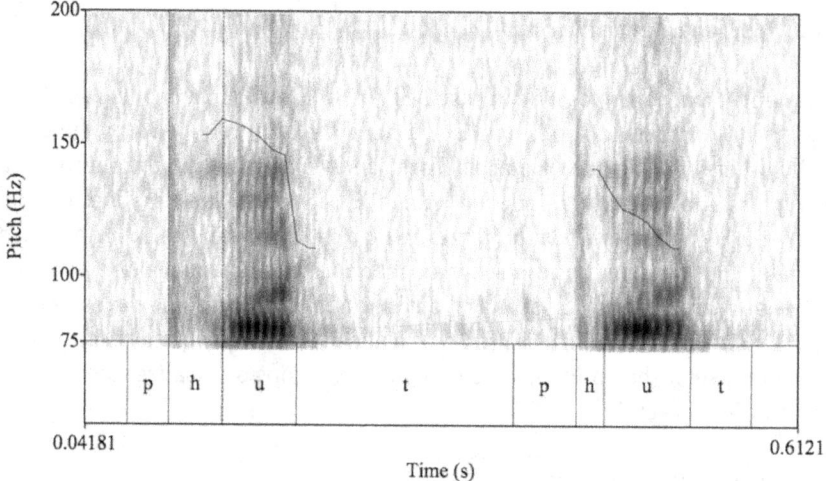

Figure 3.1(a): Spectrogram for /putput/ 'pregnant' (GM, 1990_AB).

In word-initial position there is no length contrast for voiceless/voiced stops, i.e. /p, b/ and /t, d/ all have durations around 50–100 ms. This is evident in tokens where the target words are phrase medial, as in Figure 3.4(a) below. However in word-medial intervocalic position, the contrast is of both voicing and duration, with only voiceless obstruents subject to a phonetic lengthening pattern described in the next section. Figure 3.2 illustrates the contrast, with medial voiceless /p/ closure of 172 ms, and medial voiced /b/ closure of 88 ms (cf. Walsh, 1976, pp. 320–324). Voicing is clearly visible in /b/, while /p/ lacks voicing, and has a distinctive release burst.

The voiceless stop / fricative contrast, as mentioned above, is in word-medial intervocalic onsets only. Fricatives contrast with stops by making only partial closure, during which voicing continues. For the laminal there is generally light

3.4 Obstruent voicing, closure and length — 55

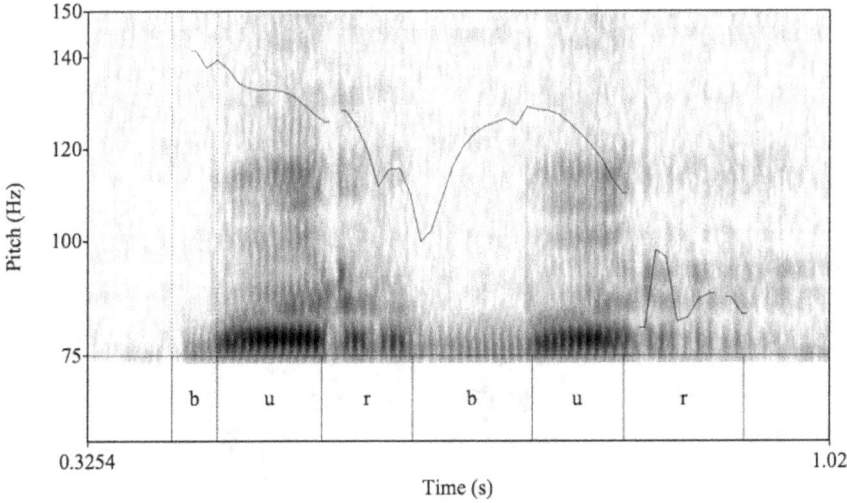

Figure 3.1(b): Spectrogram for /burbur/ 'cold' (GM, 1990_AB).

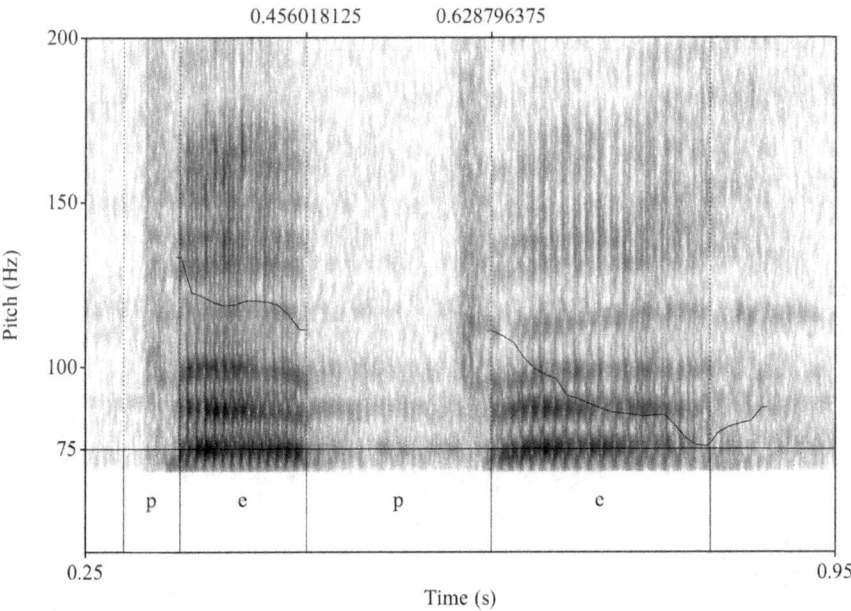

Figure 3.2(a): Word-medial intervocalic /p/, duration 172 ms (MiJa, 2013-01-08).

56 — 3 Segmental sound patterns

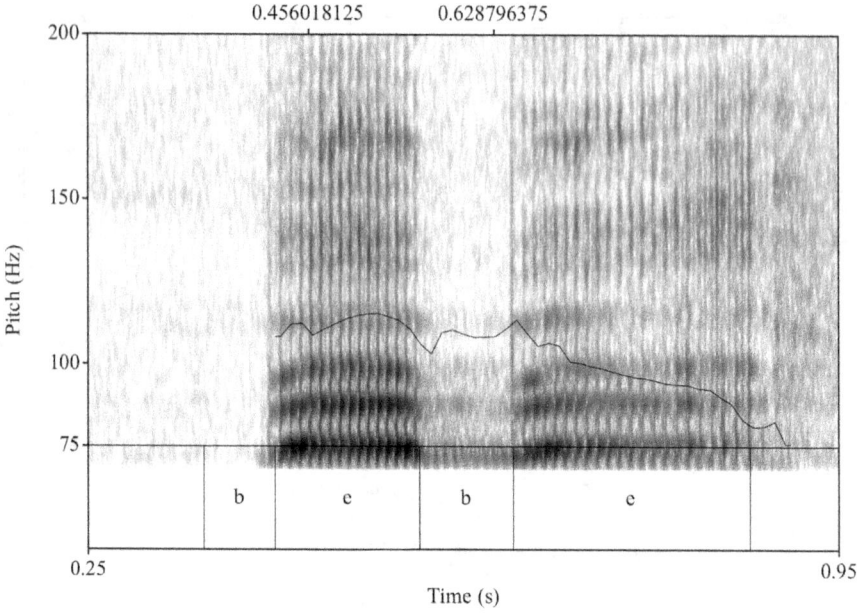

Figure 3.2(b): Word-medial intervocalic /b/, duration 88 ms (MiJa, 2013-01-08).

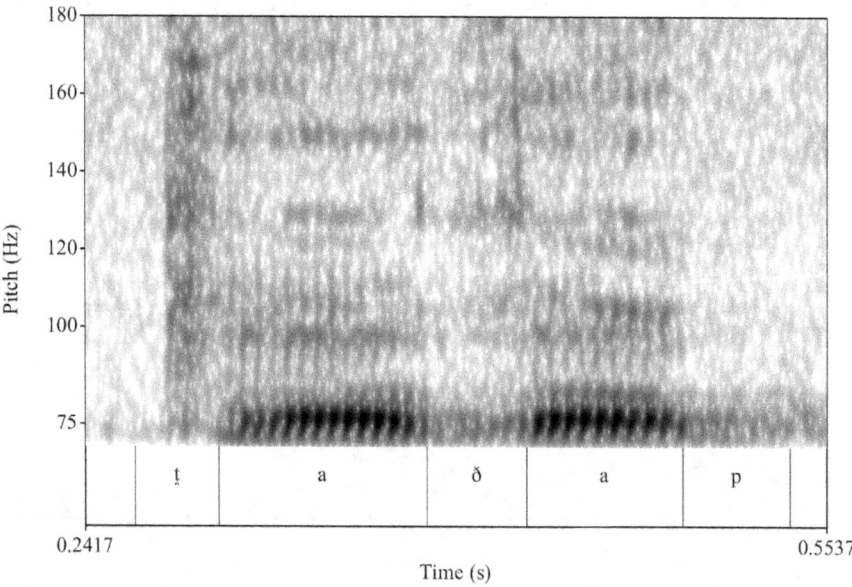

Figure 3.3(a): Acoustic realisation of laminal fricative /ð/ (JaDo, 2013-01-21).

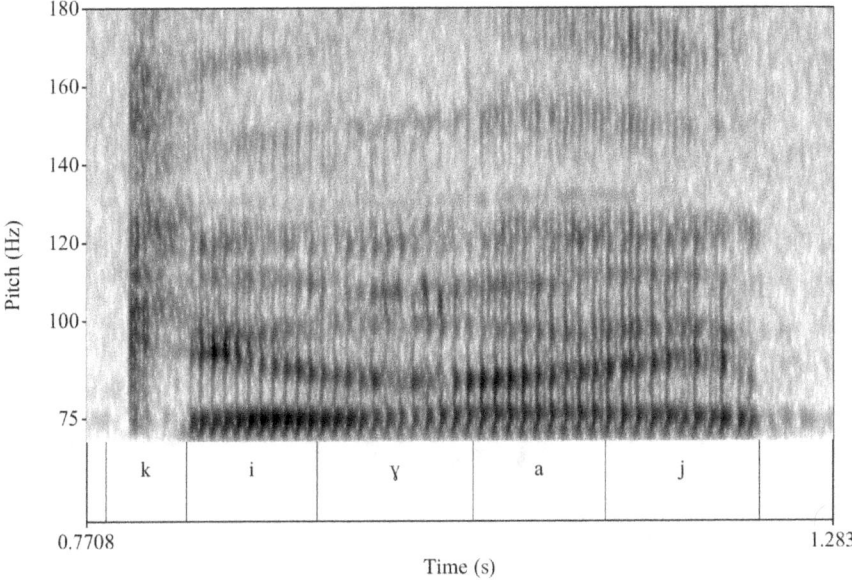

Figure 3.3(b): Acoustic realisation of dorsal fricative /ɣ/ (AxLa, 2013-01-15).

frication [ð], while for the dorsal there is either frication or merely approximation [ɣ ~ ɰ]. Figure 3.3 shows sample spectrograms.

3.4.4 Word-medial obstruent lengthening

As mentioned above, voiceless obstruents /p, ṯ, t, k/ in word-medial position have a long closure duration, typically in the range 150–200 ms, while in word-initial position both voiceless and voiced stops are around 50–100 ms. This phenomenon merits discussion because it is related to morpho-phonological lenition effects in complex words (§4.4), and because it may explain the limited distribution of the fricative obstruent phonemes /ð, ɣ/.

Figure 3.4 illustrates the positional effect on voiceless obstruent length, with tokens of /p/ in initial position (79 ms) and medial position (150 ms).

We might ask if the different obstruent lengths should be analysed as an effect of prosodic prominence, since the medial obstruents in disyllabic words always follow the vowel that anchors pitch accent /CV́C:VC/, and it has been argued for various Australian languages that post-stress consonants are lengthened (Fletcher & Butcher, 2014, pp. 120–121; Fletcher, Stoakes, Loakes, & Singer, 2015). However evidence from trisyllabic and quadrisyllabic words undermines

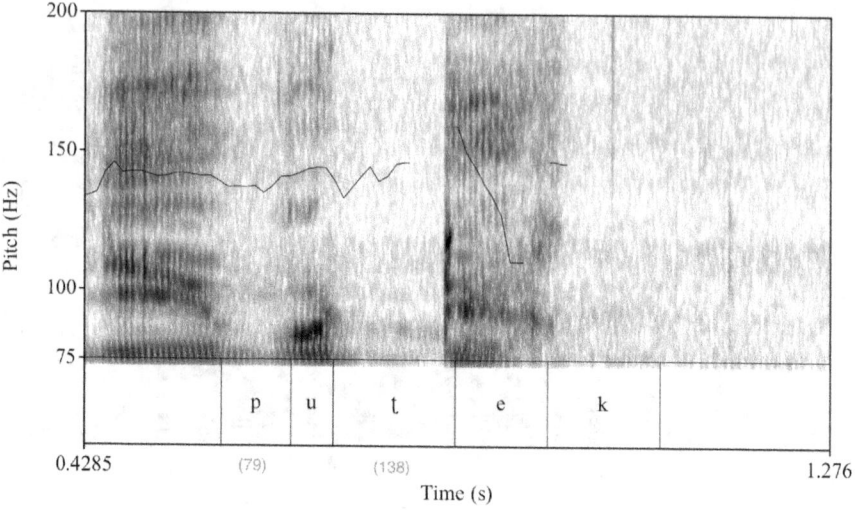

Figure 3.4(a): Short initial /p/ in [puṭek] 'dirt' (McKu, 2013-01-07).

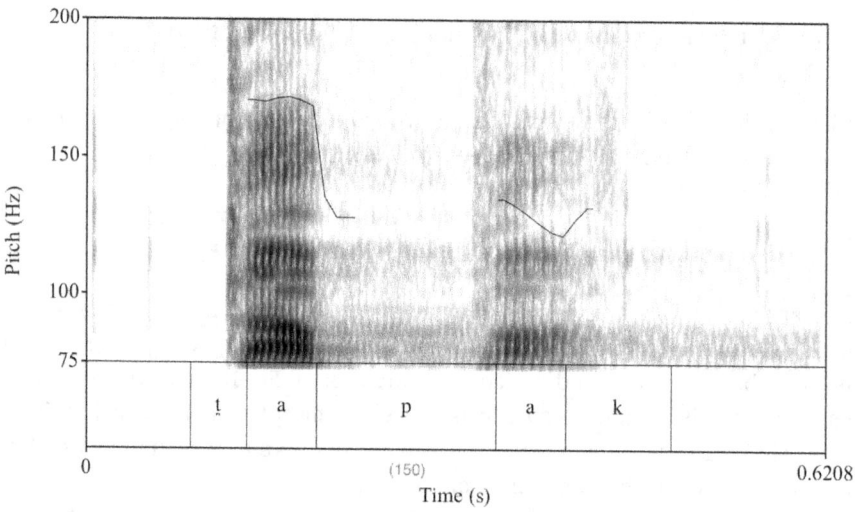

Figure 3.4(b): Long medial /p/ in [ṭap:ak] 'fog' (McJa, 2013-01-02).

this hypothesis. Obstruents in these longer words are lengthened either after or before the prominent syllable (34–38), which is always penultimate (§4.3).

Long obstruents in trisyllabic words
(34) [kumúk:uɾ] 'fighting stick' (DP, 2015-09-29_AT)
(35) [dak:á:raṇ] 'polygynous' (DP, 2015-09-29_AT)

3.4 Obstruent voicing, closure and length — 59

Long obstruents in quadrisyllabic words
(36) [kalamáːti] 'malevolent spirit known for biting people'
(37) [lametːíɲi] 'uncircumcised boy' (RaTu, 2016-07_FN)
(38) [t̪it̪ːimámpe] 'fan fern' (DP, 2015-09-29_AT)

However there does seem to be one restriction on voiceless obstruent lengthening in word-medial positions. Where a longer word contains more than one medial voiceless obstruent, only the right-most of these is long. Words with a medial voiceless obstruent only at the first syllable juncture exhibit lengthening as expected (39, 40), but words with another voiceless obstruent at the next juncture exhibit lengthening only on the right-most obstruent (41, 42, Figure 3.5).

(39) [ɲipːiliɲ] 'river'
(40) [ɲapːuɭu] 'breast'
(41) [ɲapapːa] 'sugar glider'
(42) [mutitːi] 'lower back'

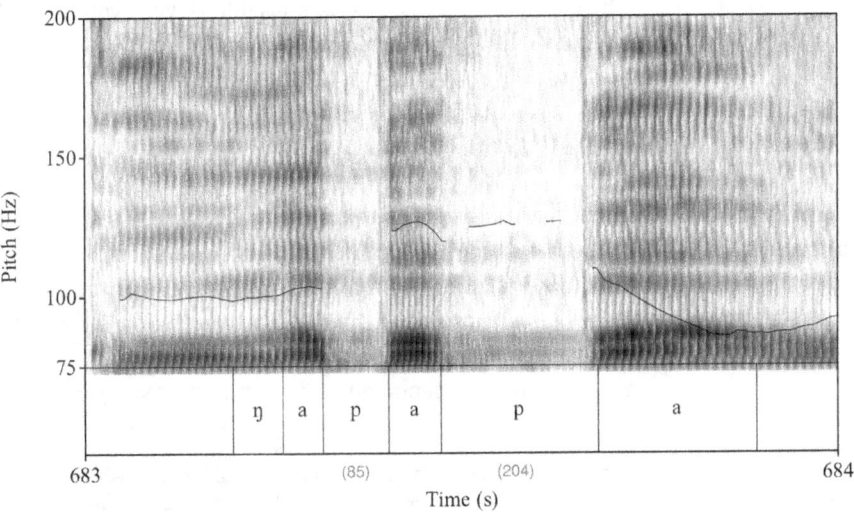

Figure 3.5: Right-most obstruent lengthening in [ɲapapːa] 'sugar glider' (DePu, 2013-01-11).

Note that multiple voiceless obstruent syllable junctures (i.e./CVKVKVC/, where /K/ = any voiceless obstruent), are rare in Murrinhpatha simple words. Examples (41, 42) appear to be historically complex: /mu-t̪i-t̪i/ ??-buttocks-PLUR 'lower back'; /ɲa-pa-pa/ ??-screech-PLUR 'sugar glider'. Apart from these lexicalised outliers, we can posit a general phonological constraint */CVKVKVC/. Indeed precisely this constraint is found in a northern Australian language, Ngalakgan, where it applies to phonemically long obstruents (Baker, 2008, p. 291). Baker analyses these as geminate onset clusters, and observes that there can only be one such cluster within a lexical word.[15]

The positionally determined lengthening of obstruents occurs only in the voiceless series /p, t̪, t, k/, and not in the voiced alternates /b, d̪/. The latter maintain about the same duration range, around 50–100 ms, in both initial and medial positions.

We will see below that non-lengthened voiceless obstruents are subject to phonetic lenition, often being articulated without full oral closure.

For independent words, the lenition of unlengthened obstruents is a phonetic variable (i.e. /p/ → [p̆ ~ β ~ w]), usually in word-initial position. But at initial position in bound lexical stems, the fricative or glide realisation is phonologised following a vowel. Voiceless obstruents therefore morpho-phonologically alternate with fricatives and glides (§4.4). This alternation may indeed be the original source of the fricative phonemes /ð, ɣ/, which as we saw above, are limited to word-medial positions, mostly at the beginning of bound morphs. The stem-medial examples, such as the synchronically unanalysable /kiɣaj/ 'young man' may of course be the residue of now opaque morphology.

3.5 Geminate sonorants and voiced stops

Murrinhpatha has contrastive single/geminate consonants of a type that is quite unusual among Australian languages.[16] Various northern Australian languages have contrastive consonant length, but in all other cases this is an obstruent contrast, usually described as a phonemic distinction between short/long stops (Butcher, 2004; Stoakes, 2013). We have just seen that in Murrinhpatha, voiceless obstruent lengthening is a phonetic phenomenon determined by word position.

---

15 Another interesting comparison is that Ngalakgan geminates in suffixes are reduced to singleton if they are preceded by any geminate, or other obstruent cluster, within the prosodic word (Baker, 2008, pp. 252ff.). Compare this to the short length of the voiceless obstruents succeeded by another voiceless obstruent in Murrinhpatha /ŋapapːa/, /mut̪it̪ːi/. The blocking of length seems to work in opposite directions in Ngalakgan and Murrinhpatha, just as the two languages assign prosodic prominence from opposite ends of the word.

16 This may also be quite unusual at a global level. An earlier work on geminate typology suggested that geminate sonorants are only found where there are also geminate obstruents (Podesva, 2002), but Blevins (2004, p. 178) uses a wider sample of languages to show that this is not the case.

3.5 Geminate sonorants and voiced stops — 61

Phonologically contrastive length applies instead to two sonorants and a voiced obstruent, all of which are apical: /n, l, ḍ/. Note that the alveolar/retroflex status of these phonemes is rather unclear (§3.6).

Contrastive geminates appear in finite verb stems, where gemination of the stem consonant marks plural subject inflection (§5.5). This type of systematic sonorant gemination has not been reported for any other Australian language except Ngan'gi (Reid, 1990, p. 407ff.), though a lexically limited contrast is attested for various other languages.[17]

The geminate contrast appears in stem alternations on nine of the 39 finite verb stems: /ni/ 'be', /nu/ 'use feet', /na/ 'use fire', /la/ 'wipe', /la/ 'eat', /ḍu/ IMPEL, as well as associated reflexive verb stems. These verb stems alternate a singleton form for singular subject with geminate form for plural subject, e.g. /ŋu-nu-ŋam/1SG-use.feet.SG-NFUT, /ŋu-nnu-ŋam/ 1PL-use.feet.PL-NFUT. The alternation is quite paradigmatically regular for the verbs in which it operates,[18] and for first-person forms it is the sole marker of plural inflection, thus forming minimal pairs as above. For second and third person it sometimes combines with alternations in the word-initial consonant, e.g. /di-la-Ø/ 3SG-wipe.SG-PST, /pi-lla-Ø/ 3PL-wipe.PL-PST (§5.5). Figure 3.6 illustrates the realisation of the length contrast, in this instance with closure durations /n/ = 50 ms and /nn/ 153 ms. These are careful speech tokens, and in spontaneous speech the durational distinction seems to be more subtle.

The historical source for contrastive geminates is a plural */ɾ(V)/ prefix that preceded finite verb stems (Green, 2003). For apical-onset stems this assimilated to the stem consonant, e.g. */ŋu-ɾ-nu/ 1-PL-use.feet > /ŋu-nnu/ 1-use.feet.PL,[19] while for labial or velar consonants it has been deleted (presuming that it also appeared with these verb stems). It is also deleted in three verbs with laminal nasal-obstruent clusters in their stems – /ṉta/ 'crouch', /ṉti/ 'perch' and /ṉti/ 'have' – though since all of these have clusters, it is unclear whether /ɾ/ has deleted because they are laminal, or because of illicit CCC clustering. In fact the /ɾ/ formative only remains present in some verbs with stems that have lost all consonants e.g. /ŋi-i-ni/ 1-sit-PST, /ŋa-ɾ-i-ni/ 1-PL-sit.PL-PST (§5.5) (Green, 2003,

---

[17] Andrew Butcher (p.c.) has drawn my attention to a scattering of attested contrasts between singleton and geminate sonorants in Adnyamathanha, Wik Mungkan and Bajjamalh. But none of these languages makes extensive use of geminate sonorants.

[18] The gemination pattern is only broken for the PST forms of /ni/ 'be', which have a singleton suppletive /di/ for both singular and plural subject.

[19] The apical assimilation has unusual consequences for the tap /ɾ/, for which Green (2003: 143) suggests reconstructions like */ŋurru/ > /ŋuɽu/ go.1SG.IRR. Murrinhpatha's flap verb-stems /ru/ 'go' and /ra/ 'watch' do indeed alternate with retroflex approximants in plural forms.

62 — 3 Segmental sound patterns

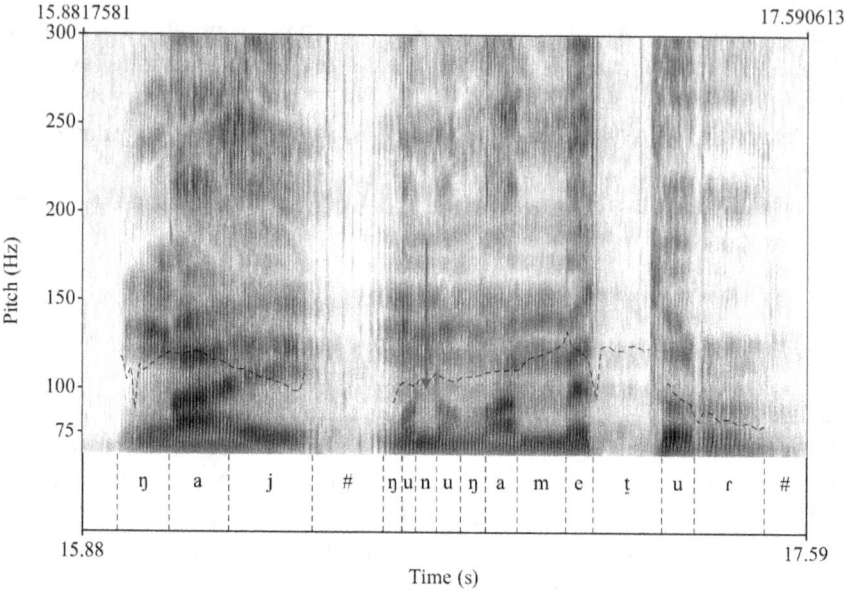

Figure 3.6(a): Singleton /n/ in /ŋaj ŋunuŋam-me-ʈur/ 'I stepped on it' (LP, 2015-07-08_LS).

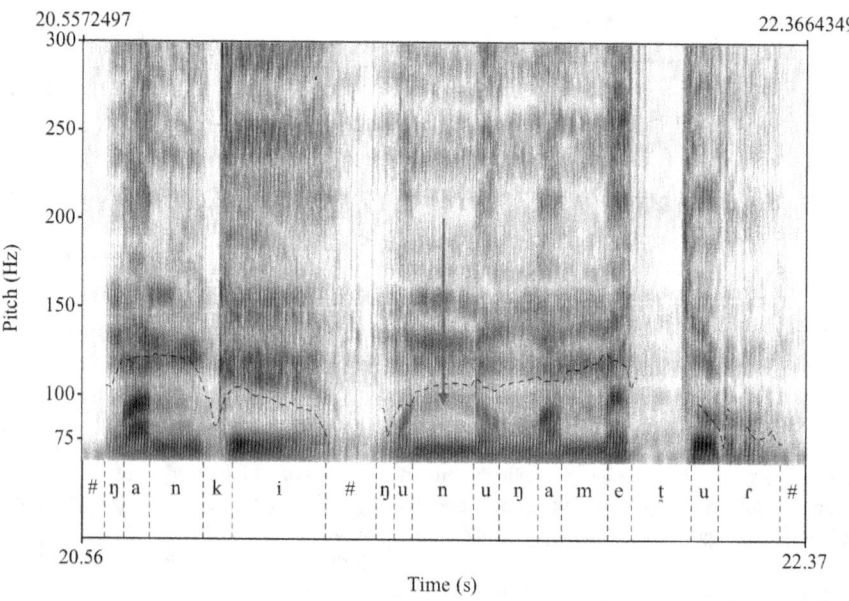

Figure 3.6(b): Geminate /nn/ in /ŋanki ŋunnuŋam-me-ʈur/ 'we stepped on it' (LP, 2015-07-08_LS).

p. 138ff.). These reconstructions explain why contrastive gemination appears for apical /n, l, ɖ/, and not for other places of articulation. The absence of gemination for *voiceless* stops may be simply because finite verb stems have no (unclustered) voiceless stops (§5.4).

I here label the long sonorant phones as 'geminates', and represent them as two-segment strings e.g. /nn/, averting the need to posit further phonemic contrasts e.g. /n, n:/. Note however that this is somewhat problematic for the geminate voiced obstruent /ɖɖ/. To maintain a two-segment analysis here we must posit a voiced obstruent in a syllable coda, e.g. /ɲuɖ.ɖan/ IMPEL.1PL.NFUT, though this is unusual since coda obstruents are otherwise voiceless. Alternatively we might posit a complex onset, i.e. /ɲu.ɖɖan/, though this would again be highly unusual, since all other onsets are simple. In summary, both possible segment/syllable analyses of gemination violate otherwise very solid phonological patterns in the language.

3.6 The intermediate status of retroflexion

Contrastive alveolar and retroflex apical consonants are found in many Australian languages, though the contrast is usually neutralised in word-initial position (Fletcher & Butcher, 2014, p. 103), and in some languages the contrast is not consistently realised (e.g. Garrwa: Mushin, 2012; Central Arrernte: Tabain, 2009). Several Daly region languages lack the contrast altogether (Dixon, 2002a, p. 565), and in Ngan'gi there is non-contrastive variation between alveolar/retroflex articulations (Reid, 1990, p. 41). In Murrinhpatha there is some evidence for contrastive retroflexion, though it is not consistently realised. Alveolar and retroflex apicals are therefore in an 'intermediate' phonological relationship, neither fully contrastive phonemes nor totally unpredictable allophones (Goldsmith, 1995; Hall, 2013). Linguists working on Murrinhpatha have not reached consistent judgements about whether particular lexemes have alveolar or retroflex phonological representations, and native speakers I have worked with do not give clear guidance on this point. Therefore acoustic data analysis would be required to rigorously investigate this topic. In this discussion I confine myself to sketching the outlines of the problem.

Street (2012) lists many lexemes as having contrastive alveolar/retroflex apicals in word-medial and word-final positions, and supportive evidence can be found for some of these in speech data from some speakers. For example, speaker AMN (b. 1962) produces distinctive vowel transitions into the word-medial laterals in /kala/ 'bandicoot' and /kaɭaj/ 'fishing net', with a subtle (to my perception) rhotic colouring for the retroflex. The most visible effect this has on formant structure is a lowering of F3 and F4. For the alveolar apical in /al/ the formants stay flat at about 2500Hz and 3500Hz respectively, while for the retroflex apical in /aɭ/ they descend to around 2000/2800Hz on transition to the consonant (Figure 3.7).

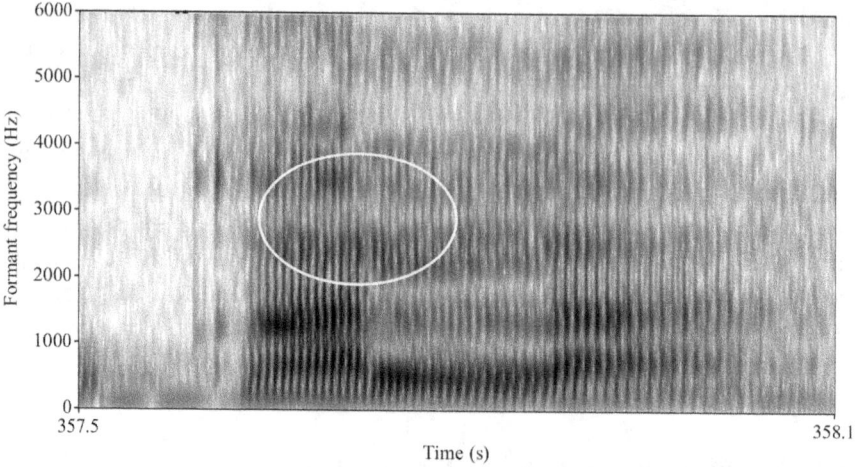

Figure 3.7(a): Alveolar apical lateral in /kala/ 'bandicoot' with highlighting on F3 and F4 transitions for /al/ (AMN, 2015-07-02_AT).

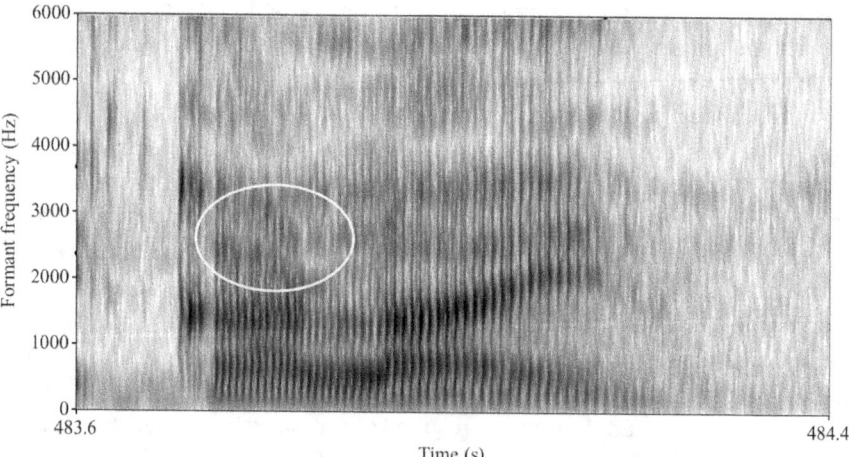

Figure 3.7(b): Retroflex lateral in /kaɭaj/ 'fishing net' with highlighting on F3 and F4 transitions for /aɭ/ (AMN, 2015-07-02_AT).

A second speaker, PeBu (b. 1958), illustrates the obstruent contrast attested by Street in the roots /-bat/ 'hit, throw' versus /-paʈ/ 'leave'. Again this is reflected in an acoustic contrast between flat F3/F4 formants for /at/ and descending transitions for /aʈ/ (Figure 3.8).

3.6 The intermediate status of retroflexion — 65

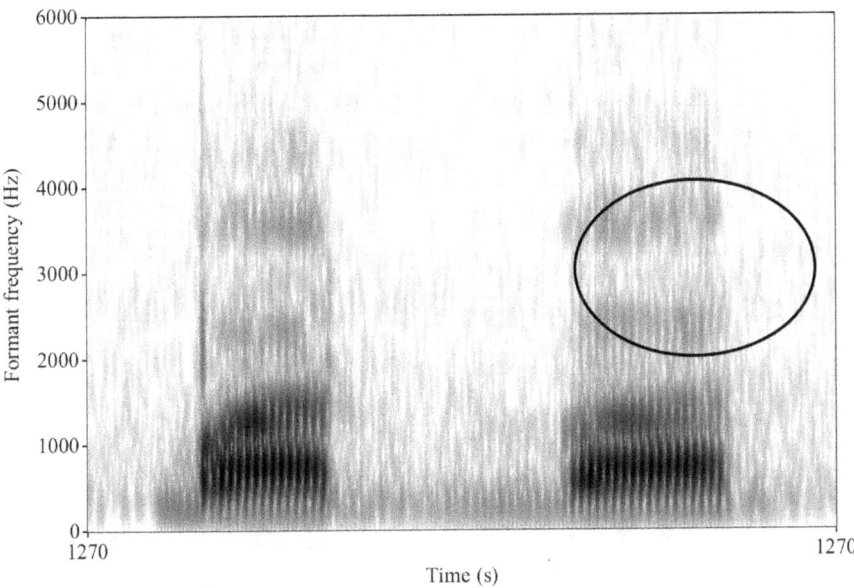

Figure 3.8(a): Alveolar apical obstruent in /bat-bat/ 'right hand' (PeBu, 1990_AB).

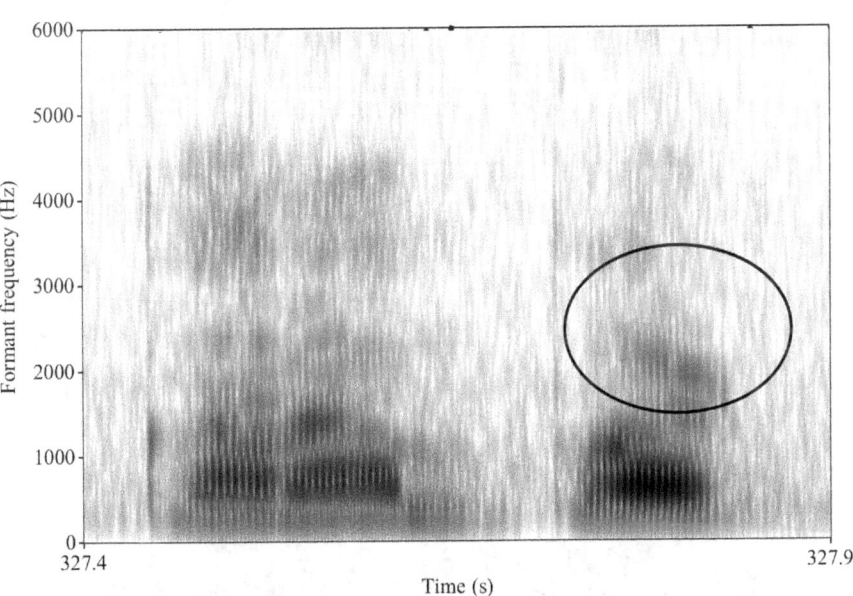

Figure 3.8(b): Retroflex obstruent in /kanam-paʈ/ 'she left it' (PeBu, 1990_AB).

However not all data supports Street's proposed contrasts. Various speakers produce /bat/ 'hit, throw' and /paṭ/ 'leave' without a clear retroflexion contrast (Figure 3.9). Most of the high-quality audio data available is for younger speakers, and it is possible that merger of the alveolar / retroflex contrast is a generational change. However there is also some evidence of non-contrastiveness from somewhat older speakers (e.g. AMN, b. 1962), and Street's (2012) dictionary

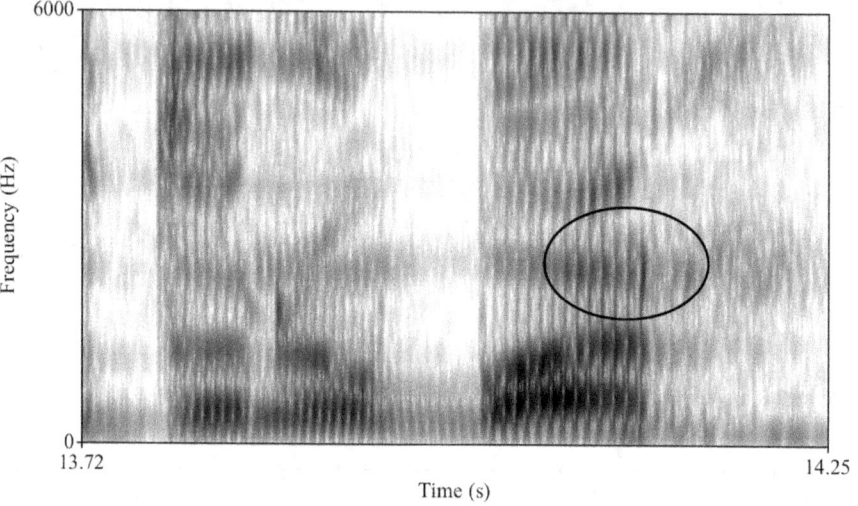

Figure 3.9(a): /ṭunu-bat/ 'throw it!' (DePu, 2016-06_AMP).

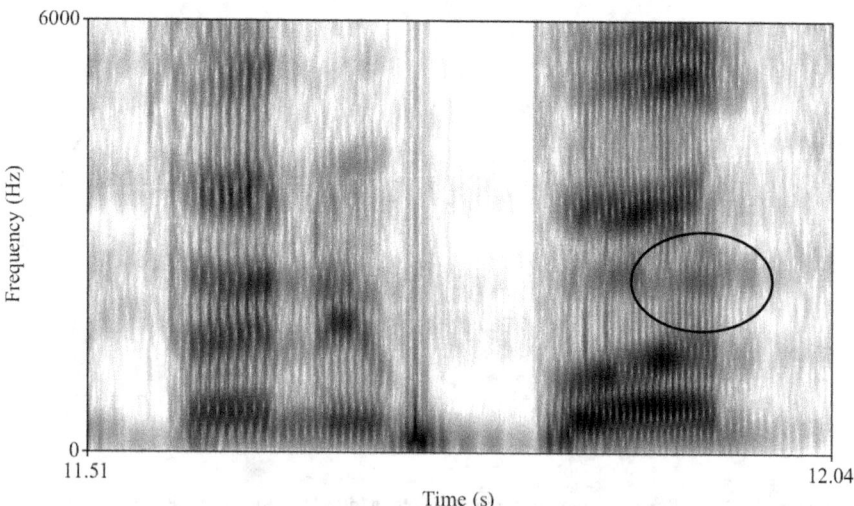

Figure 3.9(b): /ṭani-paṭ/ 'leave it!' (DePu, 2016-06_AMP).

also suggests some variability among older speakers, for example listing both /kuli ~ kuḷi/ 'bereaved parent' and /wanankal ~ waṇaŋkal/ 'healer'. More extensive acoustic data analysis would be required to delineate the distribution of the retroflexion contrast within the speech community.

In the word-initial position, which has been recognised as a neutralising context for apicals in previous studies (e.g. Street & Mollinjin, 1981), there is again variable realisation, though with a general tendency for retroflexion to occur after a vowel. In this book the representation of apicals as alveolar or retroflex generally follows the decision reached by Street (2012), except for in few cases where examples I have collected appear to directly contradict Street's version. It should be kept in mind that apicals can generally be produced with varying degrees of retroflexion, according to the speaker.

In summary, some acoustic data does support the notion of contrastive retroflexion in Murrinhpatha, while other data casts doubt upon it. One possible explanation is that this is a matter of inter-speaker variation, perhaps related to diverse personal language histories in contact with other languages of the Daly Region. Murrinhpatha sits on a historic borderline between languages to the south that have contrastive retroflexion (e.g. Jaminjung), and languages to the north and inland that do not (e.g. Marrithiyel, Ngan'gi, Malak-malak) (Dixon, 2002a, p. 565ff.). An intermediate phonological contrast may here reflect an 'intermediate' position in linguistic geography.

3.7 Connected speech processes

Phonetic reductions that occur when words are spoken together in fluent, connected speech may be seen as marginal phenomena, separable from the more systematic phonological structures of the language. However, connected speech processes are of interest as some form the basis for morpho-phonological juncture effects in complex words (§4.5). The connected speech reductions discussed here are subdivided into those that involve progressive assimilation of morpheme-initial consonants, and those that involve degemination. These are of course not the full range of connected speech reductions that occur, but they are some of the most salient because they involve phonemic segments becoming phonetically identical to other phonemic segments, e.g. /p/ → [w]. The phonetic reductions described here are systematic and frequent in connected speech, but tend to disappear in careful speech.[20]

---

[20] Note however that some of the pronunciations described here appear even in elicited, self-monitored speech tokens, especially when produced by younger male speakers (Mansfield, 2015a).

3.7.1 Progressive consonant assimilation

I describe here three progressive consonant assimilations: nasal liquidation /ln, rn/ → [ll, rr], labial glide fortition /mw/ → [mp ~ mm], and a class of intervocalic obstruent lenitions /p, t̪, k/ → [β, ð, ɣ].

Nasal liquidation

Nasal liquidation predominantly affects three suffixes beginning with /n/: /-nu/ FUT, /-nime/ PAUC.M and /-nukun/ GEN, ADVERS (43–45). There is no reason to suspect that it is specific to these morphological structures; rather, these are simply by far the most common constructions producing /ln, rn/ sequences. Unlike the other assimilations described here, nasal liquidation does not have a phonologised counterpart attested for compound word structures, however this may simply be due to the lack of /l-n, r-n/ sequences across morphological junctures in compounds. Furthermore, there are no /ln, rn/ clusters attested in simple stems, suggesting that there is a general phonological constraint against such sequences. Nasal liquidation has not been attested as a phonetic or phonological process in any other Australian language as far as I know, though it does occur in the Caucasian language Udi (Harris, 2002, p. 34).

(43) bat̪allu
 ba-t̪al-nu
 AFFECT.3SG.IRR-chop-FUT
 she will chop it

(44) kawurrime
 ka-wur-nime
 carry.3PL.IRR-drag-PAUC.M
 they (pauc.) might drag it

(45) naŋkallukun
 naŋkal-nukun
 who-GEN
 whose (is it)?

Labial glide fortition

Labial glide fortition also occurs predominantly with suffixes, /-wad̪a/ SEQ, /-wuran/ GO.IMPF, /-waɲu/ DIR (46–48). The phonetic fortition to [p ~ m] is likely not a binary choice so much as a cline of gesture timing between closure of velum and labial release (Browman & Goldstein, 1992). Labial glide fortition also occurs as a phonologised alternation, but only at compound-internal morphological junctures (§4.5).

(46) ŋunuŋampaḏa
 ŋunuŋam-waḏa
 use.feet.1SG.NFUT-SEQ
 I'm going now (FeBu, 2004-06-24)

(47) ŋara mampuran
 ŋara mam-wuran
 INTG do.3SG.NFUT-GO.IMPF
 what does it do? (AMN, 2015-01-30_Pr3-D1)

(48) jerpilammaŋu
 jerpilam-waŋu
 PLACE.NAME-TOWARDS
 towards Yerrpilam (JaLo, 2013-06-22_02)

Voiceless obstruent lenition

Voiceless obstruent lenition mainly affects morph-initial segments, and is exhibited not just in suffixes, but also at the beginning of independent words. Many lexical stems begin with voiceless obstruents, and the required context for lenition, a preceding vowel, is very frequent. Three voiceless obstruents /p, ṯ, k/ are subject to lenition, becoming realised as fricatives (often voiced), approximants or deleted altogether. For simplicity I here represent voiced fricative realisations only: [β, ð, ɣ]. The lenited variants are more common for /p, k/ at the beginning of both independent words and bound lexical stems, while for /ṯ/ lenition is mostly limited to suffixes (49–51) (Mansfield, 2015a). The apicals /t, ʈ/ do not usually exhibit phonetic lenition (52).

(49) miβaŋu βuḏanwiβaŋam
 mi-paŋu puḏan-wi-paŋam
 VEG-grass IMPEL.3PL.NFUT-smoke-BE.IMPF
 they are smoking marijuana

(50) ɣaḏuɣaɲi niɲaɲtiɣanam
 kaḏu-kaɲi niŋam-ṯi-kanam
 PERS-this use.fire.3SG.NFUT-cook-BE.IMPF
 this person is cooking

(51) naɲṯiṯapak ʈipmam wuriniwalakṯaðara
 naɲṯi-ṯapak ʈipmam wurini-palak-ta-ṯara
 THING-mist black go.3SG.PST-slither-PST-MOVE
 black mist settled

(52) kutiwuŋku
 ku-tiwuŋku
 ANIM-eagle
 eagle

Voiceless obstruent lenition generally occurs only on morpheme-initial segments because these are phonetically short, while morpheme-medial voiceless obstruents are long, and thus protected from lenition (§3.4.4). However, as we saw above, voiceless obstruents are *not* long when there is another voiceless obstruent occurring to their right within the word. In these cases phonetic lenition is just as frequent, if not more so, than in word-initial position (53). We may therefore observe that the more precise target of lenition is any non-lengthened voiceless obstruent, though for simplicity of exposition it will generally suffice to refer to 'initial obstruent lenition'.

(53) ŋaβapa
ŋapapa
sugar glider

Bound morphemes beginning with voiceless obstruents phonologise lenition when they are lexical elements of compounds (coverbs, body-part nominals; §8.4, §8.5). In the phonologised lenition, glides and fricatives are produced, and the apical obstruent is also lenited: /p, t̪, ʈ, k/ → /w, ð, ɻ, ɣ/.

3.7.2 Degemination

Murrinhpatha has geminate consonants at morphological boundaries in compounds, and in some finite verb stems where erstwhile morphological boundaries become somewhat opaque (§5.4). In both cases geminates may be reduced to singleton length in connected speech (54, 55).

(54) baŋamelmelwuran
baŋa<u>m-m</u>elmel-wuran
AFFECT.3SG.NFUT-flatten.PLUR-GO.IMPF
he is flattening it

(55) pulamaʈ
pu<u>ll</u>am-aʈ
eat.3PL.NFUT-eat
they ate it

Degemination of vowels may occur whenever these are brought together by phonetic deletion of the consonant in between (56). A few coverbs have phonologised initial consonant deletion (§8.4), and when these are brought into contact with a preceding vowel there is phonologised (obligatory) reduction to a single vowel.

For most sequences it is V₁ that remains (57), while the /ia/ sequence is merged to /e/ (58).

(56) ḍiraŋaɻaṯu
 ḍiraŋaɻa-kaṯu
 PLACE.NAME-FROM
 from Dirrangara

(57) maŋaṉṉeṯ
 maŋan-ṉe-aṯ
 use.hands.1SG.NFUT-3SG.OBJ.F-get
 I got it for her (Street, 1987, p. 110)

(58) pibet
 pibi-at
 stand.3PL.PST-stand
 they stood (Street, 1987, p. 110)

3.8 Loanwords and lexico-phonological strata

A substantial proportion of the lexicon used in contemporary Murrinhpatha speech consists of recognisable loanwords from English and Jaminjung (a Mirndi language bordering Murrinhpatha territory to the south, (Schultze-Berndt, 2000)). Loanwords have had a major effect in expanding the segmental and syllabic inventory of Murrinhpatha, though they have not affected the morpho-phonological structures of the language. Loanwords as a rule are independent lexical words,[21] and may host nominal or phrasal morphology, but cannot act as stems of finite verbs. Examples throughout this book include few English loanwords, because inherited vocabulary often provides more complete illustrations of morphology. It should be noted that examples are in this sense somewhat unrepresentative of the contemporary lexicon.

Loanwords are sometimes completely assimilated to the phonology of the receiving language (e.g. Fr. *crêpe* > Eng /kreɪp/), but in other instances they maintain phonological structures (segmental, phonotactic or prosodic) that were previously not in the phonology of the receiving language (e.g. *déjà vu* > /deɪʒavuː/).

---

[21] There are a handful of exceptions where English-derived nouns have become 'bound roots', occurring only in compounds (§7.1.1.).

The receiving language thus has distinct sound patterns associated with lexical subsets of distinct etymological provenance, and these can be labelled 'lexico-phonological strata' (Itô & Mester, 1995). Though the strata have their origin in lexical borrowing, they are ultimately defined by phonology rather than etymology. Not all loanwords from a given source language will bring with them the imported sound pattern (some words may be phonologically assimilated), and with time these strata may no longer be recognised by speakers as borrowings, even though they maintain distinctive phonological structures (e.g. Latin loanwords in English, Chomsky & Halle, 1968, pp. 171–174; Sanskrit loanwords in Malayalam, Mohanan, 1986).

Murrinhpatha is undoubtedly replete with loanwords from various neighbouring languages, which however cannot be easily distinguished on phonological grounds. But there is a clear stratum of lexemes that betray their origin in Jaminjung by their use of a post-alveolar laminal obstruent before back vowels, i.e. /ṯa, ṯu/.²² In Murrinhpatha's older hereditary stratum there is a single laminal obstruent /t̪/, which is realised with a dental place of articulation before back vowels [t̪a, t̪u], and a post-alveolar articulation before front vowels [ṯe, ṯi]. Jaminjung, by contrast, has contrastive palatals as in *thabba* 'stick out', *jab* 'get detached'. Jaminjing > Murrinhpatha loans that have the post-alveolar before a back vowel maintain the source phonology, rather than integrating to the older Murrinhpatha allophony, thus establishing a laminal contrast in Murrinhpatha. Such loanwords and loan stems include /ṯanṯu/ 'boat', /ṯalaŋka/ 'billabong', /-ṯuŋ/ 'kiss', /ṯanpa/ 'ceremony genre', /kaṯawula/ 'ceremonial head-dress', /ṯalput ~ ṯelput/ 'house', and various subsection names such as /ṯaŋala/. Loanword strata of this type have elsewhere been identified as a common source of laminal contrasts in Australian languages (Dixon, 2002a, p. 562). Murrinhpatha also has a noun classifier /ṯu/ VIOLENCE (§7.2), which may have been borrowed or otherwise influence by related forms in the sister language Ngan'gi, where laminals are usually palatal (Reid, 1990, pp. 46, 287).²³ The existence of this one apparently non-Jaminjung item in the post-alveolar contrast stratum for the moment remains unexplained.

The English lexico-phonological stratum, which at the oldest might have begun development in the late nineteenth century (Walsh, 2011), contributes a

---

22 In fact some of these could be from other languages to the south that have /ṯa, ṯu/, though Jaminjung is the most likely source, being the immediate southern neighbour and with extensive contact with Murrinhpatha (§2.2.1). Intensive social contact between Murrinhpatha and Jaminjung speakers was focused on cattle stations where the two worked alongside one another in the early twentieth century (Harvey, 2013; Stanner, 1936).

23 Potentially related forms are Ngan'gikurungurr *yuri* 'striker' and *tyun* 'large woomera' (Reid, 1990, p. 287).

much larger proportion of the contemporary Murrinhpatha vocabulary, and a much larger range of distinctive phonological structures (Mansfield, 2015b). These have been borrowed both directly from contact with Australian English speakers, but also via contact with the English-lexified Kriol spoken by many Aboriginal people across northern Australia (Sandefur, 1986), and perhaps earlier via contact with a pidgin variety used for trade and labour. The English stratum adds several new contrastive segments: fricatives /f, s, ʃ/ in syllable onsets, one new simple vowel /o/ (and, marginally, a tense vowel /ʉ/), and two diphthongs /ai, ei/ (59–63).

(59) finiț   'finish'
(60) seip   'save'
(61) ʃeip   'shape'
(62) taim   'time'
(63) tʉ   'two'

The English stratum also introduces new phonotactics for already existing segments: word-initial /ɻ/, word-initial onsetless syllables V(C), and the full range of English onset clusters, /sp, pl, tɻ/ etc (64–68).

(64) inpol   'involve'
(65) ɻait   'right'
(66) spidi   'speedy'
(67) pleit   'plate'
(68) tɻaj   'try'

Some older English borrowings, though they assimilate fricatives to the pre-existing voiceless stop series, nonetheless add further vocabulary to the laminal contrast stratum, e.g. /ṯaba/ 'afternoon' (< Eng. *supper*), /ṯuya/ 'sugar', /attaṯ/ 'outside'. The English stratum also introduces a laminal contrast to the nasals, e.g. /ɲuwan/ 'new'. On the other hand some English sound patterns are assimilated rather than imported, including the /h/ segment, various other vowels, coda obstruent manner distinctions, and coda clusters (69–74).

(69) ospaip 'hose-pipe' /həʉz/
(70) attait 'outside' /æɔtsaɪd/
(71) bek[24] 'bag' /bæg/

---

[24] I represent English voiced obstruent codas as assimilating to the non-contrastive Murrinhpatha coda obstruent series, even though in some loanword tokens the contrast does

(72) fɹit̻   'fridge' /fɹɪdʒ/
(73) fɹen   'friend'
(74) teis   'taste'

Finally, it is worth noting that some English loanwords introduce word-final accentual anchoring, breaking the general Murrinhpatha pattern of penultimate accent (75) (§4.3). On the other hand, there is some evidence of English word-initial stress lexemes being assimilated to the Murrinhpatha accentual pattern (76), though this has not been investigated extensively.

(75) antastén   'understand'
(76) keméɻa   'camera'   (MaMi, 2015-07-21)

The expanded consonant inventory of contemporary Murrinhpatha, combining the inherited lexicon with Jaminjung and English lexico-phonological strata, is illustrated in Table 3.5. Shading indicates recently absorbed phonemes. The expanded vowel inventory is illustrated in Figure 3.10.

Table 3.5: Contemporary Murrinhpatha consonant inventory. Shading indicates recently absorbed lexico-phonological strata.

		Labial	Laminal		Apical		Dorsal
			Dental	Post-alveolar	Alveolar	Retroflex	
Obstruent	Voiceless	p	t̪	ʈ͡	t	ʈ	k
	Voiced	b			d	ɖ	
	Fricative	f	ð	ʃ	s		ɣ
Nasal		m	n̪	ɲ	n	ɳ	ŋ
Lateral					l	ɭ	
Trill / tap					r		
Glide		w	j		ɻ		

---

appear to be maintained, e.g. /beg/ 'bag'. I have not yet gathered evidence sufficient to confidently attest this as an imported sound pattern.

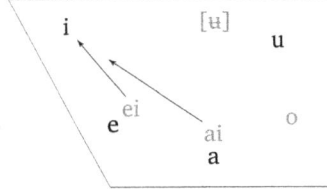

Figure 3.10: Contemporary Murrinhpatha vowel inventory including (greyed) recently absorbed lexico-phonological strata.

3.9 Summary

We have seen in this chapter that the basic phonological structure of Murrinhpatha words follows some of the typical characteristics found in other Australian languages: simple syllable shapes, maximised consonant contrasts in word-medial intervocalic position, cluster constraints. But it has rather broader possibilities than has been reported for other Australian languages, especially those of the Pama-Nyungan family: obstruent codas, obstruent manner contrasts in onsets, and a more variable satisfaction of cluster constraints. We have in addition noted an interesting pattern of phonetic obstruent lengthening at word-medial positions, which however is not applied to bound morphs with initial obstruents. The unlengthened obstruents are subject to lenition, which is phonologised as morpho-phonological juncture alternations for many bound stems, as we will see in the next chapter. The next chapter will also explore how the building blocks described here are deployed more specifically in different morphological structures, and in particular how these structures combine with supra-segmental features (vowel length and pitch) to mark out prosodic word and phrase units.

4 Morphologically specific sound patterns

4.1 Introduction

This chapter describes the morpho-phonology of Murrinhpatha – that is to say, the ways in which certain morphological structures exhibit specific phonological patterns. Some morphosyntactic classes in Murrinhpatha use restricted subsets of the full phonological inventory. A related phenomenon is allomorphic alternation where morphological elements combine. These phenomena are mediated by higher level phonological structures, i.e. the 'prosodic constituents' of prosodic word and syllable, which are introduced in this chapter. These prosodic constituents mediate the relationship between segmental phonology (described in the previous chapter) and the structure of stems, affixes, derivation and compounding (described in the following chapters).

The first part of this chapter (§4.2) introduces morphosyntactic classes, with particular attention to their phonological characteristics. Murrinhpatha phonology exhibits patterns specific to morphosyntactic classes, the most dramatic of which is that open lexical classes use obstruent codas, while the closed classes (which includes finite verb stems) have only sonorant codas. The two open classes, *nominals* and *coverbs*, are lexical stem classes in which some members are independent words, some can be either independent or compounded, and some appear only in compounds. Finite verb stems can also be considered a lexical class, though some members are highly grammaticalised, as explained in later chapters (§5, §8). Finite verb stems are a closed set of just 39 members, clearly distinguished from the other lexical classes by the fact that they always appear in inflected (finite) form. In addition to the lexical classes, I identify five classes of bound grammatical morphs. Finally, there is a small closed class of *function words*: independent words with grammatical meanings.

The second part of the chapter (§4.3) describes the prosodic word (PWord, ω), one of the key analytical concepts in this book. The PWord is the basic sound shape of a minimal utterance, and is characterised by a minimal requirement of bimoraic phonological weight. PWords may have prosodically adjunct bound morphs attached to them (§1.8), and one or more PWords together with their adjuncts form a prosodic phrase (PPhrase, φ). The PPhrase is marked by a single pitch accent, anchored on the penultimate syllable of the right-most PWord in the phrase. On this basis we can classify a few basic types of PPhrases: phrase consisting of a standalone PWord, which itself may be morphologically simplex or complex (1, 2); phrase consisting of PWord with adjuncts (3); phrase consisting of multiple PWords and any adjuncts (4).

(1) [[malkimárin]ω]φ
    vein
(2) [[ŋunuŋám-ku]ω]φ
    use.feet.1SG.NFUT-throw
    I threw it away
(3) [[puma-páṭa]ω-nu-ŋime]φ
    use.hands.3PL.IRR-make-FUT-PAUC.F
    they will make it
(4) [[kale]ω   [nukúnu]ω-ðaŋunu]φ
    mother   3SG.M-SOURCE
    from his mother

The final part of the chapter (§4.5) describes phonological alternations that occur at morphological junctures within PWords. These are specific to PWord-internal junctures, and have a tendency to mask the morphological constituents of the PWord, especially in cases where the alternations are not predictable by rules. Nonetheless there are clear patterns evident in the alternations, and these can be motivated by positing phonological constraints, the most complex of which involve consonant clusters. One of the major constraints on consonant clusters is a dispreference for peripheral-coronal place contours, *PER-COR (Hamilton, 1996). This is of considerable interest from the point of view of phonological typology, because it is the inverse of place contours observed on other continents, which exhibit a *COR-PER constraint (Blust, 1979; Lahiri, 2012).

4.2 Morphological categories and their phonological shape

I here lay out the morphological categories of Murrinhpatha, each of which will be described in more detail in the remaining chapters of the book. The morphological categories are identified by their distinct distributions – the positions they may fill in phrase structures and complex word structures – however, they also have distinctive phonological characteristics. In this chapter, our focus is on the phonological characteristics of the morphological categories, in particular their prosodic constituency and their distinctive use of the language's overall segmental inventory.

I identify three 'lexical' classes – nominals, coverbs and finite verb stems – though the last of these has only a semi-lexical character, since it is a closed class and some of its members are highly grammaticalised. Each of the lexical classes has distributional sub-categories referencing particular phrase or word structures in which some members of the class are constrained to appear – i.e. some may appear only as independent words, while others appear only in compounds. But there are other members that can be either bound or independent, thus motivating the superordinate category. The notion of 'independent word' that I draw upon here refers to morphs that can be spoken alone as a meaningful utterance, though in the final chapter I discuss alternative approaches to wordhood in Murrinhpatha (§9.4). In addition to the lexical classes, there are six grammatical classes – i.e. closed classes, whose members have more abstract semantics such as tense or number categories. These are semi-regular inflectional formatives, predicate inflectional suffixes, adverbials, discourse tags, case markers and function words.

(a) *Nominals* are an open lexical class, typically referring to either entities or properties of entities. To some extent nominals might be further subclassed into nouns and adjectives, distinguishing those that denote an entity versus those that denote a property of an entity (Wierzbicka, 1986). However there is no clear morphosyntactic distinction between these (Dixon, 1980, p. 272; Walsh, 1976, p. 126ff.), so for the purposes of this book they are treated together as a single class. However, multiple nominals can be combined in a noun phrase, the structure of which suggests further sub-categorisation into generic nouns, specific nouns, adjectives and determiners (§7.3). Some adjectives can also function as adverbs, specifying the manner of action or event.

  i. *Free nominals* are those that appear as independent words, and account for most of the category. These are mostly of a lexical, i.e. semantically specific character, but also include paradigmatic sets, in particular demonstratives, pronouns, numerals and interrogatives.

  ii. *Incorporated body parts* are a closed class of body-part nouns that are compounded to coverbs, which are in turn compounded to finite verb stems (§8.5). Some incorporated body parts also appear as free nominals, whereas others appear only as incorporated.

  iii. *Classifier nominals* are a closed class that occur both as independent words or as the first element of nominal compounds, in which they classify nominal referents according to an ontological paradigm (§7.3). In view of the latter function, they may also be considered a distinct class of bound grammatical morphs.

(b) *Coverbs* are the other open lexical class. The distinction from nominals is not sharp, because there are some lexemes that can be used both as nominals and as coverbs (Mansfield, 2016a, p. 412), and neither is there a sharp distinction in the bound morphology they host (§8.4). However we can posit distinct nominal and coverb syntactic roles, where the nominal forms part of a noun phrase (§7.3), while the coverb forms part of a phrasal verb or compound verb. In some cases the same lexeme can take on either of these roles.

i. *Free coverbs* are those that appear as distributionally independent words, and may take up the position before a finite verb in a phrasal verb construction (§8.2). Most free coverbs can also appear as bound coverbs.
ii. *Bound coverbs* are those that appear compounded to finite verb stems. The majority of coverbs are bound only, though a few can be either bound or free.

(c) *Finite verb stems* are a closed class that is sharply distinct from the categories above. These have a clear morphosyntactic distinction in that there are no non-finite or 'bare stem' forms, but only forms inflected for person, number and tense. This inflectional morphology is very unpredictable in form (§5.2), and is not shared with other word classes. In most parts of this book, finite verb stems are represented as single units, e.g. /wuran/ go.3SG.NFUT. However in sections that focus on their inflectional patterns, segmented versions are presented, e.g. /wu-ɾa-n/ 3SG-go-NFUT. Where segmentation is applied, the lexical element such as /ɾa/ 'go' is labelled an 'inner stem' (see below).

a. *Simple verb stems* are those finite verb stems that can form a verbal word along with any appropriate inflectional morphs, but without any compounded coverb. There are 11 simple verbs, and ten of these can also appear as classifier verb stems (only /ma/ 'do, say' is always simple).
b. *Classifier verb stems* are those that combine with a coverb to form a compound verb. There are 28 stems that appear as classifiers only, and some of these have lost much of their lexical semantic character (§8.3).

(d) *Semi-regular inflectional formatives* are the 'inner stems' and inflectional exponents of finite verb stems, e.g. /wu-ɾa-n/ 3SG-go-NFUT. Semi-regular formatives capture patterns shared only among subsets of the finite stem class. To the extent that some patterns occur only on a few finite stems, it is unclear whether they form part of the mental grammar of speakers (§1.7, §5.7). The exponence of an inflectional category is usually marked not by a single semi-regular formative, but rather is distributed over inner stem and affix formatives (§5.4).

(e) *Predicate inflectional suffixes* are bound inflectional exponents that exhibit fully regular patterns, i.e. without the lexical specificity of semi-regular inflectional formatives (§6). Regular inflectional suffixes can be hosted by either finite verbs or nominals, whichever has the predicating function in the clause. They specify inflectional categories of pronominal person, role, number and event TAM.

(f) *Adverbials* are a closed class of bound elements, marking fairly abstract modal, temporal or spatial categories (§7.6). Adverbials are not specific about the stem class to which they attach. They are hosted to the right of the final word in the phrase, though on verbs or predicating nouns they may be positioned amidst predicate inflectional affixes.

(g) *Discourse tags* are pragmatic elements that, like adverbials, attach to phrases rather than a specific stem class (§7.7). However, unlike adverbials, discourse tags are always the final element at the right edge of the phrase.
(h) *Case markers* indicate the semantic role of a nominal argument. They attach to the final word of the argument noun phrase (§7.5).
(i) *Function words* are a handful miscellaneous independent words not included any of the categories above. These are a multi-purpose preposition and complementiser /ŋara/[25]; negators /meɻe/ and /manaŋka/. These host only phrasal morphology that can attach to any phrase type, and thus have limited relevance to matters addressed in this book.

The morphological classes deploy rather different versions of the segmental sound patterns described in the last chapter. The open lexical classes, nominals and coverbs, use the full range of segmental patterns. Closed classes use more restricted segmental patterns: finite verb stems more closely conform to the 'standard Australian word' profile described in the last chapter, with only sonorant codas, and only homorganic clusters. Bound grammatical morphs are also somewhat closer to the standard Australian segmental structure, though unlike the lexical classes, they are not always syllabic.

4.2.1 Open lexical classes: Nominals and coverbs

Nominals deploy the full set of sound patterns described in the previous chapter, which is to say that the maximally diverse range of 'word' patterns described there can more specifically be read as a description of Murrinhpatha nominal lexemes. Coverbs use the same full range of segmental patterns exhibited by nominals, but are unusual in that the vast majority of coverb roots are monosyllabic, in some cases open CV (5–7) but more frequently closed CVC(C) (7–11). Coverbs that are not attested as independent words are here cited with a left-edge hyphen.

(5) du   'weep'
(6) -pa   'scream'
(7) -la   'climb'
(8) -paṯ   'leave'
(9) biḷ   'open eyes'

---

[25] /ŋara/ also acts as a general interrogative, but in that case it has similar morphosyntactic and prosodic behaviour to a nominal. There are also more specific interrogatives, /ṯaŋku/ 'which', /naŋkal/ 'who', /minṯiɻe/ 'when', which behave morphosyntactically as nominal.

(10) -ḷuj   'turn'
(11) -ṭaɾk   'tie'

There are a few disyllabic coverb roots (e.g. /ɣuḍuk/ 'drink', /puteṭ/ 'feel movement'), and some of these are nominals that double as coverbs (e.g. /paṭa/ 'good n., make cv.'). But coverb *lexemes* are very often multisyllabic, even though coverb *roots* are typically monosyllabic, because so much of the coverb lexicon involves compounding of coverbs with body parts (12–14, §8.5), or reduplicative derivatives which would have once marked pluractional event structure but have become lexicalised as the basic form of the coverb (15, 16, §8.6).

(12) -paɲ-ṭaɾk   'tie loincloth'
     -groin-tie
(13) -ṭe-pup   'listen'
     -ear-sit
(14) -ŋka-bat   'be surprised'
     -eye-hit
(15) -lili   'walk'
(16) -jiɾjiɾ   'boil'

The monosyllabic tendency among coverb roots may be linked to historical sources in ideophones – in some instances an ideophonic quality remains transparent, e.g. /du/ 'cry'. This pattern has been observed in other northern Australian languages that have coverbs (Warlpiri: Nash, 1982, p. 185; Jaminjung: Schultze-Berndt, 2003, p. 161). There is another interesting comparison with other coverb languages. Pama-Nyungan (PNy) languages have very limited possibilities for coda consonants, either using very limited segmental types or no codas at all (Hamilton, 1996). But in some PNy languages with coverbs, such as Warumungu, a much wider range of coda consonants (including obstruents, laterals, approximants and trill) appear just in the coverb lexicon (Simpson, 1998, p. 711). This suggests that the unusual phonotactics of coverbs in these languages may be attributed to borrowing from non-PNy languages to the north. In Murrinhpatha, by contrast, we find /CVC/ word shapes with obstruent codas not just in the coverb lexicon, but also throughout the nominal vocabulary. On the other hand, we will see below that Murrinhpatha finite verb stems and bound morphs do *not* use obstruent codas, instead adhering to PNy phonotactics.

Some coverbs appear as independent words, but many appear only in bound form, compounded to the right of finite verb stems (§8.2). Some bound coverbs have shapes that would not be permissible if they were independent words. Two consist of only an onsetless syllable (/aʈ/ 'get, /aʈ/ 'eat'), while several have complex /ŋk/ onsets (e.g. /ŋkaj/ 'probe', /ŋke/ 'prevent'). In both cases, the coverb must combine with the preceding morph in the compound to produce a permissible syllabic structure (17, 18).

(17) ma.ŋa.naʈ
 maŋan-aʈ
 use.hands.1SG.NFUT-get
 I got it

(18) ŋaŋ.kaj.nu
 ŋa-ŋkaj-nu
 PIERCE.1SG.IRR-probe-FUT
 I'll probe it (Street 2012, -*ngkay*)

Several coverbs also begin with non-word-initial continuants /ð, ɣ, ɻ/, though some or all of these cases can be analysed as the result of a lenition process applied at morpho-phonological junctures (§4.4.1), in which case we might suppose that historical free forms would have had voiceless obstruent onsets /ʈ, k, t/.

4.2.2 Finite verb stems and semi-regular inflectional elements

Murrinhpatha finite verb stems are rather unusual in their highly irregular inflectional morphology, and in the fact that they form a closed class, with just 39 members. From a phonological point of view, what makes the finite verb stems interesting is that, compared to the open classes of nominals and coverbs, they are much closer to standard Australian word shape.

Within finite verb stem forms, we can distinguish prefix, suffix and 'inner stem' elements (§5.3). Prefixes can be further broken down into consonant and vowel elements, while inner stems exhibit consonant and vowel feature alternation patterns. Example (19) shows finite verb stem structure, with prefix consonant and vowel, suffix, and a consonant feature alternation on the inner stem. Example (20) shows another example, with a vowel frontness inner stem alternation. Inner stems and inflectional formatives are unlike other classes of bound morphology in Murrinhpatha in two ways: firstly, their relationship to grammatical meanings is highly unpredictable; secondly, they are prosodically minimal, with some being less than a syllable in size, and others consisting of phonological features rather than segments. It is only the whole finite verb stem that has a word-like shape. The morphological structure of finite verb stems is discussed extensively in the next chapter.

(19) p-i-ɾi-ni
PrefC-PrefV-Inner[C:RHOTIC]-Suffix
sit.3PL.PST

(20) p-u-me-ø
PrefC-PrefV-Inner[VF:FRONT]-Suffix
do.3PL.PST

The inflected forms of finite verb stems use a restricted range of segmental patterns compared to nominals and coverbs. As we saw in the previous chapter, the open lexical classes use a range of consonants in syllable codas, supporting an analysis of word composition as built up from a common syllabic unit (21–23). But when we turn to finite verb stems, we instead find only nasals in coda position, and the only cluster type is homorganic nasal-stop (24–27). There are also geminate sonorants that are not found in the open classes at all (28, §3.5), and all intervocalic obstruents are voiced obstruents, deriving from the fact that the inner stems have only voiced obstruents and homorganic nasal-stop clusters (e.g. /ba/ AFFECT, /ɖu/ IMPEL, /n̪t̪i/ 'have'), rather than the three-way voiced/voiceless/continuant contrast of the open classes (29). Finite verb stems generally have a higher proportion of sonorant consonants than open class words, which also aligns them more closely with the general profile of Australian sound patterns (Fletcher & Butcher, 2014, p. 101).

Open class word shapes
(21) wak   'crow'
(22) maɾ.kat̪   *person's name*
(23) buk.man̪.t̪aɾ 'red'

Finite verb stem (closed class) word shapes
(24) ŋi   sit.1SG.IRR
(25) nu.ɻu   go.2PL.IRR
(26) pum.pan   go.3PL.NFUT
(27) kan̪.t̪a.ŋan   crouch.3SG.NFUT-
(28) ŋun.nu   use.feet.1PL.IRR
(29) pu.bam   AFFECT.3PL.NFUT-

One respect in which Murrinhpatha finite verb stems do *not* conform to the standard Australian word shape is that there are many monosyllabic verb stems, whereas the Australian standard is minimally disyllabic (Dixon, 1980, p. 159; Evans, 1995, p. 739).

4.2.3 Bound grammatical morphs

The various classes of bound grammatical morphology (predicate inflectional suffixes, adverbials, case markers and discourse tags) share common segmental patterns, though they have distinct prosodic constituencies. Bound morphs need not conform to syllabic structure, since they can be syllabified with the stems or other bound morphs to which they attach. However, for the most part they are made up of whole syllables and are similar phonologically to standard Australian word shapes, even though they do not appear as independent words.

All bound morphs are suffixes or enclitics and many are prosodically 'adjunct', that is to say they are external to the prosodic word unit formed by their host lexeme (§1.8). They consist of up to three syllables (30–33), and their initial consonant may be one that is not permitted word-initially (34, 35).[26]

(30) =ka   CONSTITUENT
(31) -ɲi.me   PAUC.F
(32) =wa.ḍa   SEQUENTIAL
(33) =ḍe.ji.da   ITERATIVE
(34) =ɻe   AGENTIVE, INSTRUMENTAL, PERLATIVE
(35) -ða   PAST

There are no clear examples of grammatical prefixes in the regular morphology (as opposed to semi-regular inflections on the finite verb stems, which include prefixes). However classifier nouns are substantially grammaticalised, and can be analysed as 'noun class prefixes' (§7.1.2). These are also prosodically external, and have one or two syllables (36–38).

(36) ku-   ANIMATE-
(37) ṭuŋ.ku-   FIRE-
(38) mu.riṉ-   LANGUAGE-

Bound grammatical morphs are closer to the standard Australian word shape than are the open lexical classes of Murrinhpatha. Bound morphs have only sonorant codas, though they do not have the same highly restricted set of medial consonants as finite verb stems (39–43). Murrinhpatha bound morphs thus

---

[26] I am analytically agnostic as to the underlying form of such morphs, since they alternate in manner according to the final segment of their host, and either alternant could be taken as derived from morpho-phonological process. I.e. /V=ɻe ~ C=ṭe, V-ða ~ C-ṭa/ (§4.4.1).

conform to a widely observed pattern of affixes drawing on a restricted subset of the phonological inventory (Hopper & Traugott, 2003, p. 154), though this has been shown to be a pattern rather than a universal (Bybee, 2005).

(39) =nu.kun -GENITIVE, ADVERSATIVE
(40) =ŋa.ṯa -CONDITIONAL
(41) =ŋaða -DIMINUTIVE
(42) =wan.ku -COMITATIVE
(43) ṯamul- SPEAR-

There are a few exceptions to the otherwise whole-syllable structure of bound morphs. Interestingly, these are all prosodically internal suffixes, either object (OBJ) or oblique (OBL) pronominal suffixes, or a paucal (PC) number modifier with which they combine (§6.2.4). Most OBJ/OBL pronominals do have word-like shapes (44–46), but there are also three members of the paradigm (total N = 16) that are non-syllabic, being either /CCV/ or just /C/ (47–49). The final example (49) is an allomorph phonologically conditioned by a preceding vowel, which has led to phonologised lenition of the otherwise syllabic allomorph /-wun/. But for (47, 48) there are no syllabic allomorphs, so it remains unclear what sort of historical erosion or re-analysis might explain their non-syllabic shape.

(44) -ŋa 1SG.OBL
(45) -wu 3PL.OBL
(46) -nan 2PL.OBJ
(47) -mpa 2SG.OBL
(48) -ŋku PC.OBJ
(49) -n 3PL.OBJ / V_

In the final sections of this chapter I will explain how segmental phonology is conditioned by PWord constituency. However before that it is necessary to introduce both the Murrinhpatha PWord and the PPhrase.

4.3 The prosodic word

Many points of analysis in subsequent chapters will be based on identification of the prosodic word (PWord, ω), a structural unit that has great explanatory power in Murrinhpatha, as it does for many other languages (Gordon, 2016, p. 262ff.; McCarthy & Prince, 1993). I describe here the essential characteristics of the PWord, which is a minimally bimoraic, accent-anchoring unit of speech.

The importance of PWords in Murrinhpatha has much to do with the units of speech that fall *outside* the PWord. This accounts for a significant proportion of bound morphology, which I label prosodically 'external' or 'adjunct' (§1.8). One or more PWords, together with their dependent adjuncts, together form a prosodic phrase (PPhrase, φ). There is exactly one pitch accent in each PPhrase, predictably anchored to the penultimate syllable of the right-most PWord within the PPhrase.

The PWord is a bimoraic speech unit that provides the anchor for pitch accents. If the PWord has two or more syllables, pitch accent is anchored on the penultimate syllable. Monosyllabic PWords anchor the accent on their single syllable. However not all PWords have accents, as multiple PWords combining into a PPhrase have just one accent, on the right-most PWord. The anchoring of pitch accents on PPhrase-final PWords is illustrated in (50) and Figure 4.1 (repeated from §1.8).

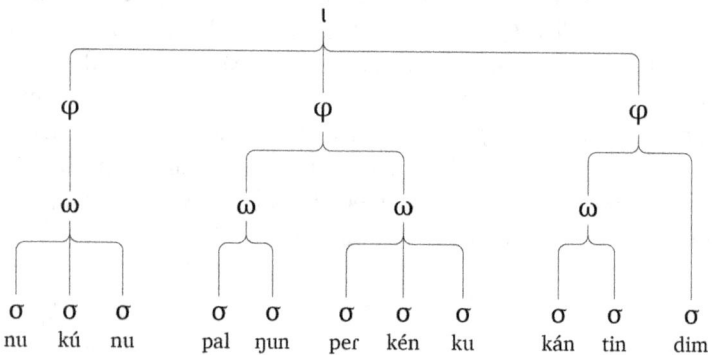

Figure 4.1: Example of Murrinhpatha prosodic constituent hierarchy.

(50) [[nukúnu]ω]φ   [[palŋun]ω [perkénku]ω]φ   [[káṉtin]ω-dim]φ
     he   woman   two   have.3SG.NFUT-SIT.IMPF
     he has two women   (LP, 2015-09-16_AT)

The PWord is coextensive with all morphologically simple words (nominals and coverbs) and with all finite verb stems including their semi-regular inflectional morphology. Accordingly, whenever these word types are right-most in a PPhrase, or indeed stand alone as utterances, they host a pitch accent on a monosyllable (51) or penultimate syllable (52–55).

(51) búrk   'great'
(52) píliṉ   'star'
(53) kaḍírak   'eyebrow'
(54) ŋunúŋam   'use.feet.1SG.NFUT'
(55) malkimárin   'vein'

There are also combinations of lexical stems and bound morphs that are prosodified within a PWord constituent. In the chapters that follow we will see several such constructs: verbs with pronominal suffixes and some number suffixes (§6.2), certain demonstrative–adverbial combinations (§7.5), predicating nominals hosting various inflectional and compound elements (§6.4), and compound verbs (§8.7).

As noted above, many Australian languages require two syllables for a minimal word. In Lardil, for example, this principle means that unaffixed monosyllabic lexemes require an epenthetic final /a/ to become pronounceable words (Wilkinson, 1988). In Murrinhpatha, as in some other non-Pama-Nyungan languages of the northern fringe, there are a substantial number of monosyllabic lexemes, and these are allowed to stand alone as words. The requirement here is not for disyllabic weight, but instead for *bimoraic* weight in a lone syllable. The bimoraic requirement is also found, for example, in Warray (Harvey & Borowsky, 1999) and Ngalakgan (Baker & Harvey, 2003). For Warray nouns only the nucleus is moraic, which means that all monosyllabic words must have a lengthened vowel, whereas for Warray verbs, and for all Ngalakgan words, the rhyme is moraic, so that either a long vowel or a closed syllable satisfies the bimoraic minimum.

Bimoraic nucleus   CV:, CV:C   (Warray nouns)
Bimoraic rhyme   CV:, CVC   (Warray verbs, Ngalakgan nouns/verbs)

Murrinhpatha follows the latter pattern, requiring a bimoraic minimal word calculated over the whole rhyme of the syllable (56, 57).

(56) ba: 'blowfly'
(57) wak   'crow'

As we will see in the next section, open monosyllabic words such as (56) have an important role in allowing us to distinguish morphological constructs that are unified as a PWord, from morphological constructs that involve prosodic adjunction.

4.4 Prosodic phrases and prominence

Most descriptions of Australian languages posit a metrical grid of alternating primary and secondary stresses, most often involving trochaic feet aligned to the left edge. However these descriptions are usually impressionistic, and phonetic evidence, where available, has not always supported the phonological description. Some of these descriptions may have been influenced by an earlier theoretical expectation, largely based on Germanic languages, that all languages have a metrical grid. More recent research in prosodic phonology has largely dispelled this assumption (e.g. Goedemans & van Zanten, 2014; Hyman, 2014).

For Murrinhpatha there have been several phonological descriptions of stress, but these have not concurred on which syllables bear stress (more on this below). While I have not attempted a phonetic study using systematic measurements in controlled contexts, I have not been able to find acoustic correlates to support any of the earlier proposals for stress in Murrinhpatha, either by careful listening or by examining wave forms in Praat (Boersma & Weenink, 2012). The occurrence of PPhrase-final, PWord-penultimate pitch peaks, however, is very consistent, and can be easily detected visually or auditorily once utterances are inspected in Praat. In view of this, and emboldened by recent findings of stresslessness in prosodic phonology, I therefore propose that Murrinhpatha probably does not have any metrical grid of alternating stressed syllables. Rejection of the metrical grid is equivalent to proposing that syllables are grouped directly into PWord and PPhrase constituents, without the mediation of metrical feet (Hayes, 1995).

The only systematic form of prominence that I have identified is the pitch accent anchored to the penultimate syllable (see below). With a metrical foot structure, longer words should have further stressed syllables. However I have not been able to detect any such prominences in terms of pitch, duration, intensity or segmental quality. Longer PWords have only a single penultimate prominence, e.g. [malkimárin]_ω 'vein', and lack other types of syllabic prominence by which we might diagnose foot structure, e.g. *[(màlki)(márin)]_ω. On the other hand, two observations are indirectly suggestive of trochaic feet: (a) pitch accent is penultimate, which could be neatly interpreted as anchoring on the final trochaic foot; (b) the PWord must be bimoraic, which could be interpreted as a requirement to map onto a bimoraic foot. But against these points we must weigh the lack of any secondary prominences that would provide positive evidence for non-final feet in longer words, especially those with uneven syllable counts, e.g. ?[kuj-(nu-ŋku)-(kéḍe)]_ω ~ ?[(kuj-nu)-ŋku -(kéḍe)]_ω 'they will tangle themselves'. Therefore I propose a 'flat' prosodic hierarchy, with the syllable directly dominated by the PWord (Figure 4.2).

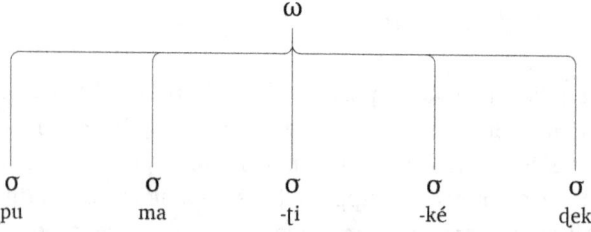

Figure 4.2: Prosodic constituency for a compound verb forming a single PWord.

(58) pumaɹiyeḑek
 puma-ṭi-keḑek
 use.hands.3PL.IRR-buttocks-finish
 they will finish it

The Murrinhpatha prosodic system therefore has no lexical contrasts, but rather has a *demarcative* function triangulating the boundary of PWord and PPhrase constituents (Hyman, 2014). The system is similar to that of French, which is also analysed as having demarcative pitch accents but no lexical stress (Jun & Fougeron, 2002); but among Australian languages no system of this type has been described.

4.4.1 The pitch accent

In pragmatically unmarked declarative sentences, the pitch accent that marks out distinct PPhrases involves a high tone immediately followed by a low tone. I tentatively analyse this as an H* pitch accent on the PWord's penultimate syllable, with a L- phrasal declarative tone anchored to the PWord's final syllable (Ladd, 2008, p. 88). In monosyllabic PWords, the H*_L- sequence is compressed into a sharp HL fall within the single, lengthened syllable (see figures 4.3 and 4.4 below). However pitch structure is not further analysed in this study. The main contribution of this study to higher-level prosodic analysis is the description of two syntactic phrase types, Noun Phrase and Preposition Phrase, that are realised prosodically as single PPhrases. I briefly explore other syntactic constituents that are *not* prosodic phrases, and defer other aspects of phrase structure to a general study of Murrinhpatha syntax.

The position of accents was determined by viewing pitch contours superimposed on spectrograms in Praat (Boersma & Weenink, 2012), though in some cases where the software fails to trace a clear pitch contour, the accent position was instead determined by listening to each syllable in isolation. Figures 4.3–4.6 illustrate accentual peaks exhibited in monosyllabic, disyllabic, trisyllabic and quadrisyllabic PWords. In each case the PWord is right-most in the PPhrase because it is the only PWord in the PPhrase.

Figure 4.7 illustrates a PPhrase containing two PWords, a possessed noun and its pronominal possessor respectively (59). Only the right-most PWord exhibits the H*_L- tone sequence.

90 — 4 Morphologically specific sound patterns

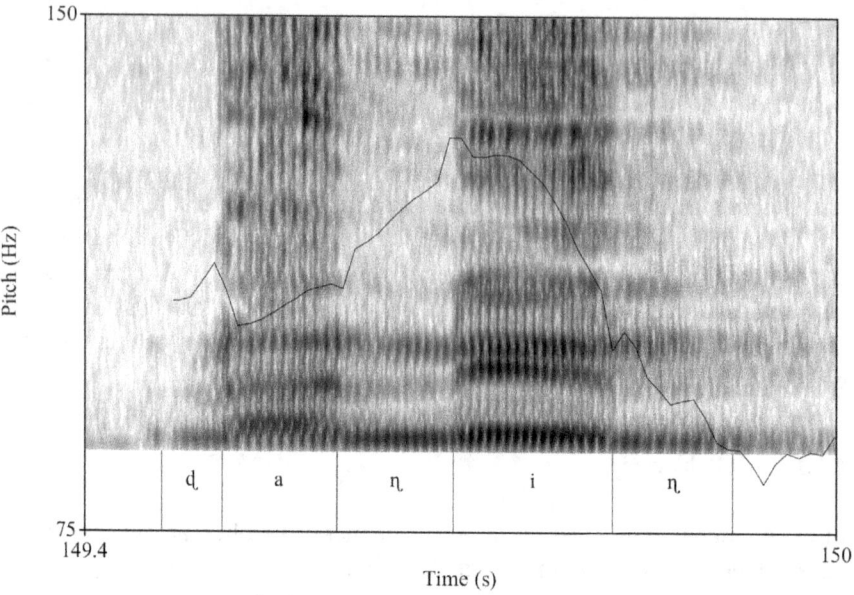

Figure 4.3: Monosyllabic PWord [ɖa-[ɳíɳ]ω]ϕ 'dream' (DP, 2015-07-07_AT).

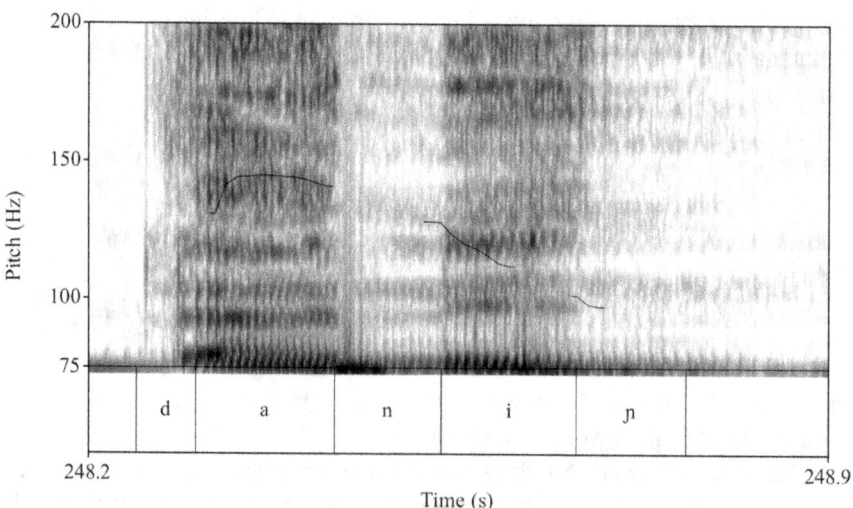

Figure 4.4: Disyllabic PWord [[dániɲ]ω]ϕ 'tree sp.' (DP, 2015-06-29_AT).

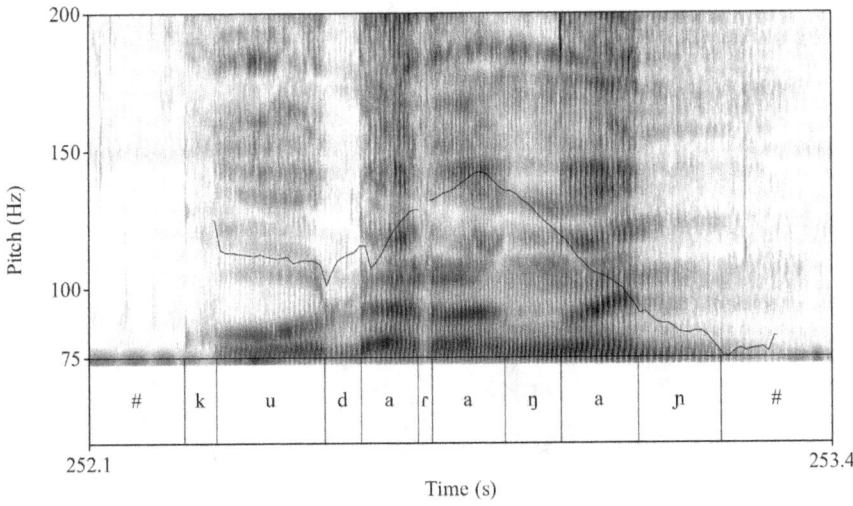

Figure 4.5: Trisyllabic PWord [ku-[daráɲaɲ]ω]φ 'John Dory fish' (DP, 2015-06-29_AT).

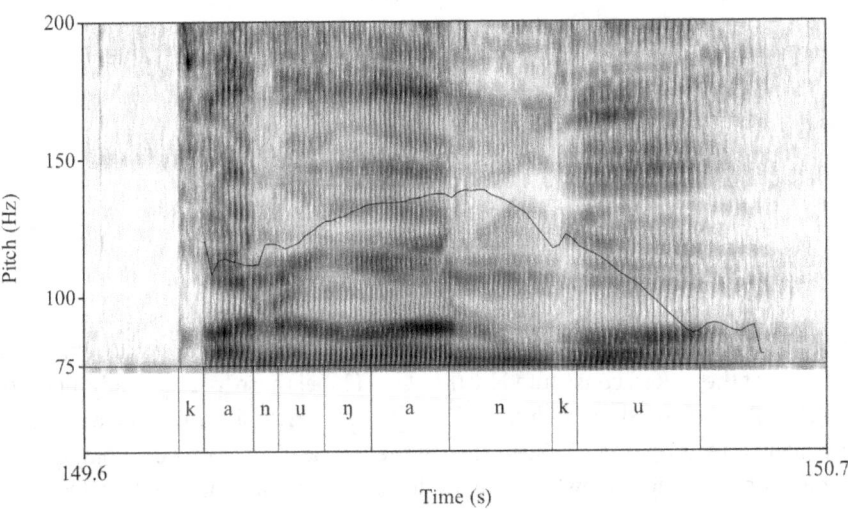

Figure 4.6: Quadrisyllabic PWord [[kanuŋánku]ω]φ 'my father's father' (DP, 2015-07-01_AT).

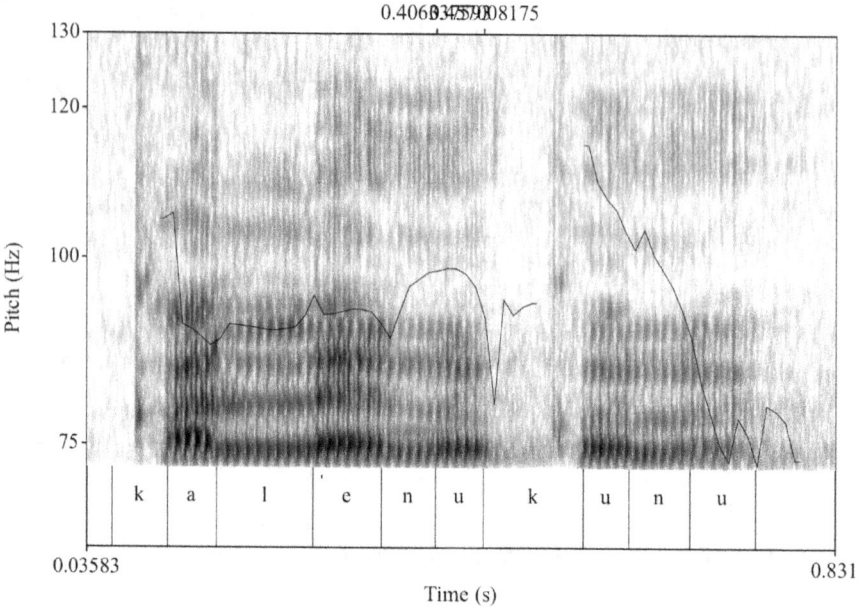

Figure 4.7: Spectrogram for (59): PPhrase containing two PWords.

(59) [[kale]_ω [nukúnu]_ω]_φ
mother 3SG.M
his mother (OwB, 2013-01-03)

4.4.2 Prosodic adjuncts

Various bound grammatical morphs are adjoined to lexical stems while remaining outside of the PWord constituted by the stem. I label these 'prosodic adjuncts', or 'external' as opposed to 'internal' bound morphs. Prosodic adjuncts are formed by many Murrinhpatha suffixes, and by the left head in NOM-NOM compounds, which includes the somewhat grammaticalised nominals that are labelled 'classifier nominals' (§7.2).

Lexical hosts that are open monosyllables /CV/ play a special role in revealing the prosodic status of bound morphs. With prosodic adjuncts, the host must satisfy the bimoraic PWord minimum on its own, which is to say that an open monosyllabic host must have its vowel lengthened (60, 61). This contrasts with internal bound morphemes or compounds, which contribute to the bimoraic minimum and therefore circumvent the need for vowel lengthening (62, 63).

(60) [náː]_ω-ða-dini
use.feet.3SG.PST-PST-SIT.IMPF
she was going along

(61) ku-[kéː]_ω
ANIM-nerite.mollusc

(62) [ná-ŋe]_ω
say.2SG.IRR-1PL.OBL
tell her

(63) [bé-puḻ]_ω
arm-wash
wash away

As mentioned above, the monosyllabic or penultimate accent anchored to the PWord is the only systematic form of prosodic prominence in Murrinhpatha. Adjuncts are prosodically weak. Where verbs have multiple suffixes, adjunction can result in long strings of weak syllables. Figure 4.8 (64) exhibits two PPhrases, the second of which has five adjunct syllables. The pitch trace shows H*_L- sequences for each PPhrase, and the lack of any further tonal events disturbing the smooth declension of the second PPhrase after the right edge of the PWord /pumaðap/.

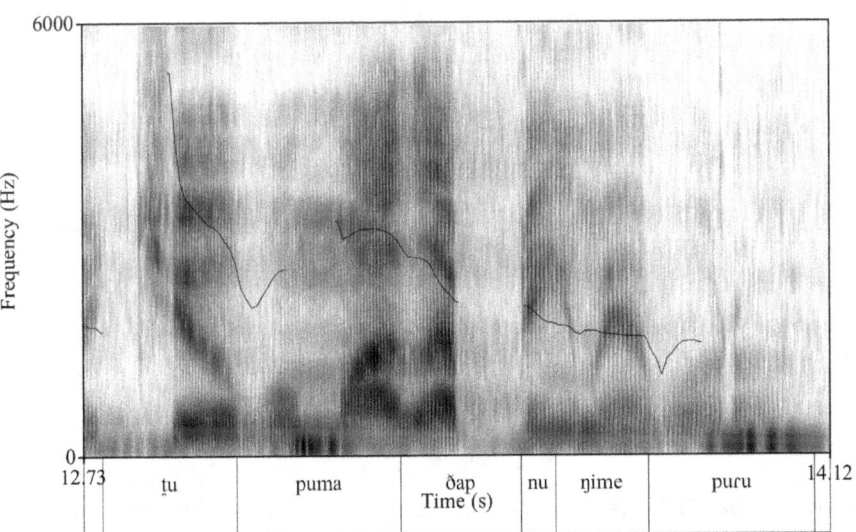

Figure 4.8: Spectrogram for (62), illustrating smooth pitch declension in external suffixes.

(64) [[t̪úː]ω]φ [[pumá-ðap]ω-nu-ŋime-puɾu]φ
     fight   use.hands.1INCL.IRR-stop-FUT-PAUC.F-GO.IMFP
     we will stop fighting   (AMN, 2015-01-29_PrT2SC1)

Figure 4.9 (65) illustrates another example of a PPhrase and its pitch countour. This time the PPhrase consists of a single polysyllabic verb, with the pitch contour ascending smoothly to the PWord-penultimate pitch accent, and smoothly declining in an adjunct suffix.

(65) [[mam-wun-ŋku-ðámdum]ω-nime]φ
     use.hands.3SG.NFUT-3PL.OBJ-PC.OBJ-squash-PAUC.M
     she is squashing them   (DP, 2015-06-29_AT)

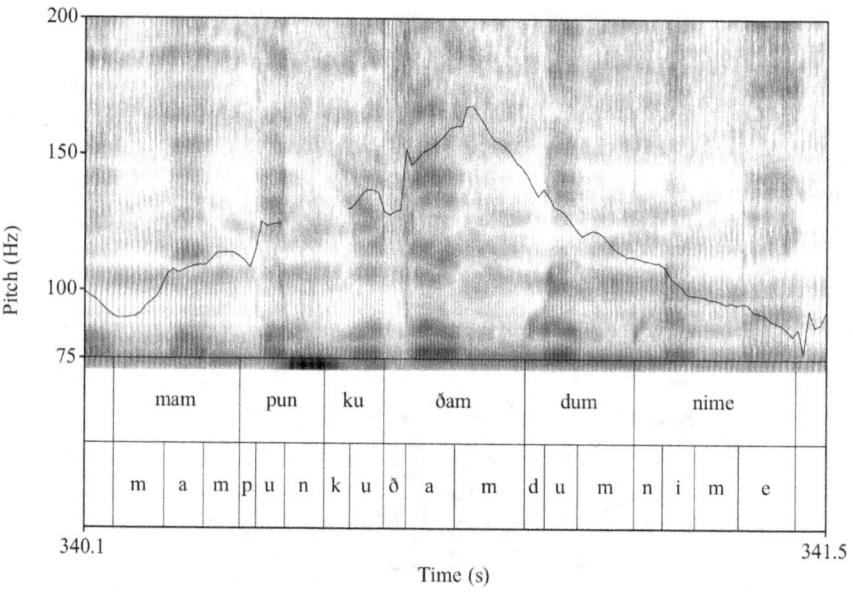

Figure 4.9: Spectrogram and pitch contour for (63), illustrating single pitch peak in a polysyllabic verb.

4.4.3 Prosodic phrase mapping to syntactic phrases

There has been relative little research into phrase structure in Murrinhpatha, and the focus of this study is on more tightly bound 'word' units (§1.7.2). However some brief comments further elucidate the prosody of the PPhrase. Only two syntactic phrase types have been identified that constitute single PPhrases. Firstly, there a noun phrase (NP) of the form [Neg Noun⁺ Adj Det]_NP (66, 67), where no element is obligatory and Det is a possessor, demonstrative or numeral (Blythe, 2009, p. 102; Mujkic, 2013). The NP is further described in (§7.2.2). Secondly, there is a prepositional phrase of the form [Prep NP]_PP (68), for which there is just a single polysemous preposition /ŋara/.

(66) [[meː]_ω [paŋu-ḍá=ŋu]_ω]_φ   [[meː]_ω [kaṉí=ŋu]_ω]_φ
     [foot   there-LOC=TOWARDS]NP [foot   here=DIR]NP
     a foot over there, a foot over here   (SeDu, 2015-07-09_SL)

(67) [mi-[ɲiː]_ω [wíje]_ω]_φ
     [VEG-penis bad]NP
     infected penis   (MNi, 2013-07_clinic)

(68) [[ŋara]_ω [ṯelput]_ω [ŋáj]_ω]_φ   [[ŋaṉe-ŋéren]_ω-ða-nime]_φ
     [LOC   house   1SG]PP   [be.1PAUC.IRR-talk-PST-PAUC.M]VP
     we were going to talk at my house   (DP, 2012-06-20_25)

As demonstrated by (66, 67), unaccented words in an NP still have PWord constituency as demonstrated by the bimoraic vowel. This is in contrast to nominal-nominal (NOM-NOM) compounds that may be constructed of exactly the same lexical components, but prosodify the head nominal as an adjunct, and produce more lexicalised (non-transparent) meanings (§7.2).

Verbs combined with subject or object argument NPs prosodify as multiple PPhrases (69, 70). There is also flexibility of word order among these elements and frequent omission of argument NPs, so there is no obvious reason to posit syntactic phrase structure (§1.2). The same prosodic and syntactic independence is found in nominal + nominal copula clauses (71). Thus there is some evidence of a relationship between PPhrase integration and syntactic constituency: NPs have a set syntactic sequence of elements, and are bound into a unified PPhrase, whereas verb + nominal or nominal + nominal copula combinations have no fixed order and are prosodically independent.

(69) [[káḍu]_ω]_φ   [[baŋam-ṯawí-bu]_ω-ḍim]_φ
     person   AFFECT.3SG.NFUT-mouth-incend-SIT.IMPF
     he's lighting up (a cigarette)   (ArM, 2013-01-05)

(70) [[mam-páṯa]_ω]_φ   [[káː]_ω]_φ
     use.hands.3SG.NFUT-fix car
     he fixed the car   (McJa, 2013-01-02)

(71) [[réddan]_ω=ka]_φ   [[pépe]_ω=waḍa]_φ
     red=CST   down=SEQ
     then the red one is downwards   (ArM, 2013-01-05)

Coverb + verb combinations, on the other hand, have fairly rigid word order, but are prosodified as two PPhrases (72, 73). This word order is not altogether rigid: the vast majority of coverb + verb combinations place the coverb first, but there are very occasional examples of the coverb following verb (74, 75). Further investigation of phrasal constituency is deferred to a study of Murrinhpatha syntax.

(72) [[bé-puḷ]ω]φ   [[wuṛíni]ω-ða]φ
     arm-wash   go.3SG.PST-PST
     he went along washing them away   (KM, 2012-06-20_26)

(73) [[ɻáɻi]ω]φ   [[dím-na]ω-kanam]φ
     worry   sit.3SG.NFUT-3SG.OBL-BE.IMPF
     he's worrying   (McKu, 2013-01-07)

(74) [kaḍu-[ŋalánṯar]ω]φ   [[panam-ka-kámpa]ω-nime]φ   [[kámpa]ω]φ
     PERS-old.man   be.3PL.NFUT-PAUC-laugh-PAUC.M   laugh
     the old men are laughing   (AnBu, 2013-01-09)

(75) [[púma]ω]φ   [[séip]ω]φ
     do.1INCL.IRR   save
     we'll save it   (PlPu, 2011-09-01_02)

4.4.4 Previous descriptions of Murrinhpatha stress

The prosodic description above is substantially at variance with previous descriptions of Murrinhpatha stress. Previous studies posit multiple stressed syllables within the PWord, though these descriptions may have been swayed by an expectation that Murrinhpatha stress should behave like the stress systems described for other Australian languages, which typically involve both primary and secondary stresses interpolated rhythmically across the length of the word. Phonetic studies of Australian stress systems have shown in some cases that earlier impressionistic descriptions were unreliable (Bowern, Alpher, & Round, 2013; Tabain, Fletcher, & Butcher, 2014).

Previous descriptions of Murrinhpatha stress assignment are particularly problematic because they do not converge in their empirical claims. The four previous descriptions disagree substantially as to which syllables are prominent, as illustrated in Table 4.1.[27] As mentioned above, this study does not posit any systematic prominence other than penultimate pitch accents.

---

[27] Where aligned words are not exactly the same, they illustrate parallel morphological structures that would be expected to have the same stress pattern. Some forms in Walsh, Street & Mollinjin and Mansfield columns are constructed from stated rules.

Table 4.1: Disagreements about prosodic prominence. The shaded cells highlight the only points on which the descriptions agree

Walsh 1976: 106–124	Street & Mollinjin 1981: 206–209	Clemens 2013: 71–80	Mansfield 2014: 176–189
?	?	dím-pàl̪	dím-pal̪
nígunú	nígunù	?	nígunu
páŋam-ká	páŋam-kà	pàŋám-ka	páŋam-ka
púru-nú	púru-nù	púru-nu	púru-nu
pán-ɲi-bát	?	pàn-ɲí-bat	pan-ɲí-bat
ŋám-ɲi-lú-wéwu	ŋàm-ɲí-lu-wéwu	ŋà-ɲi-ma-rígat-nu	?
?	píri-kájkáj-ða	pàɲi-cékcek-nu	pàɲi-cékcek-nu
?	nàm-píra	pàn-t̪át̪al	pan-t̪át̪al
?	jùɲám-nin̪t̪á-wuj	bàŋam-ŋìn̪t̪á-pal̪	mùŋam-nin̪t̪á-pal̪

4.4.5 Comparison to other Australian prosodic systems

Other prosodic systems described for Australian languages involve, canonically, primary stress on the initial syllable, followed by secondary-stressed trochaic feet, which are aligned where possible with morphological boundaries in complex words (Baker, 2014, pp. 153–164; Fletcher & Butcher, 2014, pp. 114–116). Representative examples can be illustrated from Warlpiri (76, 77).

Warlpiri stress
(76) wátijà-l̪a   tree-LOC
(77) wátija-l̪à-l̪u   tree-LOC-ERG   (Nash, 1980, p. 102)

There is some diversity of prosodic systems, especially in northern Australia, but I have not been able to identify any other Australian language that has been described as having a penultimate stress or accent, and no metrical footing. Tiwi (Osborne, 1974) is described as having a basic penultimate stress, but also with trochaic feet producing secondary accents to the left of this. Jingulu (Pensalfini, 2003), Wardaman (Merlan, 1994) and Worrorra (Clendon, 2014) are also described as having basic penultimate primary stress, again combined with foot structure, but with some trisyllabic words lexically specified as stress-initial. Gaagudju (Harvey, 2002, pp. 55–64) is the only other Australian language I have identified that is described as having words with a single pitch accent analysed as the only form of prominence in a word; this is also often penultimate, but not predictably so, and there is also ambivalent evidence for foot structure. Murrinhpatha's best-described neighbouring languages, Ngan'gi (Reid, 1990) and Marrithiyel (Green, 1989), are claimed to have the canonical Australian system of initial primary accent followed by trochaic feet. More detailed prosodic research is required for all these languages.

4.5 Prosodically internal juncture effects

We have seen above that the PWord is not always a simple lexeme, but may encompass morphological constructs including lexical compounds, and some bound grammatical morphology. The composition of such constructs may undergo a degree of phonological masking, as various phonological reductions and assimilations occur at the morphological junctures. These are distinguished from general phonetic reduction by the fact that they are phonologised (occur both in fluent speech and in careful speech), and in many cases exhibit unpredictable, lexically specified forms of reduction. Though the outcomes are not predictable by rule, we can observe some patterns in terms of interacting constraints on sonority, place of articulation, and inflectional versus lexical morphs.

4.5.1 Voiceless obstruent lenition

We saw in the previous chapter that non-lengthened voiceless obstruents, typically in morpheme-initial position, are subject to phonetic lenition. In connected speech, word-initial voiceless obstruents preceded by a vowel are frequently realised as fricatives, approximants, or deleted altogether. For many prosodically internal bound morphemes lenition is phonologised, causing voiceless obstruents to alternate with continuant or glide phonemes at the same places of articulation:

/p/   → /w/
/t/   → /ɹ/
/ṯa, ṯe/ → /ða, je/
/k/   → /ɣ/

The application of this lenition to peripherals /p, k/ is quite systematic, though not all speakers apply the dorsal lenition (see below). For coronals /t, ṯ/ there is also phonologised lenition, but it is more piecemeal, perhaps reflecting the different degrees to which the obstruents are subject to phonetic lenition (§3.7). For example, initial obstruent lenition is attested for /-ṯibaj/ 'fornicate', but not for /-tette/ 'be alarmed'; for /-ṯe/ 'ear' and /-ṯarmu/ 'shin', but not /-ṯiri/ 'wear pubic covering' or /-ṯapka/ 'be beautiful'. There are also instances where the laminal lenites despite being in a coverb-internal position, e.g. /-ða-ðap/ 'touch' PLUR, which departs from the system observed for peripherals.

The morphs to which phonologised lenition applies are bound coverbs and body part nominals, which together form compound coverbs (§8.5). Coverbs, simple or compound, are in turn compounded with finite verb stems (79–81).

(79) mawaṭanu
 ma-paṭa-nu
 use.hands.1SG.IRR-good-FUT
 I'll make it
(80) ŋunuɻiðaḷnukun
 ŋunu-ʈi-ðaḷ=nukun
 use.feet.1SG.IRR-bottom-open=ADVERS
 I might slip over
(81) ḍiepup
 ḍi-ʈe-pup
 hear.2SG.IRR-ear-sit
 listen!

Lenition does not apply to voiceless obstruents at the onset of *all* bound lexemes, as some are protected by obstruent lengthening (§3.4). For morphologically simple words we have seen that the right-most intervocalic voiceless obstruent is phonetically lengthened to around twice the duration of other voiceless obstruents, but this does not apply to obstruents that have another intervocalic obstruent to their right (82–84).

(82) daɾipːi   'skin'
(83) ɲipːiliṉ 'river'
(84) ŋapapːa   'sugar glider'

For bound lexemes, obstruent lengthening applies in a slightly different, and rather more complex set of circumstances. Firstly, lengthening applies whenever the voiceless obstruent is in the onset of a monosyllabic coverb that is the PWord's final syllable. However lengthening also applies to obstruents that are initial in a coverb *root*, but medial in a coverb *compound*. In this way, compound coverbs behave somewhat like morphologically simple PWords. Roots with initial /p/ are used to illustrate, since they show the most consistent pattern of lenition. Examples (85a–87a) demonstrate protective lengthening in monosyllabic coverb roots, while (85b–87b) demonstrate how the same roots are otherwise exposed to lenition.

(85a) diníp:it̪
 dini-[pit̪]
 sit.3SG.PST-[come.off]
 it came off
(85b) dini<u>w</u>ít̪pit̪
 dini-[pit̪-pit̪]
 sit.3SG.PST-[come.off-PLUR]
 it came off bit-by-bit
(86a) kiran̪íp:e
 kira-n̪i-[pe]
 stand.3SG.IRR-1INCL.OBJ-[head]
 he will watch over us
(86b) ban̪i<u>w</u>élip
 ba-n̪i-[pe-lip]
 AFFECT.3SG.IRR-2SG.OBJ-[head-bash]
 he'll hit you on the head
(87a) memáp:ul
 me-[ma-pul]
 use.hands.RR.3SG.IRR-hand-wash
 I will wash my hands
(87b) ma<u>w</u>úlpul
 ma-[pul-pul]
 use.hands.3SG.IRR-wash-PLUR
 I will wash (some things)

Examples (88a–89a) demonstrate protective lengthening of obstruents which are morpheme-initial, but medial within a compound coverb. These need not be in the final, post-tonic syllable of the PWord. Examples (88b, 89b) demonstrate how some of the same obstruents are otherwise exposed to lenition.

(88a) ŋun̪imep:áraŋnu
 ŋu-n̪i-[me-paraŋ]-nu
 ARC.1SG.IRR-2SG.OBJ-[foot-numb]-FUT
 I'll numb your foot (Street 2012, *parrang*)
(88b) ŋun̪i<u>w</u>áraŋnu
 ŋu-n̪i-[paraŋ]-nu
 ARC.1SG.IRR-2SG.OBJ-[numb]-FUT
 I'll stun you (DP, 2015-07-10_AT)

(89a) ḑempiṉipːíŋkaḻdim
 ḑem-[wiṉi-piŋkaḻ]-dim
 PIERCE.3SG.RR.NFUT-[impose-knee]-SIT.IMPF
 he's kneeling (Street 2012, *-winhipingkarl*)
(89b) ma<u>w</u>iŋkáḻeŋuɾu
 ma-[piŋkaḻ-ḻe]-ŋuɾu
 do.1SG.IRR-[knee-turn]-GO.IMPF
 I'll walk with my knees turned in (Street 2012, *-wingkarle*)

As mentioned above, coronals /t, ṯ/ are not lenited as systematically. For the dorsal /k/ some speakers do not produce morpho-phonological lenition in careful speech, and this non-leniting /k/ has been the version attested in previous Murrinhpatha documentation (e.g. Street 2012). However most younger speakers produce morpho-phonological lenition /k → ɣ/ (90, 91), following the same patterns as other voiceless obstruents, and consistently maintaining the alternation even in carefully articulated speech.

(90) kaḑi<u>k</u>ampaða ~ kaḑi<u>ɣ</u>ampaða
 kaḑi-kampa-ða
 be.3SG.PST-laugh-PST
 she laughed
(91) kaḑi<u>k</u>ajkajða ~ kaḑi<u>ɣ</u>ajkajða
 kaḑi-kajkaj-ða
 be.3SG.PST-call.out.PLUR-PST
 she was calling out

4.5.2 Nasal spreading

When morphs within a PWord combine to form a cluster of nasal and voiced obstruent at their juncture (i.e. /n-b, m-b, n-d, m-d/), a nasal spreading process transforms the voiced obstruent into its nasal equivalent, e.g. /n-b/ → /nm/. By assimilating nasality across the cluster, this reduces the contrastive phonological features involved. However by increasing the sonority of the second consonant, it runs contrary to a general preference for declining sonority in clusters, formulated as the Syllable Contact Law (Murray & Venneman, 1983; Parker, 2011, p. 1171). I therefore treat nasal spreading separately from the cluster harmonisation patterns described in the following sub-section, which are heavily influenced by the preference for declining sonority.

Nasal spreading appears to be categorical, or 'fully phonologised' in some compound verbs (92–94). However several other compounds show both application and non-application of nasal spreading in careful speech (95, 96). The latter may be regarded as 'partially phonologised' assimilations.

(92) panmat
 [pan-bat]_ω
 ARC.3SG.NFUT-hit
 he punched him

(93) bammat
 [bam-bat]_ω
 LOWER.RR.3SG.NFUT-hit
 it fell

(94) kanaɲɲum   (regressive place assimilation, §4.4.3)
 kanamɲum
 [kanam-ɖum]_ω
 be.3SG.NFUT-not.visible
 it is out of sight

(95) dembuɣaḷ ~ demmuɣaḷ
 [dem-buɣaḷ]_ω
 PIERCE.RR.3SG.NFUT-melt
 it's melted

(96) mampunkuðamdumnime ~ mampunkuðamnumnime
 [mam-wun-ŋku-ða-ɖum-ɖum]_ω-nime]_φ
 use.hands.3SG.NFUT-3PL.OBJ-PC.OBJ-leg-squash-PLUR-PAUC
 he's squashing them   (DP, 2015-06-29_AT)

Nasal spreading also occurs occasionally as a connected-speech variable outside the PWord (97). The limited attestation of the PWord-external version may be accounted for by the fact that prosodic adjuncts with initial voiced obstruents are not common.

(97) wurannim
 [wuran]_ω-dim
 go.3SG.NFUT-SIT.IMPF
 it's going   (AMN, 2015-01-29_Pr2-EC2)

Progressive nasal spreading to a voiced obstruent also occurs in Malayalam (Dravidian: Mohanan, 1986, p. 69) and Akan (Niger-Congo: Schachter & Fromkin, 1968). However it does not appear to be a common morpho-phonological process in languages of the world (R. Walker, 2000, p. 23ff), and in Australia it is attested for only one other language, Lardil, where its occurrence is marginal (Round, 2017).

4.5.3 Cluster harmonisation

In the last chapter it was observed that there are two constraints on consonant clusters evident within unanalysable roots: one dispreferring rising sonority clusters (*SON↑), which are rare in roots; the other banning peripheral-coronal place contours (*PER-COR), which are altogether absent. These two constraints are both also evident at prosodically internal morphological junctures, where a range of harmonisation strategies avert the dispreferred cluster types (Mansfield, 2014b, p. 165ff.; Street & Mollinjin, 1981; Walsh, 1976, p. 69ff.).[28] Most of these don't occur as phonetic effects outside the PWord, the one exception being /w→p/ fortition in onsets (§3.7). However these harmonisations are not always applied: there is inter-lexeme variation, and in some cases inter-token variation. Dispreferred clusters are not always harmonised, and there is variation among harmonisation strategies.

Harmonisation strategies deployed are (in order of frequency):
(a) deletion of either coda or onset segment to avert either *PER-COR or *SON↑;
(b) regressive place assimilation of coda to avert *PER-COR;
(c) fortition of sonorant onset to avert (*SON↑).

The two constraints *SON↑ and *PER-COR, are balanced against the impulse to maintain the phonological form of the two morphological elements contributing to the juncture (Dressler, 1984). Drawing on the terminology of Optimality Theory (Prince & Smolensky, 1993), we can treat these as 'faithfulness constraints', MAXCODA and MAXONSET, representing the impulse to maintain realisation of the coda and onset elements in the cluster respectively. The variability of outcomes prevents us from constructing an overall constraint hierarchy of the type familiar in OT analysis, but within some cluster types we can observe degrees of weighting between constraints.

Variability of resolution strategies
When the most dispreferred sonority and place profiles *SON↑ and *PER-COR, are simultaneously threatened, harmonisation strategies tend to enforce both constraints. The deletion strategy averts both problems by reducing the cluster to a single intervocalic consonant (98), while place assimilation and sonorant fortition are often found in tandem when both constraints are threatened (99).

---

[28] Previous descriptions of these phenomena have taken the form of lists of morphophonological alternations, without analyzing the underlying phonological patterns.

(98) -lukuk²⁹
-luk-luk   (*SON↑, *PER-COR)
propose.idea-PLUR
(99) dinṯel
dim-ṯel   (*SON↑, *PER-COR)
sit.3SG.NFUT-sing
he sang

On the other hand, both *SON↑ and *PER-COR are fairly frequently violated, sometimes both at the same time. The variation between enforcement and violation occurs between distinct complex lexemes that risk the same dispreferred cluster (100a, b), and also in some cases between different speech tokens of the same lexeme (101). The same lexeme may also have different resolution strategies applied in different tokens (102).

(100a) wuḍanwi
wuḍan-wi   (*SON↑, *PER-COR)
IMPEL.3SG.NFUT-inflate
he smokes
(100b) panper
pan-wer   (*SON↑, *PER-COR)
SLASH.3SG.NFUT-tremble
the engine hums
(101) demṭap ~ denṯap
dem-ṭap   (*PER-COR)
MOUTH.RR.3SG.NFUT-shut
she is shut in   (SM, 2011-08-08_2-11)
(102) dimperer ~ diwerer
dim-wer-wer
sit.3SG.NFUT-tremble-PLUR
she is trembling   (KeNa, MiJa, 2013-01)

Interaction of place and sonority contours
The morpho-phonological alternations applied to clusters demonstrate negative constraints against the most dispreferred place and sonority profiles as described above: certain place and sonority contours are *avoided*. However

---
29 Unless otherwise specified, lexical evidence presented in this section is from Street's (2012) dictionary. Some complex coverbs shown here occur only compounded to finite verbs, but this is not shown if it does not have any bearing on the morpho-phonological reduction under discussion.

we can also observe 'positive' effects related to the most harmonic place and sonority profiles, namely COR-PER and declining sonority SON↓. As we might expect, the combination of these contours is never subject to reduction (103).[30] Harmonic COR-PER clusters are never reduced in clusters with either level or declining sonority; they reduce only variably to avert the most dispreferred sonority profile, *SON↑ (104–106). But this pattern is asymmetric with the most harmonic sonority profile, SON↓, which is variably subject to reduction not just for the most dispreferred *PER-COR, but also for homorganic COR-COR profiles (unfortunately there are no forms providing evidence for PER-PER) (107, 108). In other words, the most harmonic place profile is resilient for both harmonic and 'semi-harmonic' sonority profiles, while the most harmonic sonority profile is resilient only for the most harmonic place profile. HARMONICPLACE has a more powerful positive affect in protecting clusters from reduction, compared to HARMONICSON. Place-of-articulation appears to be more important than sonority.

Most harmonic place and sonority
(103) kuḷkuḷ
 kuḷ-kuḷ   (COR-PER, SON↓)
 splash-PLUR

Most harmonic place contour
(104) -kutkut   (HARMONICPLACE > HARMONICSON)
 -kut-kut   (COR-PER, SON~)
 -collect-PLUR
(105) ṭitmut   (coverb-initial deletion, see §8.6)
 ṭi-mutmut   (HARMONICPLACE > HARMONICSON)
 ṭi-mut-mut   (COR-PER, *SON↑)
 behind-give-PLUR
 leftover food
(106) -mutut
 -mut-mut   (COR-PER, *SON↑)
 -give-PLUR

Most harmonic sonority contour
(107) nuŋanṭuk   (HARMONICSON > HARMONICPLACE)
 nuŋam-ṭuk   (SON↓, *PER-COR)
 use.feet.3SG.NFUT-search

---

30 There is a single attested exception, /biḷ biḷ/ > /bibiḷ/ 'rub off PLUR'.

(108) -ḑaḑal
      -ḑal-ḑal   (SON↓, COR-COR)
      -lean-PLUR

The harmonisation of *PER-COR heterorganic contours, contrasting with toleration of COR-PER contours, presents a typological difference between Murrinhpatha and other languages with respect to place contour constraints. As mentioned in the last chapter, Australian languages in general exhibit a discrepancy with languages of other continents on this point (Hamilton, 1996). One of the founding observations for the theory of place contour constraints is that English boundary clusters show asymmetry between place assimilation in *brown*[mp]*pear*, versus resilience in *home*[mt]*time* (Lahiri, 2012). Further support has been adduced from German and from Austronesian languages (Blust, 1979). But what we find at the juncture in Murrinhpatha compounds is the direct inverse: a strong tendency to place assimilation in /ḑam[n̪t̪]tut/ (use. mouth-rise, 'tide come in'), versus resilience to assimilation in /ban[np]pak/ (AFFECT-put, 'put down'). The *COR-PER has been proposed as a universal (e.g. Paradis & Prunet, 1991), but the evidence from Murrinhpatha and other Australian languages undermines this assertion.

Targeting codas and onsets

There is some evidence for weighting of the faithfulness constraints, MaxCoda and MaxOnset, in different patterns of coda or onset deletion applied to different cluster types. As a general rule, the coda is more vulnerable to both deletion and place assimilation, i.e. MaxOnset > MaxCoda (cf. Côté, 2000). This is evident where either of the harmony constraints is risked, and also in a few clusters that would have been quite harmonic (109–111).

(109) ŋkawaḻawaḻak   (MaxOnset > MaxCoda)
      ŋka-waḻak-waḻak   (*SON↑)
      eye-rub-PLUR
      fall asleep
(110) nuŋaṉt̪uk   (MaxOnset > MaxCoda)
      nuŋam-t̪uk   (*PER-COR)
      use.feet.3SG.NFUT-search
      she searched (for it)
(111) ṯaṯal   (MaxOnset > MaxCoda)
      ṯal-ṯal   (*harmonic*)
      cut-PLUR

However there are some cluster types where the onset is instead deleted. The first of these is in reduplicated coverbs that risk *SON↑, and that have heterorganic place contours, either the dispreferred *PER-COR, or the harmonic COR-PER. Heterorganic clusters that risk *SON↑ are only ever resolved by onset deletion (112, 113). This forms an interesting contrast with *SON↑ clusters that have *homorganic* place contours: if these resolve the violation at all, they do so either by onset deletion or by coda deletion (114, 115).

(112) ðapep   (MAXCODA > MAXONSET)
   ðap-ðap   (*SON↑, *PER-COR)
   shut-PLUR
   shut (one's mouth)

(113) wirir   (MAXCODA > MAXONSET)
   wir-wir   (*SON↑, COR-PER)
   blow-PLUR
   wind

(114) letetmam   (MAXCODA > MAXONSET)
   let-let-mam   (*SON↑, COR-COR)
   stick.PLUR-ADJZ
   sticky

(115) ḍuḍut   (MAXONSET > MAXCODA)
   ḍut-ḍut   (*SON↑, COR-COR)
   wake.someone-PLUR

There is a potential explanation for this in maintenance of root identity cues in the acoustic signal. It is well established that most consonants are better identified by their CV transition than their VC transition (J. Blevins, 2004, p. 118). The coverbs illustrated above all have a CVC form, which naturally makes their onset C more perceptually salient than their coda C. Deletion of the coda in reduplication, i.e. CV-CVC, gives the root onset two CV transitions, strengthening an already salient cue. But deletion of the onset in reduplication, i.e. CVC-VC, now gives each of the root consonants a CV transition, which ought to optimise the overall perceptual cuing of the CVC root base. For heterorganic pairs of consonants this should be especially important, since each C will have quite distinct transition cues: thus the consistent appearance of CVC-VC patterns in the *PER-COR and COR-PER clusters. But for homorganic clusters the transition cues are similar anyway, so there is less difference in transition cues between CVC-VC and CV-CVC: thus we see a mixture of the two patterns for COR-COR clusters.

Vulnerability of verb inflections

To add a final complication, the cluster harmonisations described above for reduplicated coverbs exhibit a different pattern when they occur in compound verb junctures. Some compound verbs risk a violation of *SON↑ in heterorganic clusters, but unlike reduplicated coverbs, they use only coda deletion as a harmonisation strategy (116). This is however quite consistent with the lexical signalling hypothesis proposed above, since the nasal coda that is deleted in such compound verbs is not a lexical element, but rather is an inflectional formative signalling non-future tense, which is also signalled in other parts of the finite verb stem (§5.5).

(116) nuŋalili   (MaxOnset > MaxCoda)
      nuŋam-lili   (*SON↑, *PER-COR)
      use.feet.3SG.NFUT-walk
      she walks

There is further evidence that the nasal tense inflection forming the coda in compound verb junctures is more vulnerable to deletion than lexical elements. When we examine nasal-obstruent clusters, a subtype of the harmonic SON↓ profile, we find that reduplicated coverbs and compound nouns as a rule make no reduction to the cluster, even if it has the dispreferred *PER-COR place profile (117, 118). By contrast, compound verbs risking the same cluster type are consistently reduced, either by place assimilation or by deletion to the coda nasal, again illustrating its extra-vulnerability to phonological reduction (119, 120).

(117) ṭumṭum   (MaxCoda > HarmonicPlace)
      ṭum-ṭum   (*PER-COR)
      dry-PLUR
(118) baŋmanṯaj   (MaxCoda > HarmonicPlace)
      baŋ-baṉ-ṯaj   (*PER-COR)
      pierce-pierce-tree
(119) ḍanṯuṯ   (HarmonicPlace > MaxCoda)
      ḍam-ṯuṯ   (*PER-COR)
      use.mouth.3SG.NFUT-rise
      the tide came in
(120) kanaḍi   (HarmonicPlace > MaxCoda)
      kanam-ḍi   (*PER-COR)
      be.3SG.NFUT-enter
      she enters

In summary, consonant clusters at morphological junctures are subject to interacting constraints of place and sonority profile. In a few cases, there is also evidence that morphosyntactic status has some influence, with inflectional consonants more vulnerable to deletion or assimilation than lexical consonants. We might have hoped for further evidence on morphosyntactic factors, but the types of clusters formed in compound verbs are limited to nasal codas, and therefore lack points of comparison with most cluster types exhibited in coverb reduplication and compound nouns. The interaction of place, sonority and morphosyntax in cluster phonology is subject to substantial variability between lexemes, showing that cluster alternations are to a certain degree 'lexicalised' in these often opaque constructs. But there is also variability among tokens of the same lexeme, showing that lexical specification is not a categorical effect.

4.5.4 Non-syllabifiable clusters

Murrinhpatha has a handful of bound morphs that begin with homorganic nasal-obstruent clusters. These cause no problem when preceded by a vowel-final morph, but they are not syllabifiable when preceded by a consonant-final morph, so that cluster reduction is necessary (121–124). There are not enough instances of this cluster reduction type to warrant analysis of patterns, though it is notable that in combinations of OBJ pronominals with /-ŋku/ PC.OBJ, it is always the apical coda nasal that is retained (122; §6.2.4). But in the (very common) compound verb /bam-ŋkaḍu/ 'she saw', there is variation between coda/onset deletion (124).

(121) kaṉṯimpa
 kaṉṯin-mpa
 carry.3SG.NFUT-2SG.OBL-PST
 she carries it for you

(122) panpunkubatŋime
 pan-wun-ŋku-bat-ŋime
 SLASH.3SG.NFUT-3PL.OBJ-PC.OBJ-hit-PAUC.F
 she hit them (paucal, female)

(123) meṉṯik
 mem-ṉṯik
 do.RR.3SG.NFUT-be.helpless
 he is helpless

(124) bamkaḍu ~ baŋkaḍu
 bam-ŋkaḍu
 AFFECT.3SG.NFUT-see
 she saw

4.6 Summary

In this chapter we have seen that the segmental phonology of Murrinhpatha plays out rather differently in different morphosyntactic classes. The open lexical classes, nominals and coverbs, have a distinctively non-Pama-Nyungan phonology involving many monosyllabic words, and obstruent codas. On the other hand the closed classes – finite verb stems and bound grammatical morphs – are closer to the 'standard Australian' phonology typical of Pama-Nyungan languages to the south.

On the prosodic level, nominals, coverbs and finite verb stems all share the property of instantiating a PWord constituent, in some cases encompassing both the host lexeme and bound morphemes. In many other cases bound morphemes are prosodic adjuncts, and the combination of one or more PWords together with their adjuncts constitutes a PPhrase. The latter culminates in a single pitch accent, with no evidence of metrical stress. This is at variance with other descriptions of Australian languages.

The PWord has several consequences for the phonology of morphological junctures. At PWord-internal junctures a *PER-COR place constraint is often enforced, which has been shown to be widespread in Australia (Hamilton, 1996), but appears to invert a pattern found on other continents in which PER-COR is a particularly resilient place contour in consonant clusters (J. Blevins, 2004; Blust, 1979; Lahiri, 2012). In Murrinhpatha the place constraint enters into complex interaction with a dispreference for rising sonority, as well as some morphosyntactic factors, which overall yield unpredictable phonological outcomes. These tend to make the morphological composition of PWords rather opaque. The next chapter moves onto another opaque type of morphology: the unpredictable inflectional forms of finite verb stems.

5 Finite verb stem inflection

5.1 Introduction

This chapter explores one of the most unusual features of Murrinhpatha: the exponence of inflectional categories within finite verb stems. As explained below, the term 'stem' here must be understood relative to other morphological structures in Murrinhpatha. The finite verb stem itself encompasses prefix and suffix elements, though these are sufficiently irregular that in previous work, the verb stem has usually not been presented as a morphologically complex (see references in §1.3). Meanwhile, the whole verb stem itself forms the base for more complex verb structures (§6, §8), and in this sense I label it a 'stem'. However in this chapter where its internal morphology is analysed, I analyse the verb stem's internal structure as consisting of prefix, suffix and 'inner stem'. As argued in the introduction (§1.7), I consider morphology to be a gradient phenomenon, with degrees of morphologicality corresponding to degrees of predictability or 'regularity' in the patterning of related words. The inflectional patterns discussed in this chapter show various degrees of regularity, and as a class I refer to their structural elements as 'semi-regular inflectional formatives'.

The morphological structure of finite verb stems is just one of several typologically unusual characteristics in Murrinhpatha verbs. Another unusual characteristic is that finite verb stems in Murrinhpatha are not an open class, but a closed class of 39 members, each of which appears in 42 inflecting forms. Thus in terms of lexical type count, it is a smallish closed class, but in terms of inflected forms, it is a 'large closed class' of 39×42=1638 members. However another unusual feature is the high degree of grammaticalisation in the class, with many members occurring only as bound stems in compound verbs, often without semantic compositionality (§8). Finite verb stems are therefore not altogether 'lexical' in their character, since some members lack clear lexical semantics, and the class is closed. However they are treated in this book as being more lexical than grammatical, in recognition of those finite verb stems that do behave as typical verb lexemes with meanings such as 'go', 'stand', 'have' etc.

Each of the 1638 verb stem forms combines semi-regular inflectional formatives: an inner stem, a prefix and suffix. Phonologically, these formatives are maximally /CV_{PREF}-CCV_{INNER}-CVC_{SUFF}/. In some cases, inflectional categories are also marked by phonological feature alternations, rather than concatenative formatives (Mansfield, 2016b; Mansfield & Nordlinger, 2019). For example, PL forms are sometimes marked by consonant gemination [+GEM], and PST forms sometimes marked by vowel fronting [+FRONT]. The reason why the inflectional structure of verb stems has elsewhere not been interpreted as morphology is that these patterns of inflectional exponence in some cases apply to only a few of the verb stems (Forshaw, 2016, p. 37ff.; Walsh, 1976, p. 224). For example, the PST vowel-fronting pattern applies to only 8 of the 39 stems, and in some of these does not apply consistently to all PST forms. However there are also some much more consistent patterns, such as /pV-/ PL prefixes that apply to all verb stems. These consistent morphological patterns motivate a general analysis of morphological structure in the finite verb stem, with various degrees of systematicity in the patterns. I describe these degrees of systematicity in terms of 'predictability'. This analysis draws on a partial analysis of proto-Southern Daly verb morphology (Green, 2003), adding further observations of inflectional patterns and interpreting the whole as synchronic rather than historical morphology.

The first part of this chapter provides a general description of morphological structure in finite verb stems (§5.2). This is followed by a brief introduction to the linguistic phenomenon of paradigmatic inflection classes (§5.3), and further details of how inflectional formatives exhibit paradigmatic structure in Murrinhpatha (§5.4). I then present metrics comparing the degree of unpredictability in this system to other languages (§5.5), drawing on recent typological work in this field (Ackerman & Malouf, 2013; Stump & Finkel, 2013). I then review evidence showing that the 'system' of finite verb stem inflection is not a fixed set of paradigms, but a dynamic network of intersecting word analogies, resulting in variation and change of exponence (§5.6). In the final section of the chapter, I argue that the cognitive representation of verb stems is likely to involve both whole-form storage, and internal morphological structure (§5.7).

5.2 Morphological structure in the finite verb stem

The Murrinhpatha finite verb stem is a typologically unusual structure, and requires somewhat unusual use of linguistic terminology. In particular, the unit referred to as a '(finite) verb stem' may itself include inflectional affixes, though these show varying degrees of regularity, as described in this chapter. Nonetheless, I use the term 'stem' for this structure because in most cases it is itself a base for forming morphologically complex words, rather than standing as a fully formed word in itself. Meanwhile, the fact that the verb stem in itself encompasses recognisable affixes necessitates that we must recognise a stem-within-the-stem, which I label the 'inner stem'. Thus forms like e.g. /wuɾan/ go.3SG.NFUT, /da/ AFFECT.2SG.IRR are verb stem forms. The first of these encompasses a subject agreement prefix /wu-/, a tense suffix /-n/ and an 'inner stem', /ɾa/ 'go', which show semi-regular patterns when we compare them to other forms of 'go' and other 3SG.NFUT stem forms. The second example has no segmentable affix elements, and consists of just an inner stem /da/ AFFECT, which can be represented with zero affixes, as in /ø-da-ø/ AFFECT.2SG.IRR. For some verb stems, the inner stem element does not have a consistent form across the inflectional paradigm, but rather exhibits a range of stem alternations. For example /wu-ɾa-n/ go.3SG.NFUT, /ku-ɾu-ø/ go.3SG.IRR and /pu-ɻu-ø/ go.3PL.IRR exhibit three different inner stem alternants, /ɾa, ɾu, ɻu/.

Note that '(finite) verb stem' refers to an abstract lexical entity, while '(finite) stem form' refers to any of the 42 inflected forms of a verb stem. For example, there is a verb stem meaning 'go', which appears in inflected forms such as /wuɾan, kuɾu, puɻu/, but has no uninflected bare form. Verb stems are lexical in the sense of appearing in particular lexical constructions, though only some of the verb stems have clear lexical semantics such as 'go', 'stand', 'use hands' etc. Others have highly attenuated lexical semantics, e.g. AFFECT, IMPEL, and are only meaningful as part of compound verbs, reflected in upper-case glossing for this type of verb stem (§8.4). In my analysis of inner stem alternation patterns I posit one such alternant as the underlying inner stem, and use this as a conventional representation for the verb stem as a lexical entity, e.g. /ɾu/ 'go', /ba/ AFFECT. Inner stems are phonologically minimal, never more than an open monosyllable at most. Some eroded inner stem alternants can be analysed as consisting of a vowel only, while for a few verb stems, a vowel-only form is the best candidate for an underlying form, e.g. /i/ 'sit', /i/ 'lie', /a/ PIERCE. Table 5.1 illustrates three inflected forms of three verb stems, showing examples of inner stem alternation, vowel-only inner stems, and affixal allomorphy. These are small fragments of the full 42-cell paradigms, to be described below.

Table 5.1: Examples of finite verb stem forms.

	3SG.IRR PREFIX-IN.STEM-SUFFIX	3SG.NFUT PREFIX-IN.STEM-SUFFIX	3PL.PST PREFIX-IN.STEM-SUFFIX
/la/ 'wipe'	ki-la-ø	di-la-m	pi-lla-ø
/ɾu/ 'go'	ku-ɾu-ø	wu-ɾa-n	pu-u-ɳi
/i/ 'sit'	ki-i-ø	di-i-m	pi-ɾi-ni

5.2.1 Basic and reflexive/reciprocal verb stems

The verb stem count breaks down into 27 basic verb stems, and 12 reflexive/reciprocal (RR) verb stems that are, at least etymologically, derived from transitive base stems. RR verb stems are generally distinguished from related bases by vowel fronting and sometimes raising on the inner stem (e.g. /ma/ 'do' → /me/ 'do RR'; /nu/ 'use feet' → /ni/ 'use feet RR';), though this is not altogether predictable. To varying extents the RR verb stems have become distinct verbal lexemes, taking on semantic and constructional qualities that are not transparently related to their associated bases (Nordlinger, n.d.). I therefore count RR verb stems among the full set of Murrinhpatha finite verb stems, and not as inflectional forms of their bases. Most importantly for the current discussion, the RR verb stems usually exhibit different inflectional patterns from their non-RR bases. Table 5.2 lists the 27 base stems and 12 RR stems, and associates stems with 'exponence patterns' – i.e. the complete matrix of affixes and stem alternations used for that stem's paradigm. Shading highlights stems that share exponence patterns across their full paradigms, as well as some stems that exhibit more than one exponence pattern (details below). Stems that have reasonably clear lexical semantics are glossed in lower case, while those that have lost any consistent semantic content are glossed in upper case (§8.3). Numbering of exponence patterns is not consecutive, nor is it meaningful; rather, it follows numbering established in Blythe et al (2007), with some divergences imposed by differences of analysis.[31]

5.2.2 Stem paradigms

A finite verb stem inflectional paradigm consists of 42 inflected forms. Table 5.3 illustrates a complete paradigm of inflected forms for one of the more regular verb stems, /na/ 'use fire'.

The subject participant is marked for 1/2/3 person, cross-cutting a basic SG/PL number distinction, though for some tenses this expands to a three-way SG/PL/paucal (PC) distinction. There is also a 1+2 'we inclusive' (1INCL) person

---

[31] Divergences of my exponence pattern numbers from the numbering in Blythe et al (2007) are as follows: VIII = 8, 13; X = 10, 11, 12, 15, 16. I analyse /ma/ 'do, say' and /ma/ 'use hands' as two homophonous verb stems, whereas previous works have analysed them as a single, polysemous verb stem. Similarly /a/ 'pierce' and /a/ 'use mouth'. While I analyse /ma/ 'do', /ba/ AFFECT and /ma/ 'use hands' as having two inflectional patterns each, previous works have treated each of these as a pair of two separate verb stems (respectively 8+34, 13+14, 8+9). All these differences follow from the current analysis of inner stems and inflections, as opposed to previous analyses of an unsegmentable morphological constituent (see main text).

5.2 Morphological structure in the finite verb stem — 115

Table 5.2: Murrinhpatha finite verb stems, and sharing of inflectional paradigms. Shading indicates verb stems with multiple paradigms, or paradigms that apply to multiple verb stems.

Base verb stem	Exponence patterns		Reflexive/reciprocal verb stem
/i/ 'sit'	I		
/i/ 'lie'	II		
/ra/ 'stand'	III		
/ni/ 'be'	IV		
/ṉta/ 'perch'	V		
/ru/ 'go'	VI		
/nu/ 'use feet'	VII	XXXVIII	/ni/ 'use feet RR'
/mu/ COERCE	XI		
/bu/ LOWER	XVII	XVIII	/buj/ LOWER.RR
/a/ 'use mouth'	XIX	XXI	/e/ 'use mouth RR'
/a/ PIERCE			/e/ PIERCE.RR
/a/ 'appear'	XX		
/ṉti/ 'carry'	XXII		
/u/ SLASH	XXIII	XXIV	/ju/ SLASH.RR
/ŋa/ 'put together'	XXV		
/la/ 'wipe'	XXVI	XXXVII	/li/ 'wipe RR'
/na/ 'use fire'	XXVII		
/ra/ 'watch'	XXVIII	XXXVI	/ri/ 'watch RR'
/ḏu/ IMPEL	XXIX	XXX	/ḏi/ IMPEL.RR
/la/ 'eat'	XXXI		
/ŋu/ 'pull'	XXXII	XXXIII	/ŋi/ 'pull RR'
/ṉta/ 'crouch'	XXXV		
/ba/ AFFECT	XIV		/be/ AFFECT.RR
	VIII		
/ma/ 'use hands'			/me/ 'use hands RR'
	IX		
/ma/ 'do, say'			/me/ 'do, say RR'
	XXXIV		
/mi/ 'look'	X		
/bi/ 'hear'			

TOTAL 27 VERB STEMS TOTAL 34 UNIQUE EXP. PATTERNS   TOTAL 12 VERB STEMS

Table 5.3: Inflectional paradigm of /na/ 'use fire'.

/na/ 'use fire'			NFUT (/PRSL)		IRR (/FUT)	PST	PSTIRR
SG	1		ŋinaŋam		ŋina	ŋinana	ŋinani
	2		t̪inaŋam		t̪ina	t̪inana	t̪inani
	3		ninaŋam / kinaŋam		kina / pina	nina	nina
INCL	1+2		t̪inaŋam		pina	t̪inana	t̪inani
PL	1		ŋinnaŋam		ŋinna	ŋinnana	ŋinnani
	2		ninnaŋam		ninna	ninnana	ninnani
	3		pinnaŋam / kinnaŋam		kinna / pinna	pinnana	pinnani
		PC	1		ŋinna	ŋinnana	ŋinnani
			2		ninna	ninnana	ninnani
			3		kinna / pinna	pinnana	pinnani

category, which has no number distinctions.[32] These are the core number/person categories of Murrinhpatha, but more specific sub-categories can be encoded using various suffixes outside the stem (§6.2). There are four basic tense/modality categories (henceforth 'tenses'): non-future (NFUT), irrealis (IRR), past (PST) and past irrealis (PSTIRR), as well as 'sub-tense' distinctions between NFUT vs presentational (PRSL), and IRR vs future indicative (FUT), which apply only to third-person forms. Again, these core categories can be further specified by stem-external suffixes encoding tense, modality and aspect (§6.3; Nordlinger & Caudal, 2012). Each verb stem form therefore bundles feature information about person, number and tense. Some feature distinctions are lost to syncretism in particular verb stems. The most widely found syncretisms are PL/PC, PST/PSTIRR and 1SG/3SG, each of which is found in several verb stems.

Further systematic syncretism is exhibited by younger speakers, for whom the tense syncretism has become generalised such that PST/PSTIRR and even IRR/PST/PSTIRR are neutralised throughout their inflectional systems (Mansfield, 2014b, p. 400ff.). However the inflectional system presented in this book is that

---

[32] 1INCL almost never has unique forms: it is generally identical to 2SG in NFUT, PST and PSTIRR tenses, and identical to 3SG.FUT in IRR tense. There is just one inflectional paradigm, XXXIV (§Appendix), in which there is a unique 1INCL.NFUT form.

attested by speakers in the 1970s and 1980s (Street, 1987; Walsh, 1976), with four distinct major tense categories.

In 30 out of 39 verb stems, the exponence pattern of the whole paradigm is not shared by any other stem. Just four exponence patterns are shared between multiple verb stems, the most common being 'X', which is common to five verb stems (see Table 5.2 above). This gives 34 distinct exponence patterns in total. Note also that three verb stems, /ma/ 'do', /ba/ AFFECT and /ma/ 'use hands', can each use two different exponence patterns. /ba/ AFFECT selects from patterns VIII, XIV according to compound verb constructions in which it is used, e.g. /bam-ŋkaḍu/ 'she sees', /baŋam-lele/ 'she bites'.[33] A similar relationship between compounding and inflection applies to /ma/ 'use hands', using patterns VIII, IX. /ma/ 'do' selects freely from VIII, XXXIV when it occurs as a simple verb, but uses only VIII when it forms compound verbs.

5.2.3 Eroded inner stems and lexical identity

As noted above, inner stems are phonologically minimal, and eight of the 39 verb stems have vowel-only underlying forms (others have vowel-only inner stems as alternates in plural forms, see below). The inner stems in themselves are therefore not well equipped to express lexical differences. However these verb stems generally remain distinct, despite their eroded inner stems, because they have different prefix and suffix allomorphs (1–4). The same could be said for homophony among the whole-syllable inner stems (e.g. /la/ 'wipe', /la/ 'eat'; /ma/ 'do, say', /ma/ 'use hands').

(1) ɲiniða
 [ɲi-i-ni]-ða
 1SG-sit-PST-PST
(2) ɲuða
 [ɲu-i-ø]-ða
 1SG-lie-PST-PST
(3) danibaɲṭa
 [da-a-ni]-baŋ-ða
 [3SG-PIERCE-PST]-pierce-PST
 she was stabbing

---

[33] It would be tempting to posit these lexical/inflectional relationships as categorical, but there is some evidence for variation. For example, /bam-ŋkaḍu/ 'she sees' is predominately attested with VIII, but I have also recorded an instance with XIV (LuPa, 2013-11-28_FN).

(4) punibaṉṯa
    [pu-u-ni]-baŋ-ða
    [3SG-SLASH-PST]-pierce-PST
    she was drilling

There is one pair of verb stems, /a/ 'use mouth' and /a/ PIERCE, which have both homophonous inner stems and identical exponence patterns. Therefore there is no formal reason for identifying these as separate verb stems. However I distinguish these on semantic grounds, since the set of compounds in which these forms occur encompasses two distinct semantic patterns (Nordlinger, *p.c.*).

5.3 Inflectional paradigms and inflectional classes

Nouns and verbs are said to belong to an 'inflectional class' when several lexemes share the same patterns of exponence throughout their inflectional paradigms (Stump & Finkel, 2013). Familiar examples can be found in the verb conjugation classes of Romance languages, or in English verbs that share patterns of present and past tense exponence(e.g. *sleep* PRES:: *slept* PST, *keep* PRES:: *kept* PST). An analysis of inflectional classes implies that the number of classes is substantially less than the total number of lexemes in the morphosyntactic class, and that some or most classes have substantial sets of lexical members. In other words, inflectional classes imply substantial sharing of inflectional paradigms. One can also analyse 'sub-paradigms', where lexemes have morphological relationships for subparts of their inflectional paradigms, e.g. in one tense series but not another.

5.3.1 Inflection by intersecting formatives

In some languages, the paradigm of inflectional exponences defined for each lexeme can be more elegantly analysed not as a single paradigmatic pattern, but as the intersection of several paradigmatic patterns. For example, the paradigm may have a pattern of suffix allomorphs, and also a pattern of stem ablaut or tone alternations. These can be analysed as independent morphological structures if they are independently distributed in the lexicon – i.e. if lexeme A shares its suffix pattern with lexemes B, C and D, but shares its stem ablaut pattern with C, E and F. I describe such systems as consisting of 'intersecting formatives' (Mansfield, 2016b). There does not appear to be any well-established name for this type of exponence in the morphological literature, though it has been discussed for various languages including Italian (Carstairs-McCarthy, 2011, p. 137ff.), Georgian (J. P. Blevins, 2006), Mazatec (Ackerman & Malouf, 2013; Jamieson, 1982), Russian (Brown & Hippisley, 2012, p. 71ff.) and Skolt Saami (Feist, 2015, pp. 139, 200).

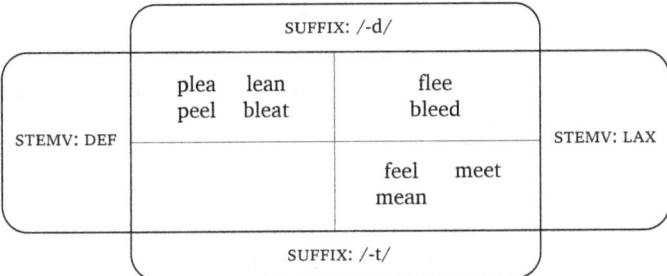

Figure 5.1: Sample of English verbs categorised according to Stem vowel and suffix formatives applying in past tense (Stump & Finkel, 2015, p. 123).

Our English past tense example is in fact an instance of intersecting formatives. For *slept*, there are two distinct formatives combining in the inflectional exponence: {PST.SUFFIX: /t/}, which is shared with a set of verbs including FEEL and MEAN; and {PST.VOWEL: [LAX]}, which is shared with a non-identical set including FLEE and MEET. Thus *slept* has inflectional relationships with two sets of verb lexemes, associated with different parts of its phonological structure; *slept* is located in the *intersection* of these two sets. The non-identity of the sets {PST. SUFFIX: /t/} and {PST.VOWEL: [LAX]} can be seen by considering the verbs FLEE, FEEL and PEEL. FLEE and FEEL are both members of {PST.VOWEL: [LAX]}, but for the suffix formative they diverge as {PST.SUFFIX: /d/} and {PST.SUFFIX: /t/}, *fled* and *felt*, respectively. A sample of verbs occupying these intersecting formatives is illustrated in Figure 5.1.[34]

Note that there may be phonological stem constraints on which intersections a verb appears in. For example it may be that in English only verbs with stem-final voicing may occupy the {PST: SUFFIX /d/, VOWEL: [LAX]} intersection occupied by FLEE and BLEED in the figure above. We will see below that a phonological constraint of this type applies to a plural stem class in Murrinhpatha (§5.4.4).

---

[34] The interpretation of suffix classes here presumes that *bled* can be represented as /bled-d/, and *met* as /met-t/.

5.4 Intersecting formatives in the finite verb stem

In Murrinhpatha, the inflectional patterns shared between one finite verb stem and another seldom account for the complete inflectional exponence of forms, but rather pattern across particular intersecting formatives. For example, /la/ 'wipe' and /na/ 'use fire' share the pattern of PL consonant gemination, but use different NFUT tense suffix allomorphs. Thus it is these intersecting formatives – the subject prefix patterns, stem suffix patterns, and stem alternation patterns – that constitute the form–meaning relationships among verb stems. The complete exponences are epiphenomenal aggregates of the semi-regular formatives, and in the complete exponences we find few shared patterns. Taking one particular paradigmatic cell as an example, in 1SG.NFUT we can distinguish quite independent allomorphies for prefix vowel and suffix. PrefV and Suffix are thus two of the intersecting formatives exhibited by the finite verb stems. Figure 5.2 illustrates their distribution for a sample of verb stems.

There are six semi-regular formative elements making up each inflectional exponence: PrefC, PrefV, InnerC, InnerV-Height (InnerVH), InnerV-Frontness (InnerVF), and Suffix. Table 5.5 shows the inflectional paradigm for /na/ 'use fire', the same verb stem that was illustrated above, but now with inflectional forms broken down into formative elements. In the illustration of the three intersecting stem features, only non-default features are labelled. For example [C:GEMINATE] indicates that InnerC = GEMINATE, InnerVF = DEFAULT and InnerVH = DEFAULT. Where all three features are default, the stem is labelled simply as [DEFAULT]. Features are spelt out in full in table headers (e.g. GEMINATE), and abbreviated in the table body (e.g. GEM). Note that some analyses assume morpho-phonological

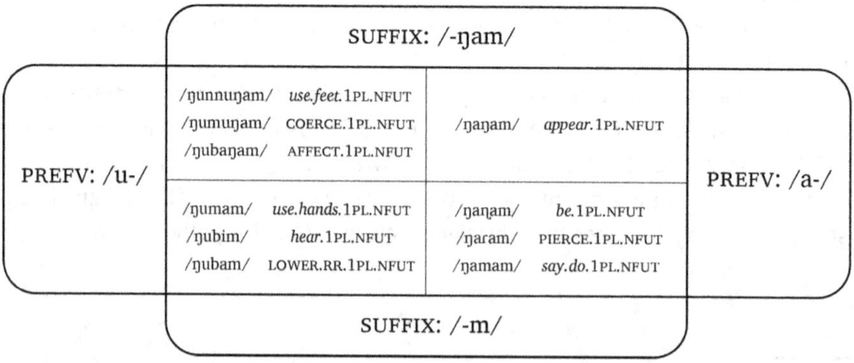

Figure 5.2: Intersection of PrefV and Suffix formative allomorphs on a sample of verb stems.

vowel merger (see §5.4.4 below), following the same pattern found elsewhere in the phonology (§3.7.2). Full formative analyses of all finite verb stems are presented in Appendix I.

Table 5.4: Sample verb stem inflection paradigm illustrating semi-regular formatives.

		/na/ 'use fire' Class: XXVII NFUT (/PRSL)	INNER STEM:	/na/ DEFAULT /nna/ C:GEMINATE /a/ C:WEAK IRR (/FUT)	PST	PSTIRR
SG	1	ŋinaŋam ŋ-i-[DEF]-ŋam		ŋina ŋ-i-[DEF]-ø	ŋinaŋa ŋ-i-[DEF]-ŋa	ŋinaŋi ŋ-i-[DEF]-ŋi
	2	t̪inaŋam t̪-...		t̪ina t̪-...	t̪inaŋa t̪-i-[DEF]-ŋa	t̪inaŋi t̪-i-[DEF]-ŋi
	3	ninaŋam / kinaŋam n-... / k-...		kina / pina k-... / p-...	niŋa n-i-[WEAK]-ŋa	niŋa n-i-[WEAK]-ŋa
INCL	1	t̪inaŋam t̪-i-[DEF]-ŋam		pina p-i-[DEF]-ø	t̪inaŋa t̪-i-[DEF]-ŋa	t̪inaŋi t̪-i-[DEF]-ŋi
PL	1	ŋinnaŋam ŋ-i-[GEM]-ŋam		ŋinna ŋ-i-[GEM]-ø	ŋinnaŋa ŋ-i-[GEM]-ŋa	ŋinnaŋi ŋ-i-[GEM]-ŋi
	2	ninnaŋam n-...		ninna n-...	ninnaŋa n-...	ninnaŋi n-...
	3	pinnaŋam / kin-naŋam p-... / k-...		kinna / pinna k-... / p-...	pinnaŋa p-...	pinnaŋi p-...
			PC 1	ŋinna ŋ-i-[GEM]-ø	ŋinnaŋa ŋ-i-[GEM]-ŋa	ŋinnaŋi ŋ-i-[GEM]-ŋi
			2	ninna n-...	ninnaŋa n-...	ninnaŋi n-...
			3	kinna / pinna k-... / p-...	pinnaŋa p-...	pinnaŋi p-...

5.4.1 PrefC

PrefC is tied to subject person/number categories. It varies primarily in 3SG forms, which have six allomorphs /p, w, d, n, j, k, ø/. Some of these allomorphs may have earlier been stem elements rather than person inflections (Green, 2003), though they now occupy the structural position of an inflectional prefix. In 1SG and 2SG forms the only allomorphy is between phonologically realised and zero forms /ŋ, ø/ 1SG; /t̪, ø/ 2SG. For PL and 1INCL forms, PrefC has fixed values, as illustrated in Table 5.5.

Table 5.5: Allomorphy of PrefC. Shading highlights that 3SG is the main locus of allomorphy.

		NFUT (/PRSL)		PST	PSTIRR	IRR (/FUT)
SG	1	ŋ, ø		ŋ, ø	ŋ, ø	ŋ, ø
	2	t̪, ø		t̪, ø	t̪, ø	t̪, ø
	3		p, w, d, n, j, k, ø			k, ø / p, ø
INCL	1/2	t̪		t̪	p	p[35]
PL	1	ŋ		ŋ	ŋ	ŋ
	2	n		n	n	n
	3	p / k		p	p	k / p
	PC 1			ŋ	ŋ	ŋ
	2			n	n	n
	3			p	p	k / p

Table 5.6: Sample of a PrefC formative paradigm.

PREFC		NFUT (/PRL)	IRR (/FUT)	PST	PSTIRR
SG	1	ŋ	ŋ	ŋ	ŋ
	2	t̪	t̪	t̪	t̪
	3	d / k	k / p	d	d
Verb stems:		/i/ 'sit', /a/ PIERCE, /e/ PIERCE.RR, /la/ 'wipe', /ra/ 'watch, /li/ 'wipe RR', /ri/ 'watch RR', /a/ 'use mouth', /e/ 'use mouth RR'			

The PrefC formative paradigm for each verb stem therefore specifies allomorphy only for SG forms, as PL forms have fixed values. One such paradigm is illustrated in Table 5.6, together with the list of verb stems that share this formative pattern.

---

[35] The one clear distinction documented for the Murrinh Kura variety (§2.2) is that its INCL.IRR verb forms begin with /ŋamp/ instead of /p/. This inflection is shared with the Ngan'gi language (Reid, 1990), which borders Murrinh Kura but not Murrinhpatha.

5.4.2 PrefV

PrefV is usually quite consistent across each verb stem's paradigm. In other words, it is associated with the verb stem itself (i.e. a 'theme vowel'), rather than any inflectional category. The most common PrefV is /u/, which is used for the most verb stems and most likely to be used consistently throughout a paradigm. Other vowels /a, e, i/ are used on fewer verb stems, and appear less consistently across a paradigms of those stems. The linking of particular PrefVs to particular verb stems probably derives from a historical pattern of vowel harmony, as suggested by the fact that /a, e, i/ PrefVs tend to match the vowel of the inner stem. Verb stem vowel harmony is found in Murrinhpatha's sister language Ngan'gi (Reid, 1990, p. 88).

Table 5.7: Sample of a PrefV formative paradigm.

PREFV			NFUT	IRR	PST	PSTIRR
SG			a	i	i	i
			i	i	i	i
			i	i	i	i
INCL			i	i	i	i
PL	1		a	u	a	a
	2		i	u	i	i
	3		i	u	i	i
	PC	1	a	a	a	a
		2	i	a	i	i
		3	i	a	i	i
Verb stems:			/i/ 'sit'			

Table 5.7 illustrates one of the PrefV inflectional paradigms that is not consistent for all paradigmatic cells. This 'irregular' paradigm is specific to a single verb stem, /i/ 'sit'. As in most other non-/u/ PrefV paradigms, the predominant vowel, /i/, matches the inner stem vowel. Note that the sub-tenses PRSL and FUT are not specified for PrefV, or indeed any other formative except PrefC. They are distinguished from their parent tenses NFUT and IRR only in prefix consonants.

There are several verb stems that have phonologically empty prefixes in SG forms – i.e. they do not realise a segment for either PrefC or PrefV. These could therefore be analysed as having distinctive PrefV paradigms with /ø/ allomorphy in some or all SG forms; but in the interest of positing fewer paradigms, I analyse these instead as having 'underlying' PrefV allomorphs for SG forms, matching the theme vowel established in the rest of the paradigm. I propose that in SG forms with empty PrefC, the PrefV cannot be realised on the surface due to the constraint against onsetless syllables (§3.3). An example of this analysis is illustrated in Table 5.8.

Table 5.8: Sample paradigm for a verb stem analysed as having a consistent /u/ allomorph for PrefV, even though this is not realised in SG forms that have an empty PrefC, due to syllable constraints.

		/ma/ 'say, do' Class: VIII	STEM:	/ma/ DEFAULT /na/ C:APICAL /me/ VF:FRONT		
		NFUT (/PRSL)		IRR (/FUT)	PST	PSTIRR
SG	1	mam Ø-u-[DEF]-m		ma Ø-u-[DEF]-Ø	me Ø-u-[FRONT]-Ø	me Ø-u-[FRONT]-Ø
	2	nam Ø-u-[APIC]-m		na Ø-u-[APIC]-Ø	ne Ø-u-[APIC, FRONT]-Ø	ne Ø-u-[APIC, FRONT]-Ø
	3	mam / mam Ø-u-[DEF]-m		ma / ma Ø-u-[DEF]-Ø	me Ø-u-[FRONT]-Ø	me Ø-u-[FRONT]-Ø
INCL	1	tumam t-u-[DEF]-m		puma p-u-[DEF]-Ø	pume p-u-[FRONT]-Ø	pume p-u-[FRONT]-Ø
PL	1	ŋumam ŋ-u-[DEF]-m		ŋuma ŋ-u-[DEF]-Ø	ŋume ŋ-u-[FRONT] Ø	ŋume ŋ-u-[FRONT] Ø
	2	numam n-...		numa n-...	nume n-...	nume n-...
	3	pumam / k-umam p-... / k-...		kuma / puma k-... / p-...	pume p-...	pume p-...
			PC 1	ŋuma ŋ-u-[DEF] Ø	ŋume ŋ-u-[FRONT] Ø	ŋume ŋ-u-[FRONT] Ø
			2	numa n-...	nume n-...	nume n-...
			3	kuma / puma k-.../ p-...	pume p-...	pume p-...

5.4.3 Suffix

Suffix formatives are tied to tense categories. Unlike the prefix string, the suffix strings do not exhibit any independent sub-parts. In other words, the suffix is best analysed as a single formative, which is maximally CVC, and is linked to tense. There are different sets of allomorphs for NFUT, PST and PSTIRR tenses

(Table 5.9), with verb stems usually selecting just one allomorph for all person/ number forms of a single tense, though in some cases a tense series switches suffix allomorphs between SG and PL forms. IRR consistently has a /ø/ suffix for all forms in all verb stems.

Table 5.9: Suffix allomorphy for finite verb stems.

NFUT	/ŋam, ŋan, m, n/
PST	/ṇa, ṇe, ṇi, ṇi, ṇa/
PSTIRR	/ṇa, ṇe, ṇi, ji, ṇi, ṇe/
IRR	/ø/

The Suffix formative exhibits 'sub-paradigm' structure across tense categories, because the allomorphy patterns that a verb stem selects for NFUT, PST and PSTIRR respectively are quite independent of one another. For example, the suffix allomorph a verb stem selects for NFUT forms is not predictable from the allomorph it selects for PST forms. Each verb stem is therefore specified by three independent formative patterns, SuffixNFUT, SuffixPST and SuffixPSTIRR, though each of these makes a very simple specification, defining the allomorph selection for each number category. Note that PC is analysed as a subcategory of PL, not always distinct (§6.2). Examples of each are illustrated in Table 5.10.

Table 5.10: Sample suffix formative paradigms.

SuffNfut		
	SG, INCL	ŋam
	PL	m
Verbs: /ø/ 'appear'		

SuffPst		
	SG, INCL	ṇi
	PL	ṇi
	PC	ṇe
Verbs: /ru/ 'go', /ø/ ARC		

SuffPstirr		
	SG, INCL	ṇi
	PL	ṇi
	PC	ṇe
Verbs: /nta/ 'perch'		

5.4.4 Inner stems

Inner stem alternations are themselves the complex intersection of three allomorphic features: consonant alternation (InnerC), vowel height alternation (InnerVH) and vowel frontness alternation (InnerVF). Inner stem alternation patterns are most often linked to tense, though they may also be linked to subject agreement. However, inner stems are the most irregular of the semi-regular inflectional formative types – i.e. their patterns are less predictable (Mansfield, 2016b). Murrinhpatha inner stem feature alternations are a particularly complex form of the 'stem grades' attested for languages such as Fula (Anderson, 1976) and Saami (Sammallahti, 1998).

For verb stems with a vowel-only default inner stem, the inner stem element is opaque in many inflected forms, since it is adjacent to a prefix vowel and therefore subject to V-V → V merger (§3.3.2), e.g. /ŋa-i-m/ → /ŋem/ sit.1SG.NFUT. The default vowel of the inner stem only becomes clear from an inner stem alternation that specifies InnerC = /ɾ/ for PL forms (see below), giving e.g. /ŋa-ɾi-m/ sit.1PL.NFUT., /ŋa-ɾa-m/PIERCE.1PL.NFUT.

InnerC

InnerC features are most strongly linked to the SG/PL number distinction (§6.2.1), with a pattern of gemination (GEM) in PL forms (e.g. /la/ → /lla/) affecting 11 verb stems. A further seven verb stems show a pattern of InnerC replacement with /ɾ/ in PL forms. These two synchronically divergent patterns actually derive from the same historic source, an erstwhile */ɾ(V)/ PL morpheme, which assimilated to following apical consonants, and simply replaced other consonants (Green, 2003). Table 5.11 illustrates a sample verb stem with the PL gemination pattern, and Table 5.12 illustrates the rhotic pattern.

InnerC SG forms exhibit a pattern of labial → apical (APIC) alternation in 2SG forms (e.g. /ma/ → /na/, /ba/ → /da/). Table 5.13 illustrates a verb stem paradigm exhibiting the apical pattern.

There are also a substantial number of suppletive InnerC alternants, which have no systematic relationship to morphosyntactic categories and thus are quite disruptive of morphological patterns. Table 5.14 illustrates a verb stem paradigm with especially irregular InnerC alternations.

InnerVH and InnerVF

Inner stem vowel alternations are again highly irregular, but have weak patterns linked to tense categories, and PC number category. In paradigms where one vowel dominates, suggesting a DEFAULT vowel status, it is the IRR tense that most consistently exhibits this vowel. Therefore, for paradigms with no clear DEFAULT vowel, the IRR vowel has been analysed as the DEFAULT.

InnerV-Height alternations show a pattern of LOW alternants /i, u → e, a/ in NFUT, PST or PSTIRR tenses, or in PC number forms. More occasionally inner stems exhibit a HIGH alternant in some tenses. InnerV-Frontness is highly unpredictable, but its strongest pattern is a FRONT alternant /a, u → e, i/, in PST and PSTIRR tenses. As with PrefV patterns (§5.4.2), InnerVH and InnerVF alternations probably derive from historical vowel harmony, in this case influenced by the vowels of the tense and number suffixes. For example, the PST = [FRONT] alternation may be related to

5.4 Intersecting formatives in the finite verb stem

Table 5.11: Sample verb stem illustrating the GEMINATE InnerC alternation in PL forms.

		/la/ 'wipe' Class: XXVI	STEM:	/la/ DEFAULT /lla/ C:GEMINATE		
		NFUT (/PRSL)		IRR (/FUT)	PST	PSTIRR
SG	1	ŋilam ŋ-i-[DEF]-m		ŋila ŋ-i-[DEF]-ø	ŋila ŋ-i-[DEF]-ø	ŋilaŋi ŋ-i-[DEF]-ŋi
	2	t̪ilam t̪-...		t̪ila t̪-...	t̪ila t̪-...	t̪ilaŋi t̪-i-[DEF]-ŋi
	3	dilam / kilam d-... / k-...		kila / pila k-... / p-...	dila d-...	dilaŋi d-i-[DEF]-ŋi
INCL	1	t̪ilam t̪-i-[DEF]-m		pila p-i-[DEF]-ø	t̪ila t̪-i-[DEF]-ø	t̪ilaŋi t̪-i-[DEF]-ŋi
PL	1	ŋillaŋam ŋ-i-[GEM]-ŋam		ŋilla ŋ-i-[GEM]-ø	ŋilla ŋ-i-[GEM]-ø	ŋillaŋi ŋ-i-[GEM]-ŋi
	2	nillaŋam n-...		nilla n-...	nilla n-...	nillaŋi n-...
	3	pillaŋam / killaŋam p-... / k-...		killa / pilla k-... / p-...	pilla p-...	pillaŋi p-...
			PC 1	ŋilla ŋ-i-[GEM]-ø	ŋilla ŋ-i-[GEM]-ø	ŋillaŋi ŋ-i-[GEM]-ŋi
			2	nilla n-...	nilla n-...	nillaŋi n-...
			3	killa / pilla k-... / p-...	pilla p-...	pillaŋi p-...

Table 5.12: Sample verb stem illustrating the RHOTIC InnerC alternation in PL forms.

		/a/ PIERCE Class: XXI	STEM:	/a/ DEFAULT /ra/ C:RHOTIC		
		NFUT (/PRSL)		IRR (/FUT)	PST	PSTIRR
SG	1	ŋam ŋ-a-[DEF]-m		ŋa ŋ-a-[DEF]-ø	ŋani ŋ-a-[DEF]-ni	ŋe ŋ-e-[DEF]-ø
	2	t̪am t̪-...		t̪a t̪-...	t̪ani t̪-...	t̪e t̪-...
	3	dam / kam d-... / k-...		ka / pa k-... / p-...	dani d-...	de d-...
INCL	1	t̪am t̪-a-[DEF]-m		pa p-a-[DEF]-ø	t̪ani t̪-a-[DEF]-ni	t̪e t̪-e-[DEF]-ø

(continued)

Table 5.12 (continued)

		/a/ PIERCE Class: XXI	STEM:	/a/ DEFAULT /ra/ C:RHOTIC		
		NFUT (/PRSL)		IRR (/FUT)	PST	PSTIRR
PL	1	ŋaram ŋa-[RHOT]-m		ŋa ŋ-a-[DEF]-ø	ŋarani ŋ-a-[RHOT]-ni	ŋera ŋ-e-[RHOT]-ø
	2	naram n-...		na n-...	narani n-...	nera n-...
	3	param / karam p-... / k-...		ka / pa k-... / p-...	pani p-...	pera p-...
			PC 1	ŋa ŋ-a-[DEF]-ø	ŋarane ŋ-a-[RHOT]-ne	ŋera ŋ-e-[RHOT]-ø
			2	na n-...	narane n-...	nera n-...
			3	ka / pa k-... / p-...	parane p-...	pera p-...

Table 5.13: Sample paradigm exhibiting 2SG apicalisation of InnerC.

		/bu/ LOWER Class: XVII	STEM:	/bu/ DEFAULT /ba/ VH:LOW	/du/ C:APICAL /da/ C:APIC, VH:LOW	
		NFUT (/PRSL)		IRR (/FUT)	PST	PSTIRR
SG	1	ban ø-u-[LOW]-n		bu ø-u-[DEF]-ø	buni ø-u-[DEF]-ni	buj ø-u-[DEF]-j
	2	dan ø-u-[LOW,APIC]-n		du ø-u-[APIC]- ø	duni ø-u-[APIC]-ni	duj ø-u-[APIC]-j
	3	ban / kuban ø-u-[LOW]-n / k-u-[LOW]-n		bu / bu ø-u-[DEF]-ø	buni ø-u-[DEF]-ni	buj ø-u-[DEF]-j
INCL	1	ṭuban ṭ-u-[LOW]-n		pubu p-u-[DEF]-ø	ṭubuni ṭ-u-[DEF]-ni	ṭubuj ṭ-u-[DEF]-j
PL	1	ŋuban ŋ-u-[LOW]-n		ŋubu ŋ-u-[DEF]-ø	ŋubuni ŋ-u-[DEF]-ni	ŋubuj ŋ-u-[DEF]-j
	2	nuban n-...		nubu n-...	nubuni n-...	nubuj n-...
	3	puban / kuban p-... / k-...		kubu / pubu k-... / p-...	pubuni p-...	pubuj p-...
			PC 1	ŋubu ŋ-u-[DEF]-ø	ŋubune ŋ-u-[DEF]-ne	ŋubuj ŋ-u-[DEF]-j

5.4 Intersecting formatives in the finite verb stem

Table 5.13 (continued)

/bu/ LOWER Class: XVII	STEM:	/bu/ DEFAULT /ba/ VH:LOW	/du/ C:APICAL /da/ C:APIC, VH:LOW
	2	nubu n̪-...	nubune n̪-...	nubuj n̪-...
	3	kubu / pubu k-... / p-...	pubune p-...	pubuj p-...

Table 5.14: Sample paradigm exhibiting highly irregular alternations of InnerC, including suppletive inner stems.

		/ru/ 'go'	STEM:	/ru/ DEFAULT /ɺu/ GEMINATE /u/ WEAK /ji/ J (SUPPL), FRONT /mpa/ MP (SUPPL), LOW	/ra/ LOW /ri/ FRONT /je/ J (SUPPL), FRONT, LOW
		NFUT (/PRSL)		IRR (/FUT)	PST	PSTIRR
SG	1	ŋuran ŋ-u-[LOW]-n		ŋuru ŋ-u-[DEF]-ø	ŋurini ŋ-u-[FRONT]-ni	ŋuri ŋ-u-[FRONT]-ø
	2	t̪uran t̪-...		t̪uru t̪-...	t̪urini t̪-...	t̪uri t̪-...
	3	wuran / kuran w-... / k-...		kuru / puru k-... / p-...	wurini w-...	wuri w-...
INCL	1	t̪uran t̪-u-[LOW]-n		puru p-u-[DEF]-ø	t̪urini t̪-u-[FRONT]-ni	t̪uri t̪u-[FRONT]-ø
PL	1	ŋumpan ŋ-u-[MP,LOW]-n		ŋuɺu ŋ-u-[GEM]-ø	ŋuɲi ŋ-u-[WEAK,-FRONT]-ɲi	ŋuji ŋ-u-[J, FRONT]-ø
	2	numpan n-...		nuɺu n-...	nuɲi n-...	nuji n-...
	3	pumpan / kumpan p-... / k-...		kuɺu / puɺu k-... / p-...	puɲi p-...	puji p-...
			PC 1	ŋa ŋ-a-[WEAK]-ø	ŋuɲe ŋ-u-[WEAK, FRONT]-ɲe	ŋuje ŋ-u-[J, FRNT, LOW]-ø
			2	na n-...	nuɲe n-...	nuje n-...
			3	ka / pa k-... / p-...	puɲe p-...	puje p-...

Table 5.15: Sample paradigm exhibiting InnerVH and InnerVF alternations associated with tense and number

		/ɖu/ IMPEL Class: XXXI	STEM:	/ɖu/ DEFAULT /ɖa/ VH:LOW /ɖi/ VF:FRONT /ɖe/ VH:LOW, VF:FRONT	/ɖɖu/ C:GEM /ɖɖa/ C:GEM, VH:LOW /ɖɖi/ C:GEM, VF:FRONT /ɖɖe/ C:GEM, VH:LOW, VF:FRONT	
		NFUT (/PRSL)		IRR (/FUT)	PST	PSTIRR
SG	1	ŋuɖan ŋ-u-[LOW]-n		ŋuɖu ŋ-u-[DEF]-ø	ŋuɖini ŋ-u-[FRONT]-ni	ŋuɖi ŋ-u-[FRONT]-ø
	2	t̪uɖan t̪-...		t̪uɖu t̪-...	t̪uɖini t̪-...	t̪uɖi t̪-...
	3	wuɖan / kuɖan w-... / k-...		kuɖu / puɖu k-... / p-...	wuɖini w-...	wuɖi w-...
INCL	1	t̪uɖan t̪-u-[LOW]-n		puɖu p-u-[DEF]-ø	t̪uɖini t̪-u-[FRONT]-ni	t̪uɖi t̪-u-[FRONT]-ø
PL	1	ŋuɖɖan ŋ-u-[GEM,LOW]-n		ŋuɖɖu ŋ-u-[GEM]-ø	ŋuɖɖini ŋ-u-[GEM,-FRONT]-ni	ŋuɖɖi ŋ-u-[GEM,-FRONT]-ø
	2	nuɖɖan n-...		nuɖɖu n-...	nuɖɖini n-...	nuɖɖi n-...
	3	puɖɖan / kuɖɖan p-... / k-...		kuɖɖu / puɖɖu k-... / p-...	puɖɖini p-...	puɖɖi p-...
		PC	1	ŋuɖɖa ŋ-u-[GEM,LOW]-ø	ŋuɖɖene ŋ-u-[GEM,-FRONT,LOW]-ne	ŋuɖɖe ŋ-u-[GEM,-FRONT,LOW]-ø
			2	nuɖɖa n-...	nuɖɖene n-...	nuɖɖe n-...
			3	kuɖɖa / puɖɖa k-... / p-...	puɖɖene p-...	puɖɖe p-...

the vowels in /-ɳi ~ -ɲi/, which are the most frequent SuffixPST formatives. Similarly the PC = [LOW] and NFUT = [LOW] alternations may be related to vowels in the /-ka/ PC.SUBJ suffix and the /-ŋam/ NFUT formative respectively. Table 5.15 illustrates a verb stem paradigm with a range of InnerVH and InnerVF alternations.

5.5 Unpredictable exponence and cross-linguistic comparison

I have described above the prolific allomorphy found in the intersecting formatives of Murrinhpatha finite verb stems. I characterise this as 'semi-regular' morphological structure, in reference to these patterns, status at the margins of morphology and unanalysable lexicon. In this section I quantify this degree of unpredictability, and compare it to measurements for other languages.

An intuitive measurement of allomorph irregularity can be reached by calculating the overall *predictability* of allomorph selection. This is not the same as number of allomorphs, because it also takes into account how evenly they are distributed in the sample. For example let us imagine five allomorphs distributed across ten verb stems. If each allomorph applies to two verb stems, [a,a,b,b,c,c,d,d,e,e], we have much less chance of predicting an allomorph, than if one particular allomorph applies to six verb stems, [a,a,a,a,a,a,b,c,d,e]. The formula for measuring the predictability of such distributions is a weighted average probability of all outcomes (i.e. all allomorphs), known as *entropy* (Shannon, 1948). Higher entropy, measured in bits, indicates a greater quantity of information is required to reduce uncertainty to zero. Informally, we can think of this as 'greater unpredictability'. For example, our six allomorphs with no particular favourite have entropy of 2.32 bits, while the same allomorphs distributed with one preferred allomorph has an entropy of 1.77 bits.

Predictability calculations for Murrinhpatha finite verb stem inflectional exponence find that inflectional cells range from 1.91 bits for 1INCL.IRR (which has no allomorphy at all in PrefV and Suffix formatives) to 4.41 bits for 2PL.NFUT and 3PL.NFUT. The average across all cells is 3.72 bits. This type of measurement may be unfamiliar in itself, but fortunately there is a cross-linguistic study of predictability in inflectional exponence that provides a point of comparison. Ackerman and Malouf (2013, p. 443) report the average predictability of cell exponence for 10 languages, including some that are informally regarded as having highly complex inflectional morphology. They find a range from 0.78 bits (for Nuer) up to 4.92 bits (for Mazatec). Added to their list, Murrinhpatha would have the third-most unpredictable exponence out of 11 languages, as shown in Table 5.17 below. However, the two languages that show higher exponence unpredictability, Mazatec and Arapesh, both have small inflectional paradigms: 6 cells and 2 cells respectively. Murrinhpatha verb stems, by contrast, specify 42 cells. Therefore Murrinhpatha inflectional morphology has among the higher rates of inflectional unpredictability observed cross-linguistically, but multiplies this unpredictability across a much larger paradigm of inflectional exponences, compared to languages attested with similar degrees of exponence unpredictability.

The effect of paradigm size on inflection predictability can be expressed with a simple extension to Ackerman and Malouf's cross-linguistic calculations, adding a 'Complete Paradigm Predictability' figure that *sums* the entropy of exponence scores for all cells, rather than averaging them. Given that entropy is the amount of information required to reduce uncertainty to zero, the addition of cell entropies represents the total amount of information required to predict all inflectional forms of a lexeme. Murrinhpatha has by far the largest Complete Paradigm Predictability score when added to Ackerman and Malouf's cross-linguistic sample. Table 5.16 illustrates the Complete Paradigm Predictability scores for the cross-linguistic sample including Murrinhpatha.[36] We see that in this measurement, Murrinhpatha is an outlier in the sample, with 156.36 bits of unpredictability in an inflectional paradigm, compared to scores ranging from 4.67–30.99 in the rest of the sample. However, this figure should be weighed against the fact that

Table 5.16: Complete Paradigm Prediction scores for cross-linguistic sample. Based on table in Ackerman and Malouf (2013, p. 443).

Language	Paradigmatic cells	Average cell predictability (bits)	Complete Paradigm Predictability (bits) (Cells x Average cell predictability)
Amele	3	2.88	8.65
Arapesh	2	4.07	8.14
Burmeso	12	1.00	12.00
Fur	12	2.40	28.47
Greek	8	1.62	12.97
Kwerba	12	0.86	10.37
Mazatec	6	4.92	29.52
Murrinhpatha	42	3.72	156.37
Ngiti	16	1.94	30.99
Nuer	6	0.77	4.67
Russian	12	0.91	10.93

Murrinhpatha finite verb stems are a closed class of 39 lexical members, while other languages in the sample apply inflectional paradigms to open lexical classes (though usually only one paradigm is applied productively). Although the very high information content of the Murrinhpatha paradigm

---

[36] See Ackerman and Malouf (2013) for a list of descriptive sources drawn on in developing this cross-linguistic comparison.

may seem problematic for learnability, speakers may be able to offset this by greater reliance on whole-form memorisation (Mansfield & Nordlinger, 2019), a question I return to below (§5.7).

The figures calculated above treat each inflectional cell as an independent problem for allomorphy prediction. However it has been argued that this is not a realistic model of language use or structure. Learners and speakers of a language are faced with a slightly different problem: predicting inflectional allomorphy of a form, given other forms that they have encountered of the same lexeme (Ackerman, Blevins, & Malouf, 2009; Ackerman & Malouf, 2013). The paradigmatic structure of languages is such that knowing the allomorphy selection of some forms generally reduces the uncertainty associated with other forms. The predictability of such implicational relations in Murrinhpatha is beyond the scope of this chapter, but has been investigated in detail in other work (Mansfield, 2016b; Mansfield & Nordlinger, 2019). This work shows that Murrinhpatha verb stem allomorphy remains highly unpredictable compared to other languages, even given the clues provided by paradigmatically related forms.

5.6 Variation and change in inflectional paradigms

The inflectional system described above is based on forms elicited from a handful of speakers in the 1970s and 1980s and documented by Street (1987). One particular speaker (GrMo, b. 1938) acted as the main informant for these paradigms (Street, *p.c.*). Representations of a grammatical system may always be to some extent a necessary reification of phenomena that are actually in flux, but this seems to be particularly the case for Murrinhpatha finite verb stem inflections. Data collected from a wider range of speakers, especially speakers born in the 1960s–90s, who contribute most of the corpus (§1.5), exhibit considerable variation and signs of diachronic change. Much of this involves variable application of the formative analogies, which reinforces the interpretation of these as active morphological elements (Mansfield & Nordlinger, 2019).

Some variation of inflection can be ascribed to phonological optimisation, either reduction or harmonisation (5, 6).

(5) ŋamam ~ ŋam   (VC haplology)
    ŋa-ma-m
    1SG-do-NFUT
(6) kuḍi ~ kuḍu   (vowel harmonisation)
    ku-ḍi-ø
    3SG-turn.RR-IRR

However many other variables are not phonological but morphological: they indicate variation in selection of formative allomorphs. These are likely to be changes in progress, because the available data suggests discrepancies between older and youngers speakers (Mansfield & Nordlinger, 2019). The change /na > nu/ go.2PL. IRR (7) provides one of the clearer examples. The earlier attested prefix vowel /a/ is unusual for a verb stem where most other forms have /u/. If we compare other verb stems that have, say, 1SG.IRR with /ŋu-/ (e.g. /ma/ 'do', /ḍu/ 'turn'), we find that they all have 2PL.IRR with /nu-/. These verb stems provide sources of analogies because their inflectional paradigms use many of the same formative allomorphs as does /ru/ 'go'.

(7) na > nu
 na-ø-ø > nu-ø-ø
 na-[WEAK]-ø > nu-[WEAK]-ø
 2PL-go-IRR   (AlBu, 2013-01-15)

Other instances alter more than one formative at a time. The change /nam > ṭamam/ do.2SG.NFUT (8) switches allomorphs for both InnerC and the PrefC, in both cases drawing on analogical sources available from various other verb stems (e.g. /ni/ 'be', /ṉti/ 'have'). The change /paŋan > piṛim/ watch.3PL.NFUT (9) switches PrefV, inner stem and suffix allomorphs, again with analogical sources for each formative (e.g. /ra/ 'stand', /ṉta/ 'perch').

(8) nam > ṭamam
 ø-na-m > ṭa-ma-m
 2SG-do-NFUT   (WaDo, 2013-01-24)
(9) paŋan > piṛim
 pa-a-ŋan > pi-ṛi-m
 pa-[WEAK]-ŋan > pi-[FRONT,HIGH]-m
 3PL-watch-NFUT   (LuPa, 2015-07-05_AM)

In summary, we see a range of variants, likely indicating change-in-progress, all of which can be attributed to switches of analogical source in selection of formative allomorphs. Research on child acquisition of finite verb stem inflection also shows that children's selection of formative allomorphs sometimes does not match adult targets (Forshaw, 2016, p. 231ff.).

5.7 Whole-form storage or morphological structure?

I return now to the existential question for semi-regular inflectional formatives: do speakers represent these in their mental grammar, or are they merely an artefact of elaborate morphological analysis? As mentioned earlier, previous work in Murrinhpatha has treated the verb stem as an indivisible unit, implicitly rejecting the morphological existence of semi-regular formatives.

Mainstream linguistic analysis usually presents the question of whole-form storage versus morphological structure as a pair of exclusive options. This follows from the traditional separation of lexicon and grammar (§1.7.3). However a constructional approach makes no such separation, and allows that Murrinhpatha stem forms may be stored as whole units, with morphological structure included in their representations. Such an approach is exemplified in (10–12). The stem form has constituency structure for inner stem, subject agreement and tense elements.[37] Inner stem alternation is represented by a diacritic. Thus where stem forms share formative elements, such as the /-m/ suffix or the LOW inner stem vowel alternation, these patterns are captured in their representations.

(10) $[_{SUBJ}[[ɲi-[la^{DEF}]_{INNER}-m]_{TNS}]]_{VS}$ → wipe.1SG.NFUT
(11) $[_{SUBJ}[[wu-[ɾa^{LOW}]_{INNER}-n]_{TNS}]]_{VS}$ → go.3SG.NFUT
(12) $[_{SUBJ}[[[da^{APIC}]_{INNER}]_{TNS}]]_{VS}$ → AFFECT.2SG.IRR

These representations, combining whole-form storage with morphological structure, capture some of the salient facts we have noted about the verb stems. Murrinhpatha verb stems have highly unpredictable inflectional exponence, and the cross-linguistic comparison above confirms that this unpredictability is typologically unusual (§5.5). However this is offset by the closed-class nature of the system, which although it is reasonably large (1638 forms), would seem to allow whole-form storage as a means of mitigating unpredictability. It is logically possible that Murrinhpatha speakers store only inner stem elements, and derive inflected stem forms via affixation and alternation processes specified in the lexical entry. But the intricacy of these derivational processes would be highly inefficient, especially for those inflectional patterns that apply to only a few stems. Some degree of whole storage seems all but inevitable, and this is captured by the representations above.

On the other hand, the entire set of 1638 inflected stem forms would require a very large amount of linguistic input to be completely memorised. Inflected forms have a Zipfian distribution in discourse (J. P. Blevins, Milin, & Ramscar, 2017), which means that while some forms occur frequently, others are vanishingly rare, and large paradigms require many millions of words to provide complete cover-

---

[37] I tentatively propose a more closely nested constituency for inner stem and tense, with subject agreement outside these, on the basis of inner stem alternations patterning more often with tense than with subject.

age (Muradoglu, 2018). For Murrinhpatha verb stems, this means that speakers must occasionally parse or produce forms that they have not encountered before, or encountered only a handful of times. Paradigmatic relations provide the implicational structure for dealing with this situation (Ackerman et al., 2009), but if whole-forms were stored without the internal constituent structure that instantiates paradigmatic relations, this would not be possible. Therefore some degree of stem-internal structure seems *a priori* necessary, though we can only guess at how the use of this structure balances out with whole-form storage. The data from variation and change in inflectional exponence (§5.6) provides some empirical evidence for implicational processes using stem-internal structure, because it shows the innovation and spread of variants that are clearly based on paradigmatic analogies, rather than purely phonological processes. The representations above capture these requirements for stem-internal morphological structure.

5.8 Summary

In this chapter we have explored a highly unpredictable system of inflectional morphology applied to finite verb stems. In the next chapter we will explore morphology that contrasts with this in having predictable phonological forms, which attach to verb stem or nominal hosts irrespective of the particular lexeme. These grammatical suffixes are attached outside of semi-regular inflectional formatives. Finite verb stems will thus continue to feature in the next chapter, as their inflected forms in turn host grammatical suffixes. Finite verb stems will also feature in a later chapter on compound verbs (§8), where their semantic characteristics and their rather ambiguous identity as 'lexical' elements will come to the fore.

6 Predicate inflectional suffixes

6.1 Introduction

Murrinhpatha has a range of suffixes that specify grammatical categories associated with a predicate, in particular its tense, aspectual and modal category, and the person, number and gender categories of its arguments. We must refer to these as 'predicate' inflections rather than verb or noun inflections, since they can be suffixed to either verb stems or nominals. However, the predicating lexeme that hosts these suffixes is much more commonly a verb, and therefore the main discussion of predicational suffixes in this chapter uses verbs as examples.

The grammatical categories encoded by predicational suffixes are integrated with the categories encoded by finite verb stem inflection, described in the last chapter. Finite verb stem inflection encodes more general categories of number and tense, while predicational morphs provide more specificity. The two types are strikingly different in their form–meaning relations. The 'semi-regular formatives' described in the last chapter are highly unpredictable in their phonological form, determined by the particular verb stem lexeme to which they attach. But the suffixes described in this chapter involve neat chunks of sound–meaning correspondence that are totally independent of lexical host.

Predicate inflectional suffixes form two distinct layers as defined by a prosodic criterion: some form a prosodic word (PWord, ω) together with their host, while others adjoin outside of the host PWord (cf. Anderson, 2005, p. 46; Selkirk, 1996). The boundary between the two layers plays a significant role in verb compounding, where a coverb attaches at the point that forms the prosodically internal/external boundary on the associated simple verb (1, coverb underlined). Compound verbs appear in many of the examples in this chapter, but discussion of compounding is deferred until Chapter §8.

Internal and external predicational morphs
(1) ŋeram-nu-ŋku-<u>bat̪</u>-nime-ŋibim
watch.RR.1PL.NFUT-RR-PAUC.OBJ-<u>look</u>-PAUC.M-STAND.IMPF
we (pauc, masc) are looking at each other   (LP, 2015-06-27_AM-02)

The two layers of predicate suffixes have somewhat different morphological structure. The internal layer is characterised by dependencies between suffixes, and by fixed ordering among those suffixes. By contrast, the outer layer has fewer dependencies among suffixes, and has considerable flexibility of suffix sequencing. Section §6.2 describes the prosodically internal layer of predicational morphs, and §6.3 the external layer. Section §6.4 provides an explicit schematic formulation of the overall verb structure. Section §6.5 describes the binding of inflection suffixes to nominals when a clause has a nominal, rather than a verbal, predicate.

6.2 The prosodically internal layer

The internal layer of predicate inflectional suffixes encodes pronominal arguments of the predicate, and number categories of these arguments. There are various dependencies in the ways that pronominal arguments and number markers combine. The general principles are (a) only one pronominal argument suffix can appear; and (b) prosodically internal number markers may only be adjacent to the pronominal argument they co-index, though further number specification can occur in the external layer. I summarise the system of pronominal and number suffixes in Figure 6.1, which shows morphotactic attachments from left to right, with arrows indicating possible attachments. Examples (2–4) illustrate some possible combinations.

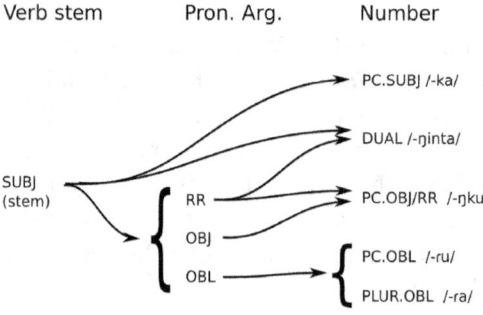

Figure 6.1: Verb stem and its internal predicate suffixes.

(2) [pumpan-ka]ω
    go.3PL.NFUT-PC.SUBJ
    they (pauc.) are going

(3) [pumem-nu-ŋku]ω
    say.RR.3PL.NFUT-RR-PC.RR
    they (pauc.) said to each other

(4) [pumam-na-ra]_ω
    say.3PL.NFUT-2PL.OBL-OBL.PLUR
    they (pl.) said to you (pl.)

As shown in Figure 6.1, the finite verb stem encodes the first pronominal argument, SUBJ, while internal suffixes may encode one (and only one) additional OBJ or OBL argument, or the reflexive/reciprocal (RR) 'pseudo-argument', which is unspecified for person and number, but indicates that the subject of the verb is also the object. Pronominal argument suffixes occur before number suffixes, and prevent the prosodically internal hosting of any number suffix that co-indexes the SUBJ of the verb stem. As noted above, the general principle is that number suffixes can be prosodically internal only if they are adjacent to their co-indexed pronominal. Thus where an OBJ/OBL/RR suffix appears, number specification of the SUBJ must appear in the external layer.

Figure 6.1 also indicates that different pronominal argument types select different number suffixes (e.g. PC.OBJ selects /-ŋku/, but PC.SUBJ selects /-ka/). Murrinhpatha predicational morphology has a cascading system of number specification: PL ('broad plural') is an under-specified plural that can be further specified as either PLUR ('specific plural') or PC ('broad paucal'); but PC in turn may be further specified with DUAL or PAUC ('specific paucal'). Cascading specification may require a series of two suffixes for a pronominal argument (e.g. /-wun-ŋku-ŋintha/ 3PL.OBJ-PC.OBJ-DUAL.F), but as shown in the figure, only the number suffix that is adjacent to the argument can be in the prosodically internal layer. The intricacies of this system are further explained in the sections below.

The prosodic integration of internal suffixes is shown by penultimate accent positioning, and the lack of bimoraic lengthening if the host is an open monosyllable (5–11).

(5) [ná-ŋa]_ω
    say.2SG.IRR-1SG.OBL
    tell me   (GbM, 2011-08-21_Ep)

(6) [mam-wí-ra]_ω
    say.3SG.NFUT-3PL.OBL-PLUR.OBL
    he told them   (ThN, 2008-09-25)

(7) [mam-ŋíṉta]_ω
    say.3SG.NFUT-DUAL.F
    they (dual) said

(8) [paṉám-ka]_ω -ŋime
    be.3pL.NFUT-PC.SUBJ-PAUC.F
    they (paucal, fem) are   (LTch, 2011-07-30)

(9) [[páṭa]ω]φ [[wuriní-ŋe]ω-ða]φ
     good   go.3SG.PST-3SG.F.OBL-PST
     he was good to her   (MnMn, 2011-07-30)

(10) [ŋunuŋám-ka]ω
     use.feet.3SG.NFUT-PC.SUBJ
     they (pauc) are going

(11) [mem-ŋiṉṭá-nu]ω
     say.3SG.RR.NFUT-DUAL.F-RR
     they (dual) said to each other

Sub-sections below describe the details of argument and number encoding in the internal layer. However we first require an outline of the grammatical number categories, which are complicated by the fact that they have different degrees of specificity in different domains.

6.2.1 Pronominal number categories

Murrinhpatha has an unusually large set of pronominal number categories, adding both dual and paucal to the standard singular/plural. Number marking uses a complex system of distributed exponence, with some morphological elements marking broader categories, and others adding specificity. Grammatical number is marked only on pronominals, and never on other nominal arguments. The analysis here draws on previous analyses of Murrinhpatha grammatical number (Blythe, 2009, p. 129ff.; Nordlinger, 2015), but reconfigures the feature analysis to make more extensive use of broad or 'underspecified' category labels.

We have seen in the previous chapter (§5.2.2) that in finite verb stem inflection, the IRR, PST, and PSTIRR tenses have a three-way number distinction, SG/PC/PLUR, while the NFUT tense collapses PC and PLUR into a more general PL category, giving a two-way SG/PL distinction. OBJ and OBL pronominal suffixes also have the SG/PL distinction, while free pronoun stems have the three-way number distinction, but in addition have a distinct 'dual sibling' category, giving a four-way SG/PC/PLUR/DUAL.SIBL (Street, 1987). Throughout the system, however, the distinctions unspecified in broad categories can nonetheless be specified using number suffixes, in either the internal or external layer. To neatly gloss this system of varying specificity, we require special abbreviations for our number categories. Table 6.1 illustrates the glossing conventions, and shows the hierarchical relationships of specificity: PL is a broad category, containing both PLUR and PC.

Table 6.1: Labels for number categories with varying degrees of specificity.

SING	Singular	One exactly (for humans); animals and inanimates are usually marked SG for any number
PL	Plural (broad)	Any number greater than one
ᴸ PLUR	Plural (specific)	More specifically, greater than paucal
ᴸ PC	Paucal (broad)	Greater than one, but not as many as plural[40]
ᴸ PAUC	Paucal (specific)	More specifically, greater than two
ᴸ DUAL	Dual	Two exactly (who are not siblings, or not known to be)
ᴸ DUAL.SIBL	Dual siblings	Two classificatory, same-sex siblings

In turn, PC is a broad category containing PAUC, DUAL and DUAL.SIBL.[38] The DUAL.SIBL number category has not been attested for any other language, and reflects the intense cultural importance of classificatory siblinghood (§2.3), as reinforced through interactional norms (Blythe, 2013).[39]

Table 6.2 shows how the broader and more specific categories are encoded in different pronominal elements. OBJ and OBL pronominals collapse PLUR/PC into the broader PL category, and use a separate suffix to mark more specific number categories where applicable. The table also shows the number categories marked on finite verb stems, depending on tense, and on free pronouns. The free pronouns have a special form distinguishing DUAL.SIBL within the PC hyper-category, but only in third person. The third-person PC free pronouns are word stems but cannot appear independently, requiring a suffix to specify PAUC or DUAL category, e.g. /peni-ɲiṉṯa/ DUAL.FEM. Gender is specified as FEMININE or MASCULINE for some 3SG and 3PC forms, and FEM is a default category, used for groups of mixed gender.

Figure 6.2 illustrates schematically how number becomes increasingly specified with the use of suffixes both internal and external. Arrows indicate

---

[38] Blythe (2009) proposes the same PC number category, but labels it 'daucal', as a portmanteau of 'DUAL' and 'paucal'. Nordlinger (2015) has a slightly different analysis that posits this as a dual category, in view of its use for encoding dual siblings when no number suffix is present.

[39] Paucal, same-sex classificatory siblings are generally encoded as PLUR category. Their only distinction from PLUR is as OBJ pronominals, where unlike PLUR number they induce the PC.OBJ suffix (Blythe, 2009, p. 129ff.). In practice the paucal sibling category is very rare.

[40] The distinction between PC and PLURAL number is arguably not so much about numerical quantity, as about recognisable reference [PC] versus non-referentiality or non-specificity [PLUR] (Blythe, 2009, p. 123).

Table 6.2: Murrinhpatha grammatical number distinctions on pronominal suffixes, finite verb stems and free pronouns (Street, 1987, p. 99; Walsh, 1976, pp. 205–209) † Portions in parenthesis are deleted post-vocalically.

		Object suffix	Oblique suffix	Verb stem (stand.NFUT)		Verb stem (stand.PST)	Free pronoun
SING	1	-ŋi	-ŋa	ŋarim		ŋiri	ŋaj
	2	-ṉi	-mpa	ṯirim		ṯiri	niṉi
	3	-ø	-ṉe FEM	pirim		piri	niɣunu FEM
			-na MASC				nukunu MASC
INCL	1/2	-ṉi	-ṉe	ṯirim		ṯiri	neki
PL	1	-ŋan	-ŋa	ŋibim	PLUR	ŋi	ŋanki
	2	-nan	-na	nibim		ni	nanki
	3	-(wu)n †	-(wi)	pibim		pi	piɣunu
					PC 1	ŋe	ŋanku
					2	ne	nanku
					3	pe PAUC,DUAL	peni- (FEM)
							peɻe- (MASC)
						DUAL.SIBL	piɣuna

morphotactic combinations from left to right, while dashed lines indicate the final number category output of each morphotactic combination. As explained below, there are distinct internal/external encoding options for dual number in subject pronominals. The internal number suffixes are further discussed in subsections below (§6.2.2, §6.2.4), while the external suffixes are discussed in the next section (§6.3). Examples (12–22) provide selected illustrations of the system.

    Verb stem subject, NFUT
(12) [kanam-ŋiṉṯa]_ω
    be.3SG.NFUT-DUAL.F
    they are (dual, fem)
(13) [paŋam-ka]_ω-ŋime
    be.3PL.NFUT-PC.SUBJ-PAUC.F
    they are (pauc, fem)

    Verb stem subject, IRR
(14) [kaŋe]_ω-ŋime
    be.3PC.IRR-PAUC.F
    they will be (pauc, fem)

6.2 The prosodically internal layer — 143

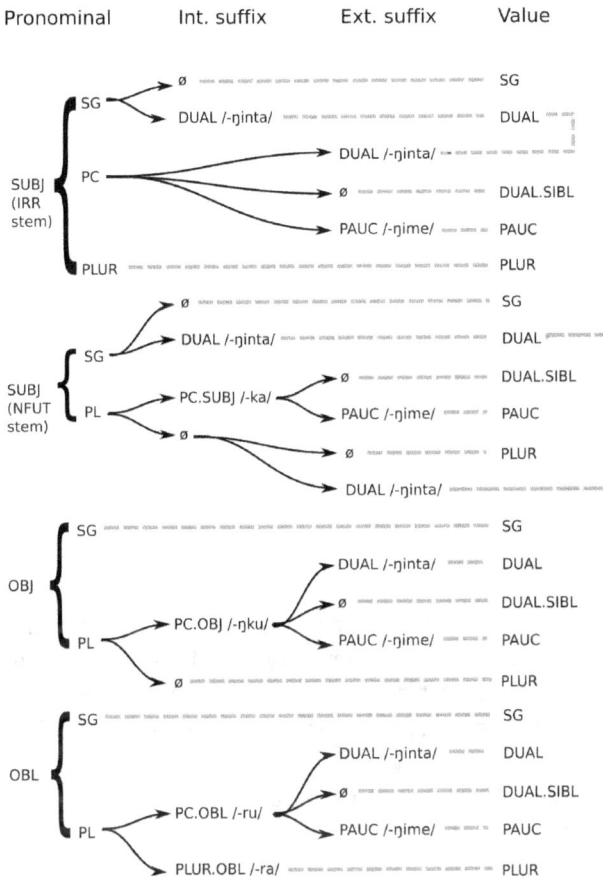

Figure 6.2: Number category specification by pronominals and number suffixes.

(15) [kaɲi]ω
be.3PLUR.IRR
they will be (plur, fem)

Object suffix PL
(16) [pan-wun-bat]ω
SLASH.3SG.NFUT-3PL.OBJ-hit
she hit them (plur)
(17) [pan-wun-ŋku-bat]ω-ɲime
SLASH.3SG.NFUT-3PL.OBJ-PC.OBJ-hit-PAUC.F
she hit them (pauc, fem)

Oblique suffix PL
(18) [mam-wi-ɾa]_ω
say.3SG.NFUT-3PL.OBL-PLUR.OBL
she said to them (plural)
(19) [mam-wi-ɾu]_ω-niṉṯa
say.3SG.NFUT-3PL.OBL-PC.OBL-DUAL.M
she said to them (dual, masc)
(20) [mam-wi-ɾu]_ω
say.3SG.NFUT-3PL.OBL-PC.OBL
she said to them (dual sibling)

Free pronoun
(21) [ŋanku]_ω
we/us (dual sibling)
(22) [ŋanku-ɲime]_ω
we/us (paucal, fem)

Younger speakers collapse one of the pronominal number distinctions, PLUR. OBL vs PC.OBL, neutralising it to the broad PL category. It is the erstwhile PLUR form that is used for the neutralised category (23), which fits with the general pattern of larger-number categories being less marked. The example also illustrates a vowel variant in the pronominal system: syllables /wi, pi/ often have a back vowel, i.e. /wu, pu/, especially for younger speakers.[41]

Youth speech
(23) muriṉ-[ɲini=maṯa]_ω   [mam-wu-ɾa]_ω-ɲime
LANG-ANAPH=EMPH   say.1SG.NFUT-3PL.OBL-PL.OBL-PAUC.F
that's just what I told them   (SL [b. 1964], 2012-06-12)

6.2.2 Single-argument verbs

Verbs with a single argument, i.e. the subject encoded in the verb stem, host only the number suffixes /-ka/ PC.SUBJ and /-ɲiṉṯa/ DUAL in the internal layer. Transitive verbs are also single-argument in terms of verb morphology if they have a 3SG object, since this particular person/number category is unmarked on the verb. As noted above, non-human referents are generally encoded as 3SG, no matter their

---

[41] Other variable vowels are /niyunu~nuyunu/ 3SG.FEM free pronoun, and /-neme~-name~-nime/ PAUC.MASC external suffix.

actual number, which contributes to a high proportion of transitive verbs lacking any object morphology.

A 'broad-paucal' subject marker /-ka/ PC.SUBJ is added in the internal layer as required if the verb is of the underspecified PL category (24, 25).⁴² This occurs only for NFUT tense verb stems, while other tenses encode PC in the stem (26, 27).⁴³

(24) [puḍḍam-<u>ka</u>-wuḷ]_ω-<u>ɲime</u>
 IMPEL.RR.3PL.NFUT-<u>PC.SUBJ</u>-return-<u>PAUC.F</u>
 they (paucal, fem) returned

(25) [puḍḍam-<u>ka</u>-wuḷ]_ω
 IMPEL.RR.3PL.NFUT-<u>PC.SUBJ</u>-return
 they (dual siblings) returned (HLK, 1997_MSC-1007)

(26) peːɲimeða
 [pe]_ω-ɲime-ða
 say.<u>3PC.PST</u>-PAUC.F
 they (paucal, fem) said

(27) [kiɻa]_ω-nu-neme
 stand.<u>3PC.IRR</u>-FUT-PAUC.M
 they (pauc, masc) will stand

Dual subject single-argument verbs host /-ɲiṉta/ DUAL.F and /-niṉta/ DUAL.M in the internal layer (for convenience I refer to both collectively as /-ɲiṉta/ DUAL, see details below). Unexpectedly this construct uses the SG subject category on the verb stem, breaking with the general pattern of larger number categories being specified by smaller ones (28). Other appearances of DUAL, either in the external suffix layer of predicates, or suffixed to free pronouns, combine with the broad PL and PC number categories (29, 30). When an external IMPF suffix is used, it agrees with the stem in subject number (Nordlinger, 2015), despite this being the 'wrong' number category for dual subject (31).

---

42 This suffix could also be posited as */-ŋka/ PC.SUBJ. Because it always appears following a nasal, the /ŋ/ in */-ŋka/ would never actually be realised, being deleted by morpho-phonological juncture rules (§4.4). The form */-ŋka/ fits better the shape of other internal bound morphs /-ŋku/ PC.OBJ, /-ŋka/ 'eye', /-mpa/ 2SG.OBL. However the /-ka/ form seems more likely given the apparent historical lenition process described in the next footnote.

43 The origin of the PC inflectional category in IRR, PST and PSTIRR tense is probably a historical reduction of /-ka/ PC.SUBJ. Verbs in these tenses all end in vowels, creating the phonological context for morph-initial voiceless obstruent lenition (§4.5.1). This would leave a vowel sequence /Va/, which by vowel degemination would lead to reductions such as /aa → a/ and /ia → e/. These are precisely the vowels we find in synchronic PC verb forms.

(28) [mam-ŋiṉṯa]_ω
say.3SG.NFUT-DUAL.F
they (dual, fem) said

(29) [pumam-ŋa]_ω-ŋiṉṯa
say.3PL.NFUT-1SG.OBL-DUAL.F
they (dual, fem) said to me

(30) [ŋanku-ŋiṉṯa]_ω
1PC-DUAL.M
we two men

(31) [mem-niṉṯa-ðaðap]_ω-dim
use.hands.RR.3SG.NFUT-DUAL-touch.PLUR-SIT.3SG.IMPF
they (dual, masc) are touching each other's hands   (JeTu, 2015-06-27_AM)

The use of a SG category for dual referents goes against the grain of the Murrinhpatha pronominal number system, where under-specification generally uses greater number categories to encompass smaller ones. Interestingly, this aberrant form of cumulative number specification, SG + DUAL = 'dual', occurs in a prosodically internal construct. Prosodically external verb constructs, by contrast, follow the more general formula PC + DUAL = 'dual' (Nordlinger & Mansfield, 2015). There is a general expectation that prosodically internal constructs should be less semantically compositional than prosodically external constructs (e.g. Baker & Harvey, 2003), however in this case we see a further type of non-compositionality, in morphosyntactic category marking rather than lexical semantics.

6.2.3 Reflexive/reciprocal valency

Reflexive/reciprocal (RR) valency is marked in the internal layer for transitive verbs, though it does not occur with predicating nominals (Nordlinger, n.d., 2011b). The valency change is obligatorily marked on verb stems, which have unpredictable alternative forms for RR valency (§5.4), and by the optional addition of an internal suffix /-nu ~ -ni/ (32–34). This suffix patterns with pronominal argument suffixes by occupying the same structural position, and combining with one of the same number suffixes as OBJ pronominals (see below). It can be thought of as encoding a special type of OBJ argument, which is co-indexed with the SUBJ argument. However /-nu ~ -ni/ RR is at best a 'pseudo-pronominal', since it does not encode person/number distinctions like the other pronominal suffixes.

(32) [dirim-nu-baṯ]_ω-dim
watch.RR.3SG.NFUT-RR-look-SIT.IMPF
he's looking at himself   (JeTu, 2015-06-27_AM)

(33) [[muriɲ]ω]φ   [[pumem-<u>nu</u>]ω-ŋime]φ
language   say.RR.3PL.NFUT-RR-PAUC.F
they (pauc fem) say to each other   (FxA, 2011-08-01_3-11)

(34) [[maŋe]ω]φ   [[mem-ma-ṉet]ω]φ
hand   use.hands.RR.3SG-hand-slice
he cut open his hand   (Nordlinger, n.d., p. 11)

For DUAL reciprocal verbs, the RR suffix combines with the DUAL suffix in either order within the internal layer (35, 36), though there is a strong preference for the DUAL-RR order. This is the only type of flexible morphotactic ordering in the internal layer, and it may be regarded as quite natural, since /-ŋiṉta/ DUAL in this construct modifies the number category of both the subject (encoded on the verb stem), and the reciprocal object (encoded in /-nu ~ -ni/), so that either may be considered an appropriate host. There are also a few instances attested with duplicate RR suffixes either side of DUAL (37), and as mentioned above, RR may also be absent (38).

(35) [[kik]ω]φ   [[mem-<u>niṉta-nu</u>]ω]φ
kick   do.RR.3SG.NFUT-<u>DUAL.M-RR</u>
they (dual masc) kicked each other   (ClW, 2015-07-13_02)

(36) [dirim-<u>ni-niṉta</u>-baṯ]ω
watch.RR.3SG.NFUT-<u>RR-DUAL.M</u>-look-SIT.IMPF
two people are looking at each other   (MN, 2015-07-06_AM2)

(37) [dirim-<u>ni-niṉta-nu</u>-ŋke]ω-waḍa
watch.RR.3SG.NFUT-<u>RR-DUAL.F-RR</u>-be.jealous-SEQ
the man and the woman became jealous of each other
(ElCu, 2004-10-16_02)

(38) [mem-niṉta-ṯaðap]ω-dim
use.hands.RR.3SG.NFUT-DUAL.M-touch.PLUR-SIT.IMPF
two people are touching each other   (JeTu, 2015-06-27_AM)

For PC reciprocal verbs, the /-ŋku/ PC.OBJ/RR suffix is optionally appended to RR within the internal layer (39, 40). For DUAL number there is one suffix form, /-ŋiṉta/ DUAL, which applies to all argument types, and can modify either the stem SUBJ argument or the suffixed RR argument. But for PC number there are distinct suffixes for distinct arguments. Thus in reciprocal verbs, the /-ka/ PC.SUBJ suffix appears only if the /-nu ~ -ni/ RR suffix is omitted, allowing /-ka/ to appear adjacent to the stem subject (41). If the RR suffix is included, then only the PC.OBJ/RR suffix can modify it (as in 39), while /-ka/ PC.SUBJ becomes ungrammatical because it is not of the right argument type to modify RR, and cannot modify stem SUBJ because the presence of the RR suffix prevents its adjacency to its co-indexed argument (42). We will see below that /-ninta/ DUAL, when blocked in from the internal layer by the non-adjacency principle, simply appears instead in the external layer. But /-ka/ PC.SUBJ does not have this flexibility, and if it is blocked from the internal layer, it does not appear at all.

(39) [ŋeram-nu-ŋku-baṯ]ω-nime-ŋibim
watch.1PL.RR.NFUT-RR-PAUC.RR-hold-PAUC.M-stand.IMPF
we (pauc, masc) are looking at each other   (LP, 2015-06-27_AM-02)

(40) [pumem-nu]ω-ŋime
say.3PL.NFUT-RR-PAUC.F
they (pauc, fem) said to themselves

(41) [pumem-ka-ṯe-bije]ω
do.RR.3PL.NFUT-PC.SUBJ-ear-unaware
they are unaware of the news   (Street 2012: -yebiye)

(42) *[pumem-nu-ka]ω-ŋime
say.3PL.NFUT-RR-PC.SUBJ-PAUC.F
they (pauc, fem) said to themselves

6.2.4 Object and oblique arguments

Any verb can potentially host an oblique (OBL) pronominal suffix, as a means of adding a non-core argument, i.e. one that is not selected for by the verb (43, 44). Some transfer verbs such as 'give' require an OBL argument to encode the recipient (45). Object (OBJ) pronominals encode the patient arguments that are inherent to transitive verbs (46). However, as mentioned above OBJ is not marked on all transitive verbs, as 3SG object is unmarked in verb morphology (47) (Nordlinger, 2011b; Street, 1987, p. 99; Walsh, 1976, p. 205ff.).

(43) [ŋem-mpa-biḻ-biḻ]ω-ŋanam
sit.1SG.NFUT-2SG.OBL-open.eyes-PLUR-BE.IMPF
I'm watching, waiting for you

(44) [mam-wi-ra]ω
say.3SG.NFUT-3PL.OBL-PLUR.OBL
she said to them (plural)

(45) [dam-na-mut]ω
pierce.3SG.NFUT-3SG.M.OBL-give
she gave it to him

(46) [pan-ɲi-bat]ω
SLASH.3SG.NFUT-1SG.OBJ-hit
she hit me

(47) [pan-bat]ω
SLASH.3SG.NFUT-hit
she hit (him / her / it)

Also syntactically transitive is a set of object-experiencer verbs, which are all compound verbs (Walsh, 1987). They are based on either transitive or RR verb stem bases, including /ma/ 'use hands', /a/ PIERCE, /e/ PIERCE.RR and /bu/ LOWER.RR. Object-experiencer verbs have fixed 3SG for the subject inflection of the verb stem, which is not referential but a 'dummy subject', while the referential participant is encoded with OBJ (48–50). Object experiencer verbs are therefore somewhat akin to nominal predicates, which use the OBJ series to mark their one-place predicates (§6.5.2).

(48) [dem-ɲi-maḍa-ɹur]ω
PIERCE.RR.3SG.NFUT-1SG.OBJ-belly-hot
I'm angry   (Street 2012, -*mardarurr*)

(49) [mam-ɲi-ŋka-wul]ω
use.hands-3SG.NFUT-2SG.OBJ-eye-submerge
you have a headache

(50) [bam-ɲi-ɹalal]ω
LOWER.RR.3SG.NFUT-1SG.OBJ-cold
I'm cold   (Street 2012, -*ralal*)

OBJ pronominal suffixes also appear where a transitive verb is derived from an intransitive using an applicative (51) (§8.5) (Nordlinger, 2011a).

(51) [[manaŋka]ω   [ŋara]ω]φ   [[pi-ɲi-ma-ʈe-pup]ω]φ
     NEG   REL   hear.3PL.IRR-2SG.OBJ-HAND.APPL-ear-sit
     they can't understand you   (SL, 2011-09-21)

The verb can only host one pronominal suffix, meaning that OBJ and OBL cannot both be marked. In many cases this is not a problem, since 3SG.OBJ is unmarked anyway, leaving room for an OBL suffix (52). When OBJ has any other person/number value, competition for the pronominal suffixal position arises (Nordlinger, 2011b, p. 710). Walsh (1976, p. 208) reports that the OBJ wins out in such situations (53). However Forshaw (*p.c.*) reports that there is free variation in encoding OBJ or OBL, but not both (54a,b).

(52) [ma-mpa-beṭi]_ω-nu
use.hand.1SG.IRR-2SG.OBL-accompany-FUT
I'll take him home for you   (Nordlinger, 2011b, p. 710)

(53) ŋaj-ɹe   ṉiṉi   ŋu-ṉi-bat-nu   nukunu-nu
1SG-AG   2SG   SLASH.1SG.IRR-2SG.OBJ-hit-FUT 3SG-DAT
I'll hit you for him   (Walsh 1976, p. 208)

(54a) ŋaj=waḍa   ma-ṉi-beṭi-nu   nukunu-nu
1SG=SEQ   use.hand.1SG.IRR-2SG.OBJ-accompany-FUT   3SG.DAT
I will take you for him   (Forshaw, p.c.)

(54b) ŋaj=waḍa   ma-ṉa-beṭi-nu   nukunu-nu
1SG=SEQ   use.hand.1SG.IRR-3SG.OBL-accompany-FUT   3SG.DAT
I will take you for him   (Forshaw, p.c.)

As mentioned above, OBJ and OBL pronominal suffixes mark a broad SG/PL number distinction, and have the number categories further specified by additional suffixes. In the internal layer these suffixes take argument-specific forms. OBL hosts /-ɾa/ to specify PLUR, and /-ɾu/ to specify PC (55, 56). OBJ hosts /-ŋku/ to specify PC, and a lack of any number suffix defaulting to PLUR (57–59). With the adjacency principle limiting the internal layer to a single number suffix, cascading number specificity can only get as far as 'broad paucal' PC for OBJ and OBL arguments. Further specification of the sub-categories PAUC and DUAL require prosodically external suffixes, as in (58, 59), to be further described below.

(55) [mam-wi-ɾa]_ω
say.3SG.NFUT-3PL.OBL-PLUR.OBL
he said to them (plur)

(56) [mam-wi-ɾu]_ω-ŋime
say.3SG.NFUT-3PL.OBL-PC.OBL-PAUC.F
he said to them (pauc)

(57) [pan-ṉan-bat]_ω
SLASH.3SG.NFUT-1PL.OBJ-hit
she hit us (plur)

(58) panŋankubatŋime[44]
[pan-ṉan-ŋku-bat]_ω-ŋime
SLASH.3SG.NFUT-1PL.OBJ-PC.OBJ-hit-PAUC.F
she hit us (paucal, female)

---

[44] Note that /-ŋku/ follows a coda consonant in most instances, which leads to the deletion of /ŋ/ according to a general syllabification constraint (§4.4.4). The full form of the suffix is only apparent in combination with /-nu/ RR.

(59) panŋankubatŋiṉṯa
 [pan-<u>nan-ŋku</u>-bat]ω-ŋiṉṯa
 SLASH.3SG.NFUT-<u>1PL.OBJ-PC.OBJ</u>-hit-DUAL.F
 she hit us (dual, female)

We have now seen that /-ŋiṉṯa/ DUAL can appear in both internal and external prosodic layers. It is internal when it combines with stem subject or RR suffix, and is adjacent to its co-indexed argument. But with OBJ or OBL suffixes it cannot be adjacent to a stem subject (due to intervention of the pronominal), or to a co-indexed pronominal argument, since these require PC suffixes /-ŋku, -ru/ before a DUAL suffix can further specify number category. This alternation between prosodically internal and external positions for /-ŋiṉṯa/ DUAL plays a special role as evidence for prosodic positioning of compounded coverbs, which is one of Murrinhpatha's more typologically unusual features (§8.7).

6.2.5 Ethical datives

A few examples are attested where a third pronominal suffix series appears. These are 'ethical dative' (DAT) arguments (Blythe, 2010a). The complete paradigm of such pronominals is not attested, though Blythe discusses some possible reconstructions. Equivalent pronominal series are found in Western Daly (Green, 1989) and in Ngan'gi (Reid, 1990, p. 134).

Ethical datives appear only occasionally in contemporary speech, but were documented in a partial description of Murrinhpatha produced in the early mission period (Flynn, 1950). Like other predicational suffixes they can attach to both verbs and nominals (60–62). Only the 3SG.F and 3SG.M forms are attested in contemporary speech, and these are homophonous with DUAL.F and DUAL.M (*modulo* some vowel variation). DAT may be prosodically internal or external, and from the limited attestations we cannot establish whether there is some grammatical determinant of positioning. This parallels the alternate internal/external positioning of DUAL, for which we have established the principle of positioning based on adjacency to co-indexed argument. Blythe (2010) hypothesises that DUAL is in fact a historical reanalysis of the 3SG.DAT pronominal.

(60) naṉṯi-[buy-<u>wiṉṯu</u>-puɾkpuɾk]ω-nu-niṉṯa
 THING-LOWER.RR.3SG.IRR-<u>3PC.DAT</u>-break.PLUR-FUT-DUAL.M
 the thing belonging to them (two males) will break
 (Flynn, 1950, p. b:6, cited in Blythe 2010a)

(61) [ŋam-ṭe-kum]_ω-**nuṉṯa**
    SLASH.1SG.NFUT-ear-forget-3SG.M.DAT⁴⁵
    I forgot him   (ClDu, 2016-07-10_07)
(62) [kaḓu-[paṭa-**ninṯa**]_ω]_φ   [ṉini]_ω-ju]_φ
    PERS-good-3SG.M.DAT   ANAPH-CLS
    he's a good person   (KaDo, 2015-07-21)

6.2.6 Verb stems and valency

We may attempt to divide Murrinhpatha verb stems into intransitives that never take OBJ (either as simple verbs, or in any of their compounds), transitives that do take OBJ (in all their compounds), and reciprocal/reflexives that are lexically related to transitives but take RR rather than OBJ (§5.4). However on this basis the verb stems /a/ PIERCE /nu/ 'use feet' would be classed as ambitransitive, as they take OBJ in some lexical compounds but only OBL in others.⁴⁶ In Table 6.3 I present an approximate classification of the finite verb stems according to transitivity – note however that the transitive class here does not include finite verb stems used for applicative transitivity, nor object-experiencer transitivity. A similar table is provided by Seiss (2013), though it does not identify exactly the same set of verb stems. Further research on this topic is deferred to a study of Murrinhpatha syntax.

Based on this tentative valency categorisation, we may note a peculiarity of the Murrinhpatha finite verb stems. Some intransitive stems occur as independent verbs, and in compounds most intransitives maintain their lexical semantics. Transitive stems and their RR alternates, on the other hand, occur only in compound verbs, and account for all the most semantically opaque stems (§8.3).

6.3 The prosodically external layer

The prosodically external layer of predicate suffixes encodes morphosyntactic categories of number (NUM), tense/modality (TENSE) and imperfective aspect (IMPF). The external layer may complete under-specified number marking established in the verb stem and the internal suffix layer, while the TENSE suffixes may further specify categories established in the verb stem, or in some cases produce

---

45 This form and its translation do not match Blythe's (2010a, p. 165) reconstructed paradigm. I elicited only this form in isolation, so my interpretation of number and gender may be unreliable.
46 E.g. dam-OBJ-ŋkaṟ 'show something to OBJ'; dam-OBL-mut 'give something to OBL'.

Table 6.3: Murrinhpatha verb stem transitivity classes.

Intransitive	/ri/ 'stand', /ni/ 'be', /ma/ 'do, say', /la/ 'eat', /i/ 'sit', /i/ 'lie', /mi/ 'look', /bi/ 'hear', /la/ 'wipe', /ø/ 'arrive', /n̪t̪a/ 'crouch', /n̪t̪a/ 'perch', /ru/ 'go', /n̪t̪i/ 'have'
Transitive	/ma/ 'use hands', /ŋa/ 'put together', /a/ 'use mouth', /na/ 'use fire', /ba/ AFFECT, /ra/ 'watch', /ɖu/ IMPEL, /mu/ COERCE, /ŋu/ 'pull', /i/ SLASH, /bu/ LOWER
Reflexive / reciprocal	/li/ 'wipe RR', /ri/ 'watch RR', /ɖi/ IMPEL.RR, /me/ 'do RR', /me/ 'use hands RR', /be/ AFFECT.RR, /buj/ LOWER.RR, /e/ 'use mouth RR', /j/ SLASH.RR, /ŋu/ 'pull RR', /e/ PIERCE.RR
?Ambitransitive	/a/ PIERCE, /nu/ 'use feet'

redundant double-marking of tense categories. One or two adverbial enclitics may also appear in the external layer, though these are addressed in the next chapter since they attach not just to verbs but also at the right edge of any prosodic phrase.

As mentioned above, the external suffixes, compared to the internal layer, have fewer dependencies and more flexible sequencing. Intricate argument-number relations as described in the previous section do not occur in the external layer. The external suffix classes are:

- Paucal and dual number (NUM: PAUC, DUAL)
- Tense/modality (TENSE)
- Imperfective (IMPF)

Positioned amongst these is one clitic class:

- Adverbial (ADV)

6.3.1 Paucal and dual number

PAUC and DUAL external suffixes add further specificity to number marking (NUM), for which broader categories are marked in the verb stem and its internal suffixes (§5.5, §6.2). We have already encountered the DUAL suffix, which can appear in the internal layer of predicational suffixes to mark the subject as dual, or in the external layer to mark any argument as dual. The external PAUC suffix also marks number for any argument, but it is an external-only suffix, quite distinct in form from the internal-layer markers PC.SUBJ, PC.OBJ, and PC.OBL. Both DUAL and PAUC have gendered forms, FEM/MASC, with the FEM category used for groups of mixed gender or unspecified gender. For convenience, most of the analysis in this book refers to the feminine (default) forms as a short-hand for forms of either gender:

	Fem. (default)	Masc. (marked)
PAUC	/-ŋime/ PAUC.F	/-neme/ PAUC.M
DUAL	/-ŋiṉṯa/ DUAL.F	/-niṉṯa/ DUAL.M

External NUM may specify number for any argument type, SUBJ, OBJ or OBL, as long as the argument has one of the broader categories PL or PC, both of which may require further specification to PAUC or DUAL categories. Thus if the subject is PL, external NUM may further specify the subject (63); if an object or oblique suffix is PC, external NUM further specifies this argument (64). However, verbs can host only one external NUM, even when there are two arguments that require further number specification. If both subject and a suffixal argument are underspecified, precedence is given to the suffixal argument, OBJ or OBL, leaving subject number underspecified (65, 66) (Nordlinger, 2015, p. 507). Notice that the external number suffix co-indexes the argument that is morphotactically closest (though usually non-adjacent) in this competition for specification.

(63) [pumam-ŋa]_ω-ŋiṉṯa
say.3PL.NFUT-1SG.OBL-DUAL.F
they (dual) said to me

(64) [mam-wi-ɾu]_ω-ŋime
say.3SG.NFUT-3PL.OBL-PC.OBL-DUAL.F
he said to them (pauc)

(65) [pumam-wi-ɾu]_ω-ŋime
say.3PL.NFUT-3PL.OBL-PC.OBL -PAUC.F
they (underspecified) said to them (pauc)

(66) [pumam-wiɾu]_ω-ŋiṉṯa
say.3PL.NFUT-3PC.OBL-DUAL.F
they (underspecified) said to them (dual)

External NUM suffixes can generally be characterised as 'obligatory'. Though only one such suffix can be hosted by the verb, if there is a PC participant then the NUM specification is almost always present. However there are a few exceptions, at least for younger speakers, where external NUM is occasionally omitted and free NPs are instead used to specify number (67, 68).

(67) ŋanku-nime   [ṉube-ŋkaḏu]_ω-ŋaḏi-ða
we.PC-PAUC.M   AFFECT.3PC.PST-see-be.IMPF-PST
we (paucal) could see it   (JaLa, 2013-01-23_VP)

(68) kaḏu-perkenku   [piɾim-wun-baṯ]_ω-dim
     PERS-two   watch.3PL.NFUT-3PC.OBJ-look-SIT.IMPF
     ŋaɾa   kaḏu-perkenkunime   paŋu
     LOC   PERS-three   there
     two people are looking at the three people there
     (McKg, 2015-07-07_Arg)

6.3.2 Tense/modality

Tense/modality (TENSE) are optional external verb suffixes, variably realised or unrealised on verbs where they might be expected. Like NUM, TENSE can add further specificity to a broad morphosyntactic category encoded in finite verb stem inflection (§5.2.2), though there are also TENSE suffixes that are uniquely selected by the stem tense category, and therefore are morphosyntactically redundant. This presumably facilitates their optional non-realisation. Table 6.4 lists the combinatoric possibilities of TENSE suffixes with finite verb stem tense categories (Nordlinger & Caudal, 2012).

Table 6.4: Verb tense categories and external tense suffixes.

Verb tense	TENSE suffix	Meaning
NFUT	*none*	Present (atelic) or Past (telic)
IRR	-nu	Future realis or irrealis
	-nukun[47]	Adversative
	-mani	Attemptive (cf. Rumsey, 2001)
	-ða	Past irrealis
PST	-ða	Past realis
PSTIRR	-ða	Past counter-factual

In addition to combinatorics, it is worth noting the distinction between /-nu/ FUT and /-ða/ PST, which have temporal meanings, and /-nukun/ ADVERSATIVE and /-mani/ ATTEMPTIVE, which have modal meanings. The latter are semantically more like the adverbial class of bound morphs (§7.5), but are here categorised with TENSE because their attachment to a verb precludes the attachment of any other TENSE suffix.

Analysis of tense and modality categories in Murrinhpatha would require several pages, and take us well outside the domain of word structure. Details can

---

[47] I have recorded one speaker (AMN, b. 1962), who consistently uses the form /-nukuj/ instead of /-nukun/. She is from the Wunh clan, who are generally identified as Murrinh Kura rather than Murrinh Patha speakers.

be found in Nordlinger and Caudal (2012), with a slightly different view proposed in Mansfield (2014b, p. 399ff.). The latter also quantifies the appearance/absence of TENSE in the speech of young men, calculating absence rates of 30–70% for /-nu/ FUT and /-ða/ PST, depending on speech style (pp. 374–387). An informal review of recordings from older speakers suggests that TENSE has similar levels of absence in their speech, though native speakers working on transcription tend to add the suffix in their careful speech renditions. In summary, in unmonitored speech TENSE only appears for about half the verbs where it is applicable.

TENSE as a general rule is attached to verbs, but there are very occasional instances where it attaches in duplicate to a verb as well as to a coverb or adverb preceding the verb. Most of these instances are temporal adverbs that attract a matching TENSE suffix (69, 70), but other adverbs or coverbs[48] are also able to host TENSE (71). However it should be stressed that, other than with temporal adverbials, there are only a couple of recorded instances of this construction.

(69) nakuḷ-nu   ŋi-ṭek-nu
     later-FUT   sit.1SG.IRR-defecate-FUT
     I'll go to the toilet later   (SbMa, 2013-01-24)

(70) kuŋiniɹe-ða   kaḍi-kumkum-ða
     yesterday-PST   be.3SG.PST-swim.PLUR-PST
     yesterday he went swimming   (JaLa, 2013-01-23)

(71) ṭara-nu   pi-ku-nu
     run-FUT   sit.3SG.FUT-run-FUT
     she's going to run   (ArMa, 2013-01-5)

6.3.3 Imperfective

A subset of finite verb stems have a secondary role, where rather than forming the base of a verb, they are appended among the external suffixes to encode imperfective aspect (IMPF). In this role they have been labelled 'serial verbs' (Caudal & Nordlinger, 2011; Nordlinger, 2010a), though they are more restrictive than other types of serial verb constructions (Aikhenvald, 2006; Baker & Harvey, 2010). IMPF secondary verb stems are not independent prosodic words, and their semantic character is more grammatical than lexical. In general, IMPF contributes imperfective viewpoint aspect to a predicate, giving it an unbounded, 'framing' function

---

[48] /ṭara/ 'run' has qualities of both a coverb and an adverb. It can in itself be a non-finite verbal predicate in the imperative /tara/ 'go on quickly!'; but it can also appear in the bound adverbial position (§7.5).

in the discourse (Smith, 1997, p. 62ff.). However in the case of telic verbs in NFUT tense, IMPF in addition contributes temporal semantics, encoding present reference for a verb that would otherwise be interpreted as past perfective (Nordlinger & Caudal, 2012).

The verbs that appear as IMPF suffixes are all intransitive verb stems that denote posture or movement (Table 6.5). They may all occur as simple verbs, i.e. without a compounded coverb (§8.2). They might therefore be referred to as 'compounded stems' rather than 'suffixes', since they are elsewhere independent lexical words. However I class them with suffixes since they are deeply grammaticalised in their IMPF role, mirroring the form of verb stems but losing both their prosodic constituency, and much of their lexico-semantic character. As IMPF suffixes they are also subject to connected speech reductions that do not apply to the associated finite verb stems (Mansfield, 2015c, p. 175).

Table 6.5: Verb stems used as IMPF suffix.

3SG.NFUT form	Gloss
/-dim/	SIT.IMPF
/-pirim/	STAND.IMPF
/-jibim/	LIE.IMPF
/-kanam/	BE.IMPF
/-pin̪tim/	PERCH.IMPF
/-wuran/	GO.IMPF
/-nuŋam/	USE.FEET.IMPF

The semantics of the verb stem deployed as IMPF sometimes contributes to the overall predicate of the verb to which it is attached (72), but in most cases is semantically bleached, contributing only imperfective aspect (73). The most frequently used, 'sit' and 'be', appear to be those most bleached of lexical content.

(72) kuɻa [mam-luluj]ω -<u>wuran</u>   ŋara   paljir
    water do.3SG.NFUT-turn.PLUR-<u>GO.IMPF</u>   LOC   hill
    (the river) winds among the hills   (SeDu, 2014-10-01_Pa1-D1)

(73) núŋamdim   kan̪iwad̪án̪u
    [núŋam]ω -<u>dim</u>   [kan̪i=wad̪a=wán̪u]ω
    use.feet.3SG.NFUT-<u>SIT.IMPF</u>   here=SEQ=TOWARDS
    now he's coming this way   (MiKu, 2011-08-21_3-1)

The tense category of IMPF always agrees with the tense of the verb stem. Person/number inflection generally also agrees with the finite verb stem, though with object-experiencer verbs (§6.2.4) it agrees variably with either the finite verb stem (which encodes a dummy subject), or OBJ (which references the experiencer) (74, 75) (Nordlinger, 2010a, p. 20).

(74) [dem-ni-ɻalal]ω-ŋuran
PIERCE.3SG.RR.NFUT-1SG.OBJ-thirst-GO.1SG.IMPF
I'm thirsty (Nordlinger, 2010a, p. 20)

(75) [mam-ni-ŋkawu]ω-dim
use.hands.3SG.NFUT-1SG.OBJ-head.ache-SIT.3SG.IMPF
I've got a headache (NoPe, 2013-01-21)

Prosodically external verb suffixes generally lack any prosodic prominence. However there are a couple of counter examples in which older speakers appear to produce secondary prominences in external suffixes. Interestingly, when one of these speakers (LTch, b. 1932) produces a prosodically independent IMPF, she adds the PC.SUBJ suffix /-ka/ if it is appropriate (76) (cf. Blythe, 2009, p. 134; Nordlinger, 2010a, p. 12). But when she pronounces IMPF as a prosodic adjunct (i.e. as a typical external suffix), it does not host the PC.SUBJ suffix (77). The occasional appearance of a prosodically independent, suffix-hosting IMPF may be the last remnant of what was previously a separate word.

(76) [pumam-wun-ŋkú-ta]ω-ninta-[pumpàn-ka]ω
use.hands.3PL.NFUT-3PL.OBJ-PC.OBJ-chase-DUAL.M-GO.IMPF-PC.SUBJ
they (pauc) are chasing two people (LCh, 2015-07-01_AM)

(77) [pumam-ɲí-jit]ω-name-pibim
use.hands.3PL.NFUT-1SG.OBJ-hold-PAUC.M-STAND.IMPF
they (pauc) are holding me (LCh, 2015-07-01_AM)

6.3.4 Adverbial clitics

Adverbial (ADV) clitics are attached at the right edge of any prosodic phrase in Murrinhpatha (§7.5), but when attaching to verbs they may take a non-final position among external suffixes (78). Both noun phrases and verbs can host two ADV suffixes on the same word (79–81).

(78) [mam-wun-ŋku-makat]ω=wada-ninta
hands.3SG.NFUT-3PL.OBJ-PC.OBJ-evade=SEQ-DUAL
now it got away from the two of them (MvM, 2011-09-13_ 3-11h)

(79) [pumpan-ŋkaḍur]_ω=waḍa=katu-ɲime
     [go.3PL.NFUT-depart]=SEQ=AWAY-PAUC.F
     then they set off   (LK, 2000-11-10)
(80) naṉṯi-maɣulkul   [kanam-ma-tkut]_ω=kama=waḍa
     THING-heart   be.3SG.NFUT-APPL-collect.PLUR=UNKNOWN=SEQ
     this heart might be pounding now   (MM, 2011-09-13_2-11)
(81) [diram-ŋalɲal]_ω=katu=wa-kanam   ku-weɟe=ju
     watch.3SG.NFUT-bark.PLUR=AWAY=SURP-BE.IMPF   ANIM-pawed.beast=CLS
     a dog is barking!   (MM, 2011-09-13_2-11)

There are not enough examples of double adverbials on verbs to determine principles of relative sequencing. However for noun phrases, where there is more extensive evidence, it has been shown that the same pair of adverbials can take alternate sequences (§7.5).

6.3.5 Variable sequencing

External suffixes show considerable variability in their morphotactic sequencing. Some speakers consistently use a particular sequence, though different speakers may use different sequences, and furthermore there are some who exhibit intra-speaker variation. Previous accounts of Murrinhpatha have posited a fixed sequence of external suffixes, -TENSE-NUM-ADV-IMPF (e.g. Blythe, 2009; Nordlinger, 2015; Walsh, 1976), following the sequence illustrated in Street's (1987) very detailed verb conjugation tables. Although this sequence certainly is attested in the data, it is only one among several variants.

The observed variation supports recent literature in which other cases of freely ordered affixes have been attested (Bickel et al., 2007; Haspelmath, 2011, p. 43). Variable suffix sequencing is problematic for some theories of linguistic structure, in which it is taken as axiomatic that morphological sequencing is fixed within the grammatical word (e.g. Anderson, 1992, p. 261; Dixon, 2002b, p. 19). However the nature of Murrinhpatha variation should be understood in a framework where I do not draw an essential distinction between affixes and clitics, but rather use these as terms of convenience (§1.7.2). The external suffixes also have some characteristics associated with the term 'clitic' (§7.7). Variable sequencing of 'clitics' is generally considered less exceptional (Anderson, 2005, pp. 77, 125; Spencer & Luis, 2012, pp. 58, 117ff.).

TENSE and NUM are the most frequent external bound morphs, and these can be attached in either relative order (82, 83). Different orders can be found even where the verb has exactly the same morphological elements (82a,b). Some speakers switch between different orders, even within a single passage of speech, as in (82a,c). Other speakers stick to one particular order. A quantitative study of these suffixes has shown that younger speakers favour -NUM-TENSE in comparison to older speakers who favour -TENSE-NUM (Mansfield, 2015c), though variation is found among speakers of all ages.

(82a) [puɲe-lili]_ω-ða-nime
 go.3PC.PST-walk-PST-PAUC
 they were walking   (FlA, 2013-07_AM)
(82b) [puɲe-lili]_ω-nime-ða
 go.3PC.PST-walk-PAUC-PST
 they were walking   (GP, 2013-07_AM)
(82c) [paḍe-lili]_ω-nime-ða
 be.3PC.PST-walk-PAUC-PST
 they were walking   (FlA, 2013-07_AM)
(83a) [punnu-wun-ŋku-bir]_ω-nu-niṉta
 feet.3NS.FUT-3PL.OBJ-PC.OBJ-spear-FUT-DUAL
 they will spear the two of them   (LTch, 2015-07-01_AM)
(83b) [pani-wura-ṭurk]_ω-niṉta-nu
 be.3SG.FUT-3PC.OBL-dive-DUAL-FUT
 he will dive in for the two of them   (GM, 1981_CS1-03A)

NUM and TENSE also exhibit variable sequencing relative to ADV (84) and IMPF (85), and the latter two vary relative to one another (86).

(84a) [mam-wun-ŋku-makat]_ω=waḍa-niṉta
 use.hands.3SG.NFUT-3PL.OBJ-PC.OBJ-evade=SEQ-DUAL
 now it got away from the two of them   (MvM, 2011-09-13_3-11h)
(84b) [ɲuḍam-ka-wul]_ω-neme=waḍa
 IMPEL.3PL.NFUT-PC.SUBJ-return-PAUC=SEQ
 then we went back   (GrMo, 1981_CS1-03A)
(85a) [paḍe-kut]_ω-nime-ða-paḍi
 be.3PC.PST-collect-PAUC.M-PST-BE.IMPF
 they were collecting it   (LuPa, 2013-11)
(85b) [pube-ṭaṭal]_ω-nime-paḍi-ða
 AFFECT.3PC.PST-chop.PLUR-PAUC.M-BE.IMPF-PST
 they were chopping (wood)   (DePu, 2013-01-11)
(86a) [mem-ðal]_ω=waḍa-dim
 use.hands.3SG.RR.NFUT-open=SEQ-BE.IMPF
 it's open now   (AMN, 2015-07-02_AT)

(86b) [me-ðal]_ω-wuṛini=waḍa
use.hands.RR.3SG.PST-open-<u>BE.IMPF=SEQ</u>
then it started to open (MgDo, 2015-07-21)

Constraints on this variation are yet to be fully explored. The sheer range of possible sequences, and rarity of some combinations, will require a large corpus to investigate. However some limits are already apparent: for example, dozens of instances consistently show NUM preceding IMPF (87). Other limitations may be specific to certain age groups, clan groups or even individual speakers; again, these will only become apparent if a large corpus can be collated and appropriately annotated.

(87a) [pumam-ka]_ω-ɲime-paɳam
do.3PL.NFUT-PC.SUBJ-<u>PAUC.F-BE.IMPF</u>
they (pauc) are doing it
(87b) * [pumam-ka]_ω-paɳam-ɲime
do.3PL.NFUT-PC.SUBJ-<u>BE.IMPF-PAUC.F</u>

6.4 Representational schemata for verb inflection

We have seen above that the Murrinhpatha verb has a complex inflectional structure, with dependencies among morphological elements. I here explore theoretical representation of these phenomena, drawing on the constructional approach. As described in the introduction, this work analyses patterns in Murrinhpatha morphology, without implying that these patterns are cognitively activated in the minds of speakers (§1.7.1). However the framing of the discussion here, and the use of a constructional approach, is intended to produce representations that have a degree of psychological plausibility.

It is common practice in morphological analysis of verbs to present an abstract template that represents all possible word structures in schematic form. This practice has been followed in most of the Murrinhpatha literature (e.g. Blythe, 2009, p. 118; Mansfield, 2015c; Nordlinger, 2010b, 2015). However an alternative approach, taken by Walsh (1976, pp. 205–211), is to posit multiple schemas for verbs with different argument structures, rather than a unified template. I here argue that the multi-schema approach is more compatible with a constructional approach to morphology, and has greater *a priori* psychological plausibility.

If we attempt to represent all verb inflection structures in a single schema, we might posit something like (88). Underlining indicates elements that are required for all instantiations of the schema (i.e. just the stem), and curly brackets indicate elements with flexible sequencing. Crucially, this schema involves a disjunctive schematic slot, indicated using an (A|B) format, in which either a pronominal suffix may occur, or a subject number suffix, but not both. As pointed out by Nordlinger (2010b), this disjunction creates a dependency for the number suffix in the prosodically external layer, as dual subject number marking may or may not occur externally, depending on which option was selected in the internal disjunctive slot.

(88) [[[Stem]-(OBJ|OBL|RR|NUM.SUBJ)-NUM]ω {-TNS-NUM-ADV-IMPF}]ᵥ

The alternative approach is to posit different schemas for different configurations of argument morphology. In this approach the only structure shared by all verbs is the configuration of stem with prosodic layers of suffixes, though the nature of these suffixes is not specified (89). This general structure is inherited by sub-schemas for single-argument verbs, and those with RR, OBJ, OBL suffixes (90–93). Superscript '+' indicates an element that can occur more than once.

(89) [[[[Stem]-SUFF+]ω{-SUFF+}]ᵥ
(90) [[[[Stem]-NUM.SUBJ]ω{-TNS-PAUC-ADV⁺-IMPF}]ᵥ
(91) [[[[Stem]{-RR-DUAL}]ω{-TNS-PAUC-ADV⁺-IMPF}]ᵥ
(92) [[[[Stem]-OBJ-NUM.OBJ]ω{-TNS-NUM-ADV⁺-IMPF}]ᵥ
(93) [[[[Stem]-OBL-NUM.OBL]ω{-TNS-NUM-ADV⁺-IMPF}]ᵥ

The multi-schema approach has an important difference from the unified schema. Each of the schemata can be fully exemplified by wordforms. In this sense the schemata follow a construction grammar approach, where abstract schemata are closely linked to concrete exemplars. But the unified schema is not fully exemplified by any wordform, because of its disjunctive nature. Any given word can exemplify only one disjunctive option, or the other. Therefore, the multiple schemata can be more directly adduced from exemplary wordforms, and more directly employed for producing new wordforms. The unified schema involves deeper abstraction over more exemplars to be learnt, or to be deployed, but it does not lead to great gains in representational efficiency or elegance. I therefore consider the multi-schema approach to be more plausible as a representation of speakers' mental grammar. In a later chapter I extend this schema to represent compound verbs (§8.7.3).

6.5 Predicating nominals

The predicate suffixes described in the previous sections attach most commonly to verbs, but may also attach to a nominal if it is the predicating element in a clause.⁴⁹ A nominal predicate may be morphologically marked for a pronominal argument using either the OBJ suffix (94), or by compounding with the semantically neutral verb /ma/ 'do' (95) (Walsh, 1996b). A large proportion of predicating nominals are compounded with body part nominals, often with a high degree of semantic opacity.

(94) [muriṉ-ṉi-ðaj]_ω
 language-2SG.OBJ-mouth
 you talk a lot (LP, 2015-09-14_AT)

(95) [wirit-pumam-ka-ṟi]_ω-neme
 bony-do.3PL.NFUT-PC.SUBJ-bottom-PAUC.M
 those people are cruel (Walsh 1996b)

The data available for investigating predicating nominals is much more limited than that for verbs. Young speakers rarely use the construction. Predicating nominals seem to have been used quite extensively by speakers born before the founding of the mission, but to have decreased sharply in usage since then. Nominal predication is possible with English loanwords, though only a single spontaneous example has been identified (96). However this is not surprising given that it is younger speakers who make heavy use of English loanwords, but older speakers who frequently use predicating nominals.

(96) ibil mup ṯara kaḏu-[ṯikin-wun-ŋku]_ω-nime
 Evil group run PERS-chicken-3PL.OBJ-PC.OBJ-PAUC.M
 Evil Warriors run away, you're chicken! (i.e. cowards) (DePu, 2011-09-01)

6.5.1 Syntactic strategies for nominal predication

There are a range of strategies for nominal predication, not all of them involving morphology. The simplest is to associate an argument with a predicate by

---

49 The predicating nominals illustrated as heads of compounds here could also be interpreted as being of the *coverb* class. I am not aware of any solid grounds for categorising them one way or the other, and the fact that the same roots in many cases alternate between coverb and nominal roles makes the question ambiguous (§8.4). I have labeled them predicating 'nominals' simply because more of the observed instances use a root that elsewhere appears as a nominal argument, than elsewhere appearing as a coverb. Furthermore most have the sorts of meanings typically associated with nouns and adjectives. In any case the labeling decision has no consequences for the analysis.

parataxis (97). The addition of a copula verb allows tense to be added in an otherwise similar structure (98).

(97) naŋkun ma-kaḍu ŋaj-ju
 [husband NEG-person]PRED [1SG-CLS]ARG
 I'm not anybody's husband (PuBr, 2013-01-18_01)

(98) Waṇamparkiṭi ŋepan paṭa kaḍi-ða
 [PERS.NAME]ARG [spirit good]PRED [be.3SG.PST-PST]TNS
 Warnamparrkithi was happy (RoMo, 2010-08-27)

6.5.2 Morphological argument indexing

The use of argument morphology offers two alternatives to the paratactic strategy above: indexing an argument by OBJ suffix, or by compounding of a finite light verb stem /ma/ 'do'. Walsh (1996b) coins the terms 'nerb' and 'voun' respectively for the two types. The construct with /ma/ 'do' has a TENSE feature, and therefore may be used to predicate with temporal or modal meanings. Also it may host the IMPF bound morph (99, 100). The construct with OBJ has no TENSE feature, and therefore may only predicate a situation as being a generalised or permanent property of the pronominal argument (101–103).

With /ma/ 'do'
(99) [pakpak-me-ma]ω-ða-ŋaḍi
 weak-do.1SG.PST-hand-PST-BE.IMPF
 I was too weak (MnMn, 2004-09-12; Blythe 2009: 138)

(100) [ḍuḍu-ma-maḍa]ω-nukun-ŋuɾu
 breathless-do.1SG.IRR-belly-ADVERS-GO.IMPF
 I might get short wind (ElCu, 2004-09-12; Blythe 2009: 138)

With OBJ suffix
(101) [mutmut-ṇi-ṭe]ω
 deaf-2SG.OBJ-ear
 you're ignorant (Street 2012, *mutmutthe*)

(102) [ḍarimuṇ-ṇi-ŋini]ω
 sugar-1SG.OBJ-body
 I have diabetes (ECu, 2004-07-04)

(103) muntákpun
 [munṭak-wun]ω
 old-3PL.OBJ
 they're old

Arguments marked on predicating nominals use the same system of cascading number specification as found in finite verbs (104, §6.2.1).

(104) [putput-wun-ŋkú-ṯi]ω-niṉṯa
stubborn.PL-3PL.OBJ-PC.OBJ-nose-DUAL.M
those two men are stubborn (Street 2012, *putputthi*)

The 'do'-compound predicational construct has been frozen to form many Murrinhpatha adjectives (105, 106). These have a demorphologised form of erstwhile /mam/ do.3SG.NFUT, which appears even where the referent is plural, or the tense of the clause past or future. In this non-finite role I gloss the morph as an ADJECTIVIZER (107, 108).

(105) ṯip-mam
dark-ADJZ
dark, black

(106) teṯe-mam
hit.PLUR-ADJZ
hard, difficult

(107) pube-nu-lṯal [...] kaḏu-ṯip-mam=wa
affect.3PL.PST-RR-cut.PLUR PERS-dark-ADJZ=SURP
they were cutting each other ... Aboriginal people! (ErDu, 2011-09-17_03)

(108) kardu-palŋun ṯip-mam=ka muriṉ pama-nu
PERS-woman dark-ADJZ=CNST language say.3SG.IRR-FUT
an Aboriginal woman will speak (MaNi, 2015-02-07_Pr3-EC1)

Walsh also records a few instances of nominal predicates with both /ma/ 'do' and OBJ attached (109). The number of attested examples for these is too small to shed light on how they might differ from tensed forms without OBJ, as in (99) above.

(109) [pakpak-mam-ŋi-be]ω-ŋuṟan
cramp-do.3SG.NFUT-1SG.OBJ.-arm-GO.IMPF
my arm is habitually cramped (Walsh 1996a: 241)

6.5.3 Grammaticalisation of /ma/ 'hand'

Most examples of predicating nominals have a body part nominal compounded to them as the right-most element in the PWord. The semantics of the compound is often quite opaque, for example, from (95) above, /wirit-ṯi/ 'bony-bottom = cruel'.

The same set of body part nominals are also compounded to coverbs, where they again have a mixture of transparent and opaque semantics. The body part nominal /ma/ 'hand' also appears in some grammaticalised instances where it no longer references hands, but may instead have applicative or associative function (94, 95, Nordlinger, in prep., 2011a). Fuller discussion of body part compounding appears in the chapter on complex verbs (§8.5).

(110) [batbat-ŋi-<u>ma</u>]_ω
 right.hand.PLUR-1SG.OBJ-<u>HAND.APPL</u>
 I'm right handed   (Street 2012, *batbat*)

(111) [palŋun-ŋi-<u>ma</u>]_ω
 woman-2SG.OBJ-<u>HAND.APPL</u>
 do you have a girlfriend/wife? (*are you a woman?)

6.6 Summary

In this chapter I have described the suffixes that attach to predicate lexemes in Murrinhpatha, associating them with pronominal arguments, number categories for those arguments, tense categories, and adverbial modifiers. I have described the two prosodic layers occupied by these morphs: the internal layer, where they form a PWord together with the lexical host, and the external layer, where they adjoin outside the PWord. The internal layer specifies arguments and their broad number categories, and exhibits complex dependencies among suffixes. The external layer adds specificity to tense and number categories, as well as adverbial modifiers, and has a looser structure, with variable morphotactic sequencing. The internal and external sets of suffixes are largely disjoint sets, though the DUAL number marker has the interesting property of appearing in the internal layer by default, or the external layer if it is blocked by other internal morphs.

Illustrations in this chapter have also featured many examples of lexical compounding, the analysis of which is deferred to the chapter on complex verbs (§8). Before that, however, we explore the rest of the bound grammatical morphology, i.e. elements that attach to nominal arguments, or to prosodic phrases irrespective of morphosyntactic category.

7 Nominal and phrasal morphology

7.1 Introduction

Murrinhpatha nominal arguments host less complex morphology than predicates. Bound morphology attaching to nominals is generally prosodically external, and lacks the complex dependencies or cascading feature specificity of the predicate inflectional suffixes described in the last chapter. The grammatical morphs most commonly bound to nominal arguments are 'classifier nouns', which have an intermediate status between lexical and inflectional. Nominal arguments also host a range of case clitics, though these are optional and somewhat infrequently used.

Case clitics bind to the right edge of the NP as a whole, rather than to the noun head, which is at the left of the NP. There are two further morphological classes that are hosted at a phrasal level, but which take any phrase type as their host. The first of these are adverbials, which modify the meaning of a predicate. The second is discourse clitics, which have no referential meaning, but instead seem to function as cues to information structure and pragmatic intent.

Given their phrase-level attachment, the latter morphological classes can be labelled 'clitics', in opposition to the word-level predicational 'affixes' described in the last chapter. However this terminology deviates somewhat from typical expectations of an affix/clitic distinction, in terms of prosodic constituency and morphotactic sequencing. The first section of this chapter discusses terminological and theoretical issues relating to the affix/clitic distinction (§7.2). The following section describes the interrelated phenomena of noun phrase structure, nominal compounding and noun classifiers (§7.3). A brief section describes two rare nominal derivational suffixes (§7.4). The remaining sections describe the three types of clitics: case, adverbial and discourse (§7.5–§7.7).

7.2 Affixes and clitics

This chapter introduces a distinction in bound morphology between 'affixes' and 'clitics', as is common in works of grammatical description. However it is worth noting the particular basis for this distinction, since there is no consensus in the literature as to the meaning of 'clitic', and Murrinhpatha clitics do not align with all possible definitions (Haspelmath, 2015).

Theoretical discussion of clitics is complicated by the lack of consensus as to how they are defined. One popular parameter is selectivity: an affix is selective in the class of words it attaches to, while a clitic is less selective (Zwicky & Pullum, 1983). Related to this is a morphosyntactic word-level vs phrase-level distinction: affixes attach to particular words, while clitics attach to a phrase, and the particular word they bind to in a given instance is merely a consequence of that word's position in the phrase (Anderson, 2005, p. 133ff.). Elsewhere, clitics are defined in terms of prosodic adjunction: a clitic is prosodically deficient in the sense of lacking PWord characteristics; it therefore depends on a host word that is a full PWord, but unlike affixes, it does not unify with the host in prosodic constituency – it remains prosodically adjunct (Spencer & Luis, 2012, p. 84ff.). Similarly, a clitic is sometimes defined as a prosodically deficient, alternative form of something that elsewhere occurs as an independent word. Finally, there is a morphotactic criterion: clitics must attach outside of affixes, and only clitics, but not affixes, can have variable morphotactic sequencing (Anderson, 1992, p. 261; Zwicky & Pullum, 1983). Combining these distinct criteria is unproblematic if one is describing a language where they happen to align: i.e. if there is one set of bound morphs that are highly selective, attach to a morphosyntactic word, and are prosodically internal, while another set are unselective, attach to a morphosyntactic phrase, and are prosodically external. But where these criteria do not align, use of the term 'clitic' becomes somewhat murky, especially if it is not explicitly defined (Embick & Noyer, 2001; Haspelmath, 2015; Spencer & Luis, 2012, p. 220). There is considerable scope for such murkiness in Murrinhpatha.

The affix/clitic question has not previously been discussed for Murrinhpatha. Street (1987) and Walsh (1976) do not identify any clitics, but they treat adverbials as separate words. Blythe (2009) and Nordlinger (2010b, 2015) gloss most bound morphs as affixes, except for discourse tags and IMPF serialised verb stems, which they gloss as clitics. Turning to the most detailed descriptions available for neighbouring languages, for Marrithiyel no distinction is drawn (Green, 1989), while for Murrinhpatha's sister language Ngan'gi a clitic category is posited based on phrase-level hosting (Reid, 1990, p. 325ff.). The use of the term 'clitic' I propose below is largely parallel to Reid's use for Ngan'gi.

The various possible criteria that could be used for splitting Murrinhpatha bound morphology into affixes and clitics do not lead to consistent evaluations (Table 7.1) (cf. Bickel & Zúñiga, 2017). If we were to draw an affix/clitic distinction in Murrinhpatha based on selectivity, we might declare case markers to be affixes, since they attach only to nominals. We might also declare predicate inflections to be affixes, since they attach only to predicating lexemes (even if these encompass both verbs and nominals), and not to nominal arguments. Adverbs and discourse tags would be clitics since they are altogether unselective, while classifier nouns would also be clitics, since although they attach most often to nominals, they can also attach to verbs (§7.1.3). A morphosyntactic word-level versus

Table 7.1: Affix/clitic categorisation according to four widely used criteria. The criterion used in this study is Word/phrase attachment.

	Predicational (internal)	Predicational (external)	IMPF serial verb stem	Classifier noun	Case markers	Adverbial, Discourse tag
Selectivity	affix	affix	affix	clitic	affix	clitic
Prosodic constituency	affix	clitic	clitic	clitic	clitic	clitic
Also occurs as indep. word	affix	affix	clitic	clitic	affix	affix
☞ Word/ phrase attachment	affix	affix	affix	affix	clitic	clitic

phrase-level analysis would reach the same conclusions for predicate inflections (affixes), adverbials and discourse tags (clitics). But case markers would now also be treated as clitics, since they attach to the right of the noun phrase, rather than to the head noun. Conversely, classifier nouns might be seen as somewhat affix-like because they occasionally attach to multiple words in an NP, and fail to gap in co-ordinate NPs. If we turn to prosodic criteria, there is yet another discrepancy in that the outer layer of predicate inflections would be treated as clitics, rather than affixes. Finally, the criterion of being a prosodically deficient alternant of what is elsewhere an independent word would pick out classifier nouns and IMPF serialised verb stems as clitics. But both of these are affix-like in that they are hosted by words rather than phrases.

In an attempt to follow widely shared conventions, while also maintaining principled categories, in this study I use 'clitic' for phrase-level morphology, i.e. case markers, adverbials and discourse tags. Other bound morphs are labelled 'affixes'. The following caveats apply to the affix/clitic distinction applied here. On the affix side (i.e. predicate inflectional suffixes, and marginally noun class prefixes), it must be noted that they attach to both verb and nominal word classes, that some have prosodically external constituency, and that the external predicational 'affixes' can have variable morphotactic sequencing (Mansfield, 2015c). On the clitic side, it must be noted that adverbial clitics, when attaching to verbs, sometimes occur inside of predicate inflectional suffixes, and also that adverbials may form lexically specified, prosodically internal bonds with demonstratives and interrogatives. These caveats take us some way from typical expectations of affix and clitic behaviour. In view of this, caution should be exercised if the affix/clitic categories are to be deployed in typological comparisons, since they are likely to have been used in quite different ways in other studies.

7.3 Noun phrases, nominal compounds and classifier nouns

Murrinhpatha has a fixed-order noun phrase (NP), within which sequences of two or three nouns can be included, either as separate words or as a compound word. The vast majority of these NON-NOM compounds are headed by one of a closed set of ten nouns, here labelled 'classifier nouns'. Classifier nouns are to some extent grammaticalised and therefore exhibit duality of function, both as nominal lexemes and as prefix-like bound elements marking noun class (Walsh, 1997). To fully appreciate the role of classifier nouns, we must further explore noun phrase structure, and generic–specific relations in the nominal lexicon. Various Australian languages have been analysed as having either generic nouns (e.g. Gaby, 2017, p. 78ff.) or semantic noun genders (e.g. Singer, 2016). We will see that Murrinhpatha combines elements of both phenomena.

7.3.1 Noun phrases and generic–specific relations

As mentioned in previous chapters, Murrinhpatha has an NP with fixed word order, [Neg Noun$^+$ Adj Det]$_{NP}$, though no element is obligatory (§4.4.3). The element 'Noun$^+$' indicates that multiple nouns can be strung together in a series, and these show a distinctive pattern of sequencing from the most generic to the most specific. This can be thought of as a 'head + modifier' pattern, also exhibited by the placement of adjectives and demonstratives further to the right. The nouns can be subcategorised into three types according to these generic–specific relations:

a) *classifier nouns* are those that are always in the most generic position on the left;
b) *generic nouns* are those that may have a classifier to their left, and/or a more specific noun on their right;
c) *specific nouns* are those that are always the right-most noun, though they may be further modified by adjectives or determiners on their right.

There are ten classifier nouns, listed in Table 7.2. Classifier nouns appear in a very high proportion of NPs, and are generally far more frequent than other types of nouns. As we will see below, classifier nouns have some characteristics of grammatical prefixes, and therefore are glossed in UPPER CASE.

Any entity can be referenced, at the expense of denotational specificity, using simply a classifier noun (1). None of the noun types is obligatory in the NP, though maximally one of each type – classifier, generic, specific – can be

7.3 Noun phrases, nominal compounds and classifier nouns

Table 7.2: Classifier nouns (Walsh, 1997).

Classifier	Gloss	Meaning
da	PLACE, TIME	Locations in space and time
kaḏu	PERS	Socially recognised (usually Aboriginal) people (Mansfield, 2018)
ku	ANIM	Animals, meat, spirit beings, non-socially recognised humans
kuɹa	WATER	Water and water-based liquids
mi	VEG	Consumable plant matter: fruit and vegetables, tobacco and marijuana
muriṉ	LANG	Languages, names, stories, songs
naṉṯi	THING	Miscellaneous inanimate objects, body parts
ṯamul	SPEAR	Types of spear
ṯuŋku	FIRE	Fire, firearms and electricity
ṯu	VIOL	Weapons, acts of violence

included.[50] Examples (1–7) illustrate the possible category combinations, in some cases with additional adjectives or demonstratives. Classifier nouns are represented as forming compounds with the following noun, while combinations of generics, specifics, adjectives and demonstratives are represented as phrasal. The basis for this distinction will be described below.

Classifier

(1) naṉṯi=kaṯu!
THING=DEMAND
give me the thing! (e.g. clothes, implement, paper, phone)

Generic

(2) ṯaj kaṉi
tree PROX
this tree

Specific

(3) menek
ironwood.tree

Classifier + generic

(4) naṉṯi-ṯaj
THING-tree
(a, the) tree

---

[50] I have observed a very few double-classifier exceptsions, such as /kaḏu-kuɹa/ PERS-WATER 'drunkard'.

Classifier + specific
(5) naṉṯi-menek
    THING-ironwood
    (a, the) ironwood

Generic + specific
(6) ṯaj menek
    tree ironwood
    (a, the) ironwood tree

Classifier + generic + specific
(7) naṉṯi-ṯaj   menek
    THING-ironwood tree
    (a, the) ironwood tree

The hierarchy of classifier, generic and specific nouns creates an implicit ontological structure in the noun lexicon, as in Figure 7.1. The structure of the NP embodies this ontological hierarchy in its left-to-right sequencing.

The set of nominals that are always in the most generic (head) position, and therefore qualify as classifier nouns, may not be diachronically stable. The list in Table 7.1 represents Murrinhpatha as documented from older speakers, who appear to use /ṯamul/ 'spear' at the top of the chain, e.g. /ṯamul-menek/ 'ironwood spear'. However younger speakers no longer use spears, and do not command as much vocabulary associated with types of spear. Unsurprisingly, they usually speak only of a generic 'spear', and classify it as part of the VIOLENCE class, /ṯu-ṯamul/.

7.3.2 NOM-NOM Compounds

When nominals combine within the NP, they may sometimes exhibit loss of prosodic wordhood, and loss or reduction of compositional semantics. Where either or both of these occur, I label the sequence a 'NOM-NOM compound'. Note that this

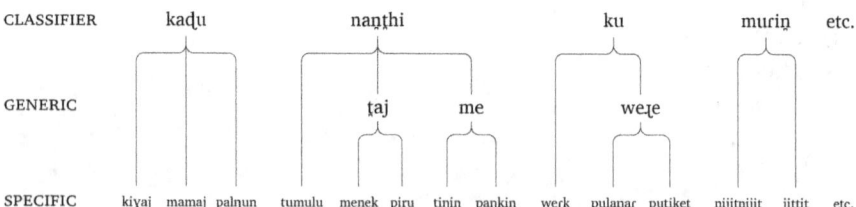

Figure 7.1: Illustrative fragment of the ontological hierarchy in the Murrinhpatha noun lexicon.

compound structure is closely related to phrasal structure, since it involves the same NOM + NOM combination as is found among independent words in the NP.

The distinction between compound and phrasal NOM + NOM combinations in Murrinhpath can be tested empirically by reference to the bimoraic minimum – nominal stems that have independent PWord constituency must be minimally bimoraic. However, because this criterion only defines minimal quantity, and not any other characteristics such as stress or intonation, it only provides evidence for PWord constituency in open monosyllabic stems. These are the only stems that do not inherently have two morae, and must therefore have their vowel lengthened when they form PWords, e.g. /ke/ → [keː]ω 'nerite shell'. As described in an earlier chapter (§4.4.3), NPs prosodify a PWord for each word element, and a single PPhrase for the whole NP, marked by a penultimate pitch accent on the final PWord (8, 9).

(8) [[meː]ω   [paŋu=dá=ŋu]ω]φ   [[meː]ω   [kaṇí=ŋu]ω]φ
     [foot   there=LOC=TOWARDS]NP   [foot   here=DIR]NP
     a foot over there, a foot over here   (SeDu, 2015-07-09_SL)

(9) [[níṇi]ω=ka]φ   [[teː]ω   [wíje]ω]φ
     [2SG]NP=CST   [ear   bad]NP
     do you have a sore ear?   (LP, 2013-07_clinic)

Compounding can be identified wherever open monosyllabic noun elements do not meet the bimoraic minimum. For example, the same head nouns that are prosodified as PWords above, are elsewhere prosodified as left-adjunct syllables, as indicated by lack of vowel lengthening (10–12). The fact that the head noun is an adjunct, rather than combining with its modifier into an integrated PWord, is confirmed by bimoraic lengthening on modifiers (13).

(10) [me-[ŋala]ω   [múp]ω=ka]φ
     foot-big   people=CST
     Big Foot people [nickname of a tribe]   (KM, 2011-08-16)

(11) [te-[páṭa]ω]φ   [[ṭím]ω]φ
     ear-good   sit.2SG.NFUT
     you know it well   (PhyBu, 2009-11-21_03)

(12) [ṭe-[wíje]ω]φ
     ear-bad
     (heavy metal music) sounds bad   (SL, 2011-09-21)

(13) [ku-[kéː]ω]φ
     ANIM-nerite.mollusc

In addition to the reduced prosodic constituency, the lexical semantics of compounded nouns may no longer be transparently present in the meaning of the whole. In some compound examples above (10–12), the concepts FOOT and EAR, are not part of the denotation in either case. The compound (12) sharpens the distinction, forming a minimal pair with the second NP in (9). The compound makes a metaphorical use of /ṯe/ 'ear' to reference a characteristic sound, in this case that of heavy metal music.

When we turn to prosodic evidence for classifier nouns, we find that open monosyllabic classifiers are usually prosodic adjuncts, and therefore part of compounds. This is generally the case when classifiers combine with generic nouns, specific nouns or both (14–17).

(14) [mi-[kílen]ω]φ
 VEG-green.plum
(15) [ku-[lawáŋka]ω]φ
 ANIM-wallaby
(16) ku-[wéɹe]ω
 ANIM-furry.quadruped
 dingo
(17) ku-weɹe-[puláɲar]ω
 ANIM-furry.quadruped-dingo
 dingo
(18) ku-weɹe-[puṯíket]ω
 ANIM-furry.quadruped-cat
 cat

Complex lexemes combining generic–specific, or classifier–generic–specific, also prosodify as compounds (19, 20). This compound structure has to some extent remained productive in coining words to describe new artefacts encountered since the arrival of Europeans (21–23, and 18 above).

(19) me-[paŋkin]ω
 foot-top
 instep
(20) naṉṯi-me-[paŋkin]ω
 THING-foot-top
 instep
(21) me-[bút]ω
 foot-boot
 shoe

(22) me-[sák]_ω
 foot-sock
 sock
(23) me-[wíl]_ω
 foot-wheel
 car wheel

By contrast, when nouns (either classifier, generic or specific) combine with adjectives of determiners, there is not consistent prosodic adjunction of the head. Limiting ourselves to classifiers, we find examples both with and without PWord lengthening in open monosyllables. Thus classifiers may either be prosodic adjuncts to adjectives and determiners (24–27), or alternatively prosodify as independent PWords (28, 29). From the examples observed (limited to monosyllabic classifiers), there is no clear pattern as to which prosodification is applied. However, what is clear is that prosodic adjunction occurs more consistently in noun-noun combinations than it does in combinations involving adjectives of determiners. Furthermore, it is among nouns that combinatoric associations tend to be specified by the lexical ontology represented in Figure 7.1 above, as opposed to the free combination of nouns and adjectives/determiners, for which no such lexical ontology exists.

(24) [mi-[páṭa]_ω]_φ [mi-[káṇi]_ω=ju]_φ
 [VEG-good]_NP [VEG-this]_NP=CLS
 this food is good   (CsMo, 2011-07-09_3-1)
(25) [ku-[ŋála]_ω]_φ
 ANIM-big
 a big creature   (MgBi, 2015-07-21)
(26) [da-[káṇi]_ω]_φ [puṭkít]_ω]_φ
 PLACE-this   place.name
 this place here, Port Keats   (KM, 2012-06-20_28)
(27) [mi-[ŋáj]_ω=wa]_φ [[káj]_ω=ju]_φ
 food-1SG=SURP this=CLS
 this food is mine!   (CP, 2011-09-09_2-5)
(28) [[kuː]_ω [ŋalŋála]_ω]_φ
 [ANIM big.VERY]_NP
 some very important white people   (MNi, 2015-02-07_Pa1SC2)
(29) muː ṭáŋku=wa   [[daː]_ω   [káṇi]_ω]_φ wuran=ju
 but INTERG=SURP [TIME   this]_NP go.3SG.NFUT=CLS
 but what is the nature of this thing time?   (MNi, 2015-02-07_Pr3SC2)

As mentioned above, empirical evidence for compounding is limited to open monosyllabic elements. Semantic non-compositionality is also associated with compounding, but since compounds may be either compositional or non-compositional, semantic evidence is also indecisive in many instances. This leaves us many instances in which polysyllabic nouns combine transparently with other nouns, and could be analysed as compounds or as phrasal structure (30a,b). The approach taken in this book is to represent such constructs as compounds (i.e. as in 30a), since the evidence from open monosyllables indicates compounding. An alternative analysis would be to posit compounding as a special property of monosyllabic head nouns, but this analysis is dispreferred since it involves an extra stipulation in the morphosyntax → prosody mapping.

(30a) [kuɻa-[ɲipíliṇ]ω]φ
 WATER-river
(30b) [[kuɻa]ω [ɲipíliṇ]ω]φ
 WATER river

7.3.3 From compounds to class prefixes

We have seen above that classifier nouns are part of a general pattern of NOM-NOM compounding in Murrinhpatha, and indeed are the most common head elements in this structure. However classifiers also exhibit a substantial degree of grammaticalisation, suggesting that they have an intermediate status between being lexical stems and inflectional prefixes. The evidence for this lies in paradigmaticity and semantic bleaching. However the limits of this grammaticalisation is evidenced by productive, semantically transparent use of classifiers, and by inconclusive syntactic evidence.

Classifier nouns have a paradigmatic character, in the sense that every generic or specific noun has some classifier that it selects as an optional preceding element in compounds. Furthermore, the ten classifiers exhaustively divide up semantic space, according to the semantic criteria outlined in Table 7.1 above. They thus 'classify' all nominal denotations into one of ten classes. But although the vast majority of specific nouns select a classifier in accordance with semantic criteria, there are some instances in which the selection of classifier is conventional rather than semantic. Compare the semantically expected classifications in (31–34) with the unexpected classifications in (35, 36).

(31) ku-ṭiriṇin   ANIM-skink   (animate)
(32) ku-ŋen   ANIM-meat   (part of animate)
(33) mi-lala   VEG-cycad.fruit   (consumable plant)

(34) mi-ṯawuy   ANIM-native.tobacco   (consumable plant)
(35) ku-tiliman   ANIM-spear.grass   (*not* animate)
(36) ku-paljiɾ   ANIM-rock = "money"   (*not* animate, or rock)

On the other hand, not all specific and generic nouns select for just one classifier. A few nouns combine with multiple classifiers, and in so doing, reverse the typical head–modifier relationship, with the classifier encoding the function or context of the entity, rather than the broader class of entities of which it is a member (37, 38) (Walsh, 1997).

(37a) naṉṯi-ṯaj   THING-wood   'wood, tree, stick'
(37b) ṯu-ṯaj   VIOLENCE-wood 'stick used for fighting'
(37c) ṯuŋku-ṯaj   FIRE-wood   'firewood'
(38a) naṉṯi-paljiɾ THING-rock   'rock'
(38b) ṯu-paljiɾ   VIOL-rock   'rock used for fighting'
(38c) da-paljiɾ   PLACE-rock   'hill'

Multiple classification also shows a few instances of productivity with recently introduced phenomena. For example, non-Aboriginal people are usually classified as /ku/ ANIM (Mansfield, 2018), leading to multiple classifications such as (39).

(39a) kaḏu-wanaŋkal PERSON-doctor 'traditional healer'
(39b) ku-wanaŋkal   ANIM-doctor   '(non-Aboriginal) doctor'

The instances of multiple classification above illustrate the lexical semantic character of classifiers. However there are other instances of multiple classification which instead show sets of compounds that are associated by conventionalised metaphors rather than transparent semantics. These entities may be related by their shape or consistency (40, 41, 42) ecological association (43; cf. Turpin, 2013) or ceremonial/mythological association (44).

(40a) naṉṯi-kamaḻ THING-eye = 'eye'
(40b) mi-kamaḻ   VEG-eye = 'seed'
(40c) kuɻa-kamal   WATER-eye = 'water-hole'
(41a) naṉṯi-ṯipuḻ THING-mucus = 'snot'
(41b) ku-ṯipuḻ   ANIM-mucus = 'egg white'
(42a) naṉṯi-ɲi   THING-penis = 'penis'
(42b) ku-ɲi   ANIM-penis = 'death adder'
(43a) naṉṯi-buɾuɾ THING-termite.mound = 'termite mound'
(43b) ku-buɾuɾ   ANIM-termite.mound = 'snake sp. that frequents termite mounds'

(44a) kaḓu-muṯiŋka   PERS-old.woman = 'old woman'
(44b) naṉṯi-muṯiŋka   THING-old.woman = 'bullroarer – a device used in the *punh* ceremony associated with a powerful female spirit'

Turning to syntactic evidence, we should expect that an inflectional morph would have the capacity to occur with multiple stems in a phrase, whereas a compounding element might not (Haspelmath, 2011, p. 47ff.; Spencer & Luis, 2012, p. 199ff.). Co-ordinate NPs provide evidence here, though it is not decisive, as both patterns are found. Some same-class coordinate NPs have a class prefix on each member, as do different-class coordinate NPs (45, 46, 48). But there are other instances where a single prefix is used for same-class coordinate NPs (Nordligner, *p.c.*) (47).

(45) paḓe-wuɾkuɾk-ṯa   ku-paŋpi   i   ku-wul̪kmanṯaj
    be.3PC.PST-catch.PLUR-PST ANIM-mullet and ANIM-catfish
    the two siblings were catching mullet and catfish   (KMB, 1958_K)
(46) kaḓu-mamaj i   ku-tedibe   ŋuɾŋuwal̪
    PERS-child   and ANIM-teddy.bear   sleep
    the child and the teddy-bear are sleeping   (KtLo, 2016-11-01)
(47) ṯuḓu-ŋa-yiṯ-mani   ṯaŋku mukmuk
    IMPEL.2SG.IRR-1SG.OBL-tell-DESID what brain
    paṉṯin-pibim   kaḓu-ṯipmam i   bamam=ju
    have.3PL.NFUT-STAND.IMPF   PERS-black   and white=CLS
    tell me, what kinds of thoughts do black people and white people have?
    (MaNi, 2015-02-07_Mark-Ninnal_NAATI-Pro1-SC2)
(48) kaḓu-nuyan̪ i   kaḓu-maḓin̪puj   dem-n̪inṯa-maḓatat
    PERS-man   and PERS-girl   PIERCE.RR.3SG-DUAL.F-stand.facing
    a man and a girl are standing facing each other   (DePu, 2015-07-05_AT)

Finally, there is evidence of semi-inflectional status of classifiers from noun + adjective combinations. In these structures a compounded lexeme would be expected to appear just once, with the adjective modifying the whole compound. An inflection element, on the other hand, might be applied to both noun and adjective. Murrinhpatha classifiers show mixed evidence here, usually attaching just to the noun (49, 50), but occasionally attaching to both a head noun and its modifying adjective (51).[51] However, prefixing just to the left-most, head noun is far more common.

---

51 Walsh (1997: 264) proposes that this does not occur. Such instances have been found only with /ku-/ ANIM and /mi-/ VEG, which are cognate with class prefixes /a-/, /mi-/ in Marrithiyel and other Western Daly languages, which also exhibit the noun/adjective double-marking pattern (Green, 1997; Reid, 1990).

(49) [ku̲-[weɻe]ω   [múlak]ω]φ
    [ANIM-pawed.beast dangerous]NP
    savage dog
(50) [da-[ʈelput]ω [munʈak]ω [n̪íni]PW=ju]φ
    [PLACE-house   old   ANAPH=CLS]NP
    that old house   (AdTu, 2015-07-13_LH)
(51) [ku̲-[karaʈ]ω ku̲-[puɻkuɻk]ω   ku̲-[téɻet]ω]φ
    [ANIM-devil   ANIM-small.numerous ANIM-many]NP
    many little devils   (DePu, 2011-07-21_3-16)

In summary, semantic, combinatoric and syntactic evidence point to an intermediate status for classifier nouns. In each of these dimensions, they behave in some ways like lexical stems in a compound structure, and in other ways like grammatical prefixes in an inflectional structure.

7.3.4 Classifiers with verbs

Prosodically adjunct classifiers most frequently occur in argument NPs, but they may also attach to either verbal or nominal predicates. Though syntactic research on this construct is still needed, it appears to cross-reference the verb to any one of its arguments (52), or in some cases to semantically classify the predicate itself (53). In (53) the class prefix /ʈu-/ could potentially cross-reference a weapon instrument, but this was in fact a description of a picture showing one man punching another. Verbal attachment is the norm for 'gender' classes in some other northern Australian languages, though in these cases the classes are less semantic and more grammaticalised (e.g. Anindilyakwa: van Egmond, 2012).

(52) ku̲-param-ka-wal̲-ða   ku̲-buliki
    [ANIM-PIERCE.3PL-PC.SUBJ-shoot-PST]PRED [ANIM-bullock]NP
    the two siblings shot a bullock   (PaPu, 2011-09-01)
(53) ʈu-[pán-bat]ω
    [VIOL-ARC.3SG.NFUT-hit]PRED
    he hit him   (ArMa, 2013-01-05)

7.3.5 Negative nominal prefix

Some classifier nominals have a further special property that sets them apart from general nouns. When used as full nouns, they may host a prosodically internal negator prefix, thus composing 'none of X' (54a, 55) (Walsh, 1976, p. 192).

This complex noun is often itself redundantly marked with a class prefix (54b). The negative nominal prefix might almost be used as a morpho-syntactic parameter distinguishing classifier nouns from general nouns, except that three of the classifiers, /muriɲ/ LANGUAGE, /ḍa/ PLACE, TIME and /t̪u/ VIOLENCE cannot host the negator prefix (Walsh, 1997, p. 258).

(54a) [má-mi]ω   NEG-VEG   'no food', 'no tobacco'
(54b) mi-[má-mi]ω   VEG-NEG-VEG   (as above)
(55) [ma-kúɻa]ω   NEG-WATER   'nothing to drink'
      (KaD, 2015-07-21)

The negator prefix may also appear on predicating nominals, if the predicate is a classifier noun (56).

(56) kardu-[ma-kura-ŋan-t̪aj]ω   ŋanki
     PERS-NEG-water-1PL.OBJ-mouth   1PL
     we're non-drinkers   (KaD, 2015-07-21)

7.4 Nominal derivations

Murrinhpatha does not have much morphology that could be characterised as 'derivational', but there are a couple of derivational suffixes for nominals. One is /-mawu/ DWELLER. It attaches to a place-referring nominal, deriving 'one that dwells at N' (57, 58). It is an 'internal suffix', i.e. it forms a PWord together with its host.

(57a) ḍa-[pút̪]ω
      PLACE-bush
(57b) kaḍu-[put̪-máwu]ω
      PERSON-[bush-DWELLER]
      person who lives in the bush   (McMi, 2015-07-21)
(57c) mi-[put̪-máwu]ω
      VEG-[bush-DWELLER]
      forageable vegetable foods   (ReWa, 2015-07-17)
(58a) ḍa-[káŋkal]ω
      PLACE-above
      the sky
(58b) [kaŋkal-máwu]ω
      [above-DWELLER]
      Jesus Christ (lit. 'sky-dweller')   (McMi, 2015-07-21)

The other is /-ṯar/ QUITE, which attaches to adjectives to moderate the degree of the adjectival property (59). It is not used productively, but rather is frozen into particular lexicalised combinations (60), in some of which the stem is not an independent word (61, where /buk/ otherwise appears as a bound coverb, but never as an independnet word).

(59) ku-ŋala-ṯar   ṉini-ṉini
    ANIM-big-QUITE ANAPH-ANAPH
    those quite large fish   (AaNe, 2017-14-03)

(60) paŋkiṯar
    paŋkin-ṯar
    back-QUITE
    rock cod sp.   (Street 1989, *pangkitharr*)

(61) bukmaṉṯar
    buk-mam-ṯar
    red-ADJZ-QUITE
    red

7.5 Case clitics

Most Pama-Nyungan (PNy) languages have a rich system of case marking at the core of their grammatical organisation. But some non-PNy languages, including Murrinhpatha, instead indicate the relation of arguments to verbs primarily through pronominal morphology attached to the verb (Dixon, 2002a, p. 131ff.; Evans, 2003b). The non-PNy languages can be characterised as 'head-marking' in contrast to the PNy 'dependent marking' languages (Nichols, 1986). Murrinhpatha does have various bound morphs that can be used optionally to indicate the semantic role of a noun phrase argument. Though these can be labelled 'case' markers, they do not have the obligatory, paradigmatic character of prototypical case systems. Murrinhpatha case markers are prosodically external and attach to the right-most word in an NP (62), indicating its thematic role. I label them 'clitics' because they exhibit phrase-level attachment. Like nominal class prefixes, case clitics do not exhibit gapping in coordinated NPs (63, 64). However there are no instances attested of case suffixes attaching to noun and dependent adjective, as do class prefixes (§5.1.3).

(62) kɹek   mam   ku-nan=ɹe
    crack do.3SG.NFUT [ANIM-whats.his.name]_NP=AGENT
    kanamkek   ŋala=ɹe
    [rainbow.serpent big]_NP–AGENT

it was cracked by what's-his-name, the great Rainbow Serpent
(KeMa, 2012-06-20_28)

(63) loda=ɹe   i   tɹak   wakal   pana=ɹe
     [loader]ₙₚ=INSTR   and   [truck   small   FAMILIAR]ₙₚ=INSTR
     (with) the loader and that little truck   (BrBe, 2012-07-19)

(64) ŋara Dawun   pumpan=ka   skul=nu   i   wuḻk=nu
     LOC Darwin   go.3PL.NFUT=CST   [school]ₙₚ=DAT   and   [work]ₙₚ=DAT
     they go to Darwin for school and work   (MaNi, 2015-02-05_Ex4)

However most NPs have no case clitic, and semantic role is induced from context and world knowledge. One case suffix, /=ɹe/, marks a disjoint range of thematic roles, while the four other case suffixes /=nu, =ḍa, =nukun, =wanku/ are all more specific (Table 7.3).

Table 7.3: Nominal case clitics.

=ɹe[52]	AGENTIVE	paŋkuj=ɹe	'the snake (did it)'
	INSTRUMENTAL	liṯpur=ɹe	'with an axe'
	PERLATIVE	kani=ɹe	'around here'
	ESSIVE	muntak=ɹe	'in the old times'
=nu	DATIVE	ɲiɲi=nu	'for you'
	ALLATIVE	dawun=nu	'to Darwin'
=ðaŋunu	SOURCE	tɹak=ðaŋunu	'from the vehicle'
=ḍa	LOCATIVE	we puyuna=ḍa	'in the sisters' paperbark' (LK, 2000-11-20)
=nukun	GENITIVE	elikapta=nukun	'of the helicopter'
=wanku ~ =wunku	COMITATIVE	palŋun=wanku	'with the woman'

Examples (65, 66) show sentences where identical semantic roles appear alternately with and without case markers. Presumably there are factors relating to discourse structure or 'expectedness' that influence the realisation or non-realisation of case markers. However this topic is deferred to a study of Murrinhpatha syntax.

(65a) ṯu-liṯpuɾ=ɹe   baŋam-ṯal
       VIOL-axe=INSTR   affect.3SG.NFUT-chop
       he's chopping (wood) with an axe   (RoDu, 2011-10-10_3-1)

---

52 Maybe the underlying form is /=ṯe/. In hyper-corrected speech one speaker pronounces it alone in this form (HLK, 1976_4372B).

(65b) ṯu-liṯpuɾ baŋam-ṯal
VIOL-axe affect.3SG.NFUT-chop
he's chopping (wood) with an axe   (AnBu, 2011-07-21_3-1)

(66a) kaṉi=ka kaḏu-ṯeɾeṯ pumpan ŋaɾa shop=nu
this=CST PERS-many go.3PL.NFUT LOC shop=ALLATIVE
all these people are going <u>to the shop</u>   (FlAl, 2011-08-01_RT-FA_3-10)

(66b) meɾe wuɾini-lili-ða ŋaɾa shop
NEG go.3SG.PST-walk-PST LOC shop
he didn't walk to the shop   (CW, 2015-07-13_PI)

Two of the adverbials described in the next section, /=(ka)ṯu/ FROM and /=(wa)ŋu/ TOWARDS, also often attach to NPs to specify semantic role. For instance, they may indicate AGENT and THEME roles respectively (67, 68). However I categorise these with adverbials, rather than case suffixes, for distributional reasons. Like adverbials, they attach not just to NPs but also to verbs, and whereas case suffixes generally appear before adverbials, /=waŋu/ and /=kaṯu/ may occur after other adverbials.

(67) mem-biḻ kaḏu-ṉini=ṯu=ju
do.RR.3SG.NFUT-look.around PERS-ANAPH=FROM=CLS
that man he looks around   (CP, 2011-09-09_2-5L)

(68) ku-weɾe=waŋu mem-ni-biḻ
ANIM-pawed.beast=TOWARD do.RR.3SG.NFUT-RR-look.around
he turns (himself) to look at the lion   (CP, 2011-09-09_2-11)

NPs host only a single case marker, there is no 'stacking' as in some other Australian languages (Dench & Evans, 1988). There are a handful of examples that arguably may combine /=ɾe/ ESSIVE with /=nu/ ALLATIVE (69–71; cited in Seiss, 2011, p. 166), however the /=nu/here could alternatively be interpreted as a future tense marker, which can attach to time-referencing nominals (§6.3.2).[53]

(69) ḍa=ka ṉini=nu=ɾe=ka
TIME=CST ANAPH=?DAT=ESS=CST
at that time   (GM, 1990_70)

(70) ḍa ŋaɾa manta=ɾe=nu
TIME LOC near=ESS=?DAT
a time to come soon   (GM, 1990_70)

---

[53] Note also that these are all found in one written text, part of the Bible translation (Wycliffe Bible Translators, 1990).

(71) ḍa   nakuḷ=ɻe=nu=ja
      TIME later=ESS=?DAT=INTJ
      at a later time   (GM, 1990_47)

7.5.1 Prefixing of comitative case

There is a distinct morphological construct for the /wunku/ COMITATIVE case morph, where the case marker is prefixed to a nominal stem. However there are only a handful of examples attested for this construct, all produced by a speakers born in the pre-mission era. Most examples are with a simple nominal lexeme (72, 73), though one additionally has a compounded body part nominal (§6.4.3) and a number suffix (74).

(72) ŋuɲe-wutpun-ða=waḍa=ṭu-ɲime   wunku-ṭiṭaj=ju
      go.1PC.IRR-carry-PST=SEQ=FROM-PAUC.F   COMIT-honey=CLS
      we were going along carrying honey (MaNa, 1980_CS1-17A-06)

(73) wankuwakal   daɲaŋɲe   kuɻawanku
      wanku-wakal   daŋam-ḍe   kuɻa=wanku
      COMIT-child   AFFECT.2SG.NFUT-punch WATER=COMIT
      you drunkenly punched her when she was with her children
      (LuTch, 2016-07-05_SCOPIC02)

(74) peɻe-ninṭa=ju   wunku-maḍa-naŋkun-ninṭa=ju
      3PC.M-DUAL.M=CLS   COMIT-belly-brother.in.law-DUAL.M=CLS
      wuḍam-ninṭa-waḷ=ðara
      IMPEL.3SG.NFUT-DUAL.M-shoot=MOVING
      the two brothers-in-law, together inside (the vehicle), shot (at the wallaby) as they were moving   (MaNa, 1980_CS1-17A-07)

7.6 Adverbial clitics

Murrinhpatha has two classes of bound morphs that attach themselves promiscuously to any word type, be it nominal, verb, coverb or the negator and complementiser 'function words' (§4.2). The two promiscuous classes are adverbials and discourse clitics (described in the next section), and I label them 'clitics' since they attach at phrase level. Murrinhpatha has VPs [Coverb Verb] (§8.2) and PPs [Prep NP]. For these two phrase types, enclitics can attach to any word in the phrase. By contrast, for NPs [Class-Noun Adj Det] (§4.3.1) they attach only to the final word in the phrase.

Adverbials have a rather miscellaneous range of functions, in various ways modifying predicate semantics, or cuing information and discourse structure

(Street, 1996, p. 214ff.). Many have a modal or epistemic character, and in general their semantics are more grammatical than lexical. However they do not have the paradigmatic, obligatory character of inflectional morphology (Stump, 2005). The fourteen adverbial bound morphs attested in my corpus are listed in Table 7.4. Adverbials are always bound morphs: they never occur as independent utterances, nor as the host for bound morphology. Nonetheless, in vernacular orthography, adverbials are usually written as separate words.

The examples below illustrate single and double adverbials, attaching to a range of nominals (75–82). The principles influencing the sequence of double adverbials are unclear, and would require a more substantial corpus collection for analysis. A substantial number of examples are provided below to illustrate some of the possibilities, including the possibility that the same pair of adverbials may have alternate sequences (81, 82).

Nominal-Adverbial(-Adverbial)
(75) [[ka:]ω [n̪ínta]ω=ŋu]φ
car   ANAPH=TOWARD
towards that car   (AnBu, 2011-07-22_3-6)
(76) [[kala]ω [kán̪i]ω=mani]φ [[kán̪i]ω=mat̪a]φ
colour this=ATTEMPT   this=EMPH
how about this colour, right here?   (MaMi, 2015-07-21)

Table 7.4: Adverbial clitics. Forms with parenthetic elements, e.g. /=(d̪a)mat̪a/, usually have the parenthesised portion deleted in fluent speech.

=nimin	CONTRASTIVE	n̪ini=nimin	'you (not someone else)'
=wad̪a	SEQUENTIAL	ŋaj=wad̪a	'me now' (cf. Ritz & Schultze-Berndt, 2015)
=(d̪a)mat̪a	EMPHATIC	kan̪i=mat̪a	'right here'
=n̪at̪a	CONDITIONAL	n̪ala=n̪at̪a	'if it were large'
=ŋa(ða)	DIMINUTION	mi=ŋa	'a bit of food'
=de(jida)	ITERATIVE	n̪ini=de	'that same one again'
=kama	UNKNOWN	kan̪i=kama	'maybe this one'
=(wa)ra	FIRST	ŋaj=wara	'me first'
=wa	UNEXPECTED	kad̪u=wa	'(look out for) the person!'
=ðat̪pir	TRUE	murin̪=ðat̪pir	'true words'
=ðara †	MOVING	dawun=ðara	'on the way to Darwin'
=(ka)t̪u	FROM	wadeje=kat̪u	'(moving/facing) from Wadeye'
	DEMAND	mi=kat̪u	'(give) some food!'
=(wa)ŋu	TOWARDS	pepi=waŋu	'towards Peppi'
=mani	ATTEMPTIVE	ŋaj=mani	'I'll try' (cf. Rumsey, 2001)
=mana	DEDUCTIVE	kan̪i=mana	'it must be this one'
=wejida	UNDESIRED	kan̪i=wejida	'this isn't the right one'

† There is a closely related coverb /t̪ara/ 'run', as seen in (83) below.

(77) [páṭa]ω=waḍa=ŋaṭa
good=SEQ=CONDIT
(it) would be fine then (AMN, 2015-01-29_Pr2-CI2)
(78) [niɣúnu]ω=waḍa=ṭu wuḍam-ṭuk
she=SEQ=FROM IMPEL.RR.3SG.NFUT-send
now she appears (MM, 2011-09-13_2-5h)
(79) [ŋáj]ω=waḍa=mani
1SG=SEQ=ATTEMPT
how about me now? (SL, 2011-08-08_SL-PM_2-3)
(80) [kúː]ω=ḍejida=waḍa
creature=ITER=SEQ
now another creature (MM, 2011-09-13_2-11)
(81) weɹe [lájan]ω=ðaṭpir=waḍa
pawed.beast lion=TRUE=SEQ
now an actual lion (MM, 2011-09-13_2-11)
(82) kuḍán-paṭ [ŋála]ω=waḍa=ðaṭpir
IMPEL.RR.3SG.PRSL-fear big=SEQ=TRUE
he's really terrified now (MM, 2011-09-13_2-11)

7.6.1 Promiscuous attachment

Adverbials generally attach to the right-most PWord in any PPhrase, though this is not their only distribution. Verbs and coverbs both host adverbials, and both these word types always constitute PPhrases in their own right (83, 84). In NPs, it is generally only the right-most PWord, also right-most in a PPhrase, that hosts adverbials (85). Thus we can almost posit a generalised PPhrase-attachment for adverbials, except that they also attach to negators, which are non-final PWords in PPhrases constituted by either NPs or VPs (86).

(83) [[ṭára]ω=waḍa]φ ŋem-ku
run=SEQ sit.1SG.IRR-run
I'm going to run now (JaLo, 2013-01)
(84) naṇṭimaɣúlkul kanammátkutkamawaḍa
naṇṭi-maɣulkul [[kanam-ma-kutkut]ω=kama=waḍa]φ
THING-heart be.3SG.NFUT-APPL-collect.PLUR=UNKNOWN=SEQ
his heart might be pounding now (MM, 2011-09-13_2-11)
(85) [[kaː]ω [ṇínta]ω=ṇu]φ
[car ANAPH=TOWARD]NP
towards that car (AnBu, 2011-07-22_3-6)

(86) [[meɹe]ω=<u>wad̪a</u> [mád̪a]ω]φ [[má-at̪]ω]φ   t̪u-kuj=ju
    [NEG=SEQ   feeling   use.hands.1SG.IRR-get]VP VIOL-fight=CLS
    now I don't like fighting   (MaNi, 2015-02-07_Pr2-D1)

When attaching to a nominal, adverbials attach after case clitics (87, 88), which is expected given that case clitics are more selective. For verbs, however, adverbials are mixed in with the variably sequenced external layer of predicational suffixes (89) (§6.3.4).

(87) pleit   [númi]ω=nu=wad̪a
    plate   one=DAT=SEQ
    for one plate now   (ClK, 2011-08-30_3-1)
(88) kuran   [pán̪u]ω=ɹe=nimin
    go.3SG.PRSL   there=PERL=CONTR
    running along there too   (MaWo, 2012-07-11)
(89) [mam-wun-ŋku-makat]ω=<u>wad̪a</u>-nin̪t̪a
    use.hands.3SG.NFUT-3PL.OBJ-PC.OBJ-evade=SEQ-DUAL
    now it got away from the two of them   (MvM, 2011-09-13_3-11h)

The morphotactic layering of nominals is therefore as in (90) (cf. Walsh, 1976, p. 265ff.). Adverbials are consistently positioned after case, and discourse clitics (see §7.6 below) are consistently positioned after adverbials.

Nominal morphotactics
(90) Classifier-[Nominal]ω=Case=Adverbial=Adverbial=Discourse

The unit of meaning affected by the adverbial is often a whole clause, rather than a verbal predicate or a nominal argument. Within the clause, adverbials do not seem to select any particular phrase as the target for attachment, though impressionistically the first phrase seems to be favoured. Examples above illustrate adverbials attaching to both first phrases (78, 83, 86), last phrases (82, 84) and being spread over multiple phrases (76). Furthermore, unlike nominal morphology discussed above, adverbials *do* exhibit gapping on co-ordinate XPs, in which case they attach to the first half of the coordination (91).

(91) kad̪u-nuyan̪   pulit̪   n̪ini=ka   dem-pin̪t̪ut̪=<u>wad̪a</u>
    PERS-man   paralysed   ANAPH=CST   [PIERCE.RR.3SG.NFUT-get.up=SEQ]VP
    i   kumpara=wara   pirim-wun-mad̪at̪   ŋara kad̪u
    and [in.front=FIRST stand.3SG.NFUT-3PL.OBJ-surprise]VP LOC   person
    then the paralysed man got up and stood before them unexpectedly
    (GrMo, 1990_Lk5:17-26-008-1)

Thus adverbials can be said to attach at a higher level syntactically, and more external level morphotactically, compared to the case clitics and classifier nouns above, and especially compared to the internal predicate inflections described in the last chapter.

7.6.2 Demonstrative and interrogatives hosting adverbials

Despite the generally phrasal attachment of adverbials, there are some special cases where they attach to demonstratives and interrogatives as prosodically internal units. There is one demonstrative and one interrogative that attach all adverbials internally, and four adverbials that attach internally to any demonstrative or interrogative. These combinations constitute exceptions to the prosodic constituency found elsewhere in phrasal structures, suggesting that they are lexically stored as constructions rather than being generated as phrases.

Murrinhpatha has six distinct demonstratives, and four interrogatives (Table 7.5). Both are closed sub-classes of the general nominal word type (§4.2). The semantics of demonstratives, which are intimately connected with pointing and other gestures, is discussed in Blythe et al. (2016).

The stems that always attach adverbials internally are the demonstrative /ṇini/ ANAPH (92–94), and the interrogative /ŋara/ 'what, where?' (95, 96). Note that in these prosodically internal constructs, the adverbial is internally adjoined even if it attaches outside a case marker or another adverbial; thus it can make other, normally external morphs internal (96). But from the evidence available, it appears that /ṇini/ and /ŋara/ internally host only one adverbial, and not a second (94).

Table 7.5: Murrinhpatha demonstratives and interrogatives. Alternate forms do not show any clear difference in meaning, and are probably related by fusion of the clitic /=ḍa/ LOCATIVE.

Demonstrative	Alternate forms	Meaning
kaṇi	kaḍa, kanta	PROXIMAL
ṇini	ṇinta	ANAPHORIC
pana		RECOGNITIONAL
paŋu		DISTAL
ṭi (less common)		?DISTAL
ŋaŋka (obsolete)		DISTAL
Interrogative		**Meaning**
ŋara		what, where?
ṭaŋku		what, which?
naŋkal		who?
miṇtiɟe		when?

(92) [n̪ini=mát̪a]ω
ANAPH=EMPH
that one, exactly (LP, 2015-07-09)

(93) [d̪a-[t̪aŋku]ω [n̪ini=wára]ω=ju]φ
TIME-year ANAPH=FIRST=CLS
last year (AMN, 2015-01-30_Pr3-D1)

(94) [ŋalan̪t̪ar [n̪ini=wád̪a]ω=d̪e]φ
old.man ANAPH=SEQ=ITER
that same old man again (McMn, 2015-07-21)

(95) [[ŋara=nímin]ω]φ ŋama-nu kan̪i=ju
what=CONTR do.1SG.IRR-FUT this=CLS
what will I do about this other one!? (SL, 2011-08-08_2-11)

(96) [ŋara=ɻe=wád̪a]ω]φ kad̪u-t̪ipmam=ju
what=INSTR=SEQ PERS-black=CLS
how do Aboriginal people... (AMN, 2015-01-30_Pr3-D2-SC2)

Four adverbials attach internally, not just to the two stems above, but to any demonstrative or interrogative. These are /=(ka)t̪u/ FROM, /=(wa)ŋu/ TOWARDS, /=kama/ UNKNOWN, and /=wara/ FIRST (97–105). Again, this condition prosodifies the adverbial internally even if it attaches outside of a case suffix or another adverbial (101, 102, 104), while adverbials attached outside it remain external (105). Also note that the directional adverbials /=(ka)t̪u/ FROM, /=(wa)ŋu/ TOWARDS, usually have their first syllables deleted when adjoining vowel-final demonstratives and interrogatives.

/=kat̪u/ FROM
(97) [ŋaŋka=kát̪u]ω
there=FROM
from there (LK, 2000-11-10)

(98) paŋát̪u
[paŋu=káthu]ω
from over there

(99) [ŋara=kát̪u]ω pin̪t̪im-kájkaj
where=FROM perch.3PL.NFUT-call.PLUR
where are (the birds) calling out from? (LP, 2015-07-09)

/=waŋu/ TOWARDS
(100) ŋaráŋu
[ŋara=wáŋu]ω
where=TOWARDS
where to? (LP, 2015 07-09)

(101) ŋaraḍéŋu
[ŋara=ḍe=wáŋu]ω
where=ITER=TOWARDS
where to again? (SeDu, 2015-07-09)

(102) núŋamtim   kaṉiwaḍáŋu
nuŋam-dim   [kaṉi=waḍa=wáŋu]ω
use.feet.3SG.NFUT-SIT.IMPF here=SEQ=TOWARD
now he's coming this way (MiKu, 2011-08-21_3-1)

/=kama/ UNKNOWN

(103) naṉṭi-nuŋam-ṭi-min [ŋara=káma]ω
THING-use.foot.3SG.NFUT-bottom-clasp where=UNKNOWN
where's he speeding off to? (LP, 2015-07-09)

(104) [naŋkal=ṭe=káma]ω
who=AGENT=UNKNOWN
who (did it)? (MaNi, 2015-02-05_Pa2-D1)

/=waɾa/ FIRST

(105) kaḍu-[paŋu=wáɾa]ω=ŋa
PERS-there=FIRST=DIMIN
how about the man there first? (SL, 2011-08-08_2-3)

7.7 Discourse clitics

The second class of phrasal morphology in Murrinhpatha is the discourse clitics, a set of three semantically empty bound morphs that attach at the right edge of any syntactic phrase. Their function is rather unclear and requires more research, but the most plausible hypotheses are that they help mark phrase edges, cue information structure and pragmatic intent (Wilmoth, 2014, p. 38). The three discourse clitics, with their rather arbitrary glosses, are as follows:

/=ka/   CONSTITUENT (CST)
/=ju/   CLAUSE (CLS)
/=ja/   INTERJECTION (INTJ)

Discourse clitics are used prolifically in hesitant, disfluent speech, suggesting that they additionally have a turn-holding function like the English 'um' and 'ah' (cf. Himmelmann, 2014, p. 942). The clitic /=ka/ CONSTITUENT usually appears on non-final phrase constituents in an utterance, while the clitic /=ju/ CLAUSE usually appears clause-finally (106–108). However /=ka/ may also appear clause-finally when an implicit question is formed by simply naming a referent with an interrogative intonation (Nordlinger, *p.c.*) (109, 110).

(106) t̪u=**ka** meɻe ŋuna-bat-ða muɳt̪ak=waɖa=**ju**
[[fight]~NP~=CST [NEG use.foot.1SG.PST-hit-PST]~VP~ [before]~NP~=SEQ]~CLAUSE~=CLS
I didn't hit her before (MaNi, 2015-02-02_Pr2-D1)

(107) t̪aj larin paɲu baŋam-t̪at̪al=**ka** t̪uŋku
[[wood dry DISTAL]~NP~ [AFFECT.3SG.NFUT-chop.PL]~VP~=CST [fire]~NP~]~CLAUSE~
he's chopping that dead wood for a fire (DaMa, 2011-08-25_3-1)

(108) kaɖu=**ka** dini-ŋurkurk-ða kaɖu=**ju**
[[person]~NP~=CST [sit.3SG.PST-sleep.PLUR-PST]~VP~ [person]~NP~]=CLS
he was asleep (SaLo, 2011-08-08_2-1)

(109) Maɟara=ka?
NAME=CST
Madjarra (is he there)?

(110) muriṉ=ka?
language=CST
language (shall we transcribe some)?

The /=ja/ clitic is usually attached to phrases with an interjective or interrogative function (111) (Wilmoth, 2014).

(111) paɲu=**ka** muriṉ-kuɻa=kama=**ja**
[[[there]~NP~=CST [LANG-water=UNKNOWN]~NP~=INTJ]~CLAUSE~
there, the talk seems incomprehensible! (lit. 'water language')
(AMN, 2015-01-30_Pr3-D1-EC1)

We saw above that adverbials generally attach at the right edge of phrases, though with exceptions relating to negators, demonstratives and variable sequencing of suffixes on verbs. Discourse clitics are attached more strictly at the right edge of syntactic phrases, which always gives them the final position in PPhrases (112, 113). They attach outside of all other classes of bound morphs, including adverbials (114, 115).

(112) [ku-[tit̪a]~ω~ [nukúnu]~ω~=**ka**]~φ~ mem-na-bil=kat̪u=waɖa
[ANIM-teacher 3SG]~NP~=CST do.RR.3SG.NFUT-3SG.OBL-look=FROM=SEQ
now his teacher looks at him (SM, 2011-08-08_2-3)

(113) [[t̪ára]~ω~]~φ~ [[ju-wiṉáɻat̪]~ω~-ða=**ka**]~φ~ ɖa-nan=mat̪a=ŋu
[run lie.3SG.PST-run-PST]~VP~=CST PLACE-whats.it=EMPH=TOWARDS
he ran all the way to what's-it-called (PaPu, 2011-09-01_02)

(114) paŋu=ɹe=ju
[there=ESS]NP=CLS
around that place (SM, 2011-08-08_2-3)

(115) munʈak=wada=ka
[before]NP=SEQ=CST
in the old days (MkN, 2015-02-07_Pr2-D1)

The corpus contains just a handful of possible counter-examples to the phrase-edge positioning of discourse clitics. These all involve monosyllabic CV classifier nouns hosting the /=ka/ clitic, and exempt the open monosyllables from bimoraic lengthening. This suggests that /=ka/ may represent a secondary strategy for achieving bimoraic weight in open monosyllables (116, 117) (§4.3.1).

(116) [[ku=ka]ω [weɹe]ω [ŋala]ω]φ
[ANIM=CST furry.quadruped big]NP
the big dog (CP, 2009-07-07_04)

(117) [[mi=ka]ω [ðiː]ω=ɹe]φ [[láwam]ω=ju]φ
[VEG=CST there=ESS]NP bread=CLS
the food over there, the bread (NoPe, 2009-07-07_04)

7.8 Summary

In this chapter we have explored the morphology of nominal arguments and phrases, which involves less complexity and looser binding, compared to verbal morphology. The first type of such nominal morphology, classifier nouns, has a mixture of lexical and inflectional characteristics. Classifier nouns are in fact a special instance of NOM-NOM compounding, but one that is exceptionally prevalent. At the right edge of the noun phrase are case clitics, which mark the semantic role of nominal arguments in clause structure, but are only used occasionally and therefore play a fairly minor role in the grammar.

Adverbials and discourse clitics attach to any type of phrase. Adverbials have more complicated distribution as they may also sit among a verb's predicational suffixes, or attach to a phrase-initial negative function word, whereas discourse clitics more strictly attach to the end of syntactic phrases. In the next chapter we return to more tightly bound structures in the verb, before reviewing the morphology as a whole in the final chapter.

8 Complex verbs and compounding

8.1 Introduction

Discussion of verbs in previous chapters has focused on the 39 finite verb stems and the inflectional affixes that attach to them. But the majority of the Murrinhpatha verb lexicon is composed of verb stems combined with coverbs. I refer to such verbs as *complex verbs*, in opposition to the *simple verbs* constituted by verb stems as independent lexemes. Complex verbs may be structured as two-word phrases, [Coverb Verb]$_{VP}$, but much more frequently are structured as compound verbs, [VerbStem[-Coverb]]$_V$. The compounding mechanism is so dominant that three quarters of the finite verb stems, and the majority of coverbs, appear only in compounds. The development of so many bound verbs and coverbs has been accompanied by substantial semantic opacity, such that in many verbs it is difficult or impossible to attribute distinct meanings to the two lexical elements. If this were not complexity enough, many coverbs are themselves compounds of a coverb root combined with a body part nominal, making the overall verb a trilexical recursive compound verb, [VerbStem[-[Bodypart-]Coverb]]$_V$. Again, the semantic contribution of the body part is often opaque.

The formation of compound verbs interacts with the internal/external layering of predicate inflectional suffixes: the coverb is attached after all internal suffixes, and before all external suffixes. Lexical compounding generally works by adjoining a second lexeme either directly to the stem of the first lexeme (as in [sabre-[tooth]]-s), or to the whole inflected form of the first lexeme (as in [milk-[teeth]]) (Anderson, 1992, p. 295). Murrinhpatha presents a third distinct type, where the adjoined lexeme is attached to a prosodic edge, which may occur either before or after various inflectional affixes, rather than attaching to a morphosyntactically specified host. 'Prosodic compounding' of this type has not been attested in any other language as far as I know (Mansfield, 2017).

The next section describes the general distinction between simple verbs, and the two complex types: phrasal verbs and compound verbs. Section §8.3 categorises finite verb stems according to their degree of independence and semantic transparency. Section §8.4 introduces the coverb lexical class, while section §8.5 describes the compounding of coverbs with body part nominals, and section §8.6 describes a reduplicative process that derives pluractional coverbs. Section §8.7 describes the attachment of coverbs to a prosodic anchor point on the finite verb stem, and the recursive prosodic word structure that is thereby constituted.

8.2 Simple, phrasal and compound verbs

The previous two chapters have focused the discussion of verb morphology on what we will call *simple verbs*, i.e. those that deploy a finite verb stem as an independent lexical item, without any further verbal lexical material (1). But Murrinhpatha makes extensive use of *complex verbs*, where the verbal predicate combines a finite verb stem with a coverb. Complex verbs may be morphologically realised either as a phrasal verb (2) or a compound (3):

(1) [wúran]$_\omega$
 go.3SG.NFUT
 she's going

(2) [[wilíli]$_\omega$]$_\varphi$ [[wúran]$_\omega$]$_\varphi$
 walk go.3SG.NFUT
 she's walking

(3) [wuran-líli]$_\omega$
 go.3SG.NFUT-walk
 she's walking

Complex verbs are a common form of verbal predication throughout north-western Australia. In most of these languages the combinations take a phrasal form (Bowern, 2014; McGregor, 2002; Nash, 1982; Schultze-Berndt, 2003), but compounding is the main lexical verb type in various other languages including Gooniyandi (McGregor, 1990), Gaagudju (Harvey, 2002), and several Daly region languages (Tryon, 1974). In both Murrinhpatha and in other north-western languages, the coverb class has considerable overlap with nominals. The coverb class, unlike the finite verb stem class, is open to lexical borrowing; but borrowed coverbs are generally used only as independent words, and not in compounds (Mansfield, 2016a).

The majority of the Murrinhpatha verbal vocabulary (excluding recent borrowings from English) occurs only in compounds. Most coverbs, and 29 of the 39 finite verb stem stems, are only attested in this bound form. Verb stems in compounds have been labelled 'classifier stems', in view of their tendency to classify events in terms of valency, aktionsart, instrument, vector and posture (Nordlinger, 2015). Classifiers make a transparent semantic contribution to some compounds (4a,b), but not to others (5a,b). As illustrated in these examples, coverbs may combine with several different classifier stems. Since there is only a small set of classifiers, it is inevitable that at least some of these must combine with many different coverbs. The two lexical classes have a many-to-many relationship in compounding.

(4a) maɻídanu
 ma-ṭiḍa-nu
 use.hands.1SG.IRR-push-FUT
 {Classifier-Coverb}
 I'll push it (by hand)

(4b) nuɲuɻídanu
 nuɲu-ṭiḍa-nu
 use.foot.3SG.IRR-push-FUT
 {Classifier-Coverb}
 I'll push it with my foot (Street, 2012: *-rirda*)

(5a) bam-ɲi-ɻalal
 AFFECT.3SG.NFUT-1SG.OBJ-discomfort
 {Classifier-PRON-Coverb}
 I'm cold

(5b) dem-ɲi-ɻalal
 PIERCE.RR.3SG.NFUT-1SG.OBJ-discomfort
 {Classifier-PRON-Coverb}
 I'm thirsty

In terms of discourse frequency, there are generally about twice as many compound verbs used as there are simple verbs (Table 8.1). It is not surprising that compound verbs should dominate, since these are a large lexical class with thousands of members, while there are only ten simple verb lexemes. But the fact that simple verbs nonetheless account for a substantial minority of discourse tokens shows that some members of this small lexicon are used very frequently. The discourse frequency of the third verb type, phrasal verbs, is quite different between younger and older speakers. For younger speakers this is a substantial category accounting for 17% of discourse verb tokens, whereas for older speakers phrasal verbs are quite rare, accounting for only 1% of verb tokens. This difference is largely accounted for by the greater use of English loanwords by younger speakers, since these are borrowed as coverbs in phrasal but not in compound form (Mansfield, 2016a).

Table 8.1: Discourse frequency of three verb types. Data is from (Mansfield, 2016a, p. 420), augmented by a further 101 tokens from one older speaker (GM, 1977-00-00), and 109 tokens from one younger speaker (DP, 2012-06-20_25).

	Simple	*Compound*	*Phrasal*	*Total N*
All tokens	30% (249)	61% (516)	9% (76)	(841)
(Older speakers)	31% (128)	68% (277)	1% (4)	(409)
(Younger speakers)	28% (121)	55% (239)	17% (72)	(432)

8.3 The verbiness of verb stems

Some finite verb stems are complete verbs in themselves, being independent words that function as lexical predicates of event semantics. Others have less verby properties in various ways. As mentioned above, the term 'classifier stem' is applied to verb stems in compounds, which we may contrast against 'simple stems' for those that form independent words. Here I further categorise verb stems with respect to their lexico-semantic status. The following analysis is based on some 400 compounds extracted from the Murrinhpatha dictionary (Street, 2012). These were arranged into sets by verb stem, to reach an impressionistic estimate as to the degree of semantic consistency in each set. Further research will be required for more comprehensive semantic analysis. The four categories of verb stem are:

Simple verb stems

    Lexical verb stem – Can occur as a simple verb, and when it occurs as a classifier in compounds, its independent meaning is usually maintained as a semantic element of the compound.

    Light verb stem – Can occur as a simple verb, but when it occurs as a classifier in compounds, its independent meaning is often not maintained.

Classifier-only verb stems

    Semantic classifier – Occurs only as a classifier, and makes a fairly consistent semantic contribution to compounds.

    Pseudo-classifier – Occurs only in compounds, and does not make a consistent semantic contribution.

The boundaries are somewhat fuzzy between the first two categories, and the second two categories, respectively, because the matter of semantic transparency is a cline of metaphorical extension.

The most clearly lexical verbs are /ɾa/ 'stand', /ṉta/ 'perch', /i/ 'lie', /ɾu/ 'go' and /ṉti/ 'carry'. Each of these may form a simple verb when appropriately inflected (§6.2), and contributes transparently to compounds as illustrated in Table 8.2. For reference, verb stems are listed along with the arbitrarily assigned classifier numbers (CN) by which they are identified in previous works (e.g. Blythe, 2009; Nordlinger, 2015; Street, 1987). As discussed in an earlier chapter (§5.2.3), there are several verb stems with homophonous inner stems, though their finite forms are nonetheless distinguished by different inflectional allomorphy.

The remaining simple verbs are less semantically transparent in compounds (Table 8.3). The label 'light verb' is appropriate for these because they have both

Table 8.2: Lexical verbs and some examples of compounds.

Verb	CN	Transparent compounds
/i/ 'lie'	2	/-ŋurkurk/ 'sleep', /-pup/ 'die', /-wal/ '(of a snake) strike'
/ra/ 'stand'	3	/-at̪/ 'stand up', /-kampa/ 'stand laughing', /-bat/ 'throw missile'
/n̪t̪a/ 'perch'	5	/-kaj/ '(of a bird) call out', /-mad̪i/ '(of a new moon) rise'
/ru/ 'go'	6	/-lili/ 'walk', /-kampa/ 'walk along laughing', /-kaḻ/ 'move in a straight line'
/n̪t̪i/ 'carry'	22	/-kum/ 'swim while holding something', /-wiṉaɻat/ 'run away with something'

Table 8.3: Light verbs and some examples of compounds.

Verb	CN	Transparent compounds	Opaque compounds
/i/ 'sit'	1	/-ɻel/ 'sing (sitting)', /-t̪ek/ 'defecate'	/-ku/ 'run', /-paḻ/ 'be broken'
/nu/ 'use feet'	7	/-ɻid̪a/ 'kick', /-wiṉaɻat/ 'run', /-ku/ 'throw',/-bir/ 'throw spear'[54]	/-wut̪/ 'be feeble'
/ma/ 'do, say'	8, 34	–	/-ɻiked̪ek/ 'finish', /-ŋkawur/ 'have a headache'
/me/ 'do, say RR'	10	–	/-biḻ/ 'turn and look'
/ni/ 'be'	4	–	/-kut/ 'gather', /-wup/ 'sit down'

independent, albeit highly generic lexical meanings, but also appear in complex predicates where their meaning is lost (Butt & Geuder, 2001). The verbs /ni/ 'be' and /ma/ 'do, say' are particularly 'light', in that even their independent usages encode aktionsart categories (state or customary action, and telic action, respectively) rather than more specifically 'lexical' semantics. Accordingly, these contribute aktionsart properties rather than lexical semantics to the compounds in which they appear.

Classifier-only stems are about equally divided into *semantic classifiers* and *pseudo-classifiers*. As mentioned in an earlier chapter, all transitive stems are classifier-only, and pseudo-classifiers, the most semantically opaque type, are all transitive verbs (§6.2.4).

---

[54] /nu/ 'use feet' appears in several compounds involving throwing projectiles. We might think of these actions as more obviously involving the hands or arms than the feet – but the feet are actually also involved in throwing projectiles with force.

Table 8.4: Semantic classifiers and examples of compounds.

Verb	CN	Compound examples
/ma/ 'use hands'	8, 9	/-paṭa/ 'make', /-puteṭ/ 'turn by hand', /-jel̪/ 'paint', /-ṭa/ 'catch'
/me/ 'use hands RR'	10	/-kurk/ 'scratch oneself', /-ṭa/ 'catch each other'
/ni/ 'use feet RR'	38	/-bir/ 'throw spears at each other'
/a/ 'use mouth'[55]	19	/-ðarpu/ 'ask, request', /-ṭiraṭ/ 'lie', /-ṭap/ 'taste', /-ŋkabir/ 'scold'
/e/ 'use mouth RR'	21	/-ŋkabir/ 'argue', /-ŋkawaj/ 'refuse'
/a/ 'appear'	20	/-ɹuðaj/ 'emerge', /-ɹuj/ 'arrive'
/ŋa/ 'put together'	25	/-pup/ 'lay objects in a pile', /-melal̪/ 'plait fibres', /-lip/ 'squash together'
/la/ 'wipe'	26	/-pul/ 'wipe', /-kurk/ 'sharpen', /-ṭum/ 'wipe dry'
/li/ 'wipe RR'	37	/-ṭum/ 'wipe oneself dry'
/na/ 'use fire'	27	/-ṭi/ 'cook', /waṭ/ 'singe', /-wu/ 'warm'
/ra/ 'watch'	28	/-baṭ/ 'watch', /-ŋalbal̪/ '(of a dog) glare barking', /-maɹit/ 'learn by observation', /-ŋke/ 'be jealous'
/ri/ 'watch RR'	36	/-ŋkaɹit/ 'gaze at one's own reflection'
/ŋu/ 'pull'	32	/-wuj/ 'eject', /-jeɣaj/ 'move something out of the way', /-jer/ '(of the tide) recede'
/ŋi/ 'pull RR'	33	/-wuj/ 'exit', /-ɹaṭtaṭ/ 'move oneself out of the way'
/mi/ 'look'	12	/-jer/ 'look around'
/la/ 'eat'	31	/-aṭ/ 'eat'
/bi/ 'hear'	16	/-jepup/ 'hear'
/nṭa/ 'crouch'	35	/-ṭa/ 'crouch', /-ŋkaḍal/ 'balance', /-te/ 'be sleepless'

Table 8.4 lists the semantic classifiers: those that occur only in compounds, but for which a lexico-semantic meaning can be posited based on a fairly consistent semantic element in those compounds. For some of these there are also a few compounds that do not fit the semantic pattern, but I focus here on exemplifying those that do fit the pattern. There are different degrees of semantic consistency among the semantic classifiers. For example, /na/ 'use fire', /la/ 'wipe' and /ra/ 'watch' have sets of compounds that are totally consistent or almost so in featuring the glossed semantic element. /ŋa/ 'put together' is also fairly consistent, but has somewhat opaque outliers /-ɣaŋaweṭ/ 'sun set' and /-baṭ/ 'have something caught in one's throat'.

---

[55] Note that /a/ 'use mouth' is homophonous with /a/ PIERCE, because both have the same default stem, and share the same inflectional paradigm (Nordlinger p.c.). Allotting opaque compounds to one of these verbs or the other is therefore somewhat arbitrary, but because /a/ 'use mouth' seems to have a slightly stronger semantic pattern, I have allotted opaque compounds to /a/ PIERCE.

The list of semantic classifiers includes several reflexive/reciprocal (RR) stems, which are derived from transitive verb stems (§5.4) (Nordlinger, n.d.). The RR stems in many cases participate in the same compound combinations as their base stems, but there are also instances where they form distinct compound lexemes not attested for their bases, and for this reason they are treated as lexically distinct. Note that RR stems fall into the same light/semantic/pseudo categories as their bases – that is to say they have about the same degree of lexico-semantic integrity. However we saw in an earlier chapter that they have different patterns of inflectional allomorphy from their bases (§5.2.1).

Three stems /la/ 'eat', /mi/ 'look' and /bi/ 'hear' have a special status, because they each occur only in a single compound. Therefore they do not have semantic patterns like other semantic stems, though neither do they have heavily grammaticalised character of pseudo-classifiers. Similarly, /n̠t̠a/ 'crouch' is attested for just three compounds, which makes it more difficult to decide whether these exhibit a semantic pattern.

Table 8.5 lists the pseudo-classifiers, those that appear only in compounds, and for which the set of such compounds has little or no semantic consistency. On the other hand, although pseudo-classifiers are semantically bleached in most compounds, Nordlinger (p.c.) reports that semantically productive usage can be elicited with some speakers. Pseudo-classifiers are all transitive or RR, and most

Table 8.5: Pseudo-classifiers and examples of compounds.

Verb	CN	Compound examples
/ba/ AFFECT	13, 14	/-ɣuḏuk/ 'drink (something)', /-maḏabu/ 'betray', /-ŋkaḏu/ 'see', /-jilil/ 'be in the middle', /-lele/ 'bite'
/be/ AFFECT.RR	15	/-ŋkaḏu/ 'see oneself', /-maḏabi/ 'meet', /-ŋkabu/ 'go too fast'
/bu/ LOWER	17	/-pak/ 'put (down)', /-bat/ 'throw down', /-ðarkat/ 'bog (a vehicle)', /-ðarmupak/ 'retaliate'
/buj/ LOWER.RR	18	/-bat/ 'fall', /-werar/ 'drop to one knee', /maḏaḏu/ 'be out of breath'
/mu/ COERCE	11	/-maḏali/ 'bend', /-wil/ 'convince', /-pal/ 'break off', /-ŋkalili/ 'follow around in a circle'
/a/ PIERCE	19	/-wal/ 'spear, shoot', /-ŋkaj/ 'poke into a hole', /-mut/ 'give', /-ɻiwak/ 'follow'
/e/ PIERCE.RR	21	/-t̠ekum/ 'poke something in one's ear', /jiji/ 'hurry', (object experiencers e.g.: /-t̠eḏe/ 'be in the sun', /-ɻalal/ 'be thirsty')
/u/ SLASH	23	/-ɣat/ 'circumcise', /-pek/ 'comb hair', /-ŋkapul/ '(of sun) rise', /-bat/ 'call by phone', /-wur/ 'measure'
/ju/ SLASH.RR	24	/-jekum/ 'forget', /-t̠elal/ 'carry on head'
/ḏu/ IMPEL	29	/-ŋkal/ 'bring back', /-at̠/ 'exchange', /-t̠uk/ 'send', /-t̠et̠it̠/ 'instruct', /-kulk/ 'soak'
/ḏi/ IMPEL.RR	30	/-wul/ 'go back', /-jir/ 'soak oneself', /-ɻalal/ 'laugh'

of them appear in large numbers of compounds. They are given notional glosses in small capitals, which only sometimes reflect any actual semantic contribution. However, again there is a cline of semantic transparency here, and the cut-off point between semantic classifiers and pseudo-classifiers is somewhat arbitrary. /bu/ LOWER, /mu/ COERCE and /a/ PIERCE all have substantial sets of compounds with shared semantic elements, as illustrated in the table. But in each of these cases I judge the semantic set to be outweighed by a larger set that breaks the semantic pattern. The verbs /ḍu/ IMPEL and /u/ SLASH have only vague semantic patterns among small subsets of the many compounds they appears in. The verb /e/ PIERCE.RR has more of a grammatical than a lexico-semantic pattern for many of its compounds: besides appearing in reflexive/reciprocal versions of /a/ PIERCE compounds, it also appears in a substantial set of object-experiencer compounds (§6.2.4).

8.3.1 Finite verb stems or inflection-class prefixes?

Pseudo-classifiers, taken on their own merits, may not be analysed as verb stems at all. They encode the subject and tense categories associated with finite verb stems, but where they do not contribute a lexico-semantic head, they are more like grammatical prefixes than lexical stems. In fact this analysis could be extended beyond pseudo-classifiers to the instances when light verbs lose their usual semantic content. On this analysis, the coverb becomes the stem of a simplex verb that has both prefixes and suffixes, and the pseudo-classifier becomes an inflectional prefix belonging to an inflectional class selected by the coverb. The differences between an inflectional prefix analysis (where 'VIII' glosses the prefix as inflectional class VIII) and the compound verb analysis are illustrated in (6).

Compound verb analysis
(6a) [[[[[pubaŋam]-ŋi]-ŋkaḍu]-ŋiṇṭa]-piṛim]
[[[[[affect.3PL.NFUT]-1SG.OBJ]-see]-DUAL.F]-SIT.IMPF]
the two of them can see me

Inflectional prefix / simplex verb analysis
(6b) [[[pubaŋam-[ŋi-[ŋkaḍu]]]-ŋiṇṭa]-piṛim]
[[[3PL.NFUT.VIII-[1SG.OBJ-[see]]]-DUAL.F]-SIT.IMPF]
the two of them can see me

The analysis in (6b) accurately represents the loss of predicational, lexical character in the /pubaŋam/ formative. However this analysis results in quite different representations of stem/affix structure for verbs with inflection class prefixes versus those with left-edge stems, and this split into separate representations leads to systematic duplication of all the morphological structures that the two verb types have in common. Since some finite verb stems such as /wuran/ go.3SG. NFUT do retain lexico-semantic character, these must be analysed as belonging to a separate morphosyntactic category from the proposed inflectional prefixes such as /pubaŋam-/ 3PL.NFUT.VIII. This divergence complicates the fact that they have the same position in terms of word structure. Some verbs would be represented as having a left-edge lexical stem, and others as having a word-medial lexical stem. To avoid these complications, and in recognition of the shared structural characteristics of all finite verb stems, the analysis applied in this book treats all complex verbs as compounds headed by a left-edge finite verb stem, while recognising that a subset of finite verb stems are heavily grammaticalised and have largely lost their lexico-semantic character. At the end of this chapter I return to the question of lexical representations for compound verbs.

8.3.2 Psychological status of finite verb stems in compounds

There is evidence that lexical verbs and light verbs appearing in compounds are separable, word-like units for native speakers. One strand of evidence is in alternate phrasal and compounded forms produced under elicitation. For example, (7a, b) were produced in succession by a speaker, suggesting that the cognitive activation of a simple verb (7a) facilitates its use as a classifier (7b).

(7a) máṭar   ŋém
     sick   sit.1SG.NFUT
     I'm sick
(7b) ŋem-máṭar
     sit.1SG.NFUT.sick
     I'm sick   (HJ, 1959_KH)

Further evidence is presented by the orthography used by native speakers who are literate in Murrinhpatha. This does not always follow the linguists' convention of writing compound verbs as single strings. A word-break is sometimes written between finite verb stem and coverb, but this is only attested with lexical verbs and light verbs (8–10). There are no examples of orthographic splitting with classifier-only stems. This raises the possiblity that speakers may in fact have distinct mental representations for lexical verb-headed vs pseudo-classifier-headed compounds, despite their apparent structural similarities. On the other hand, orthographic phenomena may be specific to the acquisition and processing of orthography, where didactic materials present models of lexical stems, but never classifiers, as separately written words. Psycholinguistic research would be required to further understand how Murrinhpatha speakers cognitively represent verb compounding.

(8) 'nanhthi pana <u>wurran bangurr</u> mere niraputh'[56]
 naɲci   pana   wuran-baɲur   meɻe niɻa-puʈ
 THING   KNOWN   go.3SG.NFUT-be.white   neg stand.2PL.IRR-throw.away
 don't throw away those white things! (plastic rubbish)

(9) 'ngipilinh <u>kurran kathuk</u> kanhi warda-wa'[57]
 ŋipiliṉ   kuran-ŋkaðuk   kaɲi-waɖa-wa
 THING   go.3SG.PRSNL-exist   PROX-now-EMPH
 a river runs there now

(10) 'thamul thangunu <u>kardi wuyitpuyitdha-yu</u>'[58]
 ʈamul-ʈaŋunu   kaɖi-pujit-pujit-ða-ju
 spear-SOURCE   be.3SG.PST-shift-PLUR-PST-CLS
 he was shifting (the ocean) with his spear

8.3.3 A recent history of grammaticalisation

There is some evidence to suggest that in recent history verb compounding was more productive, and that the nexus of the VerbStem-Coverb compound was somewhat looser. For Ngan'gi there is substantial evidence of VerbStem-Coverb fusion occurring within the last century (Reid, 2003), and though Murrinhpatha does not enjoy the same wealth of early twentieth-century linguistic records, there are nonetheless some facts suggesting a more modest transition occurring in Murrinhpatha within a similar period. The first item of evidence is that one coverb borrowed since English contact has been compounded with a finite verb stem, /ma-be-ṯigan/ 'use.hands-arm-<u>shake.hands</u>'. Since borrowed coverbs have not been compounded productively at all in recent decades, despite massive lexical borrowing, /ma-ṯigan/ suggests that at some earlier point, when 'shake

---

56 Sign posted by Thamarrurr Ranges, photographed by the author at Batchelor Education rooms, Wadeye, June 2015.
57 Transcription of Kanamkek dreaming story (LK, 2000-11-10), a creation myth produced by Dittin Aloyisius Kungul assissted by Christiane Charon, September 2008. Held at Wadeye community archive.
58 As above.

hands' was borrowed, new compounds could more productively be formed (Mansfield, 2016a, p. 404).

Another strand of evidence is found in the earliest audio recording of Murrinhpatha, recorded by Kenneth Hale in 1959. The speaker (HJ, b. ?1920) produces complex verbs that in contemporary Murrinhpatha involve pseudo-classifier compounds, but he instead pronounces them variably in phrasal and compound form. Table 8.6 shows the forms produced by HJ, in comparison to contemporary fused forms. The phrasal forms are in [Verb Coverb]$_{VP}$ order, not [Coverb Verb]$_{VP}$ as in contemporary Murrinhpatha verb phrases. As with contemporary phrasal verbs, there is a prosodic prominence on each of the two words. The same open phrase form is used for what would contemporarily be a compound based on a lexical verb. The vacilation between prosodic fusion and separation is reflected in Hale's fieldnotes from the session, where verbs are alternately written as one word or two. This could be an artefact of hyper-articulation produced for Hale's benefit, but a neat verb – coverb break of this sort is not produced when contemporary speakers hyperarticulate verbs.

Table 8.6: Comparison of phrasal forms recorded in 1959 with contemporary forms.

Forms produced by HJ (Hale, 1959)		Contemporary forms
ṭá-ŋa	mút	ṭa-ŋá-mut
PIERCE.2SG.IRR-1SG.OBL	give	PIERCE.2SG.IRR-1SG.OBL-give
give it to me!		*give it to me!*
dám-ŋa	mút	dam-ŋá-mut
PIERCE.3SG.NFUT-1SG.OBL	give	PIERCE.3SG.NFUT-1SG.OBL-give
he gave it to me		*he gave it to me*
kárim	kájkaj	karim-kájkaj
stand.3SG.PRSL	call.out.PLUR	stand.3SG.PRSL-call.out.PLUR
he's calling out		*he's calling out*

8.4 Coverbs

Coverbs are an open class of lexical roots that have some overlap with nominals. We can define a coverb as being any root that combines with a finite verb stem in either phrasal or compound form to create a complex predicate. A nominal meanwhile is a root that can host a nominal class prefix (§7.2). On these definitions, we can see that some roots appear alternately as coverbs (11, 12) or as nominals

(13). However the phrasal coverb position does not rigorously distinguish coverbs from nominals, since the adjectival nominals can freely take on an adverb role, modifying verbs rather than nouns. Thus /paṭa/ in (12) may alternatively be analysed as an adverb.

(11) mam-paṭa
 use.hands.3SG.NFUT-good
 she made/fixed it

(12) paṭa wurini-ŋe-ða
 good go.3SG.PST-3SG.F.OBL-PST
 he treated her well (DePu, 2011-07-30)

(13) mi-paṭa
 VEG-good
 good food

We might have hoped to more rigorously distinguish coverbs from adverbs by proposing that if there is a coverb present in the compounded position, any root in the pre-verbal position must be an adverb. However there are some examples where lexemes appear in both these positions and the pre-verbal root has the predicational nature of a verb, rather than a modifying adverb (14, 15). Therefore a finite verb stem can combine simultaneously with two coverbs, in phrasal and compound positions respectively (Mansfield, 2016a).

(14) <u>kampa</u> na-ðap-ḍe
 laugh do.2SG.IRR-shut-ITER
 stop laughing! (SB, 2013-07-11)

(15) waʃiɲ pillaŋam-biḷbiḷ-paŋam
 wash wipe.3PL.NFUT-shine.PLUR-BE.IMPF
 they're washing it (NoPe, 2013-01-21)

Like finite verb stems, coverbs encompass a mixture of those that appear as independent words, those that appear only in compounds, and those that do both. Compound-only coverbs account for the majority of the lexicon. In cases where a coverb can appear both in phrases and compounds, the two forms appear to be translational equivalents (as in 7a,b above), and there are also instances where two copies of the coverb appear together in phrasal and compounded positions (16).

(16) <u>kampa</u> paŋam-ka-<u>kampa</u>-nime
 laugh be.3PL.NFUT-PC.SUBJ-laugh-PAUC.M
 they (paucal, males) are laughing

8.5 Compounding body part nominals to coverbs

Coverbs host two forms of morphological structure: reduplicative derivation of pluractionality (described in the next section), and compounded body part nominals (Forshaw, 2011; Walsh, 1996a). This is the same set of body part nominals that we have already seen compounding prolifically with predicating nominals (§6.4). The full list elicited by Walsh (1976: 176) is given in Table 8.7, though this includes several forms that are unattested in more recent documentation.

Table 8.7: Bound body parts (Walsh, 1976, p. 176).

Bound body part	Free-form simile	Gloss	Bound body part	Free-form simile	Gloss
be	niṯi	arm	ŋudeŋke	ŋudeŋke	calf
bu	lawali	upper leg	ŋuru	ŋuru	side
ḍari	paŋkin	back	put	walmpu	testicles
ḍi	ḍimu	tooth	ṯi	lumpu	buttocks
kaḍari	kaḍirak	eye-brow	ṯiḍari	muṯiṯi	lower back
kaɲa	kaɲa	small of back	ṯama	ṯamal	neck
lu	wulumu	forehead	ṯanme	ṯemen	tongue
ma	maɲe	hand, finger	ṯarmu	ṯarmu	lower leg
maḍa	maḍa	belly	wanṯaj	wanṯaj	armpit
mala	lamala	shoulder	ṯawi	ṯaṯpi	mouth, lip
manṯi	manṯiɲapa	collar-bone area	paɳ	panṯa	groin
me	me	foot, toe	pe	pelpiṯ	head
mili	mikmu	hip	piŋka	piŋkal	knee
muru	ṯamuru	cheek	ṯe	ṯe	ear
ŋapa	ŋapa	back of neck	ṯi	ŋapuḻu	breast
ɲi	ɲi	penis	ṯi	ṯimu	nose
ŋka	kamaḻ	eye, face	ṯiri	ṯirimeme	pubic area

Other Daly languages with noun incorporation allow a few nominals other than body parts to be incorporated (Nordlinger, 2017). In Murrinhpatha, there is just one bound nominal attested in compound coverbs that does not denote a body part. /mulu-/ 'fire' is attested in just a few compounds (17, 18), and none used by younger speakers. This raises the question of whether historically there may have been some capacity for non-body-part compounding in coverbs. On the one hand we may suppose that fire could be an outlier, having been such a salient entity in pre-settlement life. But on the other hand, as we will see below, there are several other 'fossilised' compound elements in coverbs that have no synchronically recoverable meaning, and therefore could have been either body-part or non-body-part nominals

(17) ŋunnam-ka-<u>mulu</u>-waḷ-ŋime
 use.feet.1PL.NFUT-PC.SUBJ-<u>fire</u>-jump-PAUC.F
 we jumped over the fire (MaNa, 1970_CS1-017-A_06)
(18) ku-ṭirangi-<u>mulu</u>-puṭ-ṭa-ja
 ANIM-stand.2SG.PSTIRR-<u>fire</u>-throw-PST-INTERJ
 you should have thrown that meat on the fire! (LuTch, 2004-09-12)
(19) ku-ṭintu=waḍa=kama ṭuŋu-<u>mulu</u>-laṭ
 ANIM-mussel=SEQ=DUB pull.2SG.IRR-<u>fire</u>-extract
 maybe you should take those mussels out of the fire (ECu, 2004-09-12)

8.5.1 Relation to independent nominals

Bound body part nominals are a closed set and are not identical to the body part nominals that serve as independent words (Walsh, 1996a). In some cases a bound body part has a reduced phonological form compared to the independent body part (e.g. /kamaḷ, ŋka-/ 'eye'; /ḍimu, ḍi-/ 'tooth'), and in some cases it has a totally distinct form (e.g. /paŋkin, ḍari-/ 'back'; /niṭi, be-/ 'arm'). Independent body part words include compound forms denoting specific body parts (e.g. /me-paŋkin/ 'foot-back = instep of foot', /me-ṭiɲin/ 'foot-claw = toenail'), as well as more fossilised compounds (e.g. /pelpiṭ/ 'head', /pemaɾ/ 'hair on head'). The bound body parts associated with these are the more generic roots, which have a hypernymic relation to the more specific free forms (e.g. /me-/ '[any part of] foot'; /pe-/ '[any part of] head).

8.5.2 Compounding relations

Bound body parts are used prolifically in the coverb lexicon, though almost exclusively in coverbs bound to finite verb stems.[59] Therefore, a large proportion of Murrinhpatha verbs are tripartite combinations of lexical elements: [Stem-Bodypart-Coverb]. Just as [Stem-Coverb] compounds range from semantically transparent to opaque, body part compounding may also be transparent

---

[59] The only exceptional case of an independent coverb with compounded body part I have identified is /be-puḷ/ 'hand-sweep = sweep away' (KeMa, 2012-06-20_28).

or opaque. The more opaque body parts, appearing in coverbs that do not concretely include the body part meaning in their denotation, are by far the more frequently used, while transparent, productively compounded body parts are fairly rare in contemporary speech (Forshaw, 2011). The prominent role of transparent bound body parts in Walsh's earlier description (e.g. Walsh, 1976, pp. 176–186) suggests that this construct may have been more productive in an earlier period. Transparent body parts denote a part affected by the verbal predicate (20–22).

(20) ṇini   bam-pe-ḷip
     ANAPH   AFFECT.3SG.NFUT-head-hit
     she bashed him on the head   (FA, 2011-08-01_3-11)

(21) ku-weṛe   baŋam-ŋi-bu-laṯ
     ANIM-dog   AFFECT.3SG.NFUT-1SG.OBJ-leg-bite
     a dog bit me on the leg   (MaMu, 2011-09-13_CD)

(22) mem-nu-ŋka-puḷ
     use.hands.RR.3SG.NFUT-RR-face-wash
     she washed her face

However there are many more examples where the body part's semantics are metaphorically extended away from the concrete denotation (Walsh, 1996a, p. 360ff.). For example /maḍa-/ 'belly' may signify emotions (23) or the inner part of a physical space (24); /ṯawi-/ 'mouth' may signify speech, /ṯe-/ 'ear' signify knowledge, and /ŋka-/ 'eye' cognition or perception (25–28).

(23) niŋam-ŋi-maḍa-kat
     use.fire.3SG.NFUT-1SG.OBJ-belly-cut
     I feel angry   (Street 2012: -mardakat)

(24) ŋi-maḍa-pup-nu
     put.together.1SG.IRR-belly-sit-FUT
     I'll lay it in the middle

(25) diraŋan-ŋi-ṯawi-ṯeṇ
     watch.3SG.NFUT-1SG.OBJ-mouth-recognise
     he recognises my voice   (Street 2012: -thenh)

(26) dim-ṯe-pup
     hear.2SG.NFUT-ear-sit
     you heard, understood

(27) be-ŋka-bat
     AFFECT.RR.1SG.IRR-eye-hit
     I'll be surprised

(28a) pan-ɲi-ŋka-ṭip
 SLASH.3SG.NFUT-1SG.OBJ-eye-dark
 I am unaware of it (Street 2012: *-ngkathip*)
(28b) pam-ŋka-ṭip-dim kaɖu insait=waɖa
 SLASH.RR3SG.NFUT-1SG.OBJ-eye-dark PERS imprisoned=SEQ
 in prison, he realised his predicament (GM, 2016-06-24_01)

It is presumably via metaphorical extension that so many compound coverbs have become semantically opaque (29, 30). In many such instances, the coverb root to which a body part is bound does not appear without the body part, and so cannot be attributed any meaning separate from the whole (31–33).

(29) ma-ɲi-ŋka-ṭum-nukun
 do.3SG.NFUT-2SG.OBJ-eye-dry-ADVERS
 you might get hazy vision (Street 2012: *-ngkatum*)
(30) pan-ɲi-ŋka-ṭum
 SLASH.3SG.IRR-1SG.OBJ-eye-dry
 I had a miraculous vision (Street 2012: *-ngkatum*)
(31) ŋam-ṭe-kum
 PIERCE.1SG.NFUT-ear-forget
 I forgot
(32) na-ŋa-ŋka-ðaṭ-nu
 use.hands.2SG.IRR-1SG.OBL-eye-turn.to.face-FUT
 turn it to face me (Street 2012: *-ngkadhath*)
(33) dam-ɲi-maɖa-ṭin
 PIERCE.3SG.NFUT-1SG.OBJ-belly-sad
 I feel sad, worried

There are also some attested instances of compound coverbs with a [Coverb-Bodypart] sequence, rather than the more typical [Bodypart-Coverb]. The relative sparsity of these suggests that they may be remnants of a configuration that has not been productive in recent times (34–37). There is also at lease one compound coverb that alternates between [Bodypart-Coverb] and [Coverb-Bodypart] sequences (38, 39).

(34) paŋam-ɻuj-ŋka
 appear.3SG.NFUT-be.visible-face
 he peered over (Street 2012: *-ruyngka*)
(35) ṭani-ɻuj-pe-ða-ṭini
 appear.2SG.PST-be.visible-head-PST-SIT.IMPF
 your head was visible (ClDu, 2016-07-14_12)

(36) merk   piṉtim-ba-ḏi
     moon   perch.3SG.NFUT-pale-tooth
     the new moon is in the sky   (Street 2012: *-bardi*)
(37) pirim-na-laŋ-ma
     stand.3SG.NFUT-3SG.OBL-spread-hand
     he extended his hand to him   (MaNa, 1980_CS1-017-A_07)
(38) dim-ṯeṯ-pe
     sit.3SG.NFUT-stretch-head
     his hair stood on end   (Street 2012: *-rtertpe*)
(39) mam-pe-ṯeṯ
     do.3SG.NFUT-head-stretch
     his hair stood on end   (Street 2012: *-wertert*)

8.5.3 Fossilised compounds

Where bound body parts are semantically transparent, just one body part nominal compounds to the coverb (40). But once a body-part + coverb compound has become lexicalised (i.e. semantically opaque), a second body part can be recursively compounded to modify the meaning (41b, c). In this work I tend towards maximal morphological segmentation, glossing compounded body parts as morphological elements even where the compound is lexicalised (§1.7).

(40) mem-ŋka-puḻ
      use.hands.RR.3SG.NFUT-face-wash
      she washed her face
(41a) ŋuḍan-ŋka-wuj
      IMPEL.1SG.NFUT-eye-insert
      I have something on my mind
(41b) ŋuḍam-ṯe-ŋka-wuj
      IMPEL.RR.1SG.NFUT-ear-eye-insert
      I have confused understanding   (Street 2012: *-wengkawuy*)
(41c) ŋuḍam-ṯawi-ŋka-wuj
      IMPEL.RR.1SG.NFUT-mouth-eye-insert
      I have confused speech   (Street 2012: *-dhawingkawuy*)

There are further compounded elements that exist only in semantically opaque combinations, such that we cannot assign them any meaning, but can only presume that they were erstwhile bound nominals, either body parts or otherwise. Despite having lost meaning, these remain phonologically segmentable because they attach outside of the pluractional derivation (§8.6). The most prominent fossilised nominal of this type is /wiṇ(i)-/ (42, 43).

(42) ṭempiṇilkul
 ṭem-wiṇi-kulkul
 PIERCE.RR.2SG.NFUT-bend.over-expect.PLUR
 you bent over (several times) (Street 2012: -winhikul)

(43) dampiṇimaḍakpak
 dam-wiṇi-maḍa-pakpak
 PIERCE.3SG.NFUT-pour.into-belly-put.PLUR
 he poured it into a container (several times)

Finally, we should note that bound body parts can themselves occupy the coverb position in compound verbs (44, 45). This again shows that the category distinction between nominals and coverbs is somewhat porous.

(44) kaṇtin-<u>maḍa</u>
 hold.3SG.NFUT-<u>torso</u>
 she holds it to her chest

(45) diraŋan-<u>ŋka</u>
 watch.3SG.NFUT-<u>eye</u>
 she watches over it

8.5.4 Body-part applicatives

Two of the bound body parts /ma-/ 'hand' and /ŋka-/ 'eye', can function either as body part lexemes or as derivational valency-changing prefixes (§6.2.4) (Nordlinger, in prep., 2011a; Walsh, 1976, p. 184). Both promote a source or maleficiary to a direct object, though it is not clear from the limited attested examples if there is any semantic difference between them (46, 47).

(46) ŋanam-ṇi-<u>ma</u>-kut
 be.1SG.NFUT-2SG.OBJ-<u>hand.APPL</u>-collect
 I collected it from you (Nordlinger 2011a: 2)

(47) kaḍu   kani-ṇi-<u>ŋka</u>-ṭek-nu=kama
 PERSON   be.3SG.IRR-1SG.OBJ-<u>eye.APPL</u>-defecate-FUT=DUB
 the (child) might shit on me! (BeMa, 2015-03-30)

8.6 Pluractional coverbs

The second type of morphological complexity in coverbs is the derivation of pluractional (PLUR) coverbs by phonological reduplication (48) (Nordlinger & Caudal, 2012; Street, 1980a; Walsh, 1976, pp. 240–243). Pluractional verb roots derived by reduplication are elsewhere attested in the Daly region (e.g. Ngan'gi, Reid, 1990, p. 157ff.), in the north-west (e.g. Bardi, Bowern, 2004, p. 147ff.; Warlpiri, Nash, 1980, p. 136ff.), and in Australian more generally (Fabricius, 1998, p. 96ff). The most common form of the PLUR derivation is full reduplication of the base, though as we will see in Murrinhpatha there are several patterns of phonological reduction that render this as partial reduplication, as well as irregular changes and outright suppletion.

(48a) nuŋammat
 nuŋam-bat
 use.feet.3SG.NFUT-throw
 she threw a projectile
(48b) nuŋammatbat
 nuŋam-<u>bat-bat</u>
 use.feet.3SG.NFUT-<u>throw-plur</u>
 she threw projectiles (repeatedly)

The relationship of PLUR coverbs to their simple bases can be considered *derivational*, rather than inflectional. Standard definitions of the distinction often note that inflectional categories apply to all members of a word class, and involve the same semantic distinctions for all words in the class (e.g. Haspelmath & Sims, 2010, p. 89ff.). Morphological processes that are more lexically idiosyncratic, either in applicability or in semantics, are derivational. Thus Murrinhpatha PLUR coverbs would fall into the derivational category, since (a) some coverbs do not appear to have a PLUR form at all; (b) for some coverbs a formally PLUR coverb has become the only form, e.g. /ɲuɾk-uɾk/ 'sleep'; (c) the semantics of PLUR is somewhat unpredictable, i.e. there are lexicalised special meanings such as /biḽ/ 'turn to look', /biḽ-biḽ/ 'keep watch'; /bat/ 'throw, hit', /bat-bat/ 'right hand'.

Pluractional forms generally denote iterated (49), durative (50) or habitual (51) events. The use of PLUR in some cases, such as (51), might also be interpreted as encoding plurality of the object argument. This would not be unexpected, since transitive use of pluracational verbs in other languages is reported to have this function (Corbett, 2000, p. 247). However, we observe that when a Murrinhpatha transitive verb affects multiple patients, but affects them all in a single event, a simple coverb is used (52, 53). Conversely, a single argument affected by an iterative event uses a PLUR coverb (54), suggesting that it is the plurality of the event, rather than the argument, that is expressed by PLUR coverbs. Note that (52, 53) overtly mark their objects as plural, and (54) marks its oblique argument as singular, confirming that the number paradigm in the obj/obl pronominal system is independent of the simple/pluractional distinction on coverbs.

(49) ṭuru-lili=ka   paṉu   kereṯen   ini=ka
     go.2SG.IRR-walk=CST   grass   spear.grass   anaph=CST
     bu-ṉ-ṯeṯe
     LOWER.3SG.IRR-2SG.OBJ-spike.PLUR
     when you walk through the spear grass, (the seeds) stick into you
     (DePu, 2015-07-01_AT)

(50) ŋaj-waḍa   ŋurini-kumkum-ða-ŋini
     1SG.SEQ   go.1SG.PST-swim.PLUR-PST-SIT.IMPF
     wuḍini-ŋi-paḷ-ða=waḍa
     IMPEL.3SG.PST-1SG.OBJ-wash.along-PST=SEQ
     I kept on swimming as the tide pushed me along   (GrMo, 1981_CS1-03A)

(51) ku   paṉam-puṯpuṯ   ŋameɹe=ju
     money   be.3PL.NFUT-scatter.PLUR   some=CLS
     some people are always wasting money   (CaPe, 2009-07-07_04)

(52) kaḍu   peɹkenku   pirim-wun-baṯ-dim[60]
     person   two   watch.3PL.NFUT-3PL.OBJ-hold-SIT.IMPF
     ŋaɹa   kaḍu   peɹkenkuŋime
     LOC   person   three
     two people are looking at three people   (McKu, 2015-07-07_AM)

(53) wuḍan-wun-paḷ
     IMPEL.3SG.NFUT-3PL-wash.along
     (the waves) washed them in   (LcTch, 2009-11-21)

(54) kaḍi-ṉa-kajkaj-ða
     be.3SG.PST-3PL-call.out.PLUR-PST
     he (kept on) calling out to me   (RoB, 2015-07-17_02)

The surface form of pluractional coverbs is often not a complete reduplication of the base. However, I do not analyse this as a partial-reduplication template (McCarthy, 1982), but rather as the result of full reduplication with phonological

---

[60] This verb is spoken by a teenager (McKu, b. 1997) and does not conform with 'standard' inflectional patterns in two ways: the formatives used to inflect the stem watch.3PL.NFUT are rather different from the standard, and instead of adding a DUAL suffix in the external layer of bound morphs, an independent noun phrase is used to encode dual subject.

reduction (Inkelas & Zoll, 2005). This reduction takes two forms, both unpredictably applied: *cluster harmonisation*, which occurs at all morphological junctures within PWords (§4.4.3); and *morph-initial reduction*, which is elsewhere exhibited in Murrinhpatha (§4.4.1), but takes on a more drastic form in coverbs.

Cluster harmonisation may occur wherever a consonant-final morph abuts another morph within the PWord domain. This is particularly common in reduplicated coverbs, because the most common phonological form of coverb roots is CVC (§4.2.1), thus giving reduplicated CVC-CVC. Wherever these consonant clusters have a dispreferred sonority profile *SON↑ or a dispreferred place-of-articulation profile *PER-COR, various harmonisation strategies apply (§4.4.3). These are quite diverse in their outcomes, and to some extent are lexically specific to the compound verb in which they occur (55–58).

(55) damŋamuṯutkanam
 dam-ŋa-muṯ-muṯ-kanam
 PIERCE.3SG.NFUT-1SG.OBL-give-PLUR-BE.IMPF
 she gives me things

(56) panmeŋkaṯat
 pan-me-ŋkaṯ-ṉkat
 ARC.3SG.NFUT-foot-catch-PLUR
 she tripped them over   (Street 2012: *-mengkat*)

(57) memmibiḻwuran
 mem-biḻ-biḻ-wuran
 do.RR.3SG.NFUT-look.out-PLUR
 he's turning to look around   (Street 2012: *-birl*)

(58) dimmiḻbiḻ
 dim-biḻ-biḻ
 sit.3SG.NFUT-look.out-PLUR
 he kept watch   (Street 2012: *-birl*)

For /CV/ coverb bases, meanwhile, there is always full reduplication (59), and occasionally triplication (60), which does not appear to have any special semantic or grammatical function.

(59) kanammebe
 kanam-be-be
 be.3SG.NFUT-vomit-PLUR
 he's vomiting (repeatedly)

(60) wuranlalalakaṟim
 wuṟan-la-la-la-kaṟim
 go.3SG.NFUT-climb-PLUR-PLUR-STAND.IMPF
 he's climbing (steps)   (LTch, 2015-07-01_2-3)

The general form of morph-initial reduction in Murrinhpatha reduces voiceless obstruents /p, ṯ, k/ to continuants /w, ð̪, ɣ/ following a vowel (§3.7.1, §4.4.1). Lenition of this type occurs in coverbs, but there are also instances of more drastic reduction where the initial CV string is deleted altogether. This affects only reduplicated coverbs, and only where they occur in lexicalised compounds with body part nominals. We may suppose that this could not occur in simple coverbs, because the reduction /C/ would leave too little phonological material to signal the identity of the coverb root. But an additional reason why this should happen only in pluractional coverbs is that morph-initial reduction in coverbs depends on minimally disyllabic length (§4.4.1). As to why it occurs only in lexicalised compounds with body parts, we can only suppose that this is an effect of routinisation and loss of transparency in the compound. Coverb-initial CV deletion affects the expected /pV, ṯV, kV/ sequences (61–63). It may also affect sequences /bV, ḏV, mV/, and categorically affects /wV/ (64–67), surpassing the more general pattern that targets only voiceless obstruents for morph-initial reduction.

(61) damŋiwiṉiṯpuṯ
 dam-ŋi-[wiṉi-[puṯ-puṯ]]
 use.mouth.3SG.NFUT-1SG.OBJ-[WINHI-[scatter-PLUR]]
 he ensorcelled me (repeatedly)   (Street 2012: -winhiputh)

(62) ŋaŋkaṯuknu
 ŋa-[ŋka-[ṯuk-ṯuk]]-nu
 use.mouth.1SG.IRR-[eye-[send-PLUR]]-FUT
 I will decide (repeatedly)   (Street 2012: -ngkathuk)

(63) dininmaṯkuṯṯa
 dini-wun-[ma-[kuṯ-kuṯ]]-ð̪a
 sit.3SG.PST-3PL.OBJ-[APPL-[collect-PLUR]]-PST
 he collected it from them   (Street 2012: -makut)

(64) mamkaŋmiŋdim
 mam-[ŋka-[biŋ-biŋ]]-dim
 do.3SG.NFUT-[eye-[lift-PLUR]]-SIT.IMPF
 he's turning the pages   (Street 2012: -ngkabing)

(65) dampiṉimaḏamnum
 dam-wiṉi-[maḏa-[ḏum-ḏum]]
 PIERCE.3SG.NFUT-WINHI-[belly-[sightless-PLUR]]
 she layed them front-down   (Street 2012: -winhimardardum)

(66) t̪amɲijet̪mutt̪uran
　　 t̪am-ɲi-[t̪e-[mut-mut]]-t̪uran
　　 use.mouth.2SG.NFUT-1SG.OBJ-[ear-[deaf-PLUR]]-GO.IMPF
　　 you keep refusing me　　　　　　　　(Street 2012: -yemut)
(67) panɲiðamaɾwuɾkanam
　　 pan-ɲi-[ðama-[wuɾ-wuɾ]]-kanam
　　 ARC.3SG.NFUT-1SG.OBJ-[throat-[choke-PLUR]]-BE.IMPF
　　 I keep getting things caught in my throat　　(Street 2012: -dhamawurr)

Finally, there is a substantial number of coverbs for which the phonological relation between simple and pluractional forms shows no regularity whatsoever, and can be labelled 'suppletive'. Some of these show a hint of a historical pattern in either */ɾ/ or */ðat̪/ associating with pluractionality (68–71) (cf. §5.5.4). Others have no discernable pattern, or involve outright replacement of the whole coverb string (72, 73).

(68) ŋeŋ　　　→　　ŋeɾen
　　 talk　　　　　*talk* PLUR
(69) wit　　　→　　ɾit
　　 lay down　　　*lay down* PLUR
(70) ŋuɾu　　 →　　ŋuɾaðat̪
　　 provoke　　　*provoke* PLUR
(71) t̪iɾi　　 →　　t̪iɾaðat̪
　　 wear a naga　　*wear a naga* PLUR
(72) waɾk　　 →　　ḍaɾk
　　 lose oneself　　*lose oneself* PLUR
(73) wul̪　　 →　　lat̪
　　 return　　　　*return* PLUR

8.7 Prosodic compounding

One of the most typologically unusual characteristics of the Murrinhpatha verb is the positioning of the compounded coverb with respect to inflectional suffixes. Compounded lexical elements usually attach either to the base stem, or outside the larger unit formed by base stem plus inflections (Anderson, 1992, p. 295). The compounded lexical element should therefore be positioned either before or after inflectional affixes. But in Murrinhpatha verbs it is positioned *amidst* inflectional suffixes, at the boundary of prosodically internal and external layers. We can therefore say that it has a prosodic anchor point, rather than a position defined purely by morphosyntactic relations (Mansfield, 2017).

8.7.1 Coverb attachment to a prosodic anchor

We saw in an earlier chapter that finite verb stems host two distinct layers of inflectional suffixes: one that is prosodically internal (i.e. forming a PWord together with the host verb), and one that is prosodically external (§6.1). In compound verbs, the coverb is positioned between these layers. Thus, when a verb has no internal suffixes, the coverb is positioned directly to the right of the finite verb stem (74). But when there are internal suffixes of any type, the coverb is to the right of these (75, 76). In either case, external suffixes appear to the right of the coverb. PWord boundaries marked on these examples indicate where the PWord constituent would be on the associated simple verb – though as we will see below, compounding modifies prosodic constituency.

(74) [pume]_ω-pata-ða-ɲime
use.hands.3PL.PST-good-PST-PAUC.F
they were building (a house)

(75) [pume-ŋa]_ω-pata-ða-ɲime
use.hands.3PL.PST-1SG.OBL-good-PST-PAUC.F
they were building it for me

(76) [ma-ɲinta-nu]_ω-puḻ-nu
use.hands.3SG.IRR-DUAL.F-RR-clean-FUT
they will wash themselves

We saw in the earlier chapter that DUAL has a special status as the only suffix that can appear in either internal or external layer (§6.2.4). Where no OBJ or OBL suffix is present, DUAL appears internally. But where a pronominal suffix appears, it blocks DUAL from occurring within the internal layer, relegating it to the external layer where it has variable sequencing with other morphs. In all of these configurations, the coverb maintains its position at the right edge of the internal layer (77). The alternate positioning of DUAL provides special evidence that the coverb is not positioned with respect to any inflectional suffix as such, but rather with respect to the prosodic boundary.

(77a) [pa-ɲinta]_ω-waḻ-nu
PIERCE.3SG.FUT-DUAL.F-spear-FUT
two people will spear him

(77b) [pa-ɲi]_ω-waḻ-ɲinta-nu
PIERCE.3PL.FUT-1sg.obl-spear-DUAL.F-FUT
two people will spear me

(77c) [pa-n̪i]ω-wal̪-nu-n̪in̪t̪a
PIERCE.3PL.FUT-1sg.obl-spear-FUT-DUAL.F
two people will spear me

8.7.2 Recursive PWord constituency

Verb compounding uses the PWord edge of the associated simple verb as an anchor point for the coverb. But as mentioned above, the compound verb redefines the PWord domain. In the compound verb, a larger PWord is formed over a domain encompassing the stem, the coverb and any internal suffixes, while the PWord that would have been constituted in the associated simple verb is not phonologically evident in the compound. We find evidence for this because the penultimate pitch accent is calculated from the right margin of the whole compound, rather than the right margin of the head PWord (78). Furthermore, if a compound is built from just an open monosyllabic verb stem and open monosyllabic coverb /CV-CV/, neither undergoes bimoraic lengthening (79). This confirms that for the purpose of phonological realisation, neither element realises PWord phonological characteristics in its own right (§4.3).

(78) [[maŋán]ω-at̪]ω
use.hands.3sg.nfut-grab
she grabbed it
(79) [[t̪í]ω-ku]ω
sit.2SG.IRR-run
go away!

The same PWord-anchoring and recursive PWord formation applies when body part nominals are compounded with predicating nominals (§6.4). For this compound structure there is far less audio data permitting inspection of prosodic prominence, but those examples that are auditable are consistent with the same prosodic compounding structure as in verb-headed predicates (80, 81).

(80) [[darimuṉ-ŋi]ω-ŋíni]ω
[[sugar-1SG.OBJ]-body]
I have diabetes (ECu, 2004-07-04)
(81) [[pakpak-mé]ω-ma]ω-ða-ŋaḏi
[[weak-do.1SG.PST]-hand]-PST-BE.IMPF
I was too weak (MnMn, 2004-09-12)

Paradoxically, the PWord edge that provides the anchoring point for the coverb is not phonologically evident in the compound thus formed. In some approaches to word-formation this could be regarded as recursive PWord constituency (McCarthy & Prince, 1993; Peperkamp, 1996; Selkirk, 1996), with phonological opacity of the inner PWord (e.g. Bermúdez-Otero, 2011; Kiparsky, 2000). Opacity of PWords is not widely discussed in the literature, though a similar effect has been described for Axinaca Campa (McCarthy & Prince, 1993). The recursive constituency analysis is explored in more detail in Mansfield (2017). By contrast, the theoretical approach taken in this book interprets morphology as relations between words, rather than derivational processes by which words are formed. In this view the compound verbs do not contain an inner PWord constituent, opaque or otherwise.

8.7.3 Incorporating coverbs into the verb schemata

In my analysis of verb inflection structure I argued that a psychologically plausible representation should use a minimally specified general verb schema, with details of suffix structure specified in sub-schemas associated with pronominal argument configurations (§6.4). The shared schema contains only quite general information about stem–affix configuration and prosodic layering (82). Coverb compounding can be integrated into this general schema, because coverb positioning is linked to the prosodic layering structure, and does not change according to pronominal argument structures. Thus I posit a general compound verb schema as in (83).

Simple verb schema
(82) $[[[\text{Stem}]\text{-SUFF}^+]_\omega\{\text{-SUFF}^+\}]_V$

Compound verb schema
(83) $[[[\text{Stem}]\text{-SUFF}^+\text{-}[\text{Nom-}[\text{Cov}]]_{COV}]_\omega\{\text{-SUFF}^+\}]_V$

The compound schema indicates that the coverb itself may be a complex constituent built out of compounded nominal and coverb elements. It inherits the stem–suffix configuration of the general schema, but modifies the position of the PWord right edge, which is now to the right of the coverb, rather than the inner suffixes. The schema thus represents the fact, observed above, that coverb positioning matches the PWord edge of a related simple verb, but the compound does not itself retain that PWord constituent. My representation assumes that prosodic structure can be redefined in constructional inheritance relations – a topic that requires further research. Schemata (84–87) show the pronominally specific compound verb sub-schemata, inheriting the more general structure of (83). In the next section, I investigate how these schemata are inherited by yet more specific schemata for compound verb lexemes.

(84) [[[Stem]-NUM.SUBJ-[Nom-[Cov]]_{COV}]_ω{-TNS-PAUC-ADV⁺-IMPF}]_V
(85) [[[Stem]{-RR-DUAL}-[Nom-[Cov]]_{COV}]_ω{-TNS-PAUC-ADV⁺-IMPF}]_V
(86) [[[Stem]-OBJ-NUM.OBJ-[Nom-[Cov]]_{COV}]_ω{-TNS-NUM-ADV⁺-IMPF}]_V
(87) [[[Stem]-OBL-NUM.OBL-[Nom-[Cov]]_{COV}]_ω{-TNS-NUM-ADV⁺-IMPF}]_V

8.8 Representing compound verb lexemes

As noted above, a large proportion of both verb stems and coverbs do not appear as independent words, but only as parts of compounds. Taking a constructional approach (§1.7.3), I assume a grammar that represents these bound elements only as part of the compound lexemes in which they appear, and not as atomic units in the lexicon.

Particular compound word-forms inherit structure from schematic representations described in the previous section. For example (88) inherits structure from the oblique-argument schema above (87). For the verb stem element, an abstract diacritic USE.HANDS is added to identify the stem of which this is a particular inflectional form. (For additional constituent structure inside the verb stem, see §5.9.)

(88) [[[pumam]_{USE.HANDS}-ŋa-paṭ a]_ω-ŋime]_V
use.hands.3PL.NFUT-1SG.OBL-make-PAUC.F
they (pauc) made it for me

I add diacritic elements to verb stems to represent the paradigmatic inflectional information that speakers must deploy to parse and produce these. As described in an earlier chapter (§5), verb stems do not have any non-finite root form, but instead appear in one of 42 inflected forms. These paradigms exhibit semi-regular morphological patterning, leaving substantial unpredictability in the form taken for an inflectional cell of a particular stem. To be able to parse or produce a previously unencountered form of a compound verb, speakers must draw on their knowledge of the stem paradigm, encapsulated in other inflected forms of the same compound, and inflected forms of other compounds that use the same stem. Strictly speaking, this knowledge could be represented by a network of associated wordforms without any internal structure, linked by either paradigmatic relations (89–91) or by shared stem form (92 94).

Paradigmatically related compound forms
(89) pumamŋawaṯaŋime   they (pauc) made it for me
(90) mamŋawaṯaŋime   she made it for me
(91) numaŋawaṯaŋime   you (pauc) will make it for me

Compounds with same stem form (and same suffixes)
(92) pumamŋawaṯaŋime   they (pauc) made it for me
(93) pumamŋakuɾkŋime   they (pauc) scratched it for me
(94) pumamŋaweṯŋime   they (pauc) did an operation for me

Stem diacritics represent the paradigmatic information distributed across many such related forms. This must be stored as an abstract diacritic, distinct from the lexical semantics and grammatical category features associated with wordforms, because the stem does not necessarily contribute to the semantics of the whole word. Thus if we consider the representation of compounds that have highly opaque stem semantics, the speaker's knowledge that these share a common paradigm of stem forms must be encapsulated in an abstract diacritic, distinct from both phonological and semantic information (95–97). It is this representation of a shared paradigmatic structure that allows such forms to be morphologically associated, and collectively contribute to the knowledge required for parsing and producing new compound forms using this stem.

(95) [[[pan]$_{PIERCE}$-ŋi-wek]$_\omega$]$_V$
     PIERCE.3SG.NFUT-1SG.OBJ-comb.hair
     he combed my hair
(96) [[[ŋu]$_{PIERCE}$-mpa-bat]$_\omega$-nu]$_V$
     PIERCE.1SG.IRR-2SG.OBL-phone-FUT
     I'll phone you
(97) [[[puɳi]$_{PIERCE}$-wuɾwuɾ]$_\omega$-ða]$_V$
     PIERCE.3PL.PST-measure-PST
     they were measuring them

Abstract diacritics of this type can be compared to inflection class information that is required in other languages. Speakers use known forms of a lexeme to adduce the inflection class of a lexeme, which enables parsing and producing of unknown forms (Ackerman et al., 2009). This knowledge could be stored purely in networks of concrete wordforms, but speakers may also create more abstract representations of this distributed information. It is this potential abstraction that is represented as an inflection-class diacritic, which is neither phonological nor semantic in form. A related phenomenon is the 'morphomic structure' of stem alternants in some paradigms – for example Latin third stems, which do not adhere to any phonological or syntactic generalisation, but have a consistent distribution across paradigmatic cells (Aronoff, 1994).

However Murrinhpatha adds an extra twist to the phenomenon of abstract paradigmatic patterns. In the Murrinhpatha compound verb representations above, the abstract diacritic identifies not just inflection class, or a particular stem alternation, but the identity of the stem itself. This reflects the fact that finite verb stems in compounds have to a great extent become 'abstract stems', in some ways resembling inflection-class prefixes, as discussed above (§8.3.1). However we cannot neatly reclassify them as purely inflectional material, since many members of the class do retain characteristics of lexical stems, and there is no clear dividing line between those that are more stem-like and those that are more inflection-like.

8.9 Summary

In this chapter we have explored the fullest expression of complexity in Murrinhpatha word structure: the compound verb. We have seen that complex verbs make up most of the verbal lexicon, using phrasal and compound configurations, the latter being far more frequent. Compounding is responsible for a great degree of conventionalisation and opacity in finite verb stems, the majority of which occur only in compounds, and some of which have lost much of their lexical semantics. Coverbs, the lexical elements that compound with finite verb stems, are themselves in many cases compound structures including body part nominals with prolific metaphorical extension of semantics. Body part compounding is built on top of a pluractional derivation in coverb roots, which is highly unpredictable in its phonological form, and even more so when compounded with semantically opaque body part nominals. Finally, we have seen that the prosodic constituency of compound verbs has a typologically unusual feature, anchoring the coverb at a prosodic boundary, the right margin of the verbal PWord, rather than selecting either verb stem or whole inflected word as its morphotactic host.

9 Murrinhpatha wordhood and gradient morphology

9.1 Introduction

In the preceding chapters I have described the word-like, tightly bound structures of Murrinhpatha, and the prosodic constituents formed by these structures. In this final chapter I briefly review the main structures (§9.2, §9.3), and return to two theoretical issues raised in the introduction. The first of these is the question of wordhood – how might we distinguish Murrinhpatha words from phrases on the one hand, and word parts on the other (§9.4). I answer this by offering not one but three definitions of wordhood in Murrinhpatha, which however do not align well in the parts of the language they encompass. The second issue is how to define and identify word parts – that is to say, morphology (§9.5). I argue that morphology is a gradient phenomenon defined by form–meaning patterns among words. More rigorous attempts to identify the presence of morphology would require a method for quantifying the inherent gradience of patterns. I discuss some factors that we might consider in such a quantification, and propose, following Haspelmath (2011), that such a method may offer us a principled, though fuzzy, distinction between morphology and syntax. I conclude by reflecting on how questions about wordhood and morphology affect the conception of Murrinhpatha as a 'polysynthetic' language, and what might make polysynthetic languages special (§9.6).

9.2 Murrinhpatha phonology

The phonology of Murrinhpatha fits broadly into typical Australian patterns, with a small set of vowels, many consonantal places of articulation, a large range of sonorants, but rather few obstruent manner contrasts. However it departs from standard Australian patterns (e.g. Dixon, 1980, p. 127ff.) on several fronts: firstly, by having some degree of obstruent manner constrasts, with stop/fricative contrasts in the dental and dorsal positions, and more unusually, voiceless/voiced stop contrasts in the labial and apical positions. Word and syllable shapes are also non-standard, in that Murrinhpatha has many monosyllabic words (which are rare or absent elsewhere), and the permissibility of both sonorants and obstruents in the syllable coda (where most Australian languages have sonorant codas only). But the presence of monosyllabic words and obstruent codas is not idiosyncratic to Murrinhpatha. In fact these are attested in many non-Pama Nyungan languages, and the cluster of phonological characteristics that has sometimes been taken as a general Australian standard should be rebadged as a more specifically Pama-Nyungan archetype.[61]

Murrinhpatha phonology exhibits significant interaction with morphology and morphosyntactic classes. Firstly, the full segmental and syllabic inventory is only used by the two main lexical classes, nominals and coverbs. Finite verb stems and bound grammatical morphs use substantially restricted subsets, which interestingly are close to the sonorant, open-syllabled sound patterns found elsewhere. Sentence (1) illustrates the presence of atypical features: obstruent codas, a coda cluster, and a velar fricative, all of which are limited to noun and coverb lexemes (underlined). On the other hand, (1) also illustrates a typologically unusual geminate /nn/, which occurs only in finite verb stems.

(1) kaḏukíyaj   ṯú   punnuŋampátbat   kuwérknu
    kaḏu-<u>kiyaj</u>   ṯu   punnuŋam-<u>bat</u>-bat   ku-<u>werk</u>-nu
    PERS-young.man VIOL use.feet.3PL.NFUT-throw-throw ANIM-cockatoo-DAT
    the young men threw things at the cockatoo

The prosodic constituency of words and phrases provides further mediation between phonology and morphology. The Murrinhpatha prosodic word (PWord) is characterised by minimally bimoraic length, penultimate pitch accent when it is the final PWord in a phrase, and by various segmental assimilation processes that only apply PWord-internally. Some bound morphology is internal to the PWord constituent, while other morphology is external, i.e. 'adjunct'. The division between prosodically internal and external morphological has consequences for the phonology of complex words. Because there is far more assimilation PWord-internally, the composition of morphological structures within this domain is more opaque, compared to the quite transparent segmentation of prosodically external structure. The assimilatory effects at lexical compounding and reduplication junctures are unpredictable, exhibiting clear patterns in the types of structure they avoid, but with specific lexemes selecting different ways of avoiding (or sometimes failing to avoid) them.

Prosodic constituency above the word level is only briefly analysed in this book, but the core observation is that there is a phonological phrase (PPhrase) that encompasses NPs and PPs, but for verbs and coverbs is constituted by a single word. The PPhrase is marked by a single H* pitch accent on the penultimate syllable of the final PWord (which is often the only PWord). Other than PWord-penultimate accentual anchoring, no system of prosodic prominence has been identified. There

---

61 Even within the Pama-Nyungan family there are languages that diverge substantially from this archetype, such as Kuuk Thaayorre (Gaby, 2017).

is no evidence of alternating strong-weak syllables as has been claimed for many other Australian languages (Evans, 1995, p. 753). This again appears to be unusual in comparison to the majority of Australian phonologies, though there is little detailed research on prosodic prominence in Australian languages, and earlier impressionistic accounts of metrical structure have been disputed (Baker, 2014, p. 154).

9.3 Murrinhpatha morphology

The analysis in this book categorises bound morphology according to semantic function, distribution and prosodic constituency. The types identified are semi-regular inflectional formatives, predicate inflectional suffixes with distinct prosodically internal and external layers, nominal classifier prefixes, case, adverbial and discourse clitics. Additionally there is lexical compounding morphology in both verbs and nominals. The main characteristics of these types are reviewed and exemplified here.

Semi-regular inflectional formatives are the morphological components of finite verb stems. Finite verb stems can be broken down into prefixes, 'inner stems' and suffixes, though the patterns upon which this analysis is based are quite inconsistent from one finite verb stem to another. Prefixes are associated with subject agreement, and suffixes with tense, though the irregularity of patterning means that morphological encoding is far from biunique, and in many instances could be characterised as distributed exponence across the whole of the verb stem. However, the regularity of patterning in the inflectional formatives varies significantly. For example, non-future (NFUT) forms consistently end with one of four suffix formatives, and just one of these, /-m/ accounts for the majority of NFUT forms (2). This can be contrasted with an inner stem alternation pattern such as vowel fronting in PST and PSTIRR tenses, which occurs in just a few verb stems. These different degrees of regularity or 'predictability' beg the question of where we should draw the line in identifying morphological structure. This cline of predictability among semi-regular formatives is one of the key motivations for proposing a gradient view of morphology, as discussed below.

(2) kanam
 ka-[ni$^{\text{BACK, LOW}}$]-m
 PREF-INNER.STEM-SUFF
 be.3SG.NFUT
 she/he/it is.

Predicate inflectional suffixes mark inflectional categories associated with a predicate, which may be either verbal or nominal. In addition to the subject participant marked on verb stems, predicate suffixes mark OBJ, OBL or RR pronominal participants (3). For nominal predicates, the OBJ suffix marks the sole participant (4). Pronominal marking establishes basic number categories, and additional predicate suffixes may be added to further specify number and gender, and to mark TAM categories. Pronominal suffixes are prosodically internal, as are number markers if they are adjacent to the pronominal argument they index. Other number markers are external, as are all TAM markers.

(3) [me-ŋa-ɾu]ω-ða-ŋime
 do.3SG.PST-1PL.OBL-PC.OBL-PST-pauc.f
 she/he/it did it for us (paucal)
(4) [muɾiṉ-ṉi-ðaj]ω
 language-2SG.OBJ-mouth
 you talk a lot (LP, 2015-09-14_AT)

Lexical compounding is very prominent in Murrinhpatha, both in verbs and nouns. There are four distinct types of compounding, shown here with semantic headedness relations, and in approximate order of frequency (5–8).

(5) [ClassifierNoun]-Nominal → Noun
 kaḍu-[muḻak]ω
 person-wild
 bad-tempered person
(6) [ClassifierVerbStem]-Coverb → Verb
 [niŋan-ṭi]ω
 heat.3SG.NFUT-cook
 she/he cooked it
(7) Bodypart-[Coverb] → Coverb
 [-ṭe-pup]ω
 -ear-sit
 listen
(8) [PredNom]-Bodypart → PredNom
 [daɾimuṉ-ŋini]ω
 sugar-body
 to be diabetic

The most frequent types (5–7) are core structures in the nominal and verbal parts of the lexicon; while the last type (8) is rare in contemporary discourse. Types (5, 6) involve small classes of head elements, classifier noun and classifier verb stem, which exhibit mixed lexical and grammatical characteristics. The closed-class heads combine with large lexical classes of dependents (nouns and coverbs).

These structures have moderate degrees of semantic compositionality. The bodypart-coverb structure (7) is right-headed, while the other three are left-headed. The core nominal type (5) stands out as the only type in which one part remains prosodically independent: the open-class nominal stands alone as a PWord, while the classifier is a left adjunct, CLASS-[NOM]ω (but see §7.3.2 on evidence for the prosodic status of the classifier). The two predicating types (6, 8) host predicate inflectional suffixes in two layers, with the dependent coverb or body-part positioned between them, and the lexical compound elements prosodified as a combined PWord, [CLASS-INFL-COV]ω-INFL and [PRED.NOM-INFL-BODYPART]ω-INFL.

Finally, there are three types of phrasal morphology or 'clitics' in Murrinhpatha. The first is *case clitics*, which are optional and rather infrequent. The semantic role of participants is more often presumed to be implicit from context. When case clitics are used, they are prosodic adjuncts to the last word in the NP (9).

(9) tɟak   wakal   [pana]ω=ɹe
    truck   small   FAMILIAR=INSTR
    with that little truck   (BrBe, 2012-07-19)

The second phrasal type is *adverbials*. There are over a dozen of these, encompassing a range of meanings mostly relating to modality or epistemic stance. Adverbials attach at the end of a phonological phrase, and more than one can attach to a phrase (10).

(10) kuḍán-paṯ   [ŋála]ω=waḍa=ðaṯpiɾ
     IMPEL.RR.3SG.PRSL-fear big=SEQ=TRUE
     he's really terrified now   (MM, 2011-09-13_2-11)

The third phrasal type is *discourse clitics*, which do not have referential meaning, but rather are used optionally to reinforce constituent structure. One tag, /=ka/, marks the end of syntactic phrases, which are simultaneously phonological phrases. Another tag, /=ju/, marks the end of clauses, which are simultaneously intonation phrases (11). /=ka/ is also used as a filler in disfluent speech. The third tag, /=ja/, is reserved for interjections.

(11) ṯu=ka   meɹe ŋuna-bat-ða   munṯak=waḍa=ju
     [[fight]NP=CST   [NEG use.foot.1SG.PST-hit-PST]VP   [before]NP=SEQ]CLAUSE=CLS
     I didn't hit her before   (MaNi, 2015-02-02_Pr2-D1)

9.4 Three types of word in Murrinhpatha

In the introduction, it was observed that the concept 'word' is difficult to rigorously define, and that word-like structures show considerable cross-linguistic diversity. I here review the question of wordhood with respect to Murrinhpatha, proposing three candidates for definitional criteria, but showing that these pick out quite different sub-sets of Murrinhpatha's grammatical constructs. This criterial non-alignment may be taken as evidence that the concept 'word' is not a natural category in Murrinhpatha.

The first type of word is that which is coextensive with the PWord. This criterion shows considerable appeal in matching simple lexical words such as /muluɲ/ 'leaf' or /wakal/ 'small', which can be independent utterances, and do not themselves contain any word-like subparts. However there are other structures matching the PWord criterion that are problematic because they contain word-like subparts. These are compounds verbs such as /piɾim-kampa/ stand.3SG.NFUT-laugh 'she is (standing there) laughing', or /kaɳʈin-maɖa/ hold.3SG.NFUT-torso 'she holds it to her chest'.

The second type of word is defined by mobility and independence of distribution – i.e. appearing freely in a range of structures without depending on a specific host element. This criterion is satisfied by the PWord-coextensive structures mentioned above, but also by clitic elements such as adverbials. This expanded set is closer to the set of elements written separately in Murrinhpatha orthography, since adverbials are written separately. Speakers also tend to pronounce adverbials separately when carefully explaining a sentence. However adverbials are never pronounced as independent utterances in normal speech – they must be postposed to a host. The 'independent distribution' criterion is also problematic in that it includes case and discourse clitics, which like adverbials have a free and mobile distribution, but are not written separately in the community orthography.

The third type of word is the minimal unit that can be a complete utterance. This is the main criterion applied in this book in distinguishing phrases from complex word structures, and in the glossing of example sentences. It was noted above that the PWord criterion is problematic in that it matches compounds, which themselves contain word-like elements. This issue is exacerbated under the complete-utterance criterion, which matches not just compounds but also the entire inflected verb complex. The verb complex can encompass one or more adverbial elements, positioned amidst inflectional elements (12). Because some parts of this structure are not minimal independent utterances (e.g. /-ɲime/ PAUC.F, /-ŋkaɖuɾ/ 'depart'), wordhood must be attributed to the whole structure. But it also contains word-like elements, and it is not clear whether native speakers would think of this more like a word or a phrase.

(12) [pumpan-ŋkaɖuɾ]PW=waɖa=kaʈu-ɲime
    [go.3PL.NFUT-depart]=SEQ=AWAY-PAUC.F
    then they set off   (LK, 2000-11 10)

In summary, the main issue with Murrinhpatha wordhood is that elements with word-like properties – lexical stems, and adverbial clitics – often themselves appear in larger structures, where one or more parts of the larger structure are not word-like, so that whole structure must be considered a word. We might say that the concept 'word' does not apply very well to Murrinhpatha, given the predominance of clitics and compounds in the language.

9.5 Morphology, gradience, and methods of quantification

I have argued above that there is no clear cut-off point between words and phrases in Murrinhpatha, though in general words are constructs in which the sub-parts are more highly interdependent. I now return to the question of identifying word-internal structure, that is to say, 'morphology'. The existence of morphological structure is usually presented as self-evident, without any explicit criterion for what constitutes such structure (Anderson, 2015). But deciding on what counts as morphology may be important for cross-linguistic comparison, for example in works that analyse linguistic complexity in terms of morphological composition (e.g. Juola, 1998; Nichols, 1992).

As was stated in the introduction (§1.7), a good starting point for a definition of morphology is to view it as patterns of form–meaning relations among words. However this definition begs a deeper ontological question as to what constitutes a 'pattern'. I here consider some methodological possibilities for identifying and quantifying patterns in form–meaning relations, drawing on Murrinhpatha examples that have been described in this book. There is some recent literature that investigates information-theoretic methods for quantifying wordhood or morphological structure (Ackerman, Malouf, & Blevins, 2016; Baayen, 2003; Geertzen, Blevins, & Milin, 2016), however there is no widely accepted methodology.

In the introduction I proposed a distinction between 'descriptive' and 'cognitive' morphology, clarifying that the structures analysed in this book are proposed only as descriptive morphology (i.e. patterns observed in the data), without implying that they should necessarily be cognitive morphology (i.e. active in the mental grammar of speakers). At various points in the book I have discussed *a priori* considerations regarding the cognitive representation of some structures (§5.7, §8.3.2, §8.8), however these too remain far from being concrete claims about cognitive processes. While descriptive morphology can be distinguished from cognitive morphology, an implicit aim of descriptive work may be to identify structures that seem likely to be cognitively represented.

In the introduction I defined cognitive morphology as cognitive co-activation of words in a connectionist mental architecture (e.g. Rumelhart & McClelland, 1986), with the 'morphological' element of such co-activation being that which cannot be assigned to co-activations that are purely phonological, or purely syntactic-semantic (Cutler, 2012, p. 103ff.). I note that morphological co-activation is a gradient phenomenon, and therefore morphology in the cognitive sense is gradient, with degrees of morphologicality corresponding to degrees of co-activation. But in descriptive morphology, we may also be able to identify degrees of morphologicality, by quantifying our notion of 'patterning' in form–meaning relations among words. Indeed, the presence of the term 'pattern' in our basic definition of morphology implies a profoundly gradient notion, since patterns may be more or less 'regular' or 'predictable'. Using Murrinhpatha examples below, I investigate some ways that we might quantify this gradience. I consider the following factors for quantification:

1. Number of words sharing a pattern;
2. Proportion of words with syntactic/semantic feature that share phonological formative;
3. Phonological transparency;
4. The status of stems;
5. Semantic transparency.

The discussion below attempts neither a comprehensive theory, nor an implementable algorithm for measuring morphologicality. Rather my aim here is to make more explicit some of the considerations that are inherent in identifying morphological structure. I also show how these considerations relate to the non-essentialist definitions of wordhood sketched above, arguing for a further conception of morphology as the blurry region that connects lexicon and syntax, and ultimately prevents any rigorous distinction between the two.

9.5.1 Number of words sharing a pattern

An obvious place to start for establishing a degree of morphologicality is the number of words in which a form–meaning association occurs. It is this consideration that often appears to underlie descriptive observations of 'morphological productivity' (§1.7.1). A Murrinhpatha morph that would rate highly for number of words is the internal-layer predicate suffix /-ŋi/ 1SG.OBJ, which can appear in hundreds or thousands of transitive verb forms that have the syntactic feature 1SG.OBJ. By contrast, the semi-regular formative /wu-/ 3SG.SUBJ appears in a much smaller number of word forms, since rather than appearing in all 3SG.SUBJ forms, it appears only on those that use one of a small set of verb stems, and among these, only in NFUT, PST and PSTIRR tenses. However some other semi-regular formatives occur on larger sets of word-forms. For example /-m/ NFUT occurs in the majority of stems with NFUT tense. At the other end of the scale, we find that clitic elements such as adverbial /=waḍa/ SEQ occur in the greatest range of word-like structures, since they can adjoin essentially any word. This would suggest that the highest degree of morphologicality is found in loosely-bound elements, which as we saw above are the same elements for which we might question whether they are part of word structure or phrase structure.

Turning to lexical stem elements, a bound coverb like /-bat/ 'hit' would have only a moderate degree of morphologicality, since it appears in just a handful of stem-coverb compounds, each of which has a limited array of inflected forms. Since coverbs seem intuitively to be clear examples of morphological structure, we will need to address other considerations for quantifying their morphologicality (see below).

An additional consideration here is the contrast between type counts and token counts. The observations above are formulated in terms of number of different word-form types, but we might also consider whether appearance in highly frequent words either increases or decreases morphologicality (Baayen, 2003). As well as considering the absolute frequency of tokens, we might also consider the relative token frequencies of word-forms in which a morph appears. For example, if there are one or two word-forms that account for a very large proportion of the appearances of a morph, then we might say that it is less morphological, since in discourse distribution it is very highly correlated with particular word-forms and therefore less independent of those word-forms. For example, the Murrinhpatha case clitic /=ḍa/ LOC usually appears in just a handful of constructs, e.g. /kaṉi=ḍa/ 'here-LOC' or /paŋu=ḍa/ 'there-LOC', even though it can appear in any NP construct. This somewhat predictable distribution might make it less of an independent morph. The information-theoretic approaches mentioned above (e.g. Ackerman et al., 2016; Geertzen et al., 2016) provide models for quantifying this type of 'predictability' or 'dependence'.

9.5.2 Proportional coverage of syntactic/semantic feature

Another way that word-counts might be relativised is with respect to the overall distribution of a syntactic or semantic feature – for example, 3SG.SUBJ or 'hand'. It was noted above that /wu-/ 3SG.SUBJ is less morphological than /-ŋi/ 1SG.OBJ, because it appears in a smaller set of word-forms. But another consideration would be that /wu-/ appears in only a minority (perhaps 10%) of all word-forms that have the feature 3SG.SUBJ, while /-ŋi/ appears consistently in every word-form with the feature 1SG.OBJ. The importance of this consideration becomes clear when we consider the semi-regular /-m/ NFUT, which occurs in a high proportion of all NFUT verbs (perhaps 70%), but not all. Now if it turns out that there are many more word-forms over all with the feature NFUT, than there are with the feature 1SG.OBJ, then we would find that on an absolute count, /-m/ NFUT has greater morphologicality, but in terms of proportional coverage of its semantic contribution, /-ɲi/ 1SG.OBJ has greater morphologicality.

9.5.3 Phonological transparency

The proposals above depend on identifying a shared phonological formative among a set of words. This phonological commonality itself may have a gradient dimension, in view of degrees of transparency found in phonology. For example, the external predicate suffix /-ŋime/ PAUC.F has a unique segmental representation in the word-forms in which it occurs. The only variations in its representation are phonetic variations. The suffix /-nu/ FUT may be considered to have less transparency because it is subject to morpho-phonological processes that give it the segmental form /-nu, -lu, -ɾu/ (§3.7.1). Coverb reduplication is less transparent still. It involves a shared pattern of phonological doubling, but the segmental form of the doubling is subject to a range of reductions and assimilations, e.g. /ðap-ðap/ → /ðapep/, /ḍut-ḍut/ → /ḍuḍut/, /-mut-mut/ → /tmut/. Coverb doubling is less phonologically transparent because the morpho-phonological processes are not applied predictably to all coverb lexemes, and therefore the relationship between simple and reduplicated forms is more unpredictable. If this degree of unpredictability can be quantified (for example by measuring distribution of morpho-phonological patterns across a set of coverb lexemes), it could be factored in to the quantification of morphologicality.

9.5.4 The status of stems

I have suggested above that morphology may be identified by patterning of shared elements among sets of words. However the identification of a morphological element leads to a further question about the theoretical status of the residual portion of the word, which we would generally identify as the 'stem'. Based on word-counts, stem formatives are less morphological, because rather than appearing in large sets of words, they appear in a small set (e.g. the various inflected forms of that word). For example a Murrinhpatha noun such as /múluɲ/ 'leaf, shade' appears in just a handful of words, being those that encompass classifier prefixes or case clitics, e.g. /mimúluɲ/ 'edible leaf', /múluɲṯe/ 'leaf INSTR' etc. The absolute degree of such stem → word mapping is a simple bare stem that is not part of any complex words.

Notice that in this conception, stems are separated from grammatical morphology as a matter of degree. We may also encounter some stem elements that do occur in fairly large sets of words, though generally not as large as the sets in which affixes occur. For example, the Murrinhpatha classifier stem /mi/ 'look' occurs only in compounds with the coverb /-jer/, producing a limited set of inflected forms. By contrast, the stem /ba/ AFFECT occurs in dozens of compounds, each with the same range of inflected forms. We may thus say that /ba/ AFFECT has greater morphologicality than /mi/ 'look'. Interestingly, we have observed that the most widely used classifier stems, such as /ba/ AFFECT, tend to be those that exhibit the most 'grammaticalisation', due to extensive bleaching of lexical semantics (§8.3).

9.5.5 Semantic transparency

Form–meaning patterning also depends upon the identifiability of shared semantics. For inflectional morphology this is quite straightforward, as the shared semantic element among the morphologically related words is a grammatical feature (such as PL, FUT, 1SG) that has a highly consistent meaning from one word to another. But in stem compounding there may be different degrees of semantic transparency, and this may be another gradient factor contributing to degrees of morphologicality. For example a high proportion of Murrinhpatha coverbs have compound structure, but these vary in terms of semantic compositionality. Compounds such as /ŋka-puḻ/ 'face-wash', /pe-puḻ/ 'head-wash', /me-puḻ/ 'foot-wash' show high semantic transparency, with the left-compounded elements denoting an affected body-part. But other compounds are non-compositional, e.g. /ŋka-wuj/, 'eye-insert, be preoccupied'. This loss of semantic transparency can be interpreted as a weakening of form–meaning patterns, and therefore a lesser degree of morpholgicality. However it is not immediately clear how degrees of semantic transparency could be operationalised in the quantification of gradient morphology.

9.5.6 Lexicon, morphology and syntax

The discussions of morphologicality above, and wordhood in the preceding section, together suggest a profoundly gradient conception of linguistic structure. Language is composed of structural units with various degrees of independence from one another (capacity to stand alone, occurrence in a large range of complex structures, lower predictability of structural context). Morphology can be understood as the blurry region between lexicon and syntax, where 'lexicon' refers to those elements that have no patterned internal structure, 'syntax' refers to the most productive combinatoric patterns with highly independent elements, and 'morphology' refers to an intermediate region where there is a degree of patterning. In Murrinhpatha and in some other languages (Tallman & Epps, 2018), the intermediate region accounts for a large proportion of the grammar, and it lacks clear natural borders with syntax on the one side, and lexicon on the other.

There may still be grounds to posit a natural distinction of morphology and syntax in some languages, and perhaps in Murrinhpatha, if we can identify a 'fuzzy distinction' in the cline of dependency (Haspelmath, 2011). Here prosodic constituency may have a crucial role. For example, if quantification techniques can be developed to measure a scale of lexicon > morphology > phrase, there could turn out to be clusterings on this cline that align with levels of the prosodic hierarchy. We have seen some suggestive evidence for this in Murrinhpatha – for example, PWord-internal predicate suffixes showed greater inter-dependency in their combinatorics, compared to PWord-external predicate suffixes. Highly independent clitics are PWord-external, while highly inter-dependent semi-regular inflectional formatives are internal not just to the PWord, but in some cases are constituted below the level of the syllable. An interesting direction for future research would be to investigate whether this impressionistic association between prosodic dependency and combinatoric dependency can be confirmed by the quantification of degrees of dependency.

9.6 Concluding comments: Wordhood and polysynthesis

This book has presented detailed analysis of word structure in a language that is generally regarded as 'polysynthetic' (Nordlinger, 2017). Murrinhpatha comfortably fits this label, as it can express in a word-like structure what most other languages would express in a sentence. This is made possible by the morphological complexity of Murrinhpatha words, especially the inclusion of multiple pronominal arguments, verb–coverb compounding, incorporation of body-part nominals, and the incorporation of adverbial modifiers. However, as we have seen in this final chapter, principled analysis of wordhood in Murrinhpatha highlights extensive non-alignment of standard wordhood criteria. In the main chapters of the book, the maximally polysynthetic analysis of Murrinhpatha has been followed, with the verb complex encompassing adverbials and prosodically external suffixes treated as a word unit. This is supported by its status as a minimal independent utterance. However other wordhood criteria, such as prosodic word constituency, and distributional independence, select somewhat smaller units as words.

The polysynthetic nature of Murrinhpatha is partly grounded in lexical compounding, which is unusually prominent in the Murrinhpatha verb lexicon.

However it has elsewhere been noted that compounding has an ambivalent status with regards to wordhood, since compounds by definition contain multiple lexical elements, one or more of which may themselves be word-like (Haspelmath, 2011, p. 39), and since compounds can in some cases be viewed as special types of phrases (ten Hacken, 2017). The concept of 'compounding' is not often explicitly applied in studies of polysynthetic verbs, but it may highlight the ambiguity of wordhood in these languages. One reason why polysynthetic verbs may not be identified as compounds is that they often interpolate multiple lexical stems with affixal material. This interpolation is also found in Murrinhpatha, however analysis of prosodic constituency in the verb provides a means of analysing it as a compound. The coverb is compounded to the base stem, but is compounded using a prosodic rather than morphosyntactic anchor-point.

As has been argued elsewhere (e.g. Baker, 2018; Tallman & Epps, 2018), the distinctive feature of polysynthetic languages may not be that they have big words, but that the concept 'word' does not apply to them easily. As noted in the introduction, Murrinhpatha does not appear to have rigid grammatical structure beyond the verb complex and the noun phrase, and it is the verb complex where most structure is usually realised. There are some good reasons why the verb complex has been identified as a word rather than a phrase – complex dependencies among its inflectional elements, semantic opacity among its lexical elements, and prosodic integration of a substantial part of the structure, marked by a single accentual prominence. If however we set aside the concept of wordhood, we can see that what makes Murrinhpatha unusual is that when it does exhibit rigid grammatical structure, this is accompanied by great complexity and opacity.

Finally, the theoretical discussions in this book have cast doubt not just on the concept of wordhood, but also morphology. Morphology involves patterned form–meaning relations among words, but since patterns may be more or less regular, I have argued that morphology is a gradient phenomenon. This perspective has been provoked by analytical issues in Murrinhpatha verb stems and coverbs, where there are different degrees of regularity in form–meaning patterning across the lexicon, and therefore no obvious cut-off point between morphology and pure, unanalysable lexicon. The degree of irregularity in Murrinhpatha morphology may again point to it being a particularly complex and opaque language. For inflectional paradigms we have been able to make a quantified cross-linguistic comparison on this point, thanks to previous work (Ackerman & Malouf, 2013). For semantic opacity of compounding, and morpho-phonological opacity, there is no established method for quantitative cross-linguistic comparison. However in this final chapter I have sketched out some possible approaches for quantifying degrees of morphologicality, which may in the future provide a different approach to comparing structural complexity among languages.

Appendix I

Finite verb stem paradigms

This appendix illustrates the inflectional paradigms of all 39 finite verb stems in Murrinhpatha (Table A.1). Each paradigm is illustrated with the complete forms of inflectional exponence, together with a segmented analysis of the semi-regular formatives that make up' the exponence (§5).

Inflected stem forms that share the same number and tense categories, and differ only in person category (e.g. 1SG.NFUT, 2SG.NFUT, 3SG.NFUT) are usually differentiated only by their prefix consonant. Where this is the case, the first person segmentation is given in full, while for second and third persons only the prefix consonant is segmented.

Note that three verb stems, /ma/ "do, say", /ba/ AFFECT, and /ma/ "use hands" each have two distinct inflectional paradigms. "Pseudo-classifiers", i.e. those that lack a clear lexico-semantic meaning, are given arbitrary labels in small capitals such as /bu/ LOWER, reflecting weak patterns of meaning found among the compound verbs in which they occur.

The inflectional paradigms illustrated here were originally documented by Walsh (1976) and Street (1987). An improved presentation format is provided by Blythe et al. (2007). The inflectional analysis presented here draws on all these sources, but is not identical to any of them. Numbering of inflectional paradigms is not consecutive, nor is it meaningful; rather, it follows numbering established in Blythe et al (2007), with some divergences imposed by differences of analysis.

Table A.1: Murrinhpatha finite verb stems, and sharing of inflectional paradigms. Shading indicates verb stems with multiple paradigms, or paradigms that apply to multiple verb stems.

Base verb stem	Exponence patterns		Reflexive/reciprocal verb stem
/i/ 'sit'	I		
/i/ 'lie'	II		
/ra/ 'stand'	III		
/ni/ 'be'	IV		
/ṉta/ 'perch'	V		
/ru/ 'go'	VI		
/nu/ 'use feet'	VII	XXXVIII	/ni/ 'use feet RR'
/mu/ COERCE	XI		
/bu/ LOWER	XVII	XVIII	/buj/ LOWER.RR
/a/ 'use mouth'	XIX	XXI	/e/ 'use mouth RR'
/a/ PIERCE			/e/ PIERCE.RR
/a/ 'appear'	XX		
/ṉti/ 'carry'	XXII		
/u/ SLASH	XXIII	XXIV	/ju/ SLASH.RR
/ŋa/ 'put together'	XXV		
/la/ 'wipe'	XXVI	XXXVII	/li/ 'wipe RR'
/na/ 'use fire'	XXVII		
/ra/ 'watch'	XXVIII	XXXVI	/ri/ 'watch RR'
/ḍu/ IMPEL	XXIX	XXX	/ḍi/ IMPEL.RR
/la/ 'eat'	XXXI		
/ŋu/ 'pull'	XXXII	XXXIII	/ŋi/ 'pull RR'
/ṉta/ 'crouch'	XXXV		
/ba/ AFFECT	XIV		/be/ AFFECT.RR
/ma/ 'use hands'	VIII		/me/ 'use hands RR'
	IX		
/ma/ 'do, say'			/me/ 'do, say RR'
	XXXIV		
/mi/ 'look'	X		
/bi/ 'hear'			
TOTAL 27 VERB STEMS	TOTAL 34 EXPONENCE PATTERNS		TOTAL 12 VERB STEMS

		/i/ 'sit' Paradigm: I	STEM:	/i/ DEFAULT /ri/ C:RHOTIC /ju/ C:J (SUPPLETIVE), VH:BACK		
		NFUT (/PRSL)		IRR (/FUT)	PST	PSTIRR
SG	1	ŋem ŋ-a-[def]-m		ŋi ŋ-i-[DEF]-ø	ŋini ŋ-i-[DEF]-ni	ŋini ŋ-i-[DEF]-ni
	2	ṭim ṭ-i-[DEF]-m		ṭi ṭ-...	ṭini ṭ-...	ṭini ṭ-...
	3	dim / kem d-i-[DEF]-m / k-e-[DEF]-m		ki/ pi k-... / p-...	dini d-...	dini d-...
INCL	1	ṭim ṭ-i-[DEF].m		pi p-i.[DEF].ø	ṭini ṭ-i-[DEF]-ni	ṭini ṭ-i-[DEF]-ni
PL	1	ŋarim ŋ-a-[RHOT]-m		ŋuju ŋ-u-[J.BACK]-ø	ŋarini ŋ-a-[RHOT]-ni	ŋarini ŋ-a-[RHOT]-ni
	2	nirim n-i-[RHOT]-m		nuju n-...	nirini n-i-[RHOT]-ni	nirini n-i-[RHOT]-ni
	3	pirim / karim p-i-[RHOT]-m / k-a-[RHOT]-m		kuju / puju k-... / p-...	pirini p-i-[RHOT]-ni	pirini p-i-[RHOT]-ni
			PC 1	ŋe ŋa.[DEF].ø	ŋarine ŋ-a-[RHOT]-ne	ŋarine ŋ-a-[RHOT]-ne
			2	ne n-...	nirine n-i-[RHOT]-ne	nirine n-i-[RHOT]-ne
			3	ke / pe k-... / p-...	pirine p-i-[RHOT]-ne	pirine p-i-[RHOT]-ne

		/i/ 'lie' Paradigm: II	STEM:	/i/ DEFAULT /ri/ C:RHOTIC /ju/ C:J (SUPPLETIVE), VH:BACK /bi/ C:B (SUPPLETIVE)		
		NFUT (/PRSL)		**IRR (/FUT)**	**PST**	**PSTIRR**
SG	1	ŋabim ŋ-a-[B]-m		ŋu ŋ-i-[DEF]-ø	ŋu ŋ-u-[DEF]-ø	ŋuŋi ŋ-u-[DEF]-ŋi
	2	t̪ibim t̪-i-[B]-m		t̪u t̪-...	t̪u t̪-...	t̪uŋi t̪-...
	3	jibim / kabim j-i-[B]-m / k-a-[B]-m		ku/ pu k-... / p-...	ju d-...	juŋi j-...
INCL	1	t̪ibim t̪-i.[DEF].m		pu p-i.[DEF].ø	t̪u t̪-u-[DEF]-ø	t̪uŋi t̪-u-[DEF]-ŋi
PL	1	ŋarim ŋ-a-[RHOT]-m		ŋuju ŋ-u-[J,BACK]-ø	ŋarini ŋ-a-[RHOT]-ni	ŋarini ŋ-a-[RHOT]-ni
	2	nirim n-i-[RHOT]-m		nuju n-...	nirini n-i-[RHOT]-ni	nirini n-i-[RHOT]-ni
	3	pirim / karim p-i-[RHOT]-m / k-a-[RHOT]-m		kuju / puju k-... / p-...	pirini p-i-[RHOT]-ni	pirini p-i-[RHOT]-ni
			PC 1	ŋe ŋa-[DEF]-ø	ŋarine ŋ-a-[RHOT]-ne	ŋarine ŋ-a-[RHOT]-ne
			2	ne n-...	nirine n-i-[RHOT]-ne	nirine n-i-[RHOT]-ne
			3	ke / pe k-... / p-...	pirine p-i-[RHOT]-ne	pirine p-i-[RHOT]-ne

/ra/ 'stand' Paradigm: III		STEM:	/ra/	DEFAULT		
			/ri/	VH:HIGH, VF:FRONT		
			/ɭa/	C:GEMINATE		
			/ɭi/	C:GEMINATE, VH:HIGH, VF:FRONT		
			/bi/	C:B (SUPPLETIVE), VH:HIGH, VF:FRONT		
			/a/	C:WEAK		
		NFUT (/PRSL)	**IRR (/FUT)**	**PST**		**PSTIRR**
SG	1	ŋarim	ŋira	ŋiri		ŋiraŋi
		ŋ-a-[HIGH,FRONT]-m	ŋ-i-[DEF]-ø	ŋ-i-[HIGH,FRONT]-ø		ŋ-i-[DEF]-ŋi
	2	ṭirim	ṭira	ṭiri		ṭiraŋi
		ṭ-i-[HIGH,FRONT]-m	ṭ-...	ṭ-...		ṭ-...
	3	pirim / karim	kira / pira	piri		piraŋi
		p-i-[HIGH,FRONT]-m / k-...	k-... / p-...	p-...		p-...
INCL	1	ṭirim	pira	piri		ṭiraŋi
		ṭ-i-[HIGH,FRONT]-m	p-i-[DEF]-ø	p-i-[HIGH,FRONT]-ø		ṭ-i-[DEF]-ŋi
PL	1	ŋibim	ŋiɭa	ŋi		ŋiɭaŋi
		ŋ-i-[B,HIGH,FRONT]-m	ŋ-i-[GEM]-ø[62]	ŋ-i-[WEAK]-ø		ŋ-i-[GEM]-ŋi
	2	nibim	niɭa	ni		niɭaŋi
		n-...	n-...	n-...		n-...
	3	pibim / kibim	kiɭa / piɭa	pi		piɭaŋi
		p-... / k-...	k-... / p-...	p-...		p-...
	PC 1		ŋiɭa	ŋe		ŋiɭaŋi
			ŋ-i-[GEM]-ø	ŋ-i-[WEAK]-ø		ŋ-i-[GEM]-ŋi
	2		niɭa	ne		niɭaŋi
			n-...	n-...		n-...
	3		kiɭa / piɭa	pe		piɭaŋi
			k-... / p-...	p-...		p-...

---

[62] /r → ɭ/ is analysed as a gemination pattern by Green (2003, p. 143). This may have more of a historic than a synchronic motivation, according to which we could posit the /ɭ/ stems in this verb as synchronically suppletive.

/ni/ 'be'		STEM:	/ni/	DEFAULT	
Paradigm: IV			/na/	VH:LOW, VF:BACK	
			/ɳi/	C:RN (SUPPLETIVE)	
			/ɳe/	C:RN (SUPPLETIVE), VH:LOW	
			/ɳa/	C:RN (SUPPLETIVE), VH:LOW, VF:BACK	
			/ḍi/	C:RD (SUPPLETIVE)	
			/ḍe/	C:RD (SUPPLETIVE), VH:LOW	

		NFUT (/PRSL)	IRR (/FUT)	PST	PSTIRR
SG	1	ŋanam	ŋani	ŋaḍi	ŋani
		ŋ-a-[LOW,BACK]-m	ŋ-a-[DEF]-ø	ŋ-a-[RD]-ø	ŋ-a-[DEF]-ø
	2	ṭanam	ṭani	ṭaḍi	ṭani
		ṭ-...	ṭ-...	ṭ-...	ṭ-...
	3	kanam / kanam	kani / pani	paḍi	kani
		k-... / k-...	k-... / p-...	p-...	k-...
INCL	1	ṭanam	pani	paḍi	ṭani
		ṭ-a-[LOW,BACK]-m	p-a-[DEF]-ø	p-a-[RD]-ø	ṭ-a-[DEF]-ø
PL	1	ŋaɳam[63]	ŋaɳi	ŋaḍi	ŋaɳi
		ŋ-a-[RN,LOW,BACK]-m	ŋ-a-[RN]-ø	ŋ-a-[RD]-ø	ŋ-a-[RN]-ø
	2	naɳam	naɳi	naḍi	naɳi
		n-...	n-...	n-...	n-...
	3	paɳam / kaɳam	kaɳi / paɳi	paḍi	kaɳi
		p-... / k-...	k-... / p-...	p-...	k-...
PC	1		ŋaɳe	ŋaḍe	ŋaɳe
			ŋ-a-[RN,LOW]-ø	ŋ-a-[RD,LOW]-ø	ŋ-a-[RN,LOW]-ø
	2		naɳe	naḍe	naɳe
			n-...	n-...	n-...
	3		kaɳe / paɳe	paḍe	kaɳe
			k-... / p-...	p-...	k-...

[63] The retroflex /ɳ/ in PL stems, as opposed to apical /n/ in SG stems, is not produced by all speakers. Younger speakers especially tend to realise the PL stem instead with a geminate consonant.

		/n̪ta/ 'perch' Paradigm: V	STEM:	/n̪ta/ DEFAULT /n̪ti/ VH:HIGH, VF:FRONT		
		NFUT (/PRSL)		IRR (/FUT)	PST	PSTIRR
SG	1	ŋan̪t̪im ŋ-a-[FRONT,HIGH]-m		ŋin̪t̪a ŋ-i-[DEF]-ø	ŋin̪t̪aɲi ŋ-i-[DEF]-ɲi	ŋin̪t̪aɲi ŋ-i-[DEF]-ɲi
	2	t̪in̪t̪im t̪-i-[FRONT,HIGH]-m		t̪in̪t̪a t̪-...	t̪in̪t̪aɲi t̪-...	t̪in̪t̪aɲi t̪-...
	3	pin̪t̪im / kan̪t̪im p-i-... / k-a-...		kin̪t̪a / pin̪t̪a k-... / p-...	pin̪t̪aɲi p-...	pin̪t̪aɲi p-...
INCL	1	t̪in̪t̪im t̪-i-[FRONT,HIGH]-m		pin̪t̪a p-i-[DEF]-ø	t̪in̪t̪aɲi t̪-i-[DEF]-ɲi	t̪in̪t̪aɲi t̪-i-[DEF]-ɲi
PL	1	ŋan̪t̪im ŋ-a-[FRONT,HIGH]-m		ŋin̪t̪a ŋ-i-[DEF]-ø	ŋin̪t̪aɲi ŋ-i-[DEF]-ɲi	ŋin̪t̪aɲi ŋ-i-[DEF]-ɲi
	2	nin̪t̪im n-i-[FRONT,HIGH]-m		nin̪t̪a n-...	nin̪t̪aɲi n-...	nin̪t̪aɲi n-...
	3	pin̪t̪im / kan̪t̪im p-i-... / k-a-...		kin̪t̪a / pin̪t̪a k-... / p-...	pin̪t̪aɲi p-...	pin̪t̪aɲi p-...
			PC 1	ŋin̪t̪a ŋ-i-[DEF]-ø	ŋin̪t̪aŋe ŋ-i-[DEF]-ŋe	ŋin̪t̪aŋe ŋ-i-[DEF]-ŋe
			2	nin̪t̪a n-...	nin̪t̪aŋe n-...	nin̪t̪aŋe n-...
			3	kin̪t̪a / pin̪t̪a k-... / p-...	pin̪t̪aŋe p-...	pin̪t̪aŋe p-...

		/ru/ 'go' Paradigm: VI	STEM:	/ru/ /ṭu/ /u/ /ji/ /mpa/	DEFAULT GEMINATE WEAK J (SUPPL), FRONT MP (SUPPL), LOW	/ra/ LOW /ri/ FRONT /je/ J (SUPPL), FRONT, LOW	
		NFUT (/PRSL)		**IRR (/FUT)**		**PST**	**PSTIRR**
SG	1	ŋuran ŋ-u-[LOW]-n		ŋuru ŋ-u-[DEF]-ø		ŋuriɲi ŋ-u-[FRONT]-ni	ŋuri ŋ-u-[FRONT]-ø
	2	ṭuran ṭ-...		ṭuru ṭ-...		ṭuriɲi ṭ-...	ṭuri ṭ-...
	3	wuran / kuran w-... / k-...		kuru / puru k-... / p-...		wuriɲi w-...	wuri w-...
INCL	1	ṭuran ṭ-u-[LOW]-n		puru p-u-[DEF]-ø		ṭuriɲi ṭ-u-[FRONT]-ni	ṭuri ṭu-[FRONT]-ø
PL	1	ŋumpan ŋ-u-[MP,LOW]-n		ŋuṭu ŋ-u-[GEM]-ø		ŋuɲi ŋ-u-[WEAK,FRONT]-ni	ŋuji ŋ-u-[J,FRONT]-ø
	2	numpan n-...		nuṭu n-...		nuɲi n-...	nuji n-...
	3	pumpan / kumpan p-... / k-...		kuṭu / puṭu k-... / p-...		puɲi p-...	puji p-...
			PC 1	ŋa ŋ-a-[WEAK]-ø		ŋuɲe ŋ-u-[WEAK,FRONT]-ɲe	ŋuje ŋ-u-[J,FRNT,LOW]-ø
			2	na n-...		nuɲe n-...	nuje n-...
			3	ka / pa k-... / p-...		puɲe p-...	puje p-...

		/nu/ 'use feet' Paradigm: VII	STEM:	/nu/ DEFAULT /ni/ VF:FRONT /nuj/ VF: OFFGLIDE /na/ VH: LOW	/nnu/ C:GEMINATE /nni/ C:GEM, VF:FRONT /nna/ C:GEM, VH: LOW /nne/ C:GEM, VH: LOW, VF:FRONT	
w		NFUT (/PRSL)		IRR (/FUT)	PST	PSTIRR
SG	1	ŋunuŋam ŋ-u-[DEF]-ŋam		ŋunu ŋ-u-[DEF]-ø	ŋuna ŋ-u-[LOW]-ø	ŋuni ŋ-u-[FRONT]-ø
	2	tunuŋam t̪-...		tunu t̪-...	tuna t̪-...	tuni t̪-...
	3	nuŋam / kunuŋam ø-... / k-...		kunu / punu k-... / p-...	na[64] ø-...	nuj ø-u-[OFFGLIDE]-ø
INCL	1	tunuŋam t̪-u-[DEF]-ŋam		punu p-u-[DEF]-ø	tuna t̪-u-[LOW]-ø	tuni t̪-u-[FRONT]-ø
PL	1	ŋunnuŋam ŋ-u-[GEM]- ŋam		ŋunnu ŋ-u-[GEM]-ø	ŋunni ŋ-u-[GEM,FRONT]-ø	ŋunni ŋ-u-[GEM,FRONT]-ø
	2	nunnuŋam n-...		nunnu n-...	nunni n-...	nunni n-...
	3	punnuŋam / kunnuŋam p-... / k-...		kunnu / punnu k-... / p-...	punni p-...	punni p-...
			PC 1	ŋunna ŋ-u-[GEM,LOW]-ø	ŋunna ŋ-u-[GEM,LOW]-ø	ŋunne ŋ-u-[GEM,FRONT,LOW]-ø
			2	nunna n-...	nunna n-...	nunne n-...
			3	kunna / punna k-... / p-...	punna p-...	punne p-...

---

[64] Street (1987) in addition lists a variant /nuɹa/ use.feet.3SG.PST. This variant does not appear in my corpus data

			STEM:	/ni/ DEFAULT /na/ VF:BACK, VH: LOW		/nni/ C:GEMINATE /nna/ C:GEM,VF:BACK, VH: LOW
		/ni/ 'use feet RR' Paradigm: XXXVIII				
		NFUT (/PRSL)	**IRR (/FUT)**	**PST**		**PSTIRR**
SG	1	ŋinim ŋ-i-[DEF]-m	ŋini ŋ-i-[DEF]-ø	ŋinaŋa ŋ-i-[BACK,LOW]-ŋa		ŋinaŋa ŋ-i-[BACK,LOW]-ŋa
	2	t̪inim t̪-...	t̪ini t̪-...	t̪ina t̪-i-[BACK,LOW]-ŋa		t̪ina t̪-i-[BACK,LOW]-ŋa
	3	niŋam / kiniŋam ø-i-[DEF]-ŋam / k-...	kini / pini k-... / p-...	niŋa ø-i-[DEF]-ŋa		niŋa ø-i-[DEF]-ŋa
INCL	1	t̪iniŋam t̪-u-[DEF]-ŋam	pini p-i-[DEF]-ø	t̪inaŋa t̪-i-[BACK,LOW]-ŋa		t̪inaŋa t̪-i-[BACK,LOW]-ŋa
PL	1	ŋinnaŋam ŋ-u-[GEM,BACK,LOW]- ŋam	ŋinni ŋ-i-[GEM]-ø	ŋinnaŋa ŋ-i- [GEM,BACK,LOW]-ŋa		ŋinnaŋa ŋ-i- [GEM,BACK,LOW]-ŋa
	2	ninnaŋam n-...	ninni n-...	ninnaŋa n-...		ninnaŋa n-...
	3	pinnaŋam / kinnaŋam p-... / k-...	kinni / pinni k-... / p-...	pinna p-...		pinna p-...
	PC 1		ŋinni ŋ-u-[GEM]-ø	ŋinnaŋa ŋ-i- [GEM,BACK,LOW]-ŋa		ŋinnaŋa ŋ-i- [GEM,BACK,LOW]-ŋa
	2		ninni n-...	ninnaŋa n-...		ninnaŋa n-...
	3		kinni / pinni k-... / p-...	pinnaŋa p-...		pinnaŋa p-...

		/ma/ 'say, do' /ma/ 'use hands' Paradigm: VIII	STEM:	/ma/ DEFAULT /na/ C:APICAL /me/ VF:FRONT /ne/ C:APICAL, VF:FRONT		
		NFUT (/PRSL)		**IRR (/FUT)**	**PST**	**PSTIRR**
SG	1	mam ø-u-[DEF]-m[65]		ma ø-u-[DEF]-ø	me ø-u-[FRONT]-ø	me ø-u-[FRONT]-ø
	2	nam ø-u-[APIC]-m		na ø-u-[APIC]-ø	ne ø-u-[APIC,FRONT]-ø	ne ø-u-[APIC,FRONT]-ø
	3	mam / kumam ø-u-[DEF]-m / k-...		ma / ma ø-u-[DEF]-ø	me ø-u-[FRONT]-ø	me ø-u-[FRONT]-ø
INCL	1	ṭumam ṭ-u-[DEF]-m		puma p-u-[DEF]-ø	ṭume ṭ-u-[FRONT]-ø	ṭume ṭ-u-[FRONT]-ø
PL	1	ŋumam ŋ-u-[DEF]-m		ŋuma ŋ-u-[DEF]-ø	ŋume ŋ-u-[FRONT]-ø	ŋume ŋ-u-[FRONT]-ø
	2	numam n-...		numa n-...	nume n-...	nume n-...
	3	pumam / kumam p-... / k-...		kuma / puma k-... / p-...	pume p-...	pume p-...
			PC 1	ŋuma ŋ-u-[DEF]-ø	ŋume ŋ-u-[FRONT]-ø	ŋume ŋ-u-[FRONT]-ø
			2	numa n-...	nume n-...	nume n-...
			3	kuma / puma k-... / p-...	pume p-...	pume p-...

---

[65] Where forms have a phonologically empty PrefC, I analyse them as having an 'underlying' PrefV following whatever theme vowel pattern is established in the rest of the paradigm. In these instances the PrefV cannot be realised on the surface due to the constraint against onsetless syllables (§5.4.2).

		/ma/ 'use hands' Paradigm: IX	STEM:	/ma/ DEFAULT /na/ C:APICAL /me/ VF:FRONT /ne/ C:APICAL, VF:FRONT		
		NFUT (/PRSL)		**IRR (/FUT)**	**PST**	**PSTIRR**
SG	1	maŋan ø-u-[DEF]-ŋan		ma ø-u-[DEF]-ø	me ø-u-[FRONT]-ø	me ø-u-[FRONT]-ø
	2	naŋan ø-u-[APIC]-ŋan		na ø-u-[APIC]-ø	ne ø-u-[APIC, FRONT]-ø	ne ø-u-[APIC,FRONT]-ø
	3	maŋan / kumaŋan ø-u-[DEF]-ŋan / k-...		ma / ma ø-u-[DEF]-ø	me ø-u-[FRONT]-ø	me ø-u-[FRONT]-ø
INCL	1	t̪umaŋan t̪-u-[DEF]-ŋan		puma p-u-[DEF]-ø	t̪ume t̪-u-[FRONT]-ø	t̪ume t̪-u-[FRONT]-ø
PL	1	ŋumaŋan ŋ-u-[DEF]-ŋan		ŋuma ŋ-u-[DEF]-ø	ŋume ŋ-u-[FRONT]-ø	ŋume ŋ-u-[FRONT]-ø
	2	numaŋan n-...		numa n-...	nume n-...	nume n-...
	3	pumaŋan / kumaŋan p-... / k-...		kuma / puma k-... / p-...	pume p-...	pume p-...
	PC 1			ŋuma ŋ-u-[DEF] ø	ŋume ŋ-u-[FRONT]-ø	ŋume ŋ-u-[FRONT]-ø
	2			numa n-...	nume n-...	nume n-...
	3			kuma / puma k-... / p-...	pume p-...	pume p-...

		/ma/ 'say, do' Paradigm: XXXIV	STEM:	/ma/ DEFAULT /me/ VF:FRONT /mi/ VF:FRONT, VH:HIGH		/na/ C:APICAL /ne/ C:APICAL, VF:FRONT /ni/ C:APICAL, VF:FRONT, VH:HIGH
		NFUT (/PRSL)		IRR (/FUT)	PST	PSTIRR
SG	1	ŋamam ŋ-a-[DEF]-m		ŋama ŋ-a-[DEF]-ø	me ø-u-[FRONT]-ø	mi ø-u-[FRONT,HIGH]-ø
	2	nam ø-a-[APIC]-m		t̪ama t̪-...	ne ø-u-[APIC,FRONT]-ø	ni ø-u-[APIC,FRONT,HIGH]-ø
	3	mam / kamam ø-a-[DEF]-m / k-...		kama / pama k-... / p-...	me ø-u-[FRONT]-ø	mi ø-u-[FRONT,HIGH]-ø
INCL	1	t̪amam t̪-a-[DEF]-m		pama p-a-[DEF]-ø	t̪ume t̪-u-[FRONT]-ø	t̪umi t̪-u-[FRONT,HIGH]-ø
PL	1	ŋamam ŋ-a-[DEF]-m		ŋujema ŋ-uje-[DEF]-ø	ŋume ŋ-u-[FRONT]-ø	ŋumi ŋ-u-[FRONT,HIGH]-ø
	2	namam n-...		nujema n-...	nume n-...	numi n-...
	3	pamam / kamam p-... / k-...		kujema / pujema k-... / p-...	pume p-...	pumi p-...
	PC 1			ŋujema ŋ-uje-[DEF]-ø	ŋume ŋ-u-[FRONT]-ø	ŋumi ŋ-u-[FRONT,HIGH]-ø
	2			nujema n-...	nume n-...	numi n-...
	3			kujema / pujema k-... / p-...	pume p-...	pumi p-...

		/me/ 'say, do RR' /me/ 'use hands RR' Paradigm: X	STEM:	/me/ DEFAULT /ne/ C:APICAL		
		NFUT (/PRSL)		**IRR (/FUT)**	**PST**	**PSTIRR**
SG	1	mem ø-u-[DEF]-m		me ø-u-[DEF]-ø	mena ø-u-[DEF]-ø	mena ø-u-[DEF]-ø
	2	nem ø-u-[APIC]-m		ne ø-u-[APIC]-ø	nena ø-u-[APIC]-ø	nena ø-u-[APIC]-ø
	3	mem / kumem ø-u-[DEF]-m / k-...		me / me ø-u-[DEF]-ø	mena ø-u-[DEF]-ø	mena ø-u-[DEF]-ø
INCL	1	ṭumem ṭ-u-[DEF]-m		pume p-u-[DEF]-ø	ṭumena ṭ-u-[DEF]-ø	ṭumena ṭ-u-[DEF]-ø
PL	1	ŋumem ŋ-u-[DEF]-m		ŋume ŋ-u-[DEF]-ø	ŋumena ŋ-u-[DEF]-ø	ŋumena ŋ-u-[DEF]-ø
	2	numem n-...		nume n-...	numena n-...	numena n-...
	3	pumem / kumem p-... / k-...		kume / pume k-... / p-...	pumena p-...	pumena p-...
			PC 1	ŋume ŋ-u-[DEF]ø	ŋumena ŋ-u-[DEF]-ø	ŋumena ŋ-u-[DEF]-ø
			2	nume n-...	numena n-...	numena n-...
			3	kume / pume k-.../ p-...	pumena p-...	pumena p-...

		/ba/ AFFECT Paradigm: VIII	STEM:	/ba/ DEFAULT /da/ C:APICAL /be/ VF:FRONT /de/ C:APICAL, VF:FRONT		
		NFUT (/PRSL)		**IRR (/FUT)**	**PST**	**PSTIRR**
SG	1	bam ø-u-[DEF]-m		ba ø-u-[DEF]-ø	be ø-u-[FRONT]-ø	be ø-u-[FRONT]-ø
	2	dam ø-u-[APIC]-m		da ø-u-[APIC]-ø	de ø-u-[APIC,FRONT]-ø	de ø-u-[APIC,FRONT]-ø
	3	bam / bam ø-u-[DEF]-m		ba / ba ø-u-[DEF]-ø	be ø-u-[FRONT]-ø	be ø-u-[FRONT]-ø
INCL	1	ṭubam ṭ-u-[DEF]-m		puba p-u-[DEF]-ø	ṭube ṭ-u-[FRONT]-ø	ṭube ṭ-u-[FRONT]-ø
PL	1	ŋubam ŋ-u-[DEF]-m		ŋuba ŋ-u-[DEF]-ø	ŋube ŋ-u-[FRONT] ø	ŋube ŋ-u-[FRONT] ø
	2	nubam n-...		nuba n-...	nube n-...	nube n-...
	3	pubam / kubam p-... / k-...		kuba / puba k-... / p-...	pube p-...	pube p-...
			PC 1	ŋuba ŋ-u-[DEF] ø	ŋube ŋ-u-[FRONT] ø	ŋube ŋ-u-[FRONT] ø
			2	nuba n-...	nube n-...	nube n-...
			3	kuba / puba k-... / p-...	pube p-...	pube p-...

		/ba/ AFFECT Paradigm: XIV	STEM:	/ba/ DEFAULT /da/ C:APICAL /be/ VF:FRONT /de/ C:APICAL, VF:FRONT		
		NFUT (/PRSL)		IRR (/FUT)	PST	PSTIRR
SG	1	baŋam ø-u-[DEF]-ŋam		ba ø-u-[DEF]-ø	be ø-u-[FRONT]-ø	be ø-u-[FRONT]–ø
	2	daŋam ø-u-[APIC]-ŋam		da ø-u-[APIC]-ø	de ø-u-[APIC,FRONT]-ø	de ø-u-[APIC,FRONT]-ø
	3	baŋam / baŋam ø-u-[DEF]-ŋam		ba / ba ø-u-[DEF]-ø	be ø-u-[FRONT]-ø	be ø-u-[FRONT]-ø
INCL	1	ṭubaŋam ṭ-u-[DEF]-ŋam		puba p-u-[DEF]-ø	ṭube ṭ-u-[FRONT]-ø	ṭube ṭ-u-[FRONT]-ø
PL	1	ŋubaŋam ŋ-u-[DEF]-ŋam		ŋuba ŋ-u-[DEF]-ø	ŋube ŋ-u-[FRONT]-ø	ŋube ŋ-u-[FRONT]-ø
	2	nubaŋam n-...		nuba n-...	nube n-...	nube n-...
	3	pubaŋam / kubaŋam p-... / k-...		kuba / puba k-... / p-...	pube p-...	pube p-...
			PC 1	ŋuba ŋ-u-[DEF]-ø	ŋube ŋ-u-[FRONT]-ø	ŋube ŋ-u-[FRONT]-ø
			2	nuba n-...	nube n-...	nube n-...
			3	kuba / puba k-.../ p-...	pube p-...	pube p-...

		/be/ AFFECT.RR Paradigm: X	STEM:	/be/ DEFAULT /de/ C:APICAL		
		NFUT (/PRSL)		IRR (/FUT)	PST	PSTIRR
SG	1	bem ø-u-[DEF]-m		be ø-u-[DEF]-ø	bena ø-u-[DEF]-ø	bena ø-u-[DEF]-ø
	2	dem ø-u-[APIC]-m		de ø-u-[APIC]-ø	dena ø-u-[APIC]-ø	dena ø-u-[APIC]-ø
	3	bem / kubem ø-u-[DEF]-m / k-...		be / be ø-u-[DEF]-ø	bena ø-u-[DEF]-ø	bena ø-u-[DEF]-ø
INCL	1	t̪ubem t̪-u-[DEF]-m		pube p-u-[DEF]-ø	t̪ubena t̪-u-[DEF]-ø	t̪ubena t̪-u-[DEF]-ø
PL	1	ŋubem ŋ-u-[DEF]-m		ŋube ŋ-u-[DEF]-ø	ŋubena ŋ-u-[DEF]-ø	ŋubena ŋ-u-[DEF]-ø
	2	nubem n-...		nube n-...	nubena n-...	nubena n-...
	3	pubem / kubem p-... / k-...		kube / pube k-... / p-...	pubena p-...	pubena p-...
			PC 1	ŋube ŋ-u-[DEF] ø	ŋubena ŋ-u-[DEF]-ø	ŋubena ŋ-u-[DEF]-ø
			2	nube n-...	nubena n-...	nubena n-...
			3	kube / pube k-... / p-...	pubena p-...	pubena p-...

		/mu/ COERCE Paradigm: XI	STEM:	/mu/ DEFAULT /nu/ C:APICAL /u/ C: WEAK		
		NFUT (/PRSL)		**IRR (/FUT)**	**PST**	**PSTIRR**
SG	1	muŋam ø-u-[DEF]-ŋam		mu ø-u-[DEF]-ø	muni ø-u-[DEF]-ni	muj ø-u-[DEF]-j
	2	nuŋam ø-u-[APIC]-ŋam		nu ø-u-[APIC]-ø	nuni ø-u-[APIC]-ni	nuj ø-u-[APIC]-j
	3	muŋam / muŋam ø-u-[DEF]-ŋam		mu / mu ø-u-[DEF]-ø	muni ø-u-[DEF]-ni	muj ø-u-[DEF]-j
INCL	1	ṭumuŋam ṭ-u-[DEF]-ŋam		pumu p-u-[DEF]-ø	ṭuni ṭ-u-[WEAK]-ni	ṭumuj ṭ-u-[DEF]-j
PL	1	ŋumuŋam ŋ-u-[DEF]-ŋam		ŋumu ŋ-u-[DEF]-ø	ŋumuni ŋ-u-[DEF]-ni	ŋumuj ŋ-u-[DEF]-j
	2	numuŋam n-...		numu n-...	numuni n-...	numuj n-...
	3	pumuŋam / kumuŋam p-... / k-...		kumu / pumu k-... / p-...	pumuni p-...	pumuj p-...
	PC 1			ŋumu ŋ-u-[DEF]-ø	ŋumune ŋ-u-[DEF]-ne	ŋumuj ŋ-u-[DEF]-j
	2			numu n-...	numune n-...	numuj n-...
	3			kumu / pumu k-... / p-...	pumune p-...	pumuj p-...

		/mi/ 'look' Paradigm: X	STEM:	/mi/ DEFAULT /ni/ C:APICAL		
		NFUT (/PRSL)		IRR (/FUT)	PST	PSTIRR
SG	1	mim ø-u-[DEF]-m		mi ø-u-[DEF]-ø	mina ø-u-[DEF]-na	mina ø-u-[DEF]-na
	2	nim ø-u-[APIC]-m		ni ø-u-[APIC]-ø	nina ø-u-[APIC]-na	nina ø-u-[APIC]-na
	3	mim / mim ø-u-[DEF]-m		mi / mi ø-u-[DEF]-ø	mina ø-u-[DEF]-na	mina ø-u-[DEF]-na
INCL	1	tumim t-u-[DEF]-m		pumi p-u-[DEF]-ø	tumina t-u-[DEF]-na	tumina t-u-[DEF]-na
PL	1	ŋumim ŋ-u-[DEF]-m		ŋumi ŋ-u-[DEF]-ø	ŋumina ŋ-u-[DEF]-na	ŋumina ŋ-u-[DEF]-na
	2	numim n-...		numi n-...	numina n-...	numina n-...
	3	pumim / kumuŋam p-... / k-...		kumi / pumi k-... / p-...	pumina p-...	pumina p-...
			PC 1	ŋumi ŋ-u-[DEF]-ø	ŋumina ŋ-u-[DEF]-na	ŋumina ŋ-u-[DEF]-na
			2	numi n-...	numina n-...	numina n-...
			3	kumi / pumi k-... / p-...	pumina p-...	pumina p-...

		/bi/ 'hear' Paradigm: X	STEM:	/bi/ DEFAULT /di/ C:APICAL		
		NFUT (/PRSL)		**IRR (/FUT)**	**PST**	**PSTIRR**
SG	1	bim ø-u-[DEF]-m		bi ø-u-[DEF]-ø	bina ø-u-[DEF]-ø	bina ø-u-[DEF]-ø
	2	dim ø-u-[APIC]-m		di ø-u-[APIC]-ø	dina ø-u-[APIC]-ø	dina ø-u-[APIC]-ø
	3	bim / kubim ø-u-[DEF]-m / k-...		bi / bi ø-u-[DEF]-ø	bina ø-u-[DEF]-ø	bina ø-u-[DEF]-ø
INCL	1	ṯubim ṯ-u-[DEF]-m		pubi p-u-[DEF]-ø	ṯubina ṯ-u-[DEF]-ø	ṯubina ṯ-u-[DEF]-ø
PL	1	ŋubim ŋ-u-[DEF]-m		ŋubi ŋ-u-[DEF]-ø	ŋubina ŋ-u-[DEF]-ø	ŋubina ŋ-u-[DEF]-ø
	2	nubim n-...		nubi n-...	nubina n-...	nubina n-...
	3	pubim / kubim p-... / k-...		kubi / pubi k-... / p-...	pubina p-...	pubina p-...
			PC 1	ŋubi ŋ-u-[DEF]-ø	ŋubina ŋ-u-[DEF]-ø	ŋubina ŋ-u-[DEF]-ø
			2	nubi n-...	nubina n-...	nubina n-...
			3	kubi / pubi k-.../ p-...	pubina p-...	pubina p-...

		/bu/ LOWER Paradigm: XVII	STEM:	/bu/ DEFAULT /du/ C:APICAL	/ba/ VH:LOW /da/ C:APICAL, VH:LOW	
		NFUT (/PRSL)		IRR (/FUT)	PST	PSTIRR
SG	1	ban ø-u-[LOW]-n		bu ø-u-[DEF]-ø	buni ø-u-[DEF]-ni	buj ø-u-[DEF]-j
	2	dan ø-u-[LOW,APIC]-n		du ø-u-[APIC]-ø	duni ø-u-[APIC]-ni	duj ø-u-[APIC]-j
	3	ban / kuban ø-u-[LOW]-n / k-u-[LOW]-n		bu / bu ø-u-[DEF]-ø	buni ø-u-[DEF]-ni	buj ø-u-[DEF]-j
INCL	1	ṭuban ṭ-u-[LOW]-n		pubu p-u-[DEF]-ø	ṭubuni ṭ-u-[DEF]-ni	ṭubuj ṭ-u-[DEF]-j
PL	1	ŋuban ŋ-u-[LOW]-n		ŋubu ŋ-u-[DEF]-ø	ŋubuni ŋ-u-[DEF]-ni	ŋubuj ŋ-u-[DEF]-j
	2	nuban n-...		nubu n-...	nubuni n-...	nubuj n-...
	3	puban / kuban p-... / k-...		kubu / pubu k-... / p-...	pubuni p-...	pubuj p-...
			PC 1	ŋubu ŋ-u-[DEF]-ø	ŋubune ŋ-u-[DEF]-ne	ŋubuj ŋ-u-[DEF]-j
			2	nubu n-...	nubune n-...	nubuj n-...
			3	kubu / pubu k-... / p-...	pubune p-...	pubuj p-...

		/buj/ LOWER.RR Paradigm: XVIII	STEM:	/buj/ DEFAULT /duj/ C:APICAL	/ba/ VH:LOW /da/ C:APIC, VH:LOW	
		NFUT (/PRSL)		**IRR (/FUT)**	**PST**	**PSTIRR**
SG	1	bam ø-u-[LOW]-m		buj ø-u-[DEF]-ø	bana ø-u-[LOW]-na	bana ø-u-[LOW]-na
	2	dam ø-u-[LOW,APIC]-m		duj ø-u-[APIC]-ø	dana ø-u-[APIC,LOW]-na	dana ø-u-[APIC,LOW]-na
	3	bam / kubam ø-u-[LOW]-m / k-u-[LOW]-m		buj / buj ø-u-[DEF]-ø	bana ø-u-[LOW]-na	bana ø-u-[LOW]-na
INCL	1	t̪ubam t̪-u-[LOW]-m		pubuj p-u-[DEF]-ø	t̪ubana t̪-u-[LOW]-na	t̪ubana t̪-u-[LOW]-na
PL	1	ŋubam ŋ-u-[LOW]-m		ŋubuj ŋ-u-[DEF]-ø	ŋubana ŋ-u-[LOW]-na	ŋubana ŋ-u-[LOW]-na
	2	nubam n-...		nubuj n-...	nubana n-...	nubana n-...
	3	pubam / kubam p-... / k-...		kubuj / pubuj k-... / p-...	pubana p-...	pubana p-...
			PC 1	ŋubuj ŋ-u-[DEF]-ø	ŋubana ŋ-u-[LOW]-na	ŋubana ŋ-u-[LOW]-na
			2	nubuj n-...	nubana n-...	nubana n-...
			3	kubuj / pubuj k-... / p-...	pubana p-...	pubana p-...

		/a/ PIERCE /a/ 'use mouth' Paradigm: XIX	STEM:	/a/ DEFAULT /ra/ C:RHOTIC		
		NFUT (/PRSL)		IRR (/FUT)	PST	PSTIRR
SG	1	ŋam		ŋa	ŋani	ŋe
		ŋ-a-[DEF]-m		ŋ-a-[DEF]-ø	ŋ-a-[DEF]-ni	ŋ-e-[DEF]-ø
	2	ṭam		ṭa	ṭani	ṭe
		ṭ-...		ṭ-...	ṭ-...	ṭ-...
	3	dam / kam		ka / pa	dani	de
		d-... / k-...		k-... / p-...	d-...	d-...
INCL	1	ṭam		pa	ṭani	ṭe
		ṭ-a-[DEF]-m		p-a-[DEF]-ø	ṭ-a-[DEF]-ni	ṭ-e-[DEF]-ø
PL	1	ŋaram		ŋa	ŋarani	ŋera
		ŋa-[RHOT]-m		ŋ-a-[DEF]-ø	ŋ-a-[RHOT]-ni	ŋ-e-[RHOT]-ø
	2	naram		na	narani	nera
		n-...		n-...	n-...	n-...
	3	param / karam		ka / pa	pani	pera
		p-... / k-...		k-... / p-...	p-...	p-...
			PC 1	ŋa	ŋarane	ŋera
				ŋ-a-[DEF]-ø	ŋ-a-[RHOT]-ne	ŋ-e-[RHOT]-ø
			2	na	narane	nera
				n-...	n-...	n-...
			3	ka / pa	parane	pera
				k-... / p-...	p-...	p-...

		/e/ PIERCE.RR Paradigm: XXI	STEM:	/e/ DEFAULT /re/ C:RHOTIC		
		NFUT (/PRSL)		**IRR (/FUT)**	**PST**	**PSTIRR**
SG	1	ŋem ŋ-e-[DEF]-m		ŋe ŋ-e-[DEF]-ø	ŋena ŋ-e-[DEF]-na	ŋena ŋ-e-[DEF]-na
	2	t̪em t̪-...		t̪e t̪-...	t̪ena t̪-...	t̪ena t̪-...
	3	dem / kem d-... / k-...		ke / pe k-... / p-...	dena d-...	dena d-...
INCL	1	t̪em t̪-a-[DEF]-m		pe p-e-[DEF]-ø	t̪ena t̪-e-[DEF]-na	t̪ena t̪-e-[DEF]-na
PL	1	ŋerem ŋ-e-[RHOT]-m		ŋa ŋ-e-[DEF]-ø	ŋerena ŋ-e-[RHOT]-na	ŋerena ŋ-e-[RHOT]-na
	2	nerem n-...		ne n-...	nerena n-...	nerena n-...
	3	perem / kerem p-... / k-...		ke / pe k-... / p-...	perena p-...	perena p-...
			PC 1	ŋe ŋ-e-[DEF]-ø	ŋerene ŋ-e-[RHOT]-ne	ŋerene ŋ-e-[RHOT]-ne
			2	ne n-...	nerene n-...	nerene n-...
			3	ke / pe k-... / p-...	perene p-...	perene p-...

		/a/ APPEAR Paradigm: XX	STEM:	/a/ DEFAULT /ra/ C:RHOTIC		
		NFUT (/PRSL)		**IRR (/FUT)**	**PST**	**PSTIRR**
SG	1	ŋaŋam ŋ-a-[DEF]-ŋam		ŋa ŋ-a-[DEF]-ø	ŋani ŋ-a-[DEF]-ni	ŋe ŋ-e-[DEF]-ø
	2	ṭaŋam ṭ-...		ṭa ṭ-...	ṭani ṭ-...	ṭe ṭ-...
	3	paŋam / kaŋam p-... / k-...		ka / pa k-... / p-...	dani d-...	de d-...
INCL	1	ṭaŋam ṭ-a-[DEF]-ŋam		pa p-a-[DEF]-ø	ṭani ṭ-a-[DEF]-ni	ṭe ṭ-e-[DEF]-ø
PL	1	ŋaram ŋa-[RHOT]-m		ŋa ŋ-a-[DEF]-ø	ŋarani ŋ-a-[RHOT]-ni	ŋera ŋ-e-[RHOT]-ø
	2	naram n-...		na n-...	narani n-...	nera n-...
	3	param / karam p-... / k-...		ka / pa k-... / p-...	pani p-...	pera p-...
PC	1			ŋa ŋ-a-[DEF]-ø	ŋarane ŋ-a-[RHOT]-ne	ŋera ŋ-e-[RHOT]-ø
	2			na n-...	narane n-...	nera n-...
	3			ka / pa k-... / p-...	parane p-...	pera p-...

		/n̪t̪i/ 'carry' Paradigm: XXII	STEM:	/n̪t̪i/ DEFAULT /n̪t̪e/ VH:LOW /i/ C:WEAK		
		NFUT (/PRSL)		**IRR (/FUT)**	**PST**	**PSTIRR**
SG	1	ŋan̪t̪in ŋ-a-[DEF]-n		ŋa ŋ-a-[WEAK]-ø	ŋan̪t̪i ŋ-a-[DEF]-ø	ŋe ŋ-e-[DEF]-ø
	2	t̪an̪t̪in t̪-...		t̪a t̪-...	t̪an̪t̪i t̪-...	t̪e t̪-...
	3	kan̪t̪in / kan̪t̪in k-... / k-...		ka / pa k-... / p-...	kan̪t̪i / kan̪t̪i k-... / k-...	de d-...
INCL	1	t̪an̪t̪in t̪-a-[DEF]-n		pa p-a-[WEAK]-ø	t̪an̪t̪i t̪-a-[DEF]-ø	t̪e t̪-e-[DEF]-ø
PL	1	ŋan̪t̪in ŋa-[DEF]-n		ŋa ŋ-a-[WEAK]-ø	ŋan̪t̪i ŋa-[DEF]-ø	ŋera ŋ-e-[RHOT]-ø
	2	nan̪t̪in n-...		na n-...	nan̪t̪i n-...	nera n-...
	3	pan̪t̪in / kan̪t̪in p-... / k-...		ka / pa k-... / p-...	pan̪t̪i p-...	pera p-...
			PC 1	ŋa ŋ-a-[WEAK]-ø	ŋan̪t̪e ŋa-[LOW]-ø	ŋera ŋ-e-[RHOT]-ø
			2	na n-...	nan̪t̪e n-...	nera n-...
			3	ka / pa k-... / p-...	pan̪t̪e p-...	pera p-...

		/u/ SLASH Paradigm: XXIII		STEM:	/u/ /mpa/ /j/ /je/	DEFAULT C:SUPPL VF:FRONT VF:FRONT, VH:LOW	
		NFUT (/PRSL)		**IRR (/FUT)**	**PST**	**PSTIRR**	
SG	1	ŋan ŋ-a-[DEF]-n		ŋu ŋ-u-[DEF]-ø	ŋuni ŋ-u-[DEF]-ni	ŋuj ŋ-u-[FRONT]-ø	
	2	t̪an t̪-...		t̪u t̪-...	t̪uni t̪-...	t̪uj t̪-...	
	3	pan / kan d-... / k-...		ku / pu k-... / p-...	puni p-...	puj p-...	
INCL	1	t̪an t̪-a-[DEF]-n		pu p-u-[DEF]-ø	t̪uni t̪-u-[DEF]-ni	t̪uj t̪-u-[FRONT]-ø	
PL	1	ŋumpan ŋa-[MP]-n		ŋu ŋ-u-[DEF]-ø	ŋuɲi ŋ-u-[DEF]-ɲi	ŋuji ŋ-u-[FRONT]-ø	
	2	numpan n-...		nu n-...	nuɲi n-...	nuji n-...	
	3	pumpan / kumpan p-... / k-...		ku / pu k-... / p-...	puɲi p-...	puji k-... / p-...	
			PC 1	ŋu ŋ-u-[DEF]-ø	ŋuɲe ŋ-u-[DEF]-ɲe	ŋuje ŋ-u-[FRONT,LOW]-ø	
			2	nu n-...	nuɲe n-...	nuje n-...	
			3	ku / pu k-... / p-...	puɲe p-...	puje p-...	

		/ju/ SLASH.RR Paradigm: XXIV	STEM:	/ju/ DEFAULT /j/ VF:FRONT /je/ VF:FRONT, VH:LOW /u/ C:WEAK		
		NFUT (/PRSL)		**IRR (/FUT)**	**PST**	**PSTIRR**
SG	1	ŋam ŋ-a-[WEAK]-m		ŋuj ŋ-u-[FRONT]-ø	ŋana ŋ-a-[WEAK]-na	ŋana ŋ-a-[WEAK]-na
	2	ṭam ṭ-...		ṭuj ṭ-...	ṭana ṭ-...	ṭana ṭ-...
	3	pam / kam p-... / k-...		kuj / puj k-... / p-...	pana p-...	pana p-...
INCL	1	ṭam ṭ-a-[WEAK]-m		puj p-u-[FRONT]-ø	ṭana ṭ-a-[WEAK]-na	ṭana ṭ-a-[WEAK]-na
PL	1	ŋujem ŋu-[FRONT,LOW]-m		ŋuju ŋ-u-[DEF]-ø	ŋujena ŋ-u-[FRONT,LOW]-na	ŋujena ŋ-u-[FRONT,LOW]-na
	2	nujem n-...		nuju n-...	nujena n-...	nujena n-...
	3	pujem / kujem p-... / k-...		kuju / puju k-... / p-...	pujena p-...	pujena p-...
			PC 1	ŋuj ŋ-u-[FRONT]-ø	ŋujena ŋ-u-[FRONT,LOW]-na	ŋujena ŋ-u-[FRONT,LOW]-na
			2	nuj n-...	nujena n-...	nujena n-...
			3	kuj / puj k-... / p-...	pujena p-...	pujena p-...

		/ŋa/ 'put together' Paradigm: XXV	STEM:	/ŋa/ DEFAULT /a/ C:WEAK		
		NFUT (/PRSL)		**IRR (/FUT)**	**PST**	**PSTIRR**
SG	1	ŋiŋam ŋ-i-[DEF]-m		ŋi ŋ-i-[WEAK]-ø	ŋiŋa ŋ-i-[DEF]-ø	ŋiŋa ŋ-i-[DEF]-ø
	2	ṭiŋam ṭ-...		ṭi ṭ-...	ṭiŋa ṭ-...	ṭiŋa ṭ-...
	3	jiŋam / kiŋam j-... / k-...		ki / pi k-... / p-...	jiŋam j-...	jiŋam j-...
INCL	1	ṭiŋam ṭ-i-[DEF]-m		pi p-i-[DEF]-ø	ṭiŋa ṭ-i-[DEF]-ø	ṭiŋa ṭ-i-[DEF]-ø
PL	1	ŋiŋam ŋ-i-[GEM]-m		ŋi ŋ-i-[WEAK]-ø	ŋiŋa ŋ-i-[GEM]-ø	ŋiŋa ŋ-i-[GEM]-ø
	2	niŋam n-...		ni n-...	niŋa n-...	niŋa n-...
	3	piŋam / kiŋam p-... / k-...		ki / pi k-... / p-...	piŋa p-...	piŋa p-...
	PC 1			ŋe ŋ-i-[WEAK]-ø	ŋiŋa ŋ-i-[GEM]-ø	ŋiŋa ŋ-i-[GEM]-ø
	2			ni n-...	niŋa n-...	niŋa n-...
	3			ke / pe k-... / p-...	piŋa p-...	piŋa p-...

		/la/ 'wipe' Paradigm: XXVI	STEM:	/la/ DEFAULT /lla/ C:GEMINATE		
		NFUT (/PRSL)		IRR (/FUT)	PST	PSTIRR
SG	1	ŋilam ŋ-i-[DEF]-m		ŋila ŋ-i-[DEF]-ø	ŋila ŋ-i-[DEF]-ø	ŋilaŋi ŋ-i-[DEF]-ŋi
	2	ṭilam ṭ-...		ṭila ṭ-...	ṭila ṭ-...	ṭilaŋi ṭ-i-[DEF]-ŋi
	3	dilam / kilam d-... / k-...		kila / pila k-... / p-...	dila d-...	dilaŋi d-i-[DEF]-ŋi
INCL	1	ṭilam ṭ-i-[DEF]-m		pila p-i-[DEF]-ø	ṭila ṭ-i-[DEF]-ø	ṭilaŋi ṭ-i-[DEF]-ŋi
PL	1	ŋillaŋam ŋ-i-[GEM]-ŋam		ŋilla ŋ-i-[GEM]-ø	ŋilla ŋ-i-[GEM]-ø	ŋillaŋi ŋ-i-[GEM]-ŋi
	2	nillaŋam n-...		nilla n-...	nilla n-...	nillaŋi n-...
	3	pillaŋam / killaŋam p-... / k-...		killa / pilla k-... / p-...	pilla p-...	pillaŋi p-...
			PC 1	ŋilla ŋ-i-[GEM]-ø	ŋilla ŋ-i-[GEM]-ø	ŋillaŋi ŋ-i-[GEM]-ŋi
			2	nilla n-...	nilla n-...	nillaŋi n-...
			3	killa / pilla k-... / p-...	pilla p-...	pillaŋi p-...

		/li/ 'wipe RR' Paradigm: XXXVII	STEM:	/li/ DEFAULT /lli/ C:GEMINATE		
		NFUT (/PRSL)		IRR (/FUT)	PST	PSTIRR
SG	1	ŋilim ŋ-i-[DEF]-m		ŋili ŋ-i-[DEF]-ø	ŋili ŋ-i-[DEF]-ø	ŋiliŋi ŋ-i-[DEF]-ŋi
	2	ṭilim ṭ-...		ṭili ṭ-...	ṭili ṭ-...	ṭiliŋi ṭ-i-[DEF]-ŋi
	3	dilim / kilim d-... / k-...		kili / pili k-... / p-...	dili d-...	diliŋi d-i-[DEF]-ŋi
INCL	1	ṭilim ṭ-i-[DEF]-m		pili p-i-[DEF]-ø	ṭili ṭ-i-[DEF]-ø	ṭiliŋi ṭ-i-[DEF]-ŋi
PL	1	ŋillim ŋ-i-[GEM]-m		ŋilli ŋ-i-[GEM]-ø	ŋilli ŋ-i-[GEM]-ø	ŋilliŋi ŋ-i-[GEM]-ŋi
	2	nillim n-...		nilli n-...	nilli n-...	nilliŋi n-...
	3	pillim / killim p-... / k-...		killi / pilli k-... / p-...	pilli p-...	pilliŋi p-...
			PC 1	ŋilli ŋ-i-[GEM]-ø	ŋilli ŋ-i-[GEM]-ø	ŋilliŋi ŋ-i-[GEM]-ŋi
			2	nilli n-...	nilli n-...	nilliŋi n-...
			3	killi / pilli k-... / p-...	pilli p-...	pilliŋi p-...

		/na/ 'use fire' Paradigm: XXVII	STEM:	/na/ DEFAULT /nna/ C:GEMINATE /a/ C:WEAK		
		NFUT (/PRSL)		**IRR (/FUT)**	**PST**	**PSTIRR**
SG	1	ŋinaŋam ŋ-i-[DEF]-ŋam		ŋina ŋ-i-[DEF]-ø	ŋinaŋa ŋ-i-[DEF]-ŋa	ŋinaɲi ŋ-i-[DEF]-ɲi
	2	t̪inaŋam t̪-...		t̪ina t̪-...	t̪inaŋa t̪-i-[DEF]-ŋa	t̪inaɲi t̪-i-[DEF]-ɲi
	3	ninaŋam / kinaŋam n-... / k-...		kina / pina k-... / p-...	niŋa n-i-[WEAK]-ŋa	niŋa n-i-[WEAK]-ŋa
INCL	1	t̪inaŋam t̪-i-[DEF]-ŋam		pina p-i-[DEF]-ø	t̪inaŋa t̪-i-[DEF]-ŋa	t̪inaɲi t̪-i-[DEF]-ɲi
PL	1	ŋinnaŋam ŋ-i-[GEM]-ŋam		ŋinna ŋ-i-[GEM]-ø	ŋinnaŋa ŋ-i-[GEM]-ŋa	ŋinnaɲi ŋ-i-[GEM]-ɲi
	2	ninnaŋam n-...		ninna n-...	ninnaŋa n-...	ninnaɲi n-...
	3	pinnaŋam / kinnaŋam p-... / k-...		kinna / pinna k-... / p-...	pinnaŋa p-...	pinnaɲi p-...
			PC 1	ŋinna ŋ-i-[GEM]-ø	ŋinnaŋa ŋ-i-[GEM]-ŋa	ŋinnaɲi ŋ-i-[GEM]-ɲi
			2	ninna n-...	ninnaŋa n-...	ninnaɲi n-...
			3	kinna / pinna k-... / p-...	pinnaŋa p-...	pinnaɲi p-...

		/ra/ 'watch' Paradigm: XXVIII	STEM:	/ra/ DEFAULT /ɻa/ C:GEMINATE /a/ C:WEAK		
		NFUT (/PRSL)		IRR (/FUT)	PST	PSTIRR
SG	1	ŋiraŋan ŋ-i-[DEF]-ŋan		ŋira ŋ-i-[DEF]-ø	ŋira ŋ-i-[DEF]-ø	ŋiraŋi ŋ-i-[DEF]-ŋi
	2	ţiraŋan ţ-...		ţira ţ-...	ţira ţ-...	ţiraŋi ţ-...
	3	diraŋan / kiraŋan d-... / k-...		kira / pira k-... / p-...	dira d-...	diraŋi d-...
INCL	1	ţiraŋan ţ-i-[DEF]-ŋan		pira p-i-[DEF]-ø	ţira ţ-i-[DEF]-ø	ţiraŋi ţ-i-[DEF]-ŋi
PL	1	ŋaŋan ŋ-a-[WEAK]-ŋan		ŋiɻa ŋ-i-[GEM]-ø	ŋiɻa ŋ-i-[GEM]-ø	ŋiɻaŋi ŋ-i-[GEM]-ŋi
	2	naŋam n-...		niɻa n-...	niɻa n-...	niɻaŋi n-...
	3	paŋam / kaŋam p-... / k-...		kiɻa / piɻa k-... / p-...	piɻa p-...	piɻaŋi p-...
			PC 1	ŋiɻa ŋ-i-[GEM]-ø	ŋiɻa ŋ-i-[GEM]-ø	ŋiɻaŋe ŋ-i-[GEM]-ŋe
			2	niɻa n-...	niɻa n-...	niɻaŋe n-...
			3	kiɻa / piɻa k-... / p-...	piɻa p-...	piɻaŋe p-...

		/ri/ 'watch RR' Paradigm: XXXVI	STEM:	/ri/ DEFAULT /t̪i/ C:GEMINATE /i/ C:WEAK		
		NFUT (/PRSL)		IRR (/FUT)	PST	PSTIRR
SG	1	ŋirim ŋ-i-[DEF]-m		ŋiri ŋ-i-[DEF]-ø	ŋiri ŋ-i-[DEF]-ø	ŋirini ŋ-i-[DEF]-ni
	2	t̪irim t̪-...		t̪iri t̪-...	t̪iri t̪-...	t̪irini t̪-...
	3	dirim / kirim d-... / k-...		kiri / piri k-... / p-...	diri d-...	dirini d-...
INCL	1	t̪irim t̪-i-[DEF]-m		piri p-i-[DEF]-ø	t̪iri t̪-i-[DEF]-ø	t̪irini t̪-i-[DEF]-ni
PL	1	ŋim ŋ-i-[WEAK]-m		ŋit̪i ŋ-i-[GEM]-ø	ŋi ŋ-i-[WEAK]-ø	ŋit̪i ŋ-i-[GEM]-ø
	2	nim n-...		nit̪i n-...	ni n-...	nit̪i n-...
	3	pim / kim p-... / k-...		kit̪i / pit̪i k-... / p-...	pi p-...	pit̪i p-...
			PC 1	ŋit̪i ŋ-i-[GEM]-ø	ŋi ŋ-i-[WEAK]-ø	ŋit̪i ŋ-i-[GEM]-ø
			2	nit̪i n-...	ni n-...	nit̪i n-...
			3	kit̪i / pit̪i k-... / p-...	pi p-...	pit̪i p-...

		/ɖu/ IMPEL Paradigm: XXIX	STEM:	/ɖu/ DEFAULT /ɖa/ VH:LOW /ɖi/ VF:FRONT /ɖe/ VH:LOW, VF:FRONT	/ɖɖu/ C:GEM /ɖɖa/ C:GEM, VH:LOW /ɖɖi/ C:GEM, VF:FRONT /ɖɖe/ C:GEM, VH:LOW, VF:FRONT	
		NFUT (/PRSL)		**IRR (/FUT)**	**PST**	**PSTIRR**
SG	1	ŋuɖan ŋ-u-[LOW]-n		ŋuɖu ŋ-u-[DEF]-ø	ŋuɖini ŋ-u-[FRONT]-ni	ŋuɖi ŋ-u-[FRONT]-ø
	2	ṭuɖan ṭ-...		ṭuɖu ṭ-...	ṭuɖini ṭ-...	ṭuɖi ṭ-...
	3	wuɖan / kuɖan w-... / k-...		kuɖu / puɖu k-... / p-...	wuɖini w-...	wuɖi w-...
INCL	1	ṭuɖan ṭ-u-[LOW]-n		puɖu p-u-[DEF]-ø	ṭuɖini ṭ-u-[FRONT]-ni	ṭuɖi ṭ-u-[FRONT]-ø
PL	1	ŋuɖɖan ŋ-u-[GEM,LOW]-n		ŋuɖɖu ŋ-u-[GEM]-ø	ŋuɖɖini ŋ-u-[GEM, FRONT]-ni	ŋuɖɖi ŋ-u-[GEM, FRONT]-ø
	2	nuɖɖan n-...		nuɖɖu n-...	nuɖɖini n-...	nuɖɖi n-...
	3	puɖɖan / kuɖɖan p-... / k-...		kuɖɖu / puɖɖu k-... / p-...	puɖɖini p-...	puɖɖi p-...
			PC 1	ŋuɖɖa ŋ-u-[GEM,LOW]-ø	ŋuɖɖene ŋ-u-[GEM,FRONT, LOW]-ne	ŋuɖɖe ŋ-u-[GEM,FRONT, LOW]-ø
			2	nuɖɖa n-...	nuɖɖene n-...	nuɖɖe n-...
			3	kuɖɖa / puɖɖa k-... / p-...	puɖɖene p-...	puɖɖe p-...

		/ɖi/ IMPEL.RR Paradigm: XXX	STEM:	/ɖi/ DEFAULT /ɖa/ VH:LOW, VF:BACK	/ɖɖi/ C:GEM /ɖɖe/ C:GEM, VH:LOW /ɖɖa/ C:GEM, VH:LOW, VF:BACK	
		NFUT (/PRSL)		**IRR (/FUT)**	**PST**	**PSTIRR**
SG	1	ŋuɖam ŋ-u-[LOW,BACK]-m		ŋuɖi ŋ-u-[DEF]-ø	ŋuɖana ŋ-u- [LOW,BACK]-na	ŋuɖana ŋ-u-[LOW,BACK]-na
	2	ʈuɖam ʈ-...		ʈuɖi ʈ-...	ʈuɖana ʈ-...	ʈuɖana ʈ-...
	3	wuɖam / kuɖam w-... / k-...		kuɖi / puɖi k-... / p-...	wuɖana w-...	wuɖana w-...
INCL	1	ʈuɖam ʈ-u-[LOW]-n		puɖi p-u-[DEF]-ø	ʈuɖana ʈ-u- [LOW,BACK]-na	ʈuɖana ʈ-u-[LOW,BACK]-na
PL	1	ŋuɖɖam ŋ-u-[GEM,LOW,BACK]-n		ŋuɖɖi ŋ-u-[GEM]-ø	ŋuɖɖana ŋ-u-[GEM,LOW, BACK]-na	ŋuɖɖana ŋ-u-[GEM,LOW, BACK]-na
	2	nuɖɖam n-...		nuɖɖi n-...	nuɖɖana n-...	nuɖɖana n-...
	3	puɖɖam / kuɖɖam p-... / k-...		kuɖɖi / puɖɖi k-... / p-...	puɖɖana p-...	puɖɖana p-...
			PC 1	ŋuɖɖe ŋ-u- [GEM,LOW]-ø	ŋuɖɖana ŋ-u-[GEM,LOW, BACK]-na	ŋuɖɖana ŋ-u-[GEM,LOW, BACK]-na
			2	nuɖɖe n-...	nuɖɖana n-...	nuɖɖana n-...
			3	kuɖɖe / puɖɖe k-... / p-...	puɖɖana p-...	puɖɖana p-...

		/la/ 'eat' Paradigm: XXXI	STEM:	/la/ DEFAULT /le/ VF:FRONT	/lla/ C:GEMINATE /lle/ C:GEMINATE, VF:FRONT	
		NFUT (/PRSL)		**IRR (/FUT)**	**PST**	**PSTIRR**
SG	1	ŋulam ŋ-u-[DEF]-m		ŋula ŋ-u-[DEF]-ø	ŋule ŋ-u-[FRONT]-ø	ŋule ŋ-u-[FRONT]-ø
	2	ṭulam ṭ-...		ṭula ṭ-...	ṭule ṭ-...	ṭule ṭ-...
	3	wulam / kulam w-... / k-...		kula / pula k-... / p-...	wule w-...	wule w-...
INCL	1	ṭulam ṭ-u-[DEF]-m		pula p-u-[DEF]-ø	ṭule ṭ-u-[FRONT]-ø	ṭule ṭ-u-[FRONT]-ø
PL	1	ŋullam ŋ-u-[GEM]-m		ŋulla ŋ-u-[GEM]-ø	ŋulle ŋ-u-[GEM,FRONT]-ø	ŋulle ŋ-u-[GEM,FRONT]-ø
	2	nullam n-...		nulla n-...	nulle n-...	nulle n-...
	3	pullam / kullam p-... / k-...		kulla / pulla k-... / p-...	pulle p-...	pulle p-...
			PC 1	ŋulla ŋ-u-[GEM]-ø	ŋulle ŋ-u-[GEM,FRONT]-ø	ŋulle ŋ-u-[GEM,FRONT]-ø
			2	nulla n-...	nulle n-...	nulle n-...
			3	kulla / pulla k-... / p-...	pulle p-...	pulle p-...

/ŋu/ 'pull' Paradigm: XXXII		STEM:	/ŋu/ DEFAULT /ŋa/ VH:LOW /ŋi/ VF:FRONT		
		NFUT (/PRSL)	**IRR (/FUT)**	**PST**	**PSTIRR**
SG	1	ŋuŋan ŋ-u-[LOW]-n	ŋuŋu ŋ-u-[DEF]-ø	ŋuŋuni ŋ-u-[DEF]-ni	ŋuŋuni ŋ-u-[DEF]-ni
	2	ṭuŋan ṭ-...	ṭuŋu ṭ-...	ṭuŋuni ṭ-...	ṭuŋuni ṭ-...
	3	juŋan / kuŋan j-... / k-...	kuŋu / puŋu k-... / p-...	juŋuni j-...	juŋuni j-...
INCL	1	ṭuŋan ṭ-u-[LOW]-n	puŋu p-u-[DEF]-ø	ṭuŋi ṭ-u-[FRONT]-ø	ṭuŋi ṭ-u-[FRONT]-ø
PL	1	ŋuŋan ŋ-u-[LOW]-n	ŋuŋu ŋ-u-[DEF]-ø	ŋuŋuni ŋ-u-[DEF]-ni	ŋuŋuni ŋ-u-[DEF]-ni
	2	nuŋan n-...	nuŋu n-...	nuŋuni n-...	nuŋuni n-...
	3	puŋan / kuŋan p-... / k-...	kuŋu / puŋu k-... / p-...	puŋuni p-...	puŋuni p-...
PC	1		ŋuŋu ŋ-u-[DEF]-ø	ŋuŋune ŋ-u-[DEF]-ne	ŋuŋune ŋ-u-[DEF]-ne
	2		nuŋu n-...	nuŋune n-...	nuŋune n-...
	3		kuŋu / puŋu k-... / p-...	puŋune p-...	puŋune p-...

		/ŋi/ 'pull RR' Paradigm: XXXIII	STEM:	/ŋi/ DEFAULT /ŋe/ VH:LOW /ŋa/ VH:LOW, VF:FRONT		
		NFUT (/PRSL)		**IRR (/FUT)**	**PST**	**PSTIRR**
SG	1	ŋuŋam ŋ-u-[LOW,FRONT]-m		ŋuŋi ŋ-u-[DEF]-ø	ŋuŋana ŋ-u-[LOW,FRONT]-na	ŋuŋana ŋ-u-[LOW,FRONT]-na
	2	t̪uŋam t̪-...		t̪uŋi t̪-...	t̪uŋana t̪-...	t̪uŋana t̪-...
	3	juŋam / kuŋam j-... / k-...		kuŋi / puŋi k-... / p-...	juŋana j-...	juŋana j-...
INCL	1	t̪uŋam t̪-u-[LOW]-m		puŋi p-u-[DEF]-ø	t̪uŋana t̪-u-[LOW,FRONT]-na	t̪uŋana t̪-u-[LOW,FRONT]-na
PL	1	ŋuŋam ŋ-u-[LOW]-m		ŋuŋi ŋ-u-[DEF]-ø	ŋuŋana ŋ-u-[LOW,FRONT]-na	ŋuŋana ŋ-u-[LOW,FRONT]-na
	2	nuŋam n-...		nuŋi n-...	nuŋana n-...	nuŋana n-...
	3	puŋam / kuŋam p-... / k-...		kuŋi / puŋi k-... / p-...	puŋana p-...	puŋana p-...
	PC 1			ŋuŋe ŋ-u-[LOW]-ø	ŋuŋana ŋ-u-[LOW,FRONT]-na	ŋuŋana ŋ-u-[LOW,FRONT]-na
	2			nuŋe n-...	nuŋana n-...	nuŋana n-...
	3			kuŋe / puŋe k-... / p-...	puŋana p-...	puŋana p-...

		/n̪ta/ 'crouch' Paradigm: XXXV	STEM:	/n̪ta/ DEFAULT		
		NFUT (/PRSL)		**IRR (/FUT)**	**PST**	**PSTIRR**
SG	1	ŋan̪taŋan ŋ-a-[DEF]-ŋan		ŋan̪ta ŋ-a-[DEF]-ø	ŋan̪ta ŋ-a-[DEF]-ø	ŋan̪taŋi ŋ-a-[DEF]-ŋi
	2	t̪an̪taŋan t̪-...		t̪an̪ta t̪-...	t̪an̪ta t̪-...	t̪an̪taŋi t̪-...
	3	kan̪taŋan / kan̪taŋan k-... / k-...		kan̪ta / pan̪ta k-... / p-...	kan̪ta k-...	kan̪taŋi k-...
INCL	1	t̪an̪taŋan t̪-i-[DEF]-ŋan		pan̪ta p-a-[DEF]-ø	t̪an̪ta t̪-a-[DEF]-ø	t̪an̪taŋi t̪-a-[DEF]-ŋi
PL	1	ŋan̪taŋan ŋ-a-[DEF]-ŋan		ŋan̪ta ŋ-a-[DEF]-ø	ŋan̪ta ŋ-a-[DEF]-ø	ŋan̪taŋi ŋ-a-[DEF]-ŋi
	2	nan̪taŋan n-...		nan̪ta n-...	nan̪ta n-...	nan̪taŋi n-...
	3	pan̪taŋan / kan̪taŋan p-a-... / k-a-...		kan̪ta / pan̪ta k-... / p-...	pan̪ta p-...	pan̪taŋi p-...
			PC 1	ŋan̪ta ŋ-a-[DEF]-ø	ŋan̪ta ŋ-a-[DEF]-ø	ŋan̪taŋi ŋ-a-[DEF]-ŋi
			2	nan̪ta n-...	nan̪ta n-...	nan̪taŋi n-...
			3	kan̪ta / pan̪ta k-... / p-...	pan̪ta p-...	pan̪taŋi p-...

Appendix II

Corpus sources

This appendix lists the primary sources cited for illustrative examples throughout the book. I am grateful to Andrew Butcher, Joe Blythe, Mark Crocombe, Lucy Davidson, Bill Forshaw, Rachel Nordlinger, Chester Street and Michael Walsh, each of whom shared recordings, and in some cases transcriptions, to aid in my research. Two recordings were also provided by the Australian Institute of Aboriginal and Torres Strait Islander Studies (AIATSIS).

I am also very grateful to all the Murrinhpatha speakers who have shared their language with us over the years. Speakers remain anonymous in this work, in the interests of protecting their privacy in relation to the cited utterances.

Source identifier	Provided by	Speech type
1958_K	AIATSIS (archive) and Nordlinger (transcription); original recording by W.E.H. Stanner	Narrative
1959_KH	AIATSIS; original recording by Kenneth Hale	Elicitation
1980_CS1-17A-06	Street	Narrative
1980_CS1-17A-07	Street	Narrative
1981_CS1-03A	Street	Narrative
1990_47	Street	Translation from English
1990_70	Street	Translation from English
1990_Lk5:17-26-008-1	Street	Translation from English
1990_AB	Butcher	Word list
1997_MSC-1007	Crocombe	Narrative
2000-11-10	Crocombe	Narrative
2004-06-24	Blythe	Elicitation
2004-07-04	Blythe	Elicitation
2004-09-12	Blythe	Conversation
2008-09-25	Nordlinger	Narrative
2009-07-07_04	Blythe	Conversation
2009-11-21_03	Blythe	Narrative
2010-08-27	Blythe	Conversation
2011-07-09_3-1	Mansfield	Narrative
2011-07-21_3-12	Mansfield	Narrative
2011-07-26_2-11	Mansfield	Narrative

(continued)

(continued)

Source identifier	Provided by	Speech type
2011-07-30_04	Blythe	Narrative
2011-08-01_3-11	Mansfield	Narrative
2011-08-08_2-11	Mansfield	Narrative
2011-08-16	Mansfield	Conversation
2011-08-21_3-1	Mansfield	Narrative
2011-08-21_Ep	Mansfield	Conversation
2011-08-25_3-1	Mansfield	Narrative
2011-09-01_02	Blythe and Mansfield	Conversation
2011-09-09_2-5	Mansfield	Narrative
2011-09-13_2-11	Mansfield	Narrative
2011-09-13_3-11h	Mansfield	Narrative
2011-09-17_03	Mansfield	Conversation
2011-09-21	Mansfield	Conversation
2011-10-10_3-1	Mansfield	Narrative
2012-06-12	Mansfield	Conversation
2012-06-20_25	Mansfield	Narrative
2012-06-20_26	Mansfield	Narrative
2012-06-20_28	Mansfield	Narrative
2012-06-30	Mansfield	Narrative
2012-07-08_FN	Mansfield	Conversation
2012-07-11	Mansfield	Narrative
2013-01-02	Mansfield	Elicitation
2013-01-03	Mansfield	Elicitation
2013-01-05	Mansfield	Elicitation
2013-01-07	Mansfield	Elicitation
2013-01-08	Mansfield	Elicitation
2013-01-09	Mansfield	Elicitation
2013-01-11	Mansfield	Elicitation
2013-01-15	Mansfield	Elicitation
2013-01-18_01	Mansfield	Narrative
2013-01-21	Mansfield	Elicitation
2013-01-23	Mansfield	Elicitation
2013-01-24	Mansfield	Elicitation
2013-01-25	Mansfield	Elicitation
2013-06-22_02	Mansfield	Narrative
2013-06-25	Mansfield	Elicitation
2013-07_clinic	Mansfield	Translation from English
2013-07_AM	Mansfield	Elicitation
2013-07-11_02	Mansfield	Conversation
2014-10-01_Pa1-D1	Mansfield	Translation from English
2015-01-29_Pr2-EC2	Mansfield	Translation from English
2015-01-29_PrT2-SC1	Mansfield	Translation from English

(continued)

(continued)

Source identifier	Provided by	Speech type
2015-01-29_T2-D2-SC2	Mansfield	Translation from English
2015-01-30_Pr3-D2-SC2	Mansfield	Translation from English
2015-01-30_Pr3-D1	Mansfield	Translation from English
2015-02-05_Pa2-D2	Mansfield	Translation from English
2015-02-07_Pa1SC2	Mansfield	Translation from English
2015-02-07_Pr2D1	Mansfield	Translation from English
2015-02-07_Pr3-EC1	Mansfield	Translation from English
2015-02-07_Pr3SC2	Mansfield	Translation from English
2015-03-30	Davidson	Conversation
2015-06-27_AM-02	Mansfield	Elicitation
2015-06-29_AT	Mansfield	Elicitation
2015-07-01_AT	Mansfield	Elicitation
2015-07-01_AM	Mansfield	Elicitation
2015-07-01_2-3	Mansfield	Narrative
2015-07-02_AT	Mansfield	Elicitation
2015-07-05_AM	Mansfield	Elicitation
2015-07-07_AT	Mansfield	Elicitation
2015-07-08_LS	Mansfield	Elicitation
2015-07-09	Mansfield	Conversation
2015-07-10_AT	Mansfield	Elicitation
2015-07-13_PI	Mansfield	Elicitation
2015-07-13_LH	Mansfield	Narrative
2015-07-17	Mansfield	Conversation
2015-07-21	Mansfield	Conversation
2015-09-14_AT	Mansfield	Elicitation
2015-09-29_AT	Mansfield	Elicitation
2016-06_AMP	Mansfield	Elicitation
2016-06-24_01	Mansfield	Narrative
2016-07_FN	Mansfield	Elicitation
2016-07-10_07	Mansfield	Elicitation
2016-07-14_12	Mansfield	Elicitation
2016-11-01	Nordlinger	Elicitation

References

Ackerman, F., Blevins, J. P., & Malouf, R. (2009). Parts and wholes: Implicative patterns in inflectional paradigms. In J. P. Blevins & J. Blevins (Eds.), *Analogy in grammar: Form and acquisition* (pp.54–82). Oxford: Oxford University Press.

Ackerman, F., & Malouf, R. (2013). Morphological organization: The low conditional entropy conjecture. *Language, 89*(3), 429–464.

Ackerman, F., Malouf, R., & Blevins, J. P. (2016). Patterns and discriminability in language analysis. *Word Structure, 9*(2), 132–155.

Aikhenvald, A. (2006). Serial verbs constructions in a typological perspective. In A. Y. Aikhenvald & R. M. W. Dixon (Eds.), *Serial Verb Constructions: a cross-linguistic typology* (pp. 1–68). Oxford, U.K.: Oxford University Press.

Altman, J., & Hinkson, M. (Eds.). (2010). *Culture crisis: Anthropology and politics in Aboriginal Australia*. Sydney: University of New South Wales Press.

Anderson, S. R. (1976). On the description of consonant gradation in Fula. *Studies in African Linguistics, 7*, 93–136.

Anderson, S. R. (1992). *A-morphous morphology*. Cambridge: Cambridge University Press.

Anderson, S. R. (2005). *Aspects of the theory of clitics*. Oxford: Oxford University Press.

Anderson, S. R. (2015). The morpheme: Its nature and use. In M. Baerman (Ed.), *The Oxford handbook of inflection* (pp. 11–34). Oxford: Oxford University Press.

Aronoff, M. (1980). The relevance of productivity in a synchronic description of word formation. In J. Fisiak (Ed.), *Historical morphology* (pp. 71–82). The Hague: Mouton.

Aronoff, M. (1994). *Morphology by itself*. Cambridge, MA: MIT Press.

Austin, P. (1988). Phonological voicing contrasts in Australian Aboriginal languages. *LaTrobe Working Papers in Linguistics, 1*, 17–42.

Baayen, R. H. (2003). Probabilistic approaches to morphology. In R. Bod, J. Hay, & S. Jannedy (Eds.), *Probabilistic Linguistics* (pp. 229–287). Cambridge, MA: MIT Press.

Baayen, R. H., & Moscoso del Prado Martín, F. (2005). Semantic density and past-tense formation in three Germanic languages. *Language, 81*(3), 666–698.

Baayen, R. H., & Schreuder, R. (Eds.). (2003). *Morphological structure in language processing*. Berlin: Mouton de Gruyter.

Baerman, M. (2001). The prosodic properties of ne in Bulgarian. In G. Zybatow, U. Junghanns, G. Mehlhorn, & L. Szucsich (Eds.), *Current issues in formal Slavic linguistics* (pp. 59–68). Frankfurt: Peter Lang.

Bailey, P., & Coren, D. (1988, December). Port Keats: Tortured town. *Sunday Territorian*, p. 6.

Baker, B. (2008). *Word structure in Ngalakgan*. Stanford: CSLI Publications.

Baker, B. (2014). Word structure in Australian languages. In H. Koch & R. Nordlinger (Eds.), *The languages and linguistics of Australia: a comprehensive guide* (pp. 139–213). Berlin: Mouton de Gruyter.

Baker, B. (2018). Words are phrases and phrases are words: constructions in northern Australian languages. In G. Booij (Ed.), *The construction of words: Advances in Construction Morphology* (pp. 255–286). Berlin: Springer.

Baker, B., & Harvey, M. (2003). Word structure in Australian languages. *Australian Journal of Linguistics, 23*(1), 3–33.

Baker, B., & Harvey, M. (2010). Complex predicate formation. In M. Amberber, B. Baker, & M. Harvey (Eds.), *Complex predicates: Cross-linguistic perspectives on event structure* (pp. 13–47). Cambridge: Cambridge University Press.

Barwick, L. (2006). Marri Ngarr Lirrga songs: A musicological analysis of song pairs in performance. *Musicology Australia*, *28*, 1–25.

Barwick, L. (2011). Musical form and style in Murriny Patha Djanba songs at Wadeye (Northern Territory, Australia). In M. Tenzer & J. Roeder (Eds.), *Analytical and Cross-Cultural Studies in World Music* (pp. 316–354). Oxford: Oxford University Press.

Barwick, L., Marett, A., Walsh, M., Blythe, J., Reid, N., & Ford, L. (2009). *Wadeye song database*. Retrieved from http://sydney.edu.au/arts/indigenous_song/wadeye/

Barwick, L., Marrett, A., Blythe, J., & Walsh, M. (2007). Arriving, digging, performing, returning: an exercise in rich interpretation of a djanba song text in the sound archive of the Wadeye Knowledge Centre, Northern Territory of Australia. In R. M. Moyle (Ed.), *Oceanic Encounters: Festschrift for Mervyn McLean* (pp. 13–24). Auckland: Research in Anthropology and Linguistics Monographs.

Bennett, R., Elfner, E., & McCloskey, J. (2016). Lightest to the Right: An Apparently Anomalous Displacement in Irish. *Linguistic Inquiry*, *47*(2), 169–234.

Berko, J. (1958). The child's learning of English morphology. *Word*, *14*(2–3), 150–177.

Bermúdez-Otero, R. (2011). Cyclicity. In M. van Oostendorp, C. Ewen, E. Hume, & K. Rice (Eds.), *The Blackwell companion to phonology* (pp. 2019–2048). Malden MA: Blackwell.

Bickel, B., Banjade, G., Gaenszle, M., Lieven, E., Paudyal, N. P., Rai, I. P., ... Stoll, S. (2007). Free prefix ordering in Chintang. *Language*, *83*(1), 43–73.

Bickel, B., Hildebrandt, K. A., & Schiering, R. (2009). The distribution of phonological word domains: a probabilistic typology. In J. Grijzenhout (Ed.), *Phonological Domains: Universals and Deviations* (pp. 47–78). Berlin: Mouton de Gruyter.

Bickel, B., & Zúñiga, F. (2017). The "word" in polysynthetic languages: Phonological and syntactic challenges. In M. Fortescue, M. Mithun, & N. Evans (Eds.), *The Oxford handbook of polysynthesis* (pp. 158–185). Oxford: Oxford University Press.

Blevins, J. (2004). *Evolutionary phonology: The emergence of sound patterns*. Cambridge: Cambridge University Press.

Blevins, J. P. (2006). Word-based morphology. *Journal of Linguistics*, *42*, 531–573.

Blevins, J. P. (2016). *Word and paradigm morphology*. Oxford: Oxford University Press.

Blevins, J. P., Milin, P., & Ramscar, M. (2017). The Zipfian paradigm cell filling problem. In F. Kiefer, J. P. Blevins, & H. Bartos (Eds.), *Perspectives on morphological organization: Data and analyses* (pp. 139–158). Leiden: Brill.

Bloomfield, L. (1933). *Language*. New York: Henry Holt.

Blust, R. (1979). Coronal-noncoronal consonant clusters: New evidence for markedness. *Lingua*, *47*, 101–117.

Blythe, J. (in press). Genesis of the trinity: The convergent evolution of trirelational kin terms. In P. McConvell, P. Kelly, & S. LaCrampe (Eds.), *Skin, kin and clan: The dynamics of social categories in Indigenous Australia*. Canberra: ANU Press.

Blythe, J. (2009). *Doing referring in Murriny Patha conversation* (PhD thesis). University of Sydney.

Blythe, J. (2010a). From ethical datives to number markers in Murriny Patha. In R. Hendery & J. Hendriks (Eds.), *Grammatical Change: Theory and Description* (pp. 157–184). Canberra: Pacific Linguistics.

Blythe, J. (2010b). Laughter is the best medicine: roles for prosody in a Murriny Patha conversational narrative. In B. Baker, I. Mushin, M. Harvey, & R. Gardner (Eds.), *Indigenous language and social identity: papers in honour of Michael Walsh* (pp. 223–236). Canberra: Pacific Linguistics.

Blythe, J. (2010c). Self-association in Murriny Patha talk-in-interaction. *Australian Journal of Linguistics*, *30*(4), 447–469.

Blythe, J. (2013). Preference organization driving structuration: Evidence from Australian Aboriginal interaction for pragmatically motivated grammaticalization. *Language*, *89*(4), 883–919.

Blythe, J. (2015). Other-initiated repair in Murrinh-Patha. *Open Linguistics*, *1*, 283–308.

Blythe, J., Mardigan, K. C., Perdjert, M. E., & Stoakes, H. (2016). Pointing out directions in Murrinhpatha. *Open Linguistics*, *2*, 132–159.

Blythe, J., Nordlinger, R., & Reid, N. (2007). Murriny Patha finite verb paradigms. unpublished ms.

Boersma, P., & Weenink, D. (2012). Praat: doing phonetics by computer (Version 5.3.42). Retrieved from http://praat.org

Booij, G. (2010). *Construction morphology*. Oxford: Oxford University Press.

Borowsky, T. (1993). On the word level. In S. Hargus & E. M. Kaisse (Eds.), *Studies in lexical phonology* (pp. 199–234). San Diego: Academic Press.

Boudelaa, S., & Marslen-Wilson, W. D. (2015). Structure, form, and meaning in the mental lexicon: evidence from Arabic. *Language, Cognition and Neuroscience*, *30*(8), 955–992.

Bowern, C. (2004). *Bardi verb morphology in historical perspective* (PhD thesis). Harvard University.

Bowern, C. (2014). Complex predicates in Australian languages. In H. Koch & R. Nordlinger (Eds.), *The languages and linguistics of Australia: a comprehensive guide* (pp. 263–294). Berlin: Mouton de Gruyter.

Bowern, C., Alpher, B., & Round, E. (2013). Yidiny stress, length and truncation reconsidered. Presented at the NELS 44, Storrs, CA., University of Connecticut.

Brady, M. (2017). *Teaching "proper" drinking? Clubs and pubs in Indigenous Australia*. Canberra: Australian National University Press.

Browman, C. P., & Goldstein, L. (1992). Articulatory phonology: An overview. *Haskins Laboratories Status Report on Speech Research*, *112*, 23–42.

Brown, D., & Hippisley, A. (2012). *Network morphology: A defaults-based theory of word structure*. Cambridge: Cambridge University Press.

Butcher, A. (2004). Fortis/lenis revisited one more time: the aerodynamics of some oral stop contrasts in three continents. *Clinical Linguistics and Phonetics*, *18*(6–8), 547–557.

Butt, M., & Geuder, W. (2001). On the (semi)lexical status of light verbs. In N. Corver & H. van Riemsdijk (Eds.), *Semi-lexical categories: The function of content words and the content of function words* (pp. 323–370). Berlin: Mouton de Gruyter.

Bybee, J. L. (2005). Restrictions on phonemes in affixes: A crosslinguistic test of a popular hypothesis. *Linguistic Typology*, *9*(2), 165–222.

Bybee, J. L. (2001). *Phonology and language use*. Cambridge: Cambridge University Press.

Bybee, J. L., & Thompson, S. (1997). Three frequency effects in syntax. *Berkley Linguistic Society*, *23*, 65–85.

Carlson, K., Frazier, L., & Clifton, C. (2009). How prosody constrains comprehension: A limited effect of prosodic packaging. *Lingua*, *119*(7), 1066–1082.

Carstairs-McCarthy, A. (2011). *The evolution of morphology*. Oxford: Oxford University Press.

Caudal, P., & Nordlinger, R. (2011). A Murrinh-Patha view of counterfactuality and the irrealis. Presented at the Australian Linguistics Society Annual Conference, Canberra.

Chomsky, N. (1957). *Syntactic structures*. The Hague: Mouton.

Chomsky, N. (1970). Remarks on nominalization. In R. A. Jacobs & P. S. Rosenbaum (Eds.), *Readings in English transformational grammar* (pp. 184–221). Boston: Ginn.
Chomsky, N., & Halle, M. (1968). *The sound pattern of English*. New York: Harper and Row.
Choo, C., & McCoy, B. F. (2010). Mission dormitories: Intergenerational implications for Kalumburu and Balgo, Kimberley, Western Australia. In P. Grimshaw & A. May (Eds.), *Missionaries, Indigenous Peoples and Cultural Exchange* (pp. 166–181). Eastbourne: Sussex Academic Press.
Christiansen, M. H., & Chater, N. (2015). The Now-or-Never Bottleneck: A Fundamental Constraint on Language. *The Behavioral and Brain Sciences*, *39*, 1–52.
Clahsen, H., Sonnenstuhl, I., & Blevins, J. P. (2003). Derivational morphology in the German mental lexicon: A dual mechanism account. In R. H. Baayen & R. Schreuder (Eds.), *Morphological structure in language processing* (pp. 122–155). Berlin: Mouton de Gruyter.
Clemens, M. (2013). *Verbal stress patterns in a morphologically complex language: Murrinh-Patha* (Honours thesis). University of Melbourne, Melbourne.
Clendon, M. (2014). *Worrorra: A language of the north-west Kimberley coast*. Adelaide: University of Adelaide Press.
Corbett, G. G. (2000). *Number*. Cambridge: Cambridge University Press.
Côté, M.-H. (2000). *Consonant cluster phonotactics: a perceptual approach* (PhD thesis). Massachusetts Institute of Technology, Amherst, MA.
Croft, W. (2001). *Radical construction grammar: Syntactic theory in typological perspective*. Oxford: Oxford University Press.
Cutler, A. (2012). *Native Listening: Language Experience and the Recognition of Spoken Words*. Cambridge, MA: MIT Press.
Dahl, O. (2004). *The growth and maintenance of linguistic complexity*. Amsterdam: John Benjamins.
De Jong, N. H., Schreuder, R., & Baayen, R. H. (2000). The morphological family size effect and morphology. *Language and Cognitive Processes*, *15*(4–5), 329–365.
Dench, A., & Evans, N. (1988). Multiple case-marking in Australian languages. *Australian Journal of Linguistics*, *8*(1), 1–47.
Di Sciullo, A.-M., & Williams, E. (1987). *On the definition of word*. Cambridge, MA: MIT Press.
Dixon, R. M. W. (1980). *The languages of Australia*. Cambridge: Cambridge University Press.
Dixon, R. M. W. (2002a). *Australian languages: Their nature and development*. Cambridge: Cambridge University Press.
Dixon, R. M. W. (2002b). Word: a typological framework. In R. M. W. Dixon & A. Y. Aikhenvald (Eds.), *Word: A cross-linguistic typology* (pp. 1–41). Cambridge: Cambridge University Press.
Dixon, R. M. W., & Aikhenvald, A. Y. (Eds.). (2002). *Word: A cross-linguistic typology*. Cambridge: Cambridge University Press.
Dressler, W. (1984). Explaining natural phonology. *Phonology*, *1*, 29–51.
Elwell, V. M. R. (1982). Some social factors affecting multilingualism among Aboriginal Australians: a case study of Maningrida. *International Journal of the Sociology of Language*, *36*, 83–103.
Embick, D. (2015). *The morpheme: A theoretical introduction*. Berlin: De Gruyter Mouton.
Embick, D., & Noyer, R. (2001). Movement operations after syntax. *Linguistic Inquiry*, *32*(4), 555–595.
Evans, N. (1995). Current issues in the phonology of Australian languages. In J. A. Goldsmith (Ed.), *The handbook of phonological theory* (pp. 723–761). Cambridge, MA: Blackwell.

Evans, N. (2003a). *Bininj Gun-Wok: a pan-dialectal grammar of Mayali, Kunwinjku and Kune*. Canberra: Pacific Linguistics.

Evans, N. (2003b). Comparative non-Pama-Nyungan and Australian historical linguistics. In N. Evans (Ed.), *The non-Pama-Nyungan Languages of Northern Australia* (pp. 3–25).

Evans, N. (Ed.). (2003c). *The non-Pama-Nyungan languages of northern Australia: Comparative studies of the continent's most linguistically complex region*. Canberra: Pacific Linguistics.

Evans, N. (2007). Warramurrungunji undone: Australian languages in the 51st millennium. In M. Brenzinger (Ed.), *Language Diversity Endangered* (pp. 342–373). Berlin: Mouton de Gruyter.

Evans, N., Fletcher, J., & Ross, B. (2008). Big words, small phrases: Mismatches between pause units and the polysynthetic word in Dalabon. *Linguistics*, 46(1), 89–129.

Evans, N., & Sasse, H.-J. (2002). Introduction: problems of polysynthesis. In *Problems of polysynthesis* (pp. 1–13). Berlin: Akademie Verlag.

Fabricius, A. H. (1998). *A comparative survey of reduplication in Australian languages*. Munich: Lincom Europa.

Falkenberg, A., & Falkenberg, J. (1981). *The affinal relationship system: A new approach to kinship and marriage among the Australian Aborigines at Port Keats*. Oslo: Universitetsforlaget.

Falkenberg, J. (1962). *Kin and totem: Group relations of Aborigines in the Port Keats district*. Oslo: Oslo University Press.

Falkes, J., Docherty, R., & Gsell, F. X. (1939). Report on mission improvements and works at Port Keats. unpublished ms; accessed at Wadeye community archive.

Feist, T. (2015). *A grammar of Skolt Saami*. Helsinki: Suomalais-Ugrilainen Seura.

Fillmore, C. J., Kay, P., & O'Connor, M. C. (1988). Regularity and idiomaticity in grammatical constructions: The case of let alone. *Language*, 64(3), 501–538.

Fletcher, J., & Butcher, A. (2014). Sound patterns of Australian Languages. In *The Languages and Linguistics of Australia: a comprehensive guide* (Vol. 3, pp. 89–132). Berlin: Mouton de Gruyter.

Fletcher, J., Stoakes, H., Loakes, D., & Singer, R. (2015). Accentual prominence and consonant lengthening and strengthening in Mawng. In *Proceedings of the International Conference of Phonetic Sciences*. Glasgow, University of Glasgow.

Flynn, F. W. (1950). *Native language of Port Keats: Commonly called Murinbada*. Kensington, NSW.

Forshaw, W. (2011). *A continuum of incorporation: Noun incorporation in Murrinh-Patha* (Honours thesis). University of Melbourne, Melbourne.

Forshaw, W. (2016). *Little kids, big verbs: The acquisition of Murrihpatha bipartite stem verbs* (PhD thesis). University of Melbourne, Melbourne.

Forshaw, W., Davidson, L., Kelly, B., Nordlinger, R., Wigglesworth, G., & Blythe, J. (2017). The Acquisition of Murrinhpatha (Northern Australia). In M. Fortescue, M. Mithun, & N. Evans (Eds.), *Oxford handbook of polysynthesis* (pp. 473–494). Oxford: Oxford University Press.

Furlan, A. (2005). *Songs of continuity and change: The reproduction of Aboriginal culture through traditional and popular music*. PhD thesis, University of Sydney.

Gaby, A. R. (2017). *A Grammar of Kuuk Thaayorre*. Berlin, Boston: De Gruyter Mouton.

Gagné, C. L. (2017). Psycholinguistic approaches to morphology. *Oxford Research Encyclopedia of Linguistics* https://dx.doi.org/10.1093/acrefore/9780199384655.013.258.

Geertzen, J., Blevins, J. P., & Milin, P. (2016). Informativeness of unit boundaries. *Italian Journal of Linguistics*, 28(2), 1–24.

Goedemans, R., & van Zanten, E. (2014). No stress typology. In J. Caspers, Y. Chen, W. Heeren, J. Pacilly, N. O. Schiller, & E. van Zanten (Eds.), *Above and beyond the segments* (pp. 83–95). Amsterdam: John Benjamins Publishing Company.
Goldberg, A. (2006). *Constructions at work: The nature of generalization in language*. Oxford: Oxford University Press.
Goldsmith, J. A. (1995). Phonological Theory. In J. A. Goldsmith (Ed.), *The Handbook of Phonological Theory* (pp. 1–23). Oxford: Blackwell.
Gordon, M. K. (2016). *Phonological typology*. Oxford: Oxford University Press.
Green, I. (1989). *Marrithiyel: a language of the Daly River region of Australia's Northern Territory* (PhD). Australian National Univeristy, Canberra.
Green, I. (1997). Nominal Classification in Marrithiyel. In M. Harvey & N. Reid (Eds.), *Nominal Classification in Aboriginal Australia* (pp. 229–253).
Green, I. (2003). The genetic status of Murrinh-patha. In N. Evans (Ed.), *The non-Pama-Nyungan Languages of Northern Australia* (pp. 125–158). Canberra: Pacific Linguistics.
Gussenhoven, C., & Rietveld, T. (2000). The Behavior of H *and L* Under Variations in Pitch Range in Dutch Rising Contours. *Language and Speech*, *43*, 183–203.
Hall, K. C. (2013). A typology of intermediate phonological relationships. *The Linguistic Review*, *30*(2), 215–275.
Halle, M., & Marantz, A. (1993). Distributed morphology and the pieces of inflection. In K. Hale & S. J. Keyser (Eds.), *The View from Building 20* (pp. 111–176). Cambridge, MA: MIT Press.
Hamilton, P. J. (1996). *Phonetic constraints and markedness in the phonotactics of Australian Aboriginal languages* (PhD thesis). University of Toronto.
Harrington, J., Palethorpe, S., & Watson, C. I. (2000). Does the Queen speak the Queen's English? *Nature*, *408*(6815), 927–928.
Harris, A. C. (2002). *Endoclitics and the origins of Udi morphosyntax*. Oxford: Oxford University Press.
Harvey, M. (2001). *A Grammar of Limilngan: A language of the Mary River Region, Northern Territory, Australia*. Canberra: Pacific Linguistics.
Harvey, M. (2002). *A grammar of Gaagudju*. Berlin: Mouton de Gruyter.
Harvey, M. (2013). Reconstructing long-term limits on diffusion in Australia. *Anthropological Linguistics*, *55*(2), 158–183.
Harvey, M., & Borowsky, T. (1999). The minimum word in Warray. *Australian Journal of Linguistics*, *19*(1), 89–99.
Haspelmath, M. (2011). The indeterminacy of word segmentation and the nature of morphology and syntax. *Folia Linguistica*, *45*(1), 31–80.
Haspelmath, M. (2015). Defining vs diagnosing linguistic categories: a case study of clitic phenomena. In J. Blaszczak, D. Klimek-Jankowska, & K. Migdalski (Eds.), *How categorical are categories*. Berlin: Mouton de Gruyter.
Haspelmath, M., & Sims, A. D. (2010). *Understanding morphology* (Second edition). London: Hodder.
Hayes, B. (1995). *Metrical stress theory: Principles and case studies*. Chicago: University of Chicago Press.
Heath, J. (1981). *Basic materials in Mara: Grammar, texts, and dictionary*. Canberra: Pacific Linguistics.
Henderson, J. (2002). The word in Eastern/Central Arrernte. In R. M. W. Dixon & A. Y. Aikhenvald (Eds.), *Word: A cross-linguistic typology* (pp. 100–124). Cambridge: Cambridge University Press.
Hildebrandt, K. A. (2007). Prosodic and grammatical domains in Limbu. *Himalayan Linguistics*, *8*, 1–34.

Himmelmann, N. P. (2014). Asymmetries in the prosodic phrasing of function words: Another look at the suffixing preference. *Language, 90*(4), 927–960.

Himmelmann, N. P. (2018). Prosody and information structure in Austronesian languages of Indonesia and East Timor.

Holt, L. L., & Lotto, A. J. (2010). Speech perception as categorization. *Attention, Perception & Psychophysics, 72*(5), 1218–1227.

Hopper, P., & Traugott, E. C. (2003). *Grammaticalization* (Second Edition). Cambridge: Cambridge University Press.

Hyman, L. M. (2014). Do all languages have word accent? In H. van der Hulst (Ed.), *Word stress: Theoretical and typological issues* (pp. 56–82). Cambridge: Cambridge University Press.

Inkelas, S., & Zoll, C. (2005). *Reduplication: Doubling in morphology*. Cambridge: Cambridge University Press.

Itô, J., & Mester, R. A. (1995). Japanese phonology. In J. A. Goldsmith (Ed.), *The handbook of phonological theory* (pp. 817–838). Oxford: Blackwell.

Ivory, B. (2009). *Kunmanggurr, legend and leadership* (PhD thesis). Charles Darwin University, Darwin.

Jackendoff, R. (2008). Construction after construction and its theoretical challenges. *Language, 84*(1), 8–28.

Jamieson, C. A. (1982). Conflated subsystems marking person and aspect in Chiquihuitlán Mazatec verbs. *International Journal of American Linguistics, 48*(2), 139–167.

Jarema, G. (2007). Compound representation and processing: A cross-language perspective. In G. Libben & G. Jarema (Eds.), *The representation and processing of compound words* (pp. 45–70). Oxford: Oxford University Press.

Jun, S.-A. (2005). Prosodic typology. In S.-A. Jun (Ed.), *Prosodic typology: The phonology of intonation and phrasing* (pp. 430–458). Oxford: Oxford University Press.

Jun, S.-A. (Ed.). (2014). *Prosodic typology II: The phonology of intonation and phrasing*. Oxford: Oxford University Press.

Jun, S.-A., & Fougeron, C. (2002). The realizations of the accentual phrase in French. *Probus, 14*, 147–172.

Juola, P. (1998). Measuring linguistic complexity: The morphological tier. *Journal of Quantitative Linguistics, 5*(3), 206–213.

Jurafsky, D., Bell, A., & Gir, C. (2000). The role of the lemma in form variation. *Laboratory Phonology VII*, 3–34. Berlin: De Gruyter.

Jurafsky, D., Bell, A., Gregory, M., & Raymond, W. D. (2001). Probabilistic relations between words: Evidence from reduction in lexical production. In J. L. Bybee & P. J. Hopper (Eds.), *Frequency and the emergence of linguistic structure* (Vol. 45, p. 229). Amsterdam: John Benjamins Publishing Company.

Kiparsky, P. (1982). Lexical phonology and morphology. In I. S. Yang (Ed.), *Linguistics in the morning calm* (Vol. 2, pp. 3–91). Seoul: Hanshin.

Kiparsky, P. (2000). Opacity and cyclicity. *The Linguistic Review, 17*, 351–365.

Koch, H. (2014). Historical relations among the Australian languages: genetic classification and contact-based diffusion. In H. Koch & R. Nordlinger (Eds.), *Handbook of Australian Languages* (pp. 23–89). Berlin: Mouton de Gruyter.

Kral, I. (2014). Shifting perceptions, shifting identities: Communication technologies and the altered social, cultural and linguistic ecology in a remote indigenous context. *The Australian Journal of Anthropology, 25*(2), 171–189.

Labov, W. (1994). *Principles of linguistic change - volume 1: Internal factors*. Malden MA: Blackwell.

Ladd, D. R. (2008). *Intonational phonology* (Second edition). Cambridge: Cambridge University Press.

Lahiri, A. (2012). Asymmetric phonological representations of words in the mental lexicon. In A. C. Cohn, C. Fougeron, & M. Huffman (Eds.), *The Oxford handbook of laboratory phonology* (pp. 146–162). Oxford: Oxford University Press.

Liberman, A. M. (1957). Some results of research on speech perception. *Journal of the Acoustical Society of America, 29*, 117–123.

Lisker, L., & Abramson, A. S. (1967). Some experiments in comparative phonetics. In *Proceedings of the 6th International Congress of Phonetic Science*. Prague.

Mansfield, J. B. (forthcoming). Epistemic authority and sociolinguistic stance in an Australian Aboriginal language. *Open Linguistics*.

Mansfield, J. B. (2013). The social organisation of Wadeye's heavy metal mobs. *The Australian Journal of Anthropology, 24*(2), 148–165.

Mansfield, J. B. (2014a). Listening to heavy metal in Wadeye. In A. Harris (Ed.), *Circulating Cultures: Indigenous Music, Dance and Media across genres in Australia* (pp. 239–262). Canberra: ANU Press.

Mansfield, J. B. (2014b). *Polysynthetic sociolinguistics: The language and culture of Murrinh Patha youth* (PhD thesis). Australian National University, Canberra.

Mansfield, J. B. (2015a). Consonant lenition as a sociophonetic variable in Murrinh Patha (Australia). *Language Variation and Change, 27*(2), 203–225.

Mansfield, J. B. (2015b). Loan phonology in Murrinhpatha. In M. Harvey & A. Antonia (Eds.), *The 45th Australian Linguistic Society Conference Proceedings– 2014* (pp. 153–172). Newcastle: NOVA Open Access Repository.

Mansfield, J. B. (2015c). Morphotactic variation, prosodic domains and the changing structure of the Murrinhpatha verb. *Asia-Pacific Language Variation, 1*(2), 162–188.

Mansfield, J. B. (2016a). Borrowed verbs and the expansion of light verb phrases in Murrinhpatha. In F. Meakins & C. O'Shannessy (Eds.), *Loss and renewal: Australian languages since contact* (pp. 397–424). Berlin: Mouton de Gruyter.

Mansfield, J. B. (2016b). Intersecting formatives and inflectional predictability: How do speakers and learners predict the correct form of Murrinhpatha verbs? *Word Structure, 9*(2), 183–214.

Mansfield, J. B. (2017). Prosodic words in cyclic derivation: The strange case of Murrinhpatha compound verbs. *Morphology, 27*(3), 359–382.

Mansfield, J. B. (2018). Murrinhpatha personhood, other humans, and contemporary youth. In D. Austin-Broos & F. Merlan (Eds.), *People and change in Indigenous Australia* (pp. 117–129). Manoa: University of Hawai'i Press.

Mansfield, J. B., & Nordlinger, R. (2019). Demorphologisation and deepening complexity in Murrinhpatha. In F. Gardani & P. M. Arkadiev (Eds.), *Morphological complexity*. Oxford: Oxford University Press.

Marett, A. (2005). *Songs, Dreamings, and Ghosts: The Wangga of North Australia*. Middletown: Wesleyan University Press.

Marslen-Wilson, W. D. (2007). Morphological processes in language comprehension. *The Oxford Handbook of Psycholinguistics* (pp. 175–193). Oxford: Oxford University Press.

McCarthy, J. J. (1982). Prosodic templates, morphemic templates, and morphemic tiers. In H. van der Hulst & N. Smith (Eds.), *The structure of phonological representations I* (pp. 191–223). Dordrecht: Foris (pp. 175-193). Oxford: Oxford University Press.

McCarthy, J. J., & Prince, A. S. (1993). *Prosodic Morphology: Constraint Interaction and Satisfaction*. New Brunswick, NJ: Rutgers University Center for Cognitive Science.

McGregor, W. (1990). *A functional grammar of Gooniyandi*. Amsterdam: John Benjamins Publishing Company.
McGregor, W. (2002). *Verb classification in Australian languages*. Berlin: Mouton de Gruyter.
Merlan, F. (1994). *A grammar of Wardaman: A language of the Northern Territory of Australia*. Berlin: Mouton de Gruyter.
Mitchell, R. (2015). Ngalmun Lagaw Yangukudu: The Language of our Homeland, in Goemulgaw Lagal: Cultural and Natural Histories of the Island of Mabuyag, Torres Strait. *Memoirs of the Queensland Museum: Culture*, 8(1), 323–446.
Mohanan, K. P. (1986). *The theory of lexical phonology*. Dordrecht: Kluwer Academic Publishers.
Mühlhäusler, P. (2002). Why one cannot preserve languages (but can preserve language ecologies). In D. Bradley & M. Bradley (Eds.), *Language endangerment and language maintenance* (pp. 34–39).
Mujkic, E. (2013). *Murrinh-Patha syntax: Clausal structure and the noun phrase* (Honours thesis). University of Melbourne, Melbourne.
Muradoglu, S. (2018). *When is enough enough? A corpus-based study of verb inflection in a morphologically rich language (Nen)* (Masters thesis). Australian National University, Canberra.
Murdoch, L. (2006, May 23). Hate stalks a community where gangs rule roost. *The Age*, pp. 1–2.
Murray, R., & Venneman, T. (1983). Sound change and syllable structure in Germanic phonology. *Language*, 59, 514–528.
Mushin, I. (2012). *A grammar of (Western) Garrwa*. Berlin: Mouton de Gruyter.
Nash, D. (1980). *Topics in Warlpiri grammar* (PhD thesis). Massachusetts Institute of Technology, Amherst, MA.
Nash, D. (1982). Warlpiri verb roots and preverbs. *Work Papers of SIL-AAB*, 6, 165–216.
Nespor, M., & Vogel, I. (2012). *Prosodic phonology* (Second edition). Berlin: Mouton de Gruyter.
Nichols, J. (1986). Head-marking and dependent-marking grammar. *Language*, 62(1), 56–119.
Nichols, J. (1992). *Linguistic diversity in space and time*. Chicago: University of Chicago Press.
Nordlinger, R. (in prep.). From body parts to applicatives in the Daly languages of Northern Australia. *Ms*.
Nordlinger, R. (n.d.). *Reciprocals in Murrinh-Patha*. unpublished paper, University of Melbourne.
Nordlinger, R. (2010a). Agreement in Murrinh-Patha serial verbs. In Y. Treis & R. De Busser (Eds.), *Selected Papers from the 2009 Conference of the Australian Linguistic Society*. Retrieved from hhtp://www.als.asn.au
Nordlinger, R. (2010b). Verbal morphology in Murrinh-Patha: Evidence for templates. *Morphology*, 20(2), 321–341.
Nordlinger, R. (2011a). From body parts to applicatives. Presented at the ALT9, Hong Kong.
Nordlinger, R. (2011b). Transitivity in Murrinh-Patha. *Studies in Language*, 35(3), 702–734.
Nordlinger, R. (2015). Inflection in Murrinh-Patha. In M. Baerman (Ed.), *The Oxford handbook of inflection* (pp. 491–519). Oxford: Oxford University Press.
Nordlinger, R. (2017). The languages of the Daly River region (Northern Australia). In M. Fortescue, M. Mithun, & N. Evans (Eds.), *Oxford handbook of polysynthesis*. Oxford: Oxford University Press.
Nordlinger, R., & Caudal, P. (2012). The tense, aspect and modality system in Murrinh-Patha. *Australian Journal of Linguistics*, 32(1), 73–112.

Nordlinger, R., & Mansfield, J. B. (2015). Murrinhpatha verbs and models of morphology. Presented at the Australian Linguistics Society Conference, Sydney.

Ohala, J. J. (1983). The origin of sound patterns in vocal tract constraints. In *The Production of Speech* (pp. 189–216). Springer, New York, NY.

Ohala, J. J. (1990). The phonetics and phonology of aspects of assimilation. In J. Kingston & M. E. Beckman (Eds.), *Papers in laboratory phonology: Between the grammar and the physics of speech* (Vol. 1, pp. 258–275). Cambridge: Cambridge University Press.

Osborne, C. R. (1974). *The Tiwi language*. Canberra: Australian Institute of Aboriginal Studies.

Paradis, C., & Prunet, J.-F. (1991). Introduction: Asymmetry and visibility in consonant articulations. In C. Paradis & J.-F. Prunet (Eds.), *Phonetics and phonology* (Vol. 2, The special status of coronals: Internal and external evidence, pp. 1–28). San Diego: Academic Press.

Parker, S. (2011). Sonority. In M. van Oostendorp, C. Ewen, E. Hume, & K. Rice (Eds.), *The Blackwell companion to phonology* (pp. 1160–1184). Malden MA: Blackwell.

Paul, H. (1888). *Principles of the history of language*. (H. A. Strong, Trans.) (Translated from the second edition). London: Swan Sonnenschein, Lowrey & Co.

Pearson, N. (2000). Our right to take responsibility. Goanna Print.

Pensalfini, R. (2003). *A Grammar of Jingulu: An Aboriginal Language of the Northern Territory*. Canberra: Pacific Linguistics.

Pentland, C., & Laughren, M. (2005). Distinguishing prosodic word and phonological word in Warlpiri: Prosodic constituency in morphologically complex words. In I. Mushin (Ed.), *Proceedings of the 2004 Conference of the Australian Linguistic Society*. University of Sydney.

Peperkamp, S. (1996). On the prosodic representation of clitics. In U. Kleinhenz (Ed.), *Interfaces in phonology* (pp. 102–127). Berlin: Akademie Verlag.

Peperkamp, S. (1997). *Prosodic Words*. The Hague: Holland Academic Graphics.

Pierrehumbert, J. B. (2001). Exemplar dynamics: word frequency, lenition and contrast. In *Frequency and the emergence of linguistic structure* (pp. 135–157). Amsterdam: John Benjamins.

Pierrehumbert, J. B., Beckman, M. E., & Ladd, D. R. (2000). Conceptual foundations of phonology as a laboratory science. In N. Burton-Roberts, P. Carr, & G. Docherty (Eds.), *Phonological knowledge: Conceptual and empirical issues*. Oxford: Oxford University Press.

Pierrehumbert, J. B., & Steele, S. A. (1989). Categories of tonal alignment in English. *Phonetica*, 46(4), 181–196.

Pisoni, D. B. (1973). Auditory and phonetic memory codes in the discrimination of consonants and vowels. *Perception and Psychophysics*, 13(2), 253–260.

Pluymaekers, M., Ernestus, M., Baayen, R. H., & Booij, G. (2010). Morphological effects on fine phonetic detail: The case of Dutch -igheid. In C. Fougeron, B. Kuehnert, M. D. Imperio, & N. Valle (Eds.), *Laboratory Phonology 10* (pp. 511–531). Berlin: De Gruyter.

Podesva, R. J. (2002). Segmental constraints on geminates and their implications for typology. Presented at the LSA Annual Meeting, San Francisco.

Post, M. W. (2009). The phonology and grammar of Galo "words": A case study in benign disunity. *Studies in Language*, 33(4), 934–974.

Prince, A. S., & Smolensky, P. (1993). *Optimality Theory: Constraint interaction in generative grammar*. New Brunswick, NJ: Rutgers University Center for Cognitive Science.

Pye, B. J. M. (1972). *The Port Keats story*. Darwin: Colemans.

Pye, B. J. M. (n.d.). The Port Keats story: Part two. unpublished ms; accessed at Wadeye community archive.

Reid, N. (1990). *Ngan'gityemerri: a language of the Daly River region, Northern Territory of Australia* (PhD thesis). Australian National Univeristy, Canberra.

Reid, N. (2003). Phrasal verb to synthetic verb: recorded morphosyntactic changes in Ngan'gityemerri. In N. Evans (Ed.), *The non-Pama-Nyungan languages of Northern Australia* (pp. 95–123). Canberra: Pacific Linguistics.

Reid, N., & McTaggart, P. (2008). *Ngan'gi dictionary*. Armidale: Australian Linguistics Press.

Reynolds, R. (1999). *Catholic Sacrament Engaging with Wadeye Ritual* (PhD thesis). Northern Territory University, Darwin.

Ritz, M.-E., & Schultze-Berndt, E. (2015). Time for a change? The semantics and pragmatics of marking temporal progression in an Australian language. *Lingua*, *166*, 1–21.

Robins, R. H. (1959). In defence of WP. *Transactions of the Philological Society*, *58*(1), 116–144.

Round, E. R. (2017). The Tangkic languages of Australia: Phonology and morphosyntax of Lardil, Kayardild and Yukulta. In M. Aronoff (Ed.), *Oxford research encyclopedia of linguistics*. Oxford: Oxford University Press.

Rumelhart, D. E., & McClelland, J. L. (1986). *Parallel distributed processing, volume 1: Explorations in the microstructure of cognition*. Cambridge, MA: MIT Press.

Rumsey, A. (1993). Language and territoriality in Aboriginal Australia. In M. Walsh & C. Yallop (Eds.), *Language and culture in Aboriginal Australia* (pp. 191–206). Canberra: Aboriginal Studies Press.

Rumsey, A. (2001). On the syntax and semantics of trying. In J. Simpson (Ed.), *Forty years on: Ken Hale and Australian languages* (pp. 353–363). Canberra: Pacific Linguistics.

Russell, K. (1999). The "word" in two polysynthetic languages. In U. Kleinhenz & T. Alan (Eds.), *Studies on the phonological word* (pp. 203–221). Amsterdam: John Benjamins.

Sammallahti, P. (1998). Saamic. In D. Abondolo (Ed.), *The uralic languages* (pp. 43–95). London: Routledge.

Sandefur, J. (1979). An Australian creole in the Northern Territory: A description of Ngukurr-Bamyili dialects (Part 1). *Work Papers of SIL-AAB*, *3*, 1–185.

Sandefur, J. (1986). *Kriol of North Australia: A language coming of age*. Darwin: SIL.

Sasse, H.-J. (2002). Lexicological and lexicographic problems of word families in Cayuga. In N. Evans & H.-J. Sasse (Eds.), *Problems of Polysynthesis* (pp. 203–221). Berlin: Akademie Verlag.

Schachter, P., & Fromkin, V. (1968). A phonology of Akan: Akuapem, Asante, Fante. *UCLA Working Papers in Phonetics*, *9*.

Schiering, R., Bickel, B., & Hildebrandt, K. A. (2010). The prosodic word is not universal, but emergent. *Journal of Linguistics*, *46*(3), 657–709.

Schultze-Berndt, E. (2000). *Simple and complex verbs in Jaminjung* (PhD thesis). Katholieke Universiteit Nijmegen, Nijmegen.

Schultze-Berndt, E. (2003). Preverbs as an open word class in Northern Australian languages: synchronic and diachronic correlates. In G. Booij & J. van Marle (Eds.), *Yearbook of Morphology 2003* (pp. 145–177). Amsterdam: Kluwer Academic Publishers.

Seiss, M. (2011). Implementing the morphology-syntax interface: Challenges from Murrinh-Patha verbs. In *Proceedings of the LFG2011 Conference*. University of Hong Kong: CSLI Publications.

Seiss, M. (2013). *Murrinh-Patha complex verbs: Syntactic theory and computational implementation* (PhD thesis). Universitaet Konstanz, Konstanz.

Selkirk, E. O. (1984). *Phonology and Syntax: the relation between sound and structure.* Cambridge, MA: MIT Press.
Selkirk, E. O. (1996). The prosodic structure of function words. In J. L. Morgan & K. Demuth (Eds.), *Signal to syntax: Bootstrapping from speech to grammar in early acquisition* (pp. 187–213). Mahwah, N.J.: Lawrence Erlbaum.
Selkirk, E. O. (2011). The syntax-phonology interface. In J. A. Goldsmith, J. Riggle, & A. C. Yu (Eds.), *The handbook of phonological theory* (Second edition, pp. 435–484). Oxford: Blackwell.
Seo, M. (2011). Syllable contact. In M. van Oostendorp, C. Ewen, E. Hume, & K. Rice (Eds.), *The Blackwell companion to phonology* (pp. 1245–1262). Malden MA: Blackwell.
Shannon, C. E. (1948). A mathematical theory of communication. *Bell System Technical Journal*, 27(3), 379–423.
Simon, H. A. (1962). The architecture of complexity. *Proceedings of the American Philosophical Society*, 106(6), 467–482.
Simpson, J. (1998). Warumungu. In A. Spencer & A. M. Zwicky (Eds.), *The handbook of morphology* (pp. 707–736). Oxford: Blackwell.
Singer, R. (2016). *The Dynamics of Nominal Classification, Productive and Lexicalised Uses of Gender Agreement in Mawng.* Berlin, Boston: De Gruyter Mouton.
Skousen, R. (1989). *Analogical modeling of language.* Dordrecht: Kluwer.
Smith, C. S. (1997). *The parameter of aspect* (Second edition). Dordrecht: Kluwer Academic Publishers.
Sommer, B. A. (1969). *Kunjen phonology: Synchronic and diachronic.* Canberra: Pacific Linguistics.
Sommer, B. A. (1976). Umbuygamu: The classification of a Cape York Penninsular language. *Papers in Australian Linguistics*, 10(2), 13–29.
Spencer, A., & Luis, A. R. (2012). *Clitics: An introduction.* Cambridge: Cambridge University Press.
Stanner, W. E. H. (1936). Murinbata kinship and totemism. *Oceania*, 7, 186–216.
Stanner, W. E. H. (1937). Aboriginal modes of address and reference in the north-west of the Northern Territory. *Oceania*, 7, 300–315.
Stanner, W. E. H. (1959). Durmugam a Nangiomeri. In J. B. Casagrande (Ed.), *In the Company of Man* (pp. 63–100). New York: Harper.
Stanner, W. E. H. (1966). *On Aboriginal religion.* Canberra: Oceania Monographs.
Stoakes, H. (2013). *An acoustic and aerodynamic analysis of consonant articulation in Bininj Gun-wok* (PhD thesis). University of Melbourne, Melbourne.
Street, C. (1980a). Reduplication in Murinbata. *Papers in Australian Linguistics*, 12, 1–21.
Street, C. (1980b). The Relationship of Verb Affixation and Clause Structure in Murinbata. *Papers in Australian Linguistics*, 12, 83–113.
Street, C. (1987). *An introduction to the language and culture of the Murrinh-Patha.* Darwin: Summer Institute of Linguistics.
Street, C. (1996). Tense, aspect and mood in Murrinh-Patha. In *Studies in Kimberley Languages in Honour of Howard Coate* (pp. 205–225). Munich: Lincom Europa.
Street, C. (2012). *Murrinhpatha to English dictionary.* Unpublished MS, Wadeye, Australia.
Street, C., & Kulampurut, H. P. (1978). The Murinbata mode of existence. *Papers in Australian Linguistics*, 11, 133–141.
Street, C., & Mollinjin, G. P. (1981). The phonology of Murinbata. *Work Papers of SIL-AAB, Series A, Volume 5*, 183–244.

Stump, G. T. (2001). *Inflectional morphology: A theory of paradigm structure*. Cambridge: Cambridge University Press.
Stump, G. T. (2005). Word-formation and inflectional morphology. In P. Štekauer & R. Lieber (Eds.), *Handbook of word-formation* (pp. 49–71). Amsterdam: Springer.
Stump, G. T., & Finkel, R. (2013). *Morphological typology: From word to paradigm*. Cambridge: Cambridge University Press.
Stump, G. T., & Finkel, R. (2015). Contrasting modes of representation for inflectional systems: Some implications for computing morphological complexity. In M. Baerman, D. Brown, & G. G. Corbett (Eds.), *Understanding and measuring morphological complexity* (pp. 119–140). Oxford: Oxford University Press.
Sutton, P. (1978). *Wik: Aboriginal society, territory and language at Cape Keerweer, Cape York Peninsula, Australia* (PhD thesis). University of Queensland, St Lucia.
Sutton, P. (1991). Language in Aboriginal Australia: social dialects in a geographic idiom. In S. Romaine (Ed.), *Language in Australia* (pp. 49–66). Cambridge: Cambridge University Press.
Tabain, M. (2009). An EPG study of the alveolar vs. retroflex apical contrast in Central Arrernte. *Journal of Phonetics, 37*, 486–501.
Tabain, M., Fletcher, J., & Butcher, A. (2014). Lexical stress in Pitjantjatjara. *Journal of Phonetics, 42*, 52–66.
Taft, M., & Forster, K. (1975). Lexical storage and retrieval of prefixed words. *Journal of Verbal Learning and Verbal Behaviour, 14*, 638–647.
Tallman, A. J. (2016). *Phonological synthesis in Chácobo (Pano)* (Qualifying paper). Austin, TX, University of Texas at Austin.
Tallman, A. J., & Epps, P. (2018). Morphological complexity, autonomy, and areality in western Amazonia. In F. Gardani & P. M. Arkadiev (Eds.), *Morphological complexity*. Oxford: Oxford University Press.
Taylor, J. (2010). *Demography as destiny: Schooling, work and Aboriginal population change at Wadeye*. Canberra: CAEPR.
ten Hacken, P. (2017). Compounding in morphology. In M. Aronoff (Ed.), *Oxford research encyclopedia of linguistics*. Oxford: Oxford University Press.
Toohey, P. (2008). *Last drinks: The impact of the Northern Territory intervention*. Melbourne: Quarterly Essay / Black Inc.
Tryon, D. (1974). *Daly family languages, Australia*. Canberra: Pacific Linguistics.
Turpin, M. (2013). Semantic extension in Kaytetye flora and fauna terms. *Australian Journal of Linguistics, 33*(4), 488–518.
Vallduvi, E., & Engdahl, E. (1996). The linguistic realisation of information packaging. *Linguistics, 34*, 459–519.
van Egmond, M.-E. (2012). *Enindhilyakwa phonology, morphosyntax and genetic position* (PhD thesis). University of Sydney.
Vaughan, J. (in press). Translanguaging and the construction of difference in north central Arnhem Land. In G. Mazzaferro (Ed.), *Translanguaging in everyday practice*. Berlin: Springer.
Walker, J. A. (2012). Form, function, and frequency in phonological variation. *Language Variation and Change, 24*, 397–415.
Walker, R. (2000). *Nasalization, neutral segments and opacity effects*. Hove: Psychology Press.
Walsh, M. (1976). *The Murinypata language of north-west Australia* (PhD thesis). Australian National Univeristy, Canberra.

Walsh, M. (1987). The impersonal verb construction in Australian languages. In R. Steele & T. Threadgold (Eds.), *Language topics: essays in honour of Michael Halliday, Volume 1* (pp. 425–438). Amsterdam: John Benjamins Publishing Company.

Walsh, M. (1990). *Language socialization at Wadeye*. AIATSIS, Canberra.

Walsh, M. (1996a). Body parts in Murrinh-Patha: Incorporation, grammar and metaphor. In H. Chappell & B. McGregor (Eds.), *The Grammar of Inalienability: A Typological Perspective on Body Part Terms and the Part-Whole Relation*. Berlin: Mouton de Gruyter.

Walsh, M. (1996b). Vouns and nerbs: A category squish in Murrinh-Patha (northern Australia). In W. McGregor (Ed.), *Studies in Kimberley languages in Honour of Howard Coate* (pp. 227–252). Munich: Lincom Europa.

Walsh, M. (1997). Noun classes, nominal classification and generics in Murrinhpatha. In M. Harvey & N. Reid (Eds.), *Nominal Classification in Aboriginal Australia* (pp. 255–290). Amsterdam: John Benjamins Publishing Company.

Walsh, M. (2007). Indigenous languages of Australia. In *The Vanishing Languages of the Pacific Rim* (pp. 221–238). Oxford: Oxford University Press.

Walsh, M. (2011). From Port Keats to Wadeye: Contact among Australian and other languages. Presented at the Australian Languages Workshop, North Stradbroke Island.

Ward, S. T. (1983). *The peoples and their land around Wadeye: Murrinh kanhi ka kardu i da putek pigunu*. Wadeye: Wadeye Press.

Wierzbicka, A. (1986). What's in a noun? (Or: How do nouns differ in meaning from adjectives?). *Studies in Language*, *10*(2), 353–389.

Wilkinson, K. (1988). Prosodic structure and Lardil phonology. *Linguistic Inquiry*, *19*, 325–334.

Wilmoth, S. (2014). *Discourse markers in Murrinhpatha* (Honours thesis). University of Melbourne, Melbourne.

Wycliffe Bible Translators. (1990). *Murrinh ngarra Jesus nukunu*. Orlando, FL: Wycliffe Bible Translators.

Zwicky, A. M., & Pullum, G. K. (1983). Cliticization vs. inflection: English N'T. *Language*, *59*(3), 502–513.

Index

Ablaut 118
Accentual phrase 22
Acquisition 35, 134, 202
Adjectives 78, 170, 175, 178
Adjuncts 174
Adverbs/adverbials 79, 158, 184–189, 204
Adversative 155
Agent 183
Alcohol 33
Allomorphs/allomorphy 118, 130
Animacy 4
Applicatives 166, 210
Argument 138
Aspirated 54
Assimilation 68, 103
Australian languages 44, 49, 87, 97, 106, 179

Bilingualism 39
Bimoraic 85, 87, 92, 139, 173, 192
Body part 163, 205

Case markers/marking 80, 168, 181
Catholic mission 31
Ceremony groups 30
Christian/Christianity 34, 37
Clans 26, 30
Classifications 177
Classifier nouns 78, 168, 170
Classifier verb stems 79, 194
Clitics 158, 167, 181–184
Coda 46
Coda consonants 81
Cognitive 13
Comitative 184
Competition 154
Complementiser 80
Complex codas 44, 45
Complexity 228
Complex verbs 194
Compounds/compounding 172–176, 194, 205–209, 225, 232
Connected speech 67, 102
Consonants 43, 60
Construction Grammar 17

Coordinate 178, 181, 187
Copula 95
Coronals 43, 48, 101
Coverbs 78, 99, 203

Daly River 35
Darwin 35
Dative 151
Degemination 70
Demonstratives 188
Derivational 180
Descriptive morphology 13
Determiners 78, 170, 175
Diacritic 219
Digital diglossia 40
Digital media 40
Diphthongs 73
Discourse tags 80, 168
Disfluent 190
Distributed morphology 16
Docherty, Richard 31
Dormitories 36
Dual 141, 145, 153–155, 216
Dummy subject 149
Duration 54, 57

English 38–40, 71
Entropy 131
Epistemic 185
Evil warriors 33
Exponence 120

Faithfulness 103
Feature 230
Final syllable 89
Finite verb stems 79, 82, 112, 139
Formants 64
Form–meaning relations 228
Fortis/lenis 51
Fortition 68, 103
Fossil 209–210
Frequency 10, 14, 195, 230
Freshwater 37
Fricatives 51, 52, 73

https://doi.org/10.1515/9781501503306-012

Frontness 125
Front vowels 43
Function words 80

Gangs 33
Geminates 70, 126
Gender 141
Generic nouns 170
Glides 43
Gradience 12, 14, 228–233
Graffiti 40
Grammaticalise 199

Harmony 123
Height 125
Heterosyllabic clusters 48
Homophony 117
Hunter gatherers 25, 29

Ideophones 81
Imperfective 156
Incorporated body parts 78
Inflectional class 118
Inflectional paradigms 19, 114, 118
Information structure 190
Inner stems 79, 113, 117, 125
Inter-marriage 37
Intermediate phrase 22
Interrogatives 188
Intersecting formatives 118
Intonation 21
Intonational phrase 22
Intransitive 152
Irregular 126
Inflectional 82

Jaminjung 29, 31, 36, 71
Judas Priest 33

Kardu Numida 32
Katherine 35
Kinship 29
Kriol 35, 38–40, 73
Kununurra 35

Laminals 43
Language and place 1, 28, 36, 45

Learnability 133
Lenition 60, 69, 98–101, 214
Lexical borrowings 38, 39
Lexical phonology 8, 11
Lexical representation 11
Lexicon 17, 172, 195, 204, 232–233
Lexico-phonological strata 72
Light verbs 196, 200
Lingua franca 35
Literacy 40
Loanwords 71, 163, 195
Low vowels 43

Magati Ke 28, 36
Manthathpe 32
Marri Amu 28, 36
Marri Ngarr 28, 36
Marrithiyel 97, 168
Marri Tjevin 28, 36
Mendhe 28, 36
Mental representations 134, 201
Metaphor 207
Metrical foot 22, 87
Modality 116, 155, 185
Moiety 30
Monosyllabic 80, 86, 113, 139, 173, 192
Morphemic 11, 220
Morphology 11, 13
Multilingualism 26, 35
Multiple classifications 177
Murrinh Kura 26, 28 38

Nasal liquidation 68
Nasal spreading 101
Negator 80, 179
Neutralization 53
Ngalakgan 9
Ngan'gi 36, 97, 123, 168, 202
Nganmarriyanga 35
Nilinh 32
Nominals 78
Non-human referents 144
Non-Pama-Nyungan languages 45
Northern Territory Emergency Response 33

Noun phrase 3, 95, 170
Number 116, 138, 140, 153

Object 148, 212
Object-experiencer 149
Oblique 148, 212
Obstruent codas 45, 81
Onset 46
Onset clusters 73
Onsetless syllables 124
Opacity 218
Optimality theory 103
Orders 4
Orthography 201, 227

Palumpa 35
Pama-Nyungan 81
Paucal 141, 153–155
Penultimate 93, 139
Peppimenarti 35
Person 116
Phonological phrase 22, 86, 93, 186
Phonology 10
Phrasal verb 194
Pidgin 73
Pitch accent 57, 86, 88, 89
Pitch contour 89
Place-of-articulation 103, 105, 213
Pluractional 210–215
Plural 141
Polysynthetic 233
Population 26, 32
Pragmatic 190
Predicate 163
Predicating nominals 180, 217
Predictability 131
Prefixes 120, 121, 200
Preposition 3, 80, 95
Prepositional phrase 95
Presentational 116
Productive/productivity 14, 177, 181, 199, 202, 207
Pronominal 148
Prosodic adjunction 22, 92, 168, 174
Prosodic compounding 215–219
Prosodic constituencies 21, 84, 216
Prosodic morphology 8

Prosodic phrase 86, 158
Prosodic structure 21
Prosodic words 8, 22, 85–87, 92, 95, 137, 173, 186, 217, 227
Psycholinguistic experiments 13

Reciprocal 114, 146, 152, 199
Recursive PWord 217
Reduplication 211
Reflexives 114, 146, 152, 199
Relative clause 3
Release burst 54
Retroflexion 63–67
Rhyme 87

Saltwater 37
School 39
Secondary stress 87
Semantic 196, 232
Semi-regular 130
Serial verbs 156
Shapes 45
Sibling 140
Simple verbs 194
Socialization 37
Social organisation 29–31
Social problems 32
Sonorant consonants 83
Sonority 48, 101, 103, 213
Sound-meaning relations 13
Southern Daly 26
Speakers 205
Stem 112, 231
Stress 88, 96
Strict layering 22
Sub-paradigms 118, 125
Subsection 30
Suppletive 126, 215
Syllable 44, 84, 86, 88
Syncretisms 116
Syntactic constituency 95

Tap 43
Template 212
Tense 116, 124, 155
Thamarrurr 32
Thematic role 4

Theme 183
Third person 141
Totemic 30
Transitive 145, 148, 152
Trill 43
Trochaic feet 87, 97

Underspecified 140, 145, 154
Unemployment 34
Unpredictable 211

Valency 146, 152
Variable 133–134, 144, 149, 159–161

Vocabulary 38
Voicing 51, 54
Vowels 43

Western Daly 28, 36
Word 1, 18, 15, 45, 227
Wordhood 15, 227, 233
Word-initial 67
Word-medial 46, 51

Young speakers 38–39, 134, 144, 154, 160, 163, 172, 195, 205

Zero 121

www.ingramcontent.com/pod-product-compliance
Lightning Source LLC
Chambersburg PA
CBHW071813230426
43670CB00013B/2439